OCR

GOVERNMENT AND POLITICS

Political Ideas
and C

g together to provide better support for you

Diane Canwell
Jonathan Sutherland
Consultant: David Binney

www.heinemann.co.uk

✓ Free online support
✓ Useful weblinks
✓ 24 hour online ordering

01865 888080

Heinemann is an imprint of Pearson Education Limited, a company incorporated in England and Wales, having its registered office at Edinburgh Gate, Harlow, Essex, CM20 2JE. Registered company number: 872828

www.heinemann.co.uk

Heinemann is a registered trademark of Pearson Education Limited

Text © Jonathan Sutherland and Diane Canwell 2009

First published 2009

13 12 11 10 09
10 9 8 7 6 5 4 3 2 1

British Library Cataloguing in Publication Data
A catalogue record for this book is available from the British Library.

ISBN 978 0 435466 92 3

Edited by Alexander Gray
Typeset by TechType
Cover photo/illustration © David Robertson/Alamy
Printed in Italy by Rotolito

Websites
There are links to relevant websites in this book. In order to ensure that the links are up to date, that the links work, and that the sites are not inadvertently linked to sites that could be considered offensive, we have made the links available on the Heinemann website at www.heinemann.co.uk/hotlinks. When you access the site, the express code is 6923P

Crown Copyright
Crown Copyright material reproduced by permission of the controller of Her Majesty's Stationery Office and the Queen's Printer for Scotland.

Photographs

The author and publisher would like to thank the following individuals and organisations for permission to reproduce photographs:

TOK56/Fotolia.com p 15; Pavel Parmenov/Fotolia.com p 26; Parliamentary copyright p 29; Tatarszkij/Fotolia.com p 52; flashkralove/Fotolia.com p 62; Martin Spurny/Fotolia.com p 68; Simon Gurney/Fotolia.com p 82; Damn designs/Fotolia.com p 96; Rene Drouyer/Fotolia.com p 122; TekinT/Fotolia.com p 136; Ritu Jethani/Fotolia.com p 141; govicinity/Fotolia.com p 170; Robert Kelly/Fotolia.com p 189; Darryl Sleath/Fotolia.com p 190; Pierre-jean G./Fotolia.com p 193; Esther Hildebrandt/Fotolia.com p 219; lily/Fotolia.com p 231; Willee Cole/Fotolia.com p 248; Walter Luger/Fotolia.com p 252; Nimbus/Fotolia.com p 258; Leonid Shcheglov/Fotolia.com p 270.

Extracts

Page 30–31: Tables showing age and gender of MPs taken from House of Commons Library Standard Note 1528 'Social background of MPs', reproduced with the permission of the House of Commons Library.

Page 31: Table showing occupational background of MPs taken from Butler et al. (2005) *The British General Election of 2005* (and earlier editions), Palgrave Macmillan, reproduced with the permission of Palgrave Macmillan.

Page 167: Annual Diversity Statistics table © Crown Copyright material is reproduced with the permission of the Controller, Office of Public Sector Information (OPSI) Click Use Licence No. C2008002327.

Page 213: Beveridge quote © Crown Copyright material is reproduced with the permission of the Controller, Office of Public Sector Information (OPSI) Click Use Licence No. C2008002327.

Page 201: Taxation, health service reform and forced marriages policy announcements taken from www.conservatives.com/Policy.aspx, reproduced with the permission of the Conservative Party.

Page 227: Sir Menzies Campbell and Charles Kennedy quotes reproduced with permission of the Liberal Democrats.

Every effort has been made to contact copyright holders of material reproduced in this book. Any omissions will be rectified in subsequent printings if notice is given to the publishers.

This textbook has been written and designed specifically to help you deal with the requirements of the OCR A2 Optional Units focusing on Political Ideas and Concepts examinations. You should find that, together with some background reading and getting into the habit of paying attention to political stories in the media, this book will prepare you for anything the examiners might want to throw at you. This book is structured so that it successively deals with each of the two parts of the A2 syllabus related to Political Ideas and Concepts (units F854 and F856). You will find all of the key terms and phrases defined and important concepts highlighted and illustrated with examples. Each of the topics within the syllabus is dealt with either in single, double or triple sections. The book has several key features, which include:

- specific learning objectives for every section
- key words or phrases defined
- links to additional reading and research
- discussion-style questions for each section
- an exam café feature at the end of each topic, with expert knowledge and guidance from an OCR examiner.

The A2 is the second half of the complete A Level. It is made up of two optional units, both of which are externally assessed. The units are:

- A2 Unit F854: Political Ideas and Concepts
- A2 Unit F856: Political Ideas and Concepts in Practice

Unit F854 is worth 25 per cent of the overall A Level mark. You will be required to sit a two-hour written paper with 100 marks available. You will have to answer question 1, which is a structured question and contains stimulus material. The questions could require you to provide answers from any of the eight topic areas in the unit. You will then have to choose three questions from a range of seven to show your understanding of:

- democratic theory
- the state, nation, sovereignty and globalisation
- power, authority and legitimacy
- rights, liberty and equality
- law, order, justice and obligation
- conservatism and nationalism
- liberalism and socialism
- alternative ideologies.

Unit F856 is also worth 25 per cent of the total A Level mark. It is also a two-hour paper with 100 marks available. You will be required to answer two questions from a choice of eight. You will be expected to draw on your knowledge of:

- British politics
- political ideas and concepts
- other political systems
- European Union.

It is important to note that this unit is synoptic. Synoptic means that the examinations test your understanding of the connections between different elements of government and politics.

In our exam café pages you will find lots of ideas to help you prepare for these exams. You will find an exam café at the end of each topic. Our first exam café shows you how to relax and prepare to write political theory essays, and there is handy revision advice from teachers and examiners. All of the other exam cafés have a **Refresh your memory** feature, with summaries, checklists and revision tips for the key ideas you need to revise. There are also **Get the result!**

features, with practice exam-style questions, accompanied by hints and tips for getting the very best grades.

The exam café explains the assessment objectives for government and politics to you. The assessment objectives are:

- **A01** – This requires you to demonstrate knowledge and understanding of relevant institutions, processes, political concepts, theories and debates.

- **A02** – This requires you to analyse and evaluate political information, arguments and explanations, and where appropriate identify parallels, connections, similarities and differences between aspects of the political systems studied, including the EU.

- **A03** – This requires you to construct and communicate coherent arguments making use of a range of appropriate political vocabulary.

The more assessment objectives you can cover in your answers, the greater the chance you have of achieving a high grade in the examinations.

Exam cafés will also show you how the examiner allocates marks for each question. You should get into the habit of offering more than just facts, as this will only gain you A01 marks (demonstrate knowledge and understanding). You need to argue, analyse and evaluate in order to achieve A02 (analyse and evaluate). To achieve A03 (communicate) your English needs to be as precise as possible and your sentences and arguments must be well structured. The exam cafés will also give you an idea about hot topics and the style of questions that may crop up.

Over the duration of the course you should try and organise your notes in the best way possible, making sure that you note down any useful contemporary examples. Make sure you understand what the syllabus is asking you to do. There is a high probability that any part of it could form the basis of a question, and it is a difficult and dangerous business to try to predict what the examiner may or may not ask. You need to know the topics thoroughly and answer the questions. A common complaint from examiners is that students simply write down everything they know about a particular topic and do not pay attention to the question.

Government and politics is a constantly developing subject. Politics is never out of the media, and there is always something new happening. New political personalities, as well as political ideas, constantly emerge and others disappear. Make sure that you do not use out-of-date examples when more recent ones are always available in the news. Keeping up to date is half the battle.

Try to follow stories through. See who is involved, who makes the decisions, why have those decisions been made and what their consequences are. Develop your own strategy for keeping up to date. The BBC's political coverage is excellent and can be watched online or even downloaded. Make sure that you also pay attention to Radio 4's political coverage and key political stories on *News 24*.

The course and the book

F854: Political Ideas and Concepts along with F856: Political Ideas and Concepts in Practice fit together perfectly to allow you to first explore a range of political ideas, democratic theories and systems and then to turn your attention to the application of those ideas and theories, to the practice of politics in Britain and in the EU.

F854 will give you an opportunity to look at the role of the state, the processes of government and the relationship between the individual and the state. You will also be introduced to a wide range of different political thinkers.

In F856 you will look at a range of different political theories, thinkers and systems and you will need to be aware of world political events.

There are eight topics in this book. Each of them examines both F854 and F856. Each of the spreads looks at a different aspect of the topic and you will find that each spread has either an F854 or an F856 heading. What we have tried to do is to present the theoretical aspects in the F854 spreads and the practical application and examples in the F856 spreads. The book is structured in the following way.

Topic or section	F854	F856
Opening exam café	All topics	All topics
Democratic theory and democracy in practice	Democratic theory	Democracy in practice
The state, nation, sovereignty and globalisation	The state, nation, sovereignty and globalisation	The state, nation, sovereignty and globalisation in practice
Power, authority and legitimacy	Power, authority and legitimacy	Power, authority and legitimacy in practice
Rights, liberty and equality	Rights, liberty and equality	Rights, liberty and equality in practice
Law, order, justice and obligation	Law, order, justice and obligation	Law, order, obligation and justice in practice
Conservatism and nationalism	Conservatism and nationalism	Contemporary conservatism and nationalism
Liberalism and socialism	Liberalism and socialism	Contemporary liberalism and socialism
Alternative ideologies	Alternative ideologies	The impact of alternative ideologies
Concluding exam café	All topics	All topics

At the end of each of the topics you will find an exam café, which relates to both F854 and F856 aspects for the examinations. You will see that there are common features in these exam cafés, with sample essays for both units, revision aids, lists of key theorists or ideas and example essay questions, along with sample essays with comments.

The first introductory exam café following this spread gives you valuable ideas to help you answer essays for both F854 and F856. It also shows you how you should prepare each of the essays and how to allocate your time. There is also a vital section that shows you what to avoid doing when you write an essay.

At the end of the book is a final exam café, which gives you key ideas to help you prepare for your exams, the rights and wrongs of revision and how to impress the examiner. You will also find a useful list of other books that may be valuable to you in preparing for the F854 and F856 examinations.

No single book on political ideologies could possibly provide you with absolutely everything that you will need or that will be expected of you in the examination. It is vital that you read as widely as possible. If you have the opportunity, make sure that you try to read some of the political theories from the original source. The vast majority of the political theorists' books are still in print, even those that were written centuries ago.

There are some books that you will find of particular value for looking at specific issues, such as liberalism or socialism. There is also no real substitute for taking notice of political debates and the ideological foundations behind different points of view, standpoints, manifesto promises and policies, some of which become legislation.

The book should provide you with the bulk of the information that you will need to appreciate the complexities of some of the political ideologies and how, over time, they have been applied to real-life political situations. Above all, you should remember that politics is a constantly changing discipline and that ideas and views, whilst based on key political ideas of the past, may be interpreted in many different ways by many different people.

Political theory is not a dry or abstract topic. Political theory determines the nature of government, its policies and legislation, and ultimately our view of the world.

ExamCafé
Relax, refresh, result!

How to use the exam café

At the end of each chapter there will be an opportunity for you to think more closely about how to use the information you have just read. In each exam café there will be hints on how to focus on the key issues; guidance will be given on how to revise the different topic areas, including several essay questions of a type that could occur in your exams, sample essay plans and answers, and also suggestions for additional reading. The first of these exam cafés is about how to write political theory essays, something that will be very new to you and possibly quite daunting. So pour yourself an invigorating cappuccino and let's get started.

How to write political theory essays

Below are suggestions for how to structure your essays for the two ideas and concepts units. When writing future essays for these units use them as a guide.

Writing unit F854 essays

The basics

For this unit you will need to answer a compulsory two-part question, based around the reading of a source, and then three further essay-style questions. Overall you should spend 30 minutes on each question, making the exam two hours in length.

What to focus on

For the compulsory question

Carefully read the short source accompanying the question – it may contain hints on what to focus upon in your answers. Give yourself approximately five minutes to make sure you understand the source and the questions before you start writing.

For part A questions (10 marks)

All that is required is knowledge and understanding (examiners refer to this as Assessment Objective 1 – AO1 for short) of a concept, or concepts, raised in the source. Give a clear definition and extend it to cover some of the relevant themes. Illustrate where possible with the ideas of related theorists. Avoid getting side-tracked into debates (this is required in part B). Above all keep your answer fairly short and to the point as you will have only about 10 minutes to write it.

For part B questions (15 marks)

All the marks are for analysis and evaluation (Assessment Objective 2 – AO2), thus your answer must focus on debate. Depending upon the specific question asked, this could be comparing and contrasting, evaluating the strengths and weaknesses of a particular theory, or considering the relative importance of key factors. Here you will have slightly longer to develop your ideas, 15 minutes in all, but still not long enough to get side-tracked into irrelevant arguments. There will be no need to give extensive supporting evidence, nor will you have to illustrate your arguments with relation to the ideas of political thinkers.

For the optional essays (each 25 marks)

- Make sure you read all seven questions before you choose which ones to answer. If you don't you may find there were others further down the list that you would have been more comfortable answering.
- Plan your answer – spend approximately five minutes making sure that you fully understand each question and planning each answer.
- At the beginning of each essay clearly define the concept/theory or ideology that is the focus of the question. Make sure you also show the examiner that you fully understand what the question

Writing unit F854 essays – continued

requires you to do by outlining the key areas you intend to cover (this is called a hypothesis).

- Deal with each relevant argument in a separate paragraph – this may be a point of comparison, strength or a weakness, or relevant perspective.
- Try and illustrate each argument with the views of a particular theorist or ideological perspective – there is no need to learn extensive quotes, accurate paraphrasing is just as good.
- Avoid just listing or describing points, instead consider issues such as the extent of similarity/difference, the relative importance of each factor, or whether the strengths outweigh the weaknesses in a particular idea.
- Conclude by emphasising the most important factors you have considered in a manner that directly addresses the question set and give, where appropriate, some personal reasoned perspective upon the topic – this shows evaluation of the arguments.

What to avoid when writing F854 essays

- There is no need to include specific illustrative factual examples, as evidence comes in the form of the use of theorists and ideological perspectives in this paper.
- Avoid hypothetical scenarios unless they are ones used by theorists – they can make your essay sound vague.
- Finally, avoid writing one-sided essays or essays from a single viewpoint – especially avoid essays that constantly use 'I think…'

Writing unit F856 essays

The basics

For this unit once again you will have two hours to answer the questions, however here you only have to write two essays, thus spending an hour on each.

For each essay

- Make sure you read all eight questions before you choose which to answer. If you don't you may find there were others further down the list that you would have been more comfortable answering.
- Plan out your answer – having an hour to write each essay you should be able to spend between 5 and 10 minutes planning each answer and making sure that you fully understand the question set.
- As with F854, start each answer by clearly defining the central concept or theory covered in the title. Having planned your essay you should be able to outline your hypothesis.
- Each paragraph should relate to a particular argument/point of comparison or issue and should be analytical in the way it deals with the issues raised. Avoid just describing arguments, also consider their validity/importance.
- For each argument/comparison raised you will need to illustrate through use of specific theory and by applying the idea to the operation of modern politics.
- When applying your points to modern politics use specific examples (events, statistics, case studies etc.) These should mainly be taken from your study of British and EU politics at AS, but where appropriate you could also use your knowledge of other contemporary political systems or events.
- As with conclusions for F854 essays, your answers should directly address the question set, highlighting the most important arguments, issues or comparisons made and, where appropriate, offer a personal perspective.

What to avoid when writing F856 essays

- Avoid writing an F854 essay without any application to modern politics. If you do, this will significantly limit your potential mark.
- Likewise, avoid writing an AS-style essay devoid of any political theory. This will have the same impact as above.
- Avoid broad generalisations or anecdotal-style evidence – this will reveal to the examiner that you have a lack of real understanding or knowledge of modern politics.
- Avoid describing ideas, instead try and analyse and evaluate – this will often come through testing the validity of a point by applying it to the operation of modern politics.

A useful hint – the skeleton model

For F856 essays think of your essay as if you were creating a human being. Think of the concepts and theories as if they were the skeleton that holds the essay together. However, without 'fleshing out' the skeleton through applying the theory to modern politics you would have only a partially complete body. And yet if your essay only consisted of modern politics without the theory you would effectively have nothing more than a mound of flesh – once again an unattractive and useless proposition!

The citizens of many countries throughout the world, including the UK, live under some form of democratic government. This means that they have chosen who they want to govern them. They do this by voting for the candidates of political parties in a national election. If they are chosen, these candidates will represent the citizens in parliament or congress. The political party which wins the election will become the governing party (the government) and that party's leader will become the head of government – the prime minister, president, or whatever. The winning of an election gives a party legitimacy to govern. At the same time the government is accountable to the electorate for its actions.

The theory is that parliamentary representatives forming the government will act on behalf of all the citizens in managing the affairs of state, including devising and implementing the policies by which they will govern and conceiving and passing laws by which they will manage the behaviour of citizens. In return the government must take into account the interests and wishes of the citizens and refrain from interfering (in various respects) in the way they live their lives.

In practice it is said that democracy works positively in that citizens are committed to engaging in the process of electing a government and taking an interest in the affairs of state, which in turn encourages the development of citizens who are more informed and therefore more capable of making decisions about who they should vote for at an election. It also works in generating the impulse towards bringing about social changes through freely objecting to anomalies and injustices in society.

On the other hand, the system is criticised. It is said to be one in which power is in the hands of an elite, that the population is generally not sufficiently well educated in matters of state and that economic inequalities prevail. The system also favours the majority and undermines or represses the minority, a phenomenon known as 'the tyranny of the majority'. In Britain, it is questionable whether the first-past-the-post voting system ensures that the consent of citizens is exercised in elections. There has also been a decline in the participation of citizens in elections. They are now involved in politics in other ways, as in the case of pressure groups. Public opinion of politicians has also declined and whenever elections are a foregone conclusion there is a loss of interest.

There are alternatives to the political electoral system for expressing discontent and striving for change. In the United States, referenda are much more commonly used than in Britain. Americans also use initiatives to put specific issues to the vote, for example California's Proposition 13, and citizens' juries are used for public consultations. Pressure groups in this country also play a role in the political process, however some of them are granted greater favours than others and therefore exercise a disproportionate amount of power.

The media have an important role in possessing the power to publicly hold politicians accountable. The problem is the impartiality of the media in favouring certain political parties over others and therefore failing to balance its exercise of power.

To be effective democracy needs citizens to be actively involved.

These are some of the issues covered in this chapter, in which the following are key themes.

- The nature of democracy
- The different types of democracy

- The nature of dictatorship

- The different types of dictatorship

- The differences between dictatorships and democracy

- The advantages and disadvantages of democracy

- Democracy in practice

In covering these themes the chapter is broken down into the following topics.

The chapter finishes with an exam café feature on page 44.

The meaning of democracy

The term democracy has a literal meaning of rule by the people. It is derived from two Greek words, which give a clue to its origins. The word *demos* means people and *kratos* means rule. This then literally means ruled by the demos, or the many. The term can be traced back to the 5th century BC, as it described a political system that was used by some cities in Greece, notably Athens.

Modern-day definitions are somewhat different and the term is often used as a derogatory rather than a positive one, implying that a state is ruled by the uneducated masses. There is also the implication that democracy stifles liberty and wisdom. In fact both these were criticisms made by Plato and Aristotle and influenced views of democracy until at least the 19th century.

As we will see, the practical application of democracy has changed over the years, although broadly there are two main forms of democracy.

- **Direct democracy** – This was practised in relatively small communities, such as Greek city states. Due to the relatively small numbers of citizens it was easy for them to gather together in an assembly to discuss problems, pass laws and adopt policies by a majority vote.

- **Representative democracy** – This was developed in Europe and in North America in the 18th century. This is a system that allows citizens to elect a small number of representatives to discuss problems, adopt policies and pass laws on their behalf.

Defining the term democracy in modern society is rather more difficult because there is still intense political debate revolving around three key questions, as can be seen in the following table.

Democracy debate	Explanation
Who are the people?	Theoretically the people are all the people, but in many cases participation is often restricted.
What is meant by rule?	Essentially democracy should be based on the concept of government by the people, in other words people govern themselves, taking part in crucial decision-making. On the other hand, there is the concept of government for the people, which does not imply a great deal of participation by the people. In its most extreme version this is a dictatorship, where the leaders claim that they are operating in the interests of the people.
How far should this rule extend?	This is essentially a debate between the public and the private. To what extent should democracy and decision-making impinge upon the private lives of individual citizens? Theoretically democracy should only extend to areas that relate to the community and do not infringe the personal liberties of individuals.

Aristotle on democracy

Aristotle was conscious of the fact that participation by citizens was desirable, but he was worried that without restraints democracy could turn into mob rule. He therefore preferred a system that contained elements of democracy and **oligarchy**, which he called **polity**.

Oligarchy

A Greek term that means ruled by a few.

Polity

A Greek term that Aristotle intended to mean that only a minority of adult males could have voting rights as citizens.

Lincoln's Gettysburg address

In this famous speech made in 1863, President Abraham Lincoln used the phrase 'government of the people, by the people, and for the people'. This is a classic definition of democracy that has two different notions. 'By the people' means that citizens participate in government and govern themselves, that is, self-government. 'For the people' suggests that government benefits the people even if this means that citizens do not rule themselves.

The characteristics of democracy

It would be wrong to jump to the conclusion that the term *demos* refers to all people. Throughout history there has always been a problem with defining who is a citizen. In the Greek city states it was generally a small proportion of the males. Foreigners, slaves and women were not eligible to vote. It has only been ninety years since women have been allowed to vote in Britain (1918) and eighty years since universal suffrage or the equalisation of voting (1928). In the United States only forty or so years ago African-Americans finally gained the vote in the southern states, after a constitutional enforcement of the vote. In Switzerland women did not attain the vote until 1971.

Broadly, it is often a question of what constitutes an adult citizen. This can be a question of the age of the individual, or their current status, for example as to whether they are imprisoned or are certifiably insane. It is perhaps more accurate to reject the concept of 'the many' or 'the people' and replace it with 'the majority'.

Different countries at different times have dabbled with different forms of democratic popular participation. They have even tried forms of direct and continuous involvement in the decision-making process. Examples include referendums, mass meetings and interactive voting using television or the Internet.

Elections are the most common form, but it is important to remember that not only are elections competitive, they ultimately choose individuals who will make decisions on behalf of the voters.

The other key issue is the spread or scope of democracy. In other words, how much of a citizen's life should be determined by decisions made by a democratic process and how much of it should be left to the individual citizen? Again there is no accepted level of 'interference'.

Democracy should establish a framework of laws within which citizens operate. In theory democracy should restrict itself to issues that affect the community as a whole. If it goes beyond this then it infringes liberty. Perhaps this is why direct and participatory forms of democracy are rare.

Some socialists and radical democrats believe that citizens have a basic right to participate in any decisions that could affect their lives and democracy is the way of achieving this goal. Karl Marx described political democracy as giving power to 'the executive committee of the bourgeoisie'. Radical democrats, such as Tom Bottomore, saw continuous participation through direct democracy by the citizens in decision-making as enhancing civic virtue.

Plato and his guardians

In *The Republic*, Plato argued that many ordinary citizens were not competent enough to rule wisely. He therefore believed that government should be dominated by philosopher kings or guardians who were, in effect, enlightened dictators. Plato believed in natural inequality. In other words, that people were born to fulfil a particular role in life; some would be leaders and some would be followers.

A statue of Plato

Schumpeter on democracy and the rule of the politician

Joseph Schumpeter's theory of democracy suggested that the democratic process was just a battleground in which power-seeking politicians sought to win citizens' votes. He said 'democracy means only that the people have the opportunity of accepting or refusing the men who are to rule them'.

Crick on the meaning of democracy

Bernard Crick wrote 'Democracy is perhaps the most promiscuous word in the world of public affairs.' What he meant by this is that democracy can literally mean almost anything to anyone. This could mean that the term may end up actually meaning nothing at all. There is no settled model of democracy, even though the West tends to use forms of liberal democracies.

DISCUSSION POINT (?)

Is it possible to come to a single definition of democracy?

Learning objectives

- Direct democracy
- Representative democracy
- Models of representation
- Similarities and differences
- Key thinkers on direct and representative democracy

Direct democracy

Direct democracy is a system of government where decisions are made by the collective choice of citizens rather than representatives.

Ancient Greece was not a single country, but a patchwork of independent city states. Around 600 BC the Athenian statesman Solon put forward a constitutional reform package, which laid out the bare bones of a democratic system. A hundred years later it was taken up by Cleisthenes. He championed political reform, which in 508 BC introduced the Athenian Democratic Constitution.

This form of democracy differed enormously from what we now understand to be democracy. It was smaller in scale, participation was limited and individuals had to be eligible. The Athenian population totalled no more than 250,000. Only around 30,000 of these were citizens, defined as adult males of Athenian birth with full citizen status. Only 5000 of these would actually regularly attend the assembly (*ecclesia*), which met around forty times a year on a hill called the Pnyx overlooking the city.

The assembly would make decisions on questions submitted to it by the Council of 500 (Boule). After discussion, voting was conducted by a show of hands, with a simple majority determining the result.

- In terms of scale, 6000 citizens were selected to be jurymen to staff the jury courts, with the average jury size of 501.

- To make participation as fair as possible most officials and jurymen were selected by lot, because elections were believed to be flawed, as they would favour the rich, the famous and the powerful.

- In terms of eligibility, only adult males could involve themselves in democratic government. Also both their parents had to be Athenians. In effect, the citizen body was a closed political elite.

Aristotle defined the democratic citizen as a man 'who has a share in [legal] judgement and office'.

Serious threats to democracy were dealt with by a form of reverse election. A citizen who presented a threat could be ostracised, which in effect meant they would be exiled for ten years. Citizens would scratch or paint the name of the individual to be ostracised on a piece of pottery. It would need 6000 citizens to vote in favour of the ostracism for it to be valid. This system was later replaced by a legal procedure delegated to the jurors of the peoples' courts.

Administrative officials were generally selected by lot in boards of ten. They were responsible for ceremonial issues, military affairs and management of the treasury. There were enormous numbers of offices and official duties, all of which were taken very seriously. Significantly, experienced orators, such as Demosthenes, were able to fundamentally influence the voting of the assemblies in a way that has never quite been replicated, even in today's mass media communications world. There are, however, criticisms of the Athenian system, as set out in the following table.

Criticism or question	Explanation
Is it right that all men are equal?	No. Slaves, women and foreigners are excluded and those with time and expertise can have more influence.
How can traditional customs and values of society be protected against temporary majorities?	It can be seen as undemocratic, as only a small proportion of adults could vote, but the ultimate right of all citizens to vote would protect traditions.
How can the rule of law be protected?	Athenians did not see the rule of law in the same way. They focused on ad hoc discretionary decision-making, as opposed to what we would call the rule of law.
Democracy encourages the emergence of factionalism, losing sight of the national interest.	Factions were a reality and in one extreme case in 411 BC the democratic assembly was replaced by the Council of 400. Political enemies were executed or forced into exile.

Representative democracy

Representative democracies are political systems in which voters elect representatives, rather than engage in direct democracy. Modern-day democracy bears little relation to the Athenian model. Government and decision-making is in the control of a handful of professional politicians. It is they who have the responsibility to make decisions on behalf of the people.

Representative democracy can therefore be described as being a rather limited and indirect form of democracy. It is limited in the sense that citizens' actual involvement in the democratic process is restricted to a handful of voting opportunities in elections throughout their lives. It is indirect in the sense that the citizens only choose who should govern and they do not exercise power themselves. However, the ability of citizens to radically change their voting habits if they are unhappy with the present government goes some way to ensuring public accountability.

Returning to Lincoln's view of democracy, representative democracy does not really address government by the people. But it does reflect government for the people.

John Stuart Mill on the dangers of democracy

Mill believed that not all political opinions had equal value and rejected the idea of political equality. Mill believed that society only had the right to interfere with the freedom of an individual when that individual's actions or inactions could cause harm to other people. If their actions or inactions would only harm themselves then government and society should allow the individual to go ahead and not interfere. Mill was in favour of extending the franchise to all educated men and women, albeit giving greater influence to the most educated.

Models of representation

There is considerable debate around the four key models of representation, with differing views, as set out in the following table.

Edmund Burke's gloomy view

Edmund Burke strongly criticised the French Revolution. He was opposed to the ideas of liberty, equality and fraternity, believing instead that good government resides in the institutions and practices that have survived several generations. He believed that government, although capable of preventing evil, actually rarely promotes good.

Thomas Paine and the rights of man

Paine believed that the concept of society is so embedded that government is barely necessary to maintain it. Paine was a radical democrat. He did recognise the need for representation. He proposed that regular elections were needed to ensure a frequent change of views between representatives and their constituents. This was to ensure that 'the elected might never form to themselves an interest separate from the electors'.

Representation model	Explanation
Trustee	This model suggests that a representative should be in a position to exercise their judgement on matters of importance. The problem is that the representative may actually only represent their own interests and not the interests of the electorate.
Delegate	This is a representative who should act on behalf of the voters on the basis of receiving clear instructions from them. A delegate should not exercise their own judgement, they should just perform as they have been instructed. This means that the representative acts for their constituents primarily and not necessarily for the good of the nation.
Resemblance	This assumes that a representative should be representative of the group that they actually represent. Whilst on an individual basis this may be difficult, across the whole of an assembly there should be a fair gender split and ethnic minority representation. This system does assume that only those that have a resemblance to a group can represent their interests.
Mandate	This model suggests that individuals are elected on the basis of the party that they represent, rather than on the basis of their own personal abilities. It assumes that representatives should ensure that they implement their manifesto promises. It does not take into account that voters may not necessarily agree with the full range of policies.

Similarities and differences

High levels of participation as typified in direct democracy are really only workable in small communities. Mass meetings involving perhaps millions of citizens is unworkable. Equally, if citizens are consulted on every single issue and given the opportunity to be involved in the debate then the country would become ungovernable and decision-making impossible. In addition, most citizens are seen to lack the time, knowledge and willingness to become more directly involved.

Representative democracy, therefore, provides an alternative. It produces a group of individuals who can devote all their time to government and perhaps do a better job than the average citizen.

However, government needs to be responsive and not bureaucratic, otherwise citizens become disengaged from the democratic process, as evidenced by falling levels of voting in elections. Often voting is seen as little more than a meaningless ritual and as having little to do with democracy.

DISCUSSION POINT (?)

How compatible are methods of direct and indirect democracy?

Models of democracy

There are rival theories or models of democracy. They each consider the different democratic forms and the mechanisms that a democracy might use. They also consider the foundations upon which there is a justification for democratic rule. There are four models.

- Classical democracy
- Developmental democracy
- People's democracy
- Protective democracy

Learning objectives

- Models of democracy
- Key thinkers

Classical democracy

Classical democracy is the oldest of the four models, dating back to ancient Greece in the 4th and 5th centuries BC. The model features a form of direct democracy used by Athens. Some believe it to be the purest form of participation and government.

In effect government and decision-making took the form of mass meetings (known as an assembly or *ecclesia*). A council of 500 acted as the executive for the assembly. A 500-strong committee made proposals to the council. The assembly itself met at least forty times a year. The president of the committee could only hold the post once in their lifetime, and only for one day.

The success of Athenian democracy was the widespread involvement of the citizens. Not only did many take active roles in decision-making, but large numbers were prepared to take public office. In reality there were drawbacks and limitations. Only Athenian-born males over the age of twenty could participate. Women and foreigners had no political rights; neither did the bulk of the population, the slaves. Indeed it was the very existence of slaves that enabled Athenians to throw themselves into political activity. Slaves carried out the hard labour and women handled domestic responsibilities.

Classical democracy lives on in township meetings in New England in the United States and in the communal assemblies of the Swiss cantons. More broadly it can be seen as being the basis behind electronic democracy, people's panels, referendums and initiatives.

Developmental democracy

Developmental democracy focuses on concerns for the development of the individual and the community. Theorists such as Jean-Jacques Rousseau believed that democracy was a way in which individuals could achieve freedom by obeying laws to which they subscribe themselves. In other words, a citizen has freedom when they can participate in a direct way in the decisions that shape the future of the community in which they live. Rousseau believed that adherence to the general will would produce a more virtuous society.

Rousseau did not believe that democracy based on elections was necessarily the way forward. He believed representative assemblies would inevitably become corrupt, placing their own selfish interests above the general will. Indeed, subsequent theorists have translated this into a belief that citizens can only develop by participating in decisions that shape their lives. This means that democracy has to be open, accountable and decentralised. Many refer to this as being 'grass roots' democracy. Early socialist theorists, such as Fourier and Owen, advocated

Rousseau on democracy

In *The Social Contract* Rousseau argued that citizens were only free when they were electing members of parliament. But once the MPs had been elected the citizens became enslaved. They only had a brief moment of freedom. He argued that citizens needed to have obedience to the general will – the collective interests of citizens – and only then would they act selflessly.

Bourgeoisie

The ruling class in a capitalist society that owns the means of production and therefore wealth.

Capitalism

An economic system in which wealth is privately owned and the market dictates prices for commodities.

Egalitarian

The belief that the promotion of equality is the main driving force in politics and public life.

Proletariat

This refers to not just the working class in a capitalist society, but to any individual who has to sell their labour to survive.

Totalitarian

It means a dictatorship that pretends to be a democracy. In effect it is a state in which a single party rules and in which opposition is not tolerated.

communal-style democracies in which the residents themselves would govern their own affairs. In the 1990s the communitarian ideas of Amitai Etzioni were influential in suggesting that as stakeholders in their own communities, people should be given opportunities to express their common values to help improve the quality of their daily lives.

One of the problems is that the general will can be manipulated by interest groups, but claim that their views represent the general will. Rousseau's ideas are therefore criticised on the basis that they could bring about a **totalitarian** democracy. J. L. Talmon argued that elevating the collective interest above that of the individual would lead to the loss of freedom in society. Rousseau himself referred to how those who disagreed with the general will must be 'forced to be free'.

There are less radical forms of developmental democracy, such as those suggested by the liberal John Stuart Mill. He saw democracy as an educational experience to broaden understanding. He wanted powerful local authorities, capable of making decisions, thus broadening public office to more of the population.

Mill on democracy

Mill did not believe in political equality. He proposed that unskilled workers would have a single vote, skilled would have two and graduates and professionals would have five or six. He had a fear that individual liberties and minority rights would be threatened by democracy and that debate and criticism would be stifled by the will of the majority.

People's democracy

This term can be used to describe the different democratic models generated by Marxist ideas, particularly those systems used in Eastern Europe after the Second World War. Although Marxists saw traditional forms of democracy as being too associated with **capitalism**, they recognised that they were **egalitarian**. Common ownership of wealth would bring about social democracy, yet political democracy was not considered desirable. Lenin advocated that the true interests of the proletariat would be better served by a vanguard party acting upon Marx's own version of the general will, 'species being'. Thus decisions would be taken by the process of democratic centralism, where the party elite would make the decisions based upon the scientific tenets of Marxism and these would be submitted for discussion amongst the masses through various tiers of worker councils.

Marx on democracy

Marx believed that democracy could only be achieved if capitalism was overthrown. He believed that once the **bourgeois** democracy was swept away and replaced with a **proletarian** democracy, problems between classes would gradually disappear. There would then be no need for government, as he defined this as the organised exploitation of one class by another, instead society would be run according to the maxim 'from each according to their ability to each according to their need'. Democracy would, in effect, be redundant.

One of the key problems with Marx's concept of the transfer of power from the bourgeoisie to the proletariat was that power actually remained in the hands of the Communist Party. There was no mechanism to check the power of the party and hold it accountable to the proletariat that it represented.

Fourier on democracy

Fourier was an early radical socialist, much criticised by later writers, such as Marx, who believed his views to be too idealistic. Fourier suggested independent communities where production would be a communal activity. Everything would be shared on an equal basis and all decisions made on a collective basis. His views have many similarities with the Israeli kibbutz system.

Protective democracy

This model suggests that democracy is not necessarily concerned with political participation, but more to do with how a citizen can protect his or herself from government. The early liberals supported this view, as they believed in individual liberties: citizens needed to be protected from over-powerful governments. John Locke had written 'life, liberty and property' and Thomas Jefferson 'life, liberty and the pursuit of happiness'. Locke believed that government needed to be based on the consent of citizens and that there was a possibility that this consent could always be withdrawn. This is one of the principles upon which the US Constitution is based, one with checks and balances on different branches of the government to prevent one from dominating the others.

The right to vote was seen as a fundamental inalienable right that could not be removed by government. Voting was largely based on property ownership and if government could take property from citizens through taxation then, as a balance, citizens should have the right to control and decide who sets those taxes. This is the basis of 'no taxation without representation', which was a call by American colonists in the run up to the American War of Independence.

Central to protective democracy is the accountability of those who are involved in government. Liberty should also be guaranteed by a separation of powers (Montesquieu emphasised the need to fragment government power through a separation of powers) and the maintenance of freedoms and rights, but above all citizens should have the opportunity to live as they please without interference. In modern politics supporters of the New Right (such as Friedman and Hayek) can be considered to be protective democrats.

DISCUSSION POINT

Which model of democracy is the most attractive and why?

Learning objectives

- What is a liberal democracy?
- Liberal and democratic ideas
- Modern appeal of liberal democracy
- Key thinkers on liberal democracies

Pluralist (or Pluralism)

This is the notion that the distribution of political power limits the ability of any one group to dominate the political system.

Pressure group

A group of individuals who share a common interest or cause and try to influence government to further that cause or interest.

Thomas Jefferson's limited government

Thomas Jefferson became the third president of the United States and was the main author of the US Declaration of Independence. He believed that democracy should mean rule by a natural aristocracy that was committed to limited government and **laissez-faire**.

What is a liberal democracy?

Liberal democracies came into existence from the middle of the 19th century and can possibly be traced back to the US Constitution of 1776. They have now spread across the world, encompassing countries as diverse as Britain, Japan and India. However, the term liberal democracy is often used as a political idea and it is probably more accurate to describe this system, using Robert Dahl's term, as a polyarchy. It is a modern form of representative democracy, which literally means 'ruled by many'.

Polyarchies are quite crude versions of democracy. There are institutions that force those who rule to take into account the interests and the wishes of the electorate. Generally, they have elected officials to run the government and there are regular, free and fair elections. The right to vote, extended to nearly all adults, there are generally few restrictions on running for office and there is constitutional protection of citizens' rights, including free expression, free assembly and protest. Citizens have access to information through a free media, there are many groups and associations that operate independently of government and the economic system is based largely on free-market capitalism.

The liberal part of liberal democracy actually goes back to the time before countries could be described as being truly democratic. The liberal approach existed when voting rights were still limited. The liberal part of the phrase simply implies limited government and that citizens should have a degree of protection from the state. Government is considered to be a necessary evil and as it could impose itself on individuals, checks and balances need to be put in place, in order to restrict its impact.

Liberal democracies have a form of electoral democracy. This means that government derives its authority or legitimacy through a popular vote. A state that restricts the eligibility of citizens to vote in any way is therefore not considered to be truly democratic. Further, elections must be regular, open and competitive. Politicians also need to be called to account for their actions.

Liberal democracies tend to incorporate a mix of rule by an elite (in this case professional politicians) along with popular participation (free, fair and regular elections). In effect, the voter uses their political power in exactly the same way as a consumer would use their economic power to buy products and services in a marketplace.

Accountability is reinforced by the right of citizens to create **pressure groups** in order to influence decision-makers. In this respect liberal democracies are often described as **pluralist** democracies. Accountability is also aided by the ability of the media to scrutinise the activities of politicians. This means that political power is widely spread amongst competing groups and that each group has access to the government. Dahl's ideas on pluralism were largely based upon his empirical study on how decisions were made in the New England town of New Haven.

Liberal and democratic ideas

Liberal democracies are not wholly supported by all theorists and points of view. There are a number of critics of the system.

- Elitists believe that political power is concentrated in the hands of the few and that power is actually exercised by elites. Gaetano Mosca and Vilfredo Pareto saw elites ruling in democracies through a combination of force and cunning (lions and foxes).

- C. Wright Mills believed that society was controlled by the power elite – based on the military-industrial complex (the relationship between government, the armed forces and industry).

- The elite controlled the hierarchies and organisations and were non-elected bodies, such as the military, the judiciary and the police. Mills argued that political equality and even the electoral process were irrelevant.

- Liberals and conservatives argue that capitalism is a precondition for democracy and that the right to own property is an essential part of this.

- Revolutionary Marxists disagree and believe that there cannot be a democratic way to socialism. Other Marxists disagreed and believed that democracy could bring about major social change. Essentially, however, Marxists believe that a real democracy can only be brought about by economic equality and this is not present in a liberal democracy.

- Radical democrats reject liberal democracies on the basis that they reduce participation to just a ritual. Citizens do not rule and there is an enormous gulf in interests and understanding between those in government and those that have elected them. Radical democrats are firm supporters of referendums and the use of information technology, but they also argue that power needs to be decentralised and that pressure groups should play a greater role in decision-making.

Modern appeal of liberal democracy

In 1989, Francis Fukuyama, a US State Department policy planner, suggested that ideological struggles were over and that western liberal democracy had proved to be the best way to run a society. He was writing at a time when the Cold War was finally over and liberal democracies had won the ideological war against the Marxists of Eastern Europe.

Fukuyama had in fact borrowed the concept from Hegel who believed that history would be over when societies had reached the final stage of their ideological evolution. Fukuyama believed that although there would still be conflict between states, the ideological war was over and won. Since he wrote his essay, we have seen countries such as Hungary, Poland and the former Soviet Union grope towards some form of liberal democracy.

Fukuyama also believed that Maoism as seen in China was an anachronism and it would only be a matter of time before China embraced market liberalisation, a process that we have certainly seen in recent years. He believed that if western-style liberal democracies were too alien to the Chinese, there was a close example that they could follow and understand – Japan. However, Japan is often assumed to be a western liberal democracy, because that is the form of government imposed by the Allies after Japan's surrender in 1945 at the end of the Second World War, but the substance of power in Japan has always been separate from its form. Career government officials, not elected political leaders, set the budget, write most legislation and make major policy decisions.

John Locke's natural rights

John Locke was an important theorist in the development of early liberalism. He believed in representative government and toleration. He identified natural rights, which were the rights to life, liberty and property. Locke was not a democrat by our standards; he only believed that those who owned property should vote. But he believed that democracy should mean a system of 'government by consent'.

Laissez-faire

In effect this means that government should not involve itself in trying to control the flow of money in an economy. This should be left to market forces and governments should not be trusted to have this amount of control over the economy. In effect it means a free market.

Alexis de Tocqueville on tyranny of the majority

Alexis de Tocqueville influenced both liberals and conservatives. He was a French politician. He believed that liberty was threatened by public opinion, which he called the tyranny of the majority. He believed that individuality, self-assurance and liberty could be lost if the majority imposed uniformity. He was in favour of decentralised government, the use of a constitution to shape society and the creation of mechanisms to ensure democratic politics.

DISCUSSION POINT ?

Why are liberal democracies so common across the world?

Learning objectives

- Characteristics of dictatorships
- Different types of dictatorships
- Differences between dictatorships and democracies
- Key thinkers on dictatorships

Autocracy

This literally means self-rule, where an individual holds all the power and can exercise that power in an arbitrary way. Laws might appear to limit the power, but they can be revoked and disobeyed by the individual.

Characteristics of dictatorships

Dictatorship is most closely associated with the exercise of absolute power by a single individual and in this respect it is very similar to the concept of **autocracy**.

The term dates back to the early Roman Republic, when supreme magistrates were sometimes given unrestricted emergency powers, thus creating a form of constitutional dictatorship. We now more broadly view dictatorships as being situations when an individual acts above the law and without constitutional constraint.

Typical examples in more recent history include Adolf Hitler, Benito Mussolini and Saddam Hussein.

In Roman times the power was only to last for six months or until such time as the crisis passed. Julius Caesar assumed dictatorial powers in 46 BC and held them for ten years before his assassination.

Dictatorships are also closely associated with the term despotism. This derives from a Greek word that originally meant 'master' and is now applied to situations where an individual assumes power over people such that the condition can be compared to that of slavery. It is often used to describe arbitrary or tyrannical governments.

Different types of dictatorships

There are several different types of dictatorship that have been identified by various political theorists and commentators, as outlined in the following table.

Type of dictatorship	Explanation
Class dictatorship	Essentially this is a version of dictatorship of the proletariat, in which revolutionary change is considered to be the permanent state of affairs. In effect society should be run by the majority class and new institutions should reflect the dominance of that class. This was the view of the Irish Republican Socialist Party led by James Connolly.
Party dictatorship	This is a situation when a party gains political power and then effectively strips all other parties of opportunities to fairly contest elections or to allow them to criticise government. A prime example in modern-day politics is the Zanu-PF of Robert Mugabe in Zimbabwe. He came to power in 1980.
Military dictatorship	This is a form of government where political power resides solely in the hands of military chiefs (sometimes referred to as a stratocracy). Usually these come to power via a *coup d'état*. Typical examples in modern-day politics include Burma, Pakistan and Libya. Some military dictatorships are typified by a cult of personality as a particular military leader comes to the fore and creates a heroic public image for him or herself, for example Idi Amin (President of Uganda 1971–79) and Muammar al-Gaddafi (Leader and Guide of the Revolution, Libya 1969 to date).
Personal dictatorship	This is the situation when a prominent individual assumes dictatorial powers and focuses their efforts into creating a positive public image for themselves, in which they are portrayed as an idealised figure, against which all others should be compared. It is often referred to as a cult of personality. Examples include Kim Il-Sung and his son in North Korea, Adolf Hitler, Joseph Stalin and Saddam Hussein.

Type of dictatorship	Explanation
Dictatorship of the proletariat	This was a term used by Karl Marx, but adapted from the French revolutionary Louis Auguste Blanqui. It implies the need for a temporary revolutionary elite to extinguish any remaining features of capitalism and impose a revolutionary programme on the people, whether they want it or not.
Autocracy	This is unchecked and overriding political power given to an individual in high office. It implies absolute or unlimited power, such as was found in hereditary monarchs (absolute monarchies). Government is carried out in the name of the individual inheriting the title. In these examples the monarch has unbridled power and does not have to share authority with a legislative assembly.
Authoritarian oligarchy	This is when political power is lodged in the hands of a small number of people that make a single, cohesive elite, such as a one-party state. Examples include the Communist seizure of power in Russia in 1917 and the emergence of Stalin as an autocratic ruler in 1922 until his death in 1953. There has been an authoritarian oligarchy in power in China since 1949.
Absolute democracy	Essentially, this is a democratic but unconstitutional government. Other terms used to describe this are majoritarian dictatorship, popular despotism or tyranny of the majority. Absolute democracy is characterised by absolute unlimited rule of the majority, regardless of whether or not it is a slim majority. There are no restraints on the power of the majority. Examples include ancient Athens and more recently the reign of terror period (1793–94) during the French Revolution.

Differences between dictatorships and democracies

There are key differences between democracies and dictatorships, as outlined in the following table.

Theme	Democracy	Dictatorship
Who makes the decisions?	In theory, it is the people who make decisions in a democracy by voting or becoming a candidate or assisting in election campaigns.	There is a monopoly of political power; the masses are excluded from politics.
Existence of political associations	In theory, most political groups are acceptable, providing they are not seen to be acting to fundamentally undermine democracy.	There is a one-party state led by an all-powerful leader.
Attitudes towards individual rights	There is a distinct split between the public and the private sphere. Liberty and civil rights are upheld.	There is an abolition of civil society. The private sphere is no longer private but of state concern.
Extent of state control	State control extends only to areas that concern the community in general.	There is a system of terror-based policing and state control of all aspects of economic life.
Attitude towards toleration and dissent	Toleration towards dissident groups is ensured through legislation, providing these views do not impinge on the civil rights of others.	There is little or no toleration and acceptance of dissent. Open terror and brutality are used to combat them.

Thomas Hobbes on absolutism and anarchy

Hobbes believed that stability and order could only be ensured by an absolute and unlimited state, the Leviathan, whose power could not be challenged or questioned. He felt there was a choice between **absolutism** and **anarchy**.

Hannah Arendt on social movements

Arendt believed that social movements, or collectivist ideas, such as nationalism, were inevitable stepping stones towards totalitarianism or dictatorial governments.

Karl Marx

Karl Marx's dictatorship of the proletariat

Marx did not actually explain what he meant by dictatorship but he did suggest the rule of the proletariat. His phrase is now used to describe the nature and the legitimacy of state power during the transition period from revolution to communism. Marx's ideas were used as a basis by Lenin, Mao and other communist leaders to justify Communist Party rule.

Jean-Jacques Rousseau on man's nature

Rousseau believed that direct democracy was the only way to ensure that everyone has equality and the rights to determine government and how society should function. He believed that this form of democracy was the sole route to legitimacy. This form of non-representative democracy means that the individual has to surrender themselves to it, as they are overridden by the rest of the community when the individual's choice conflicts with theirs, that is, the majority.

Absolutism

This is a government that is not limited in any way by an agency internal to itself, in other words there are no constitutional checks and balances.

Anarchy

A society that lacks institutions of state, rejects authority and favours spontaneous action.

DISCUSSION POINT ?

Compare and contrast dictatorships and democracies.

Pros and cons of democracy

There are a number of pro-democracy arguments, including the following.

- Expert elites in government should not be trusted with absolute unchecked power. Undemocratic elites become remote from the people and fail to understand their needs and desires. As society is made up of a great number of different groups, no elite can know what is best for everyone. The democratic elements of a political system mean that decisions take this into account and prevent decisions being dominated by elites.

- Governments would prefer to rule by consent than by force and democracy provides the basis for legitimacy, as well as social and political stability and cohesion. It creates commitment. Democracies are often associated with liberal capitalism and social welfare. These aim to ensure individual freedoms and education. These types of societies are relatively well governed, they are prosperous and cohesive.

- Democracy encourages the development of the citizen, so that they have knowledge of major issues. If the population is informed it can be responsible and take its limited role in the democratic process seriously. The government benefits from this, as new individuals are attracted into government and into party politics.

- There is also a moral claim for participation, as all citizens have a stake in society. Morality, as far as democrats are concerned, demands that individuals have a right to participate. They go further to suggest that it is not just a moral right but a moral duty to become involved.

- Democracy is also seen as an engine of social change, as it drives reform, given that voters will not continually support an unjust society. Mass democratic movements can force improvements in society, end social injustices or tackle grievances.

There are, of course, arguments against democracy.

- The first is that government actually needs a specialised elite because most people know very little about politics, issues and decision-making. Government should therefore be left to specialists who know best.

- Nineteenth-century liberals were also concerned about the dangers of majority rule by an ill-educated population. Some believed that it was important to restrict democratic rights to those who could show reasoned thought. This has come back as an issue, as allegations are made about dumbing down political debates.

- The focus on political democracy ignores economic democracy as far as Marxists are concerned. Social and economic inequalities exist, which undermine the democratic system. Equal political rights are just a sham, as people are still being governed and exploited.

- Feminists would also criticise democracy on the basis that due to the roles assigned to women in a male-dominated society, women are prevented from making their true contribution to society felt.

Perspectives on democracy

There is a considerable amount of disagreement about what is meant by democracy and its significance. The following table outlines five key perspectives.

Perspective	Explanation
Pluralist	The key theorists include Locke, Montesquieu, Madison and Dahl. Broadly, the pluralist view on democracy is somewhat similar to what we understand to be liberal democracy. In other words, democracy is based on a system of competitive elections fought by a number of different parties. Democracy operates through organised groups that try to articulate popular demands and influence government. It is slightly different to parliamentary democracy and majoritarianism, as a pluralist democracy aims to have the widest possible spread of political powers amongst a number of groups. However within each group the leadership is responsive to the views of their membership and government is in fact neutral and fragmented and allows a number of groups to access and influence them simultaneously.
Neo-pluralist or corporatist	This view of democracy is often described as corporatist or tripartite. It suggests that democracy is most effective when state officials, employers' groups and unions work directly with one another. They believe that it is possible to create a form of representation that reflects individuals' views and interests through membership of groups, rather than through competitive elections. Most believe that this tripartite approach is actually anti-democratic. Groups that have access to the government, or insider groups, have political power. Those that do not have access or are outsider groups have no power. The government can choose which organisations they will work with, which means that radical ideas and demands are excluded. Policy is created through negotiation with powerful economic groups and not driven by electoral or parliamentary democracy. There is also the issue that the groups themselves are not publicly accountable. In Mussolini's fascist Italy corporatism was based on the belief that businesses and labour were inseparable as a single entity. But in practice this version of corporatism was used to intimidate big business and smash trade unions.
Marxist	Marxist criticisms of liberal democracies focus on the tension between democracy and capitalism. On the one hand liberal democracy claims to provide political equality, whilst on the other hand the existence of capitalism generates social inequality. Marxists believe that this means that liberal democracies are therefore controlled and manipulated by the powers of the ruling classes. Antonio Gramsci referred to the process by which the bourgeoisie were able to control the masses as bourgeoisie hegemony. In other words, those who own the productive wealth of the country. They also believe that political power cannot be equally shared whilst there are differences in the power of the classes. Marxists suggest that the ruling classes will always pursue their own interests and only make concessions to other groups in order to stabilise capitalism and to ensure the continuance of unequal class power. This does not mean that they completely reject elections as a democratic process. Democracy forces governments to spend more money and expand the role and responsibility of the state. In the long term Marxists believe that higher spending governments fuel high inflation and that high tax is a disincentive to business. Balancing economic problems with ever increasing democratic pressures will cause huge legitimacy problems for governments. Jurgen Habermas argued that capitalism will ultimately undergo a crisis of legitimacy and that this was the basis of the economic and political problems encountered across the world in the 1970s.
Elitist	Key theorists include Pareto, Mosca and Michels. Classical elitists believed that democracy was nothing more than a sham and that power actually belonged to a relatively small number of people with everyone else having very little power. This has been an approach that even more modern-day elitists have followed, but it has been refined in as much as they appreciate that the electorate can decide which elite rules, but not the fact that power is always in the hands of an elite. Politicians in competitive elections have to work hard to gain the vote of the electorate and the party that wins most closely reflects the values, policies and philosophies of the majority of the voters. Democracy is seen as just a political method, a way of making political decisions. The better informed and the better skilled politicians win elections. Through competition they are accountable, but this makes for a weak form of democracy, as elites can only be removed by simply voting in another one.
New Right	The primary focus on the New Right view is that political systems are in danger of 'democratic overload' because they are open to enormous pressures from groups and the electorate. Although the New Right are supporters of the free market and believe that governments should stay out of the economy, it is corporatism they believe that can cause the most damage. Groups make demands on government and if they are well placed they can influence government which means that the government then intervenes, causing economic problems. The theory goes on to suggest that politicians have to compete by making ever more unrealistic promises to voters. In effect they try to outbid one another. This causes high inflation due to public spending and high taxes, which stunts economic growth and places a burden on businesses. The key theorists include Friedman and Hayek.

DISCUSSION POINT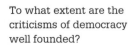

To what extent are the criticisms of democracy well founded?

Role of MPs

The concept of democracy is one of the most cherished aspects of the British political system. In Britain we have representative democracy. This means that every citizen over a certain age has the right to vote on issues that affect him or her and for the majority decision of their vote to lead to legislation being passed. It means that everyone has a right to be involved and hold political office; representative democracy encourages people to participate in the choice of individuals that will represent the majority in parliament.

However, how many of the electorate have the time and the inclination to read the full policy proposals of a party or the intentions of candidates? How many have the time to devote to direct participation in politics at any level? As a result of this, our democracy boils down to voting for a candidate every five or so years. Once they become MPs, the candidates debate and legislate on our behalf. The electorate, effectively, hands over the responsibility of decision-making and legislation to representatives.

Once they are a part of the House of Commons, MPs soon discover that democracy is a frail concept. They are bound by their party, its leadership, overwhelmed by information, and harassed by pressure and interest groups. Balancing their own personal consciences, the demands of their constituents, their party and countless other groups makes democratic, free decision-making very difficult, even in the place so closely linked with the democratic process and its values.

Learning objectives

● Role of MPs

● Which model of representation best describes the role of MPs?

● How representative is the House of Commons?

Which model of representation best describes the role of MPs?

In many cases two types of MP emerges. There are those who act in line with their consciences, regardless of what the party might say or what the electorate may want. This is generally based on a trustee model. While this gives them flexibility, it questions democracy, as they were elected on the basis of supporting specific manifesto promises.

The other type of MP tends to believe that they should react to the wishes of both their party and the electorate, to which they owe allegiance. The closest model that this equates to is the mandate model.

The following table outlines the nature of the four models of representation, as far as House of Commons MPs are concerned.

The House of Commons

Model	Realities	How and why?
Trustee	By virtue of better education and a more informed understanding the MP represents the interests of the less fortunate. It assumes that the general public are ill-educated and ill-informed and it also assumes that education assists moral decision-making and makes the more educated more likely to want to perform citizenship duties. The problem is that MPs exercise their own judgement and do not necessarily represent the interests of the electorate.	Edmund Burke would have suggested that MPs should use 'mature judgement' and 'enlightened conscience'. The trustee model suggests that the MP has a formal responsibility for the affairs of others. In other words, individuals who would act wisely on the electorates' behalf, rather than simply reflecting voters' views (this was the view of J. S. Mill).

Delegate	This cannot necessarily be perceived as a way in which either our political system aims to produce representatives, or the views of the representatives themselves. A true delegate merely follows instructions from those that elected the individual. They are not free to make broader decisions that are at variance with the wishes or the interests of their constituency. This would make political life impossible, as they would be unable to exercise their own will.	The MP is supposed to represent the interests of all their constituents and be at their service. Collectively, MPs are said to represent the country as a whole. The burden on MPs is considerable; in addition to direct parliamentary work they fulfil the role of a welfare officer/social worker to constituents and as a promoter of local interests. Thomas Paine believed that there should be 'frequent interchange' between representatives and their constituents to ensure that constituents' views were represented.
Mandate	The mandate model assumes that individual MPs, as members of a larger organisation that has received a mandate from the electorate, can only implement policies within the manifesto. In practice this is also an impossible model, as it would mean that MPs would be restricted to decision-making based on promises that they have already made. It would not give them the opportunity to react to new circumstances or new issues. In effect any decisions contrary or in addition to the manifesto would not have been endorsed by the voters.	The MP is elected (usually) on the basis of the party policies rather than as an individual. The MP is therefore in the House to speak and vote as a representative of the party. However, there have been rebellions, such as on the war in Iraq, ID cards and the extension of the 28-day detention for terror suspects. Edmund Burke (1774) believed that MPs should, above all, be independent and serve nothing but their own judgement.
Resemblance	This model suggests that the role of the MP is to be an example of the group that they actually represent. Therefore MPs should represent a cross-section of the community. In practice the working classes and ethnic minorities in particular, as well as women, are under-represented. The model suggests that only those that have a resemblance to the group can actually represent the group's interests, which of course is not necessarily the case.	MPs can be sponsored (by a trade union, etc.), they may be paid as an adviser, consultant or a director to an organisation or a business. They may meet regularly with professional lobbyists. An MP may receive financial support or information from particular groups. An MP may be influenced by their outside occupation (part-time work as a journalist, company director, lawyer, etc.) The Nolan Report (1995) suggested ways to control outside interests and since 1975 MPs are required to declare their interests at the beginning of a debate. Although an MP may have links and be influenced by a sectional interest, Rousseau believed that there was a danger that these sectional interests could supersede the general will.

How representative is the House of Commons?

To some extent MPs reflect the broadest range of different types of people; they have different motives and reasons for seeking to become an MP.

The average age of MPs dropped in 1997, mainly due to ten MPs under 30 being elected and there being fewer MPs over the age of 60. Since then the average age has risen. The following table shows the average age of MPs from 1992 to 2005.

Year	Average age	18–29	30–39	40–49	50–59	60–69	70+
1992	50	1	82	259	211	95	3
1997	48.8	10	92	254	227	68	8
2001	49.8	4	79	236	247	83	10
2005	50.6	3	89	191	249	100	14

Source: House of Commons Library

This table shows the age of MPs elected at the 2005 general election by party.

Party	Number	Average age	Under 40	41–59	60+
Labour	355	52.2	10%	71%	19%
Conservative	198	49.3	17%	65%	18%
Lib Dem	62	46.0	31%	60%	10%
Others	31	50.8	13%	77%	10%
All	646	50.6	14%	68%	18%

Source: House of Commons Library

The problem with the age of MPs reflecting the age profile of the population in general is that there are often questions of experience. In the 2008 local elections the youngest councillor elected was just 18.

The balance of gender has also changed, with women MPs now being 1 in 5, the highest ever proportion. The following table shows the proportion of male and female MPs elected to parliament from 1979 to 2005.

Election	Male	Female	Total	Female %
1979	616	19	635	3
1983	627	23	650	4
1987	609	41	650	6
1992	591	60	651	9
1997	609	120	659	18
2001	541	118	659	18
2005	609	127	646	20

Source: House of Commons Library

Labour currently has the highest proportion of female MPs, with 28 per cent, followed by the Liberal Democrats (16%) and the Conservatives (9%).

The occupational background of MPs is varied; broadly, they can be split into four major groups.

- Professions – barristers, solicitors, doctors, civil servants and teachers
- Business – directors, etc.
- Miscellaneous – professional politicians, publishers and journalists
- Manual workers – miners, etc.

The following table shows in percentages the occupational backgrounds of MPs in 2005.

Occupation	Labour	Conservative	Lib Dem
Professions	40	38	40
Business	7	38	29
Miscellaneous	43	23	29
Manual workers	10	1	2

Source: Butler et al. (2005)

In the 2005 general election, 15 MPs from ethnic minorities were elected; this was up by 3 MPs from 2001. The first non-white MPs were elected in 1987 (4 Labour MPs). In the 2005 election 2.3 per cent of MPs were non-white (compared to 8% of the population).

DISCUSSION POINT (?)

Does it matter if the House of Commons is not representative of the UK at large?

Learning objectives

- Dangers of majoritarianism
- Problems with the operation of electoral systems
- Declining participation
- Dangers of widening participation

Dangers of majoritarianism

Majoritarianism is the theory that priority should be given to the will of the majority. In its basic form, it suggests that there is a degree of insensitivity towards individuals and minorities. In practice in a democratic majoritarian political system the majority would not exclude any minority from participation in the democratic process.

The greatest fear about democracy derived from Alexis de Tocqueville's 'tyranny of the majority', in other words the fact that democracy would always have the threat that individual liberties and the rights of minorities can be overwhelmed in the name of the people. Equally, Mill believed that democracy would ultimately sweep away debate, criticism and intellectual life. The 19th century US Governor of Massachusetts, Elbridge Gerry, suggested, 'The evils we experience flows from the excess of democracy'. The key concerns of majoritarianism are therefore:

- the dangers of majority tyranny
- repression of minority rights
- tendency towards dull conformity
- what guarantees that the majority view is always right.

In Northern Ireland (1922–98), the solution to the long-term issues were found in power sharing and stipulated majority voting. The will of the majority, through the ballot box, was imposed on the minority.

Checks and balances can be incorporated to prevent the ill-effects of majoritarianism. Voting in the EU Council is through QMV (quality majority voting) and checks are built in to prevent major states dominating the voting.

However, in some tribal-based societies in Africa, such as Rwanda, a majority tribe was able to implement genocide on a minority population. In the US, the solution is the separation of powers and constitutional safeguards of minority rights in order to prevent majority tyranny. James Madison (1751–1836) aimed to ensure that there was rule in the US by multiple minorities in order to prevent the property-less majority from gaining political power; this was seen as a way to safeguard private ownership.

In Britain there is a tendency of rule by the largest minority – in recent elections this minority has fallen (in 2005 only 22% of all eligible voters voted for Labour). This has enormous implications for the mandate theory on which political parties justify their right to pursue manifesto promises and political agendas.

Problems with the operation of electoral systems

Practically, consent of the governed is exercised by the vote in elections. John Locke held that government arises out of the agreement or consent of the governed as outlined in his social contract theory.

In Britain however, the question needs to be asked whether our first-past-the-post system achieves this.

Advantages	Disadvantages
It is simple and straightforward to operate.	Votes cast for candidates (or parties) that did not receive a simple majority are wasted (the voter cast their vote for a candidate that was not elected).
It produces a clear outcome, both at constituency level and at national level, with one party usually achieving a majority of seats.	Seats won are not in proportion to the number of votes cast for each party. Regional imbalances exist where a party can consistently win 20 per cent of the vote, but not actually win a single seat.
Each constituency has a named representative to look after their interests, with a clear link between the MP and a particular area.	The winning party usually only ever represents a minority of the voters. Voters' choice is limited; they may support a candidate but not the party.
The system tends to produce a government, despite the fact that the party with the most seats may not have won the majority of the votes.	Safe seats are created where only one party ever has a chance of gaining the majority of the vote. Marginal seats become all-important. A small swing in the vote in a handful of constituencies can mean winning or losing an election.

The 2008 Zimbabwe elections illustrate the necessity for a healthy democratic culture of freedom, toleration and political pluralism for elections to be legitimate. The main complaints were:

- the MDC, backed up by human rights groups, claimed their supporters were attacked around the country

- MDC rallies were banned, with the police citing security concerns

- Morgan Tsvangirai was arrested on several occasions when he tried to go on tours

- the state-controlled broadcaster ZBC refused to take campaign adverts from the MDC

- western observers were banned, as President Mugabe accused them of bias in favour of the MDC

- the MDC accused the government of using food aid as a political weapon

- the MDC was also fearful of rigging and ballot box-stuffing on election day.

Declining participation

In a liberal democracy, aside from being actively involved in party politics, voting in elections is one of the only accurate ways of judging levels of participation. Membership of the three main parties in Britain has been in gradual decline since the mid to late 1990s. Several theories have suggested reasons for this trend, which has been identified since the 1950s.

- People are participating in politics in different ways, such as joining pressure groups. Specific objectives of pressure groups have greater appeal, rather than broader political ideas and policies associated with parties.

- The relatively poor image of politicians, particularly among people not wishing to be associated with sleaze.

- The increasing power of the European Union makes many political parties that focus on local or national policies appear irrelevant.

- It is no longer necessary to join a party to stay up to date in terms of policies and ideas, as there are many other sources of information available. Membership of a party does not mean that an individual's views are heard or acted upon.

- The politics of contentment – voters do not vote as they feel they have no serious grievances and are not concerned that the present government will be defeated.

- Elections that are seen as a foregone conclusion, with polls and pundits predicting comprehensive victories and the feeling among the electorate that their vote would not matter.

- The lack of choice – that there no longer appears to be any real difference between the main parties.

- Alienation among the electorate – a deliberate rejection of the democratic system as the voter does not feel involved.

- Social capital – voting is no longer a priority, it is too difficult and there are other personal issues that are more important.

There was great concern after the 2001 election over the massive decline in the electoral turnout. Until 1997 the percentage of eligible voters casting their votes had been relatively stable, at between 72 and 83.9 per cent. In 2001 turnout tumbled to 59.4 per cent. The fear was that if the trend continued it would be difficult for governments to claim they had a mandate to follow policy programmes.

Some suggested that this was a temporary blip and that the opinion polls were to blame. Throughout the duration of the parliament 1997 to 2001, the Labour government had a clear lead in opinion polls over the Conservatives. A 'poll of polls' of the opinion polls in the last six months of the parliament gave Labour an average twelve-point lead. Many voters, it is argued, believed the result was a foregone conclusion and opted not to bother to vote.

Some even suggest that this was the case in 2005, when the turnout was 61.3 per cent, despite the fact that Labour did not have a commanding lead. On average they were just five points ahead. As a result, the turnout increased modestly and it is argued that a closer contest in the future will result in a far higher turnout.

Other key reasons for voters not voting include the following.

Reason	Explanation
Voter mobility	The young are more geographically mobile and do not feel involved.
Apathy	Voters could not be bothered to vote: only 37 per cent of the young voted in 2005.
Abstention	Many feel alienated from politics and choose not to vote.
Boredom	The election campaign was too long and voters lost interest.
Class	In 2005 70 per cent of AB voters voted and only 54 per cent of DE voters voted.
De-alignment and party identification	Voters no longer feel it their duty to support their party and may not feel attached to a party.

Whilst voter turnout is a major aspect of voting behaviour, an important part of the turnout issue is the level of abstention. There are two major issues here.

- Firstly, although it is a legal obligation to register to vote, not everyone does register. There is an increasing number of non-registrations. Some studies suggest the figure may be as high as six million.

- Secondly, although a voter may be registered to vote they may choose not to exercise their democratic right. They have made the decision not to vote.

It is generally accepted that there are two types of abstainer.

- Passive abstainers – they have little or no interest in politics, and they are often referred to as being apathetic. The individual simply cannot be bothered to cast a vote, as politics is not relevant to their lives.

- Active abstainers – they are interested in politics, but choose not to vote for political reasons. Some disagree with the whole political system, others do not vote in order to register their disapproval, whilst others choose not to vote as none of the standing candidates matches their ideals.

There is compulsory voting in countries such as Australia and Belgium. The compulsory nature of the systems does have a potential impact upon individual liberty. Voting is seen as a civil right rather than a civic duty. Voters can exercise their rights, but are not compelled to do so.

Dangers of widening participation

True participatory democracy aims to broaden access to the decision-making process for as many citizens as possible. Taken to its logical conclusion, it would involve creating mass direct democratic processes, which would enable the vast majority of citizens to become involved in the entire decision-making process. This is being examined and piloted through the use of information technology, as we will see when we look at direct democratic systems.

One of the major problems, however, with the extension of participation is the danger that it may impede, or stagnate, decision-making. In recent years, despite a number of promises to the contrary, there have been very limited numbers of referendums used in Britain. Referendums provide an opportunity for the government to pose a specific question or series of questions to the electorate and then to act on their wishes. However, in some cases the government always takes the precaution of reserving the right to reject the electorate's advice. Classical elitist theory suggests that wider participation is undesirable; they suggest that majority views on capital punishment and immigration are good practical examples to show how the majority view is sometimes unpalatable.

DISCUSSION POINT ?

How far do the practical problems associated with democracy undermine the views of its supporters?

Learning
objectives

- The Westminster model
- The US presidential model
- How liberal democratic is the UK?

The Westminster model

The Westminster model in Britain aims to ensure free elections, freedom of speech and open and equal treatment in law. The strength and stability of the system rests on its gradual development and its flexible, unwritten constitution. Institutions have been built up over the years, along with traditions and laws.

However, not everyone believes that the Westminster model is the perfect one and point to issues such as an apathetic electorate, an overburdened legislative system, a centralised and remote ruling elite (regardless of the party in power), a party system that is unrepresentative, politicians that lack new ideas, a media that is hostile and unhelpful to government, and an economy that teeters on the brink of collapse.

There are other issues, not least the fact that Gordon Brown took over the premiership from Tony Blair in 2007 without an electorate mandate. Political sleaze is also a major concern. The following table outlines some key examples.

Labour	Conservative
Peter Mandelson – the former trade secretary resigned twice from the cabinet, initially over allegations he misled the Britannia Building Society in his mortgage application by not disclosing he had a £373,000 loan from former Labour minister Geoffrey Robinson. The second time was over the Hinduja passport affair.	Jonathan Aitken – the former defence procurement minister lied over who paid for a stay at the Ritz Hotel in Paris and ended up in jail for perjury and attempting to pervert the course of justice.
David Blunkett – the former home secretary also resigned twice. The first time followed reports that a visa application for his lover's nanny had been speeded up. He resigned again over allegations he had not revealed his financial involvement with a private DNA testing company.	Dame Shirley Porter – the former Tory leader of Westminster council was ordered to pay a surcharge of £27 million for her part in the 'council home sales for votes' scandal of the 1980s. The Law Lords said attempts to gain political support by selling off council homes in marginal wards to potential Tory voters was 'a deliberate, blatant and dishonest misuse of public power'.
Tessa Jowell – she survived her husband's entanglement with the Italian prime minister and multi-millionaire businessman Silvio Berlusconi.	Neil Hamilton – the former corporate affairs minister's career ended in disgrace after he faced accusations he had accepted cash from Harrods' owner Mohamed Al Fayed in exchange for asking parliamentary questions.

In theory, a working democratic system would surely draw more people into the political process in order to demand change. However, political participation is at low ebb. Sweeping reforms on devolution, human rights, parliamentary changes and a host of other policies have failed to energise the electorate.

A frequent criticism of the Westminster model is based on the very foundation of our democratic process: the electoral system. Election after election has seen more voters cast their votes for alternate parties to the party that ultimately wins the most number of seats and forms the government. This cuts to the core of a representative democracy, in other words the mandate to govern.

Parliamentary sovereignty is a vital part of the Westminster model. Parliament is the final law-making body of the nation. As A. V. Dicey stated, the legal right to exercise power lies with elected MPs. Parliament is charged with acting in the public interest and enforcing the public will. Parliament can remove governments, it can reject legislation and it can oppose government plans to raise finance. Yet the party system controls and manipulates MPs, regardless of public sentiment.

Ministerial responsibility is also an issue. Ministers are ultimately held accountable for the actions of their departments, not merely their own decisions. Yet on countless occasions ministers have refused to take the ultimate responsibility for mistakes and resign. In fact this is all the more problematic because day-to-day decision-making in our representative democracy is not in the hands of MPs, but in the hands of ministers. In 2007, the Northern Rock bank was revealed to be in dire financial straits. Alistair Darling, the Chancellor of the Exchequer, authorised enormous cash injections to prop up the bank. Darling had agreed to guarantee all of the deposits of savers. There were calls for his resignation, which he resisted, as critics claimed he had not taken responsibility for the crisis.

The US presidential model

In the United States there is a clear separation of powers, unlike that in Britain, where it is often blurred. The US idea was that there should never be an over-powerful executive, specifically the president, that could assume sweeping powers. Therefore the US president, the Congress and the Supreme Court are all separate. Each has the power to constrain one another. Congress can make law but the president can veto that law. The president may have the power to make judicial appointments, but they have to be confirmed by the Senate.

The major criticism of the presidential model is that by building in these checks and balances there is always conflict between the different branches of government. There is often deadlock, added to which the president is often from one party and Congress is dominated by another. Since the 2006 mid-term elections, the Democratic Party has been the majority party for the 110th Congress. George W. Bush (Republican) became president for the second time in 2005 and retained this position until 2009.

Despite the difficulties, and the fact that legislative power is separated from executive power, the system works well to protect individual rights and liberties.

Although in recent years Britain has, to some extent, adopted a presidential-style approach, particularly to election campaigns, there are still marked differences. The United States has highly personalised election campaigns, particularly for president. Brand image is all-important and the electorate is presented with the preferred candidates of the two major parties as the only credible and electable presidential options.

At least US voters can vote directly for their president. In Britain, electors, whilst voting for individual MPs who represent a particular political party, do so in the knowledge that the leader of that party will automatically become the prime minister should that party win the majority of seats.

There is no such link in the United States. Not only do presidential elections, elections to Congress and to the Senate take place at different times, but there is also no reason why a Democratic president should not be voted into power whilst Congress is dominated by the Republicans.

The prime minister has more power within government than the US president. In the US, the president's power is restricted by the constitution. This is to ensure that the executive never becomes more powerful (or independent) than the legislature. The following are the major differences.

US president	British prime minister
Ministerial appointments vetted by Congress (parliament)	Ministerial appointments decided by the prime minister
Congress may have an opposition majority	House of Commons always has a majority of MPs from the prime minister's party
President has limited powers to introduce new legislation	Legislation driven by the prime minister
Congress has greater control over spending and foreign policy	Prime minister, chancellor and foreign secretary determine these policies
Certain areas of policy are out of the hands of the president (such as education)	Prime minister involved in all areas of policy
President has limited influence over the economy	Through the chancellor the prime minister has great influence over the economy (but not interest rates)

How liberal democratic is the UK?

It is important to examine whether Britain can truly be considered a liberal democracy. The following table outlines the key criteria.

Criteria	Explanation	Complications
Protection of individual rights	Civil liberties, including freedom of speech, freedom of thought, freedom of assembly, freedom of religion etc. (within the confines of the law) are of great importance. There is equality before the law.	The rule of law protects citizens from human rights abuses.
Existence of a free media	There is a free press and media.	There are alternative sources of information (including independent media to which citizens have politically unfettered access).
Capitalist economic system	Britain has a largely private-sector-orientated economic system which aims to ensure that competition is encouraged for the benefit of consumers and the economy as a whole.	A short-term focus on supporting the economic system can lead to longer term difficulties.
Limited and separated government	There is transparent government and a separation of powers. There are also elected officials in all sectors of government.	In theory, executive power is constrained by the autonomy of the government institutions, such as an independent judiciary, parliament and other mechanisms of horizontal accountability.
Free, fair and open elections	The electorate has the right to free speech, every candidate is given the chance to send a message to his constituents before polling day and there is a secret ballot and universal suffrage.	A first-past-the-post system – not every vote counts and numbered ballot slips allow votes to be traced.
Operation of political pluralism	There is tolerance and pluralism, widely differing social and political views, and even those viewed as extreme are permitted to co-exist and compete for political power on a democratic basis.	In practice, elections are nearly always won by groups who support liberal democracy; thus the system perpetuates itself.

DISCUSSION POINT ?

Examine the strengths and weaknesses of the US and UK models of liberal democracy.

Referendums

In theory a referendum should make Britain more democratic. They are a valuable addition to general elections. In voting for a party, the electorate appears to be endorsing every aspect of a party's programme. Elections are never fought on single issues, but referendums can be and in holding one direct democracy can be exercised without unduly affecting representative democracy.

The following are examples of the use of referendums in Britain.

Issue	Turnout	Result
1975 retention of common market membership	64%	67% of voters supported the Labour government's campaign to stay in the EEC
1979 Devolution for Scotland and Wales	Scotland: 63.8% Wales: 58.8%	Scotland: Yes 51.6% Wales: No 79.7%
1997 Devolution for Scotland and Wales	Scotland: 60.4% Wales: 50.1%	Scotland: Yes 74.3% Wales: Yes 50.3%
1998 Good Friday agreement	80%	In favour: 71%
2001 Bristol council tax	40%	Almost 54% backed no increase in the council tax
2005 Edinburgh congestion charge	61.8%	133,678 votes against and 45,965 in favour
2004 Regional Assembly for the North East	48%	Yes 25%

Referendums are fairly rare in Britain, but are common across Europe and in individual states in the United States. There are a number of advantages and disadvantages of holding referendums, as can be seen in the following table.

Advantages	Disadvantages
They are very democratic.	They are fundamentally against parliamentary tradition and take power from elected representatives. Critics also believe that they undermine parliamentary sovereignty.
Important constitutional issues need to be approved by citizens, not parliament alone.	They are often associated with totalitarianism and are used to claim legitimacy for policies, often in the absence of freedom of speech or in the face of suggestions of electoral fraud, and a government might only choose to hold a referendum when they can win.
They encourage greater participation.	The wording can be misleading.
Moral questions can be settled, particularly if there is no clear party line on the issue.	Some issues are too complex for a simple 'yes' or 'no'.
They give the government clear consent on a specific issue.	A decision made by a referendum imposes an obligation on the government.
They can be used to settle divisive issues.	A majority may use a referendum to impose restrictions on a minority and the funding of 'yes' or 'no' supporters may not be equal.

Learning objectives

- Referendums
- Initiatives
- Town hall democracy
- Citizens' juries
- 'Ethenian' democracy

2011 A.V
Turnout: 42.2%
YES: 32.1%
NO: 67.9%

Initiatives

An initiative is often referred to as a popular or citizens initiative and in effect it is a petition. It requires a certain number of registered voters to force a public vote on a specific issue.

Initiatives can be either direct or indirect. Direct initiatives aim to put an issue directly to the vote after the petition and indirect ones are referred to the legislature and then put to a popular vote if the legislature does not respond.

In the United States, for example, a number of uses have been made of initiatives. In the European Union the rejected European Constitution included a limited indirect initiative right for citizens. It proposed that one million citizens from a specified number of different member states could request that the European Commission consider any proposal laid down in an initiative. In France an indirect initiative was used in 2003 with regard to the French Constitution.

Frequent referendums concerning changes to the constitution as well as laws are the key element of Switzerland's unique and well-established tradition of direct democracy. More than 100 years of experience with referendums on national, cantonal and communal level have shown that Switzerland's system of referendums guarantees not only a maximum amount of self-determination to the citizens but also a stable political system.

Town hall democracy

In 1992 one of the US presidential candidates, Ross Perot, put forward the notion of electronic town halls, in which every week a major issue would be explained in detail to people. A response would be sought from the people, which would be analysed by congressional districts. In this way, Congress would know what the people want.

Perot did not win the presidential election and many people breathed a sigh of relief. One columnist said that the electronic town hall was 'one of the leading rotten idea breakthroughs of all time'.

However, town hall democracy, albeit not electronic democracy, is alive and well in a number of US states. The system allows citizens to attend meetings that address local issues and to vote on laws for their townships. They are used in New England states, such as Vermont and New Hampshire.

The system is quite an old form of direct democracy. It was used in Iceland for centuries, where assemblies were called in order to pass laws and settle disputes.

Citizens' juries

The term citizens' jury was coined in the 1980s in the United States. It was also developed in Britain by ippr (Institute for Public Policy Research, a British progressive think tank). It is a form of public consultation. The jury is made up of individuals that are selected, ideally, at random. The jurors can cross question specialists who have different perspectives on a particular topic. The jury then produces a summary of their conclusions. The process is supervised by an oversight panel.

In July 2007 Gordon Brown announced that citizens' juries would be used to allow voters to exercise their right to influence government policy. The first citizens' jury met in Bristol in September 2007, focusing on education and children's services. Future citizens' juries were promised on the NHS, crime and communities. This was an integral part of Gordon Brown's promise of a 'new type of politics'. in which he pledged to broaden consultation.

'Ethenian' democracy

Deriving its name from the ancient Athenian form of direct democracy, where all adult male citizens had the right to attend and vote at assemblies, Ethenian democracy is a process that seeks to use the Internet as a way of connecting with the electorate and discovering their views. In effect this is electronic democracy.

It has been promoted as a way of bypassing traditional decision-making processes. There have been several projects in California, Hawaii and Alaska, which aimed to try to harness the Internet as a part of the democratic process.

In Holland there was another initiative known as the Amsterdam Digital City, which was supported by the city council and aimed to create a virtual community to encourage political debate, initiatives and online polling. In the 1990s some city authorities, such as Athens, Berlin, Bologna and Manchester, tried to develop their own version of the Amsterdam Digital City, focusing on e-democracy. In 1997 in the London Borough of Brent there was an online poll focusing on local environmental concerns, particularly the future of Wembley Stadium.

Whilst paying lip service to the development of e-democracy, many governments have shied away from it, in the belief that it could undermine the democratic process. Equally, any system such as this is open to abuse or cyber attack.

The Internet may overcome the practical obstacles to greater use of direct democracy. There is increasing use of the Internet by politicians, such as the Webcameron and Cameron Direct. To see this, go to www.heinemann.co.uk/hotlinks, insert the express code 6923P and click on the relevant link.

18 Doughty Street was a British political Internet-based broadcaster that hosted a webcast from its studio at 18 Doughty Street in Bloomsbury, London. The directors of the company were Conservative Party members. 18 Doughty Street stopped broadcasting on 19 November 2007 claiming that it was being taken off air to make a range of improvements.

DISCUSSION POINT ?

To what extent do these direct democratic ideas undermine our representative democratic system?

Learning objectives

- Parties, pressure groups and the media
- The democratic deficit

Madison and Dahl

James Madison, a US statesman and political philosopher, noted that there were countless different groups and interests all competing with one another. He believed that unless they all had a political voice then there was a danger to the stability and order of society.

Robert Dahl, a US political scientist, recognised that although some politically privileged and economically powerful groups had more influence than others, there was no permanent elite that dominated the political process.

Parties, pressure groups and the media

Pluralism is often used to describe the way in which political power is distributed. Classical pluralists believe that power is equally and widely spread and not concentrated in the hands of the elite. Pluralists assume that:

- citizens belong to groups and in fact many citizens belong to a number of groups
- groups are roughly equal and that each group has access to government and that none of the groups has a dominant position in their access to government
- there is internal responsiveness within groups and that the leaders are accountable to the members
- the state itself is neutral and that the government is fragmented and thus allows a number of different groups to access it
- groups have competing interests, but groups in general support the political system and value its openness and competitive nature.

How far this is actually true is open to debate. But we can identify that there are three key groups operating: parties, pressure groups and the media. As we will see, none of them seem to accord with the assumptions that pluralists suggest.

Back in 1775 Edmund Burke said 'parties must never exist in a free country'. They do of course and they have limited membership, in fact a falling membership, and yet it is the members that decide who will be their leader.

The processes of deciding a leader is an internal matter and not open to public scrutiny or input. It is only party members that really have the opportunity to decide or even discuss party policy that will form the backbone of the array of offerings that the party will make to the electorate at the next election. However, not even a democratic process within the party can guarantee that party members' voices will even be heard by the party hierarchy and that once in power there is no guarantee that any promises made by parties verbally or in writing will find their way onto the statute books or even be given any form of priority. In this respect political parties, as part of the democratic process, can be seen to fail the system.

Pressure groups have unequal power. Some can be classed as insider groups; those that have some form of direct connection and access to the government. This is regardless of their size or their public support. Others that may enjoy more widespread public support may be considered to be outsider groups, with little or no influence even though they may have mass membership. Certain pressure groups therefore receive preferential treatment, such as the National Farmers' Union, the Confederation of British Industry or the Law Society. Others are considered to be rather more difficult to handle and consult with, such as the Friends of the Earth or Greenpeace. The Animal Rights Movement is also almost universally ignored, largely due to the unfounded associations with radical direct action.

There are upwards of 350,000 voluntary organisations in Britain. There are 7000 organisations that routinely lobby government. Even this disparity in numbers suggests that not all groups are equal and have fair access and influence on government.

Mancur Olson's analysis of how special interests can weaken democracy helped to shape the policies of Tory governments in the 1980s. But Olson did not believe that all government was bad. He favoured a limited government able to encompass wide, not narrow interests. He argued that people only join interest groups to secure public goods; individuals become 'free riders', obtaining the benefits of the group's action without actually having to get involved. He also believed that strong group action could undermine the overall economic performance of a country.

The media is an important part of a pluralist liberal democracy. The broadcast media in particular is a vital way in which leading politicians can be seen to be held accountable for their actions in a public arena. Media scrutiny is vital, as it can challenge government claims, facts and figures in a way in which an ordinary citizen cannot.

For the print media in particular there is always the question of their loyalty towards a particular party or a particular point of view. Many commentators believe, for example, that *The Sun* newspaper, with around 12 million readers, had a significant impact on the elections in 1997 and 2001. Prior to these elections they had been strong supporters of Thatcherism and the Conservatives, but they then decided that they would endorse the Labour Party under Tony Blair. It is believed that they played an enormous part in persuading a considerable number of their readers to also switch allegiance.

The media can also play a disproportionate role in shaping the political agenda, as well as manipulating public opinion. But they are also susceptible to changes in public opinion themselves, as the media is largely a privatised industry and must therefore provide products and services in line with the views, wishes and beliefs of their customers.

Thomas Jefferson said of the media: 'Were it left to me to decide whether we should have a government without newspapers, or newspapers without government, I would not hesitate to prefer the latter.'

The democratic deficit

Democratic deficit refers to the apparent absence of public accountability in an institution that claims to have that accountability. This is a major complaint that is often made against institutions within the European Union. The criticism is that they often attain powers and privileges without being accountable for the exercise of those powers and privileges. Further they are charged with ignoring the votes of those in whose interests they profess to be acting.

In response, the European Union has been systematically strengthening the power of the European Parliament at the expense of other institutions on the basis of reinforcing democratic legitimacy within their institutions. The Maastricht Treaty brought in the concept of co-decision-making powers. It is also suggested that there is very limited scrutiny of EU directives from national parliaments.

Effective democracy relies on the active participation of citizens, but fewer and fewer are exercising their democratic rights and the argument is that this affects the legitimacy of all aspects of government. In order to arrest the alarming trend that has seen general election turnouts fall, from around 80 per cent in the 1950s to below 60 per cent in 2001 and 2005, action needs to be taken.

Efforts to improve the mechanics of voting have largely failed. Voters are now entitled to apply for postal votes for almost any reason. But all this has achieved is widespread electoral fraud. Some 3.5 million people have actually disappeared from the electoral rolls over the past few years because so little has been done to make sure that the necessary paperwork has been completed.

This leads us to another democratic deficit issue; that of consent. This is often referred to as having a mandate. As already mentioned, it is perfectly possible for a political party to gain the majority of seats in a general election but not to win the popular vote. By this we mean that the party with the largest number of seats has not received a majority of the votes; in fact more votes have been cast against that party, but they have been spread (and therefore the inference is that they are wasted) on candidates that failed to win in a particular constituency.

Voting fraud

In 2004, a judge quashed the results of two local council elections in Birmingham after deciding there had been systematic large-scale postal vote-rigging. Between 2000 and 2006 about 2000 illegal ballots were known to have been cast, out of 123 million votes in total. This resulted in at least 42 convictions.

DISCUSSION POINT ?

Are pressure groups on the whole beneficial to democracy?

ExamCafé

Relax, refresh, result!

Unit F854

Relax and prepare

When revising this topic try to do the following revision exercises. They will help you structure your notes and give you a guide as to what you will need to know for the different papers. Remember to work through unit F854 first as this will provide the theory base you will need for F856.

When revising for unit F854, think about how you would answer the following questions.

- Compare and contrast direct and indirect democracy.
- Why is democracy such a difficult concept to define?
- How democratic is liberal democracy?
- How different is democracy to dictatorship?

- Evaluate the validity of the advantages of democracy.
- How similare are the classical and protective models of democracy?

Refresh your memory

In revising for unit F854, copy out the following table and for each of the following areas try and identify relevant issues and arguments. Also insert the names and a brief description of the views of relevant thinkers.

Content	Issues and arguments	Relevant thinkers
Defining democracy		
Key characteristics of democracy		
Direct democracy		
Representative democracy		
Models of democracy		
Liberal democracy		
Democracy vs dictatorship		
Advantages and disadvantages of democracy		

To help fill in the table above you may want to consider the following theorists:

Plato, Socrates, J. J. Rousseau, C.L. Montesquieu, A. de Tocqueville, J. S. Mill, K. Marx, C. Wright Mills, J. Schumpeter, R. Dahl, T. Bottomore

Different ideological perspectives on democracy

Copy out and complete the following table. For each of the following perspectives, summarise their attitude towards democracy and identify relevant thinkers who support this view.

Perspective	Attitude towards democracy	Relevant thinker
Elitist		
Pluralist		
Conservative		
Liberal		
Socialist		
Marxist		
Radical Democrat		

Get the result !

There will be a compulsory question on the F854 paper and it will be split into two parts.

Here is the style of two-part compulsory question for you to practise on.

Source extract

'In the Gettysburg Address, delivered at the time of the American Civil War, Abraham Lincoln extolled the virtues of what he called, "government of the people, by the people, and for the people". In so doing he defined the two contrasting notions of (direct and indirect) democracy.' (Andrew Heywood (2004), *Political Theory: An Introduction*, Palgrave)

1 (a) Explain what is meant by the term direct democracy. [10 marks]

(b) Discuss the differences between direct and representative democracy. [15 marks]

Exam tips

Remember, in the exam you would have approximately 30 minutes to answer this question. You are therefore advised to spend approximately 10 minutes on question 1 (a) and 20 minutes on 1 (b).

The following are tips on how to answer the question.

Question 1 (a)

Eight of the 10 marks are for knowledge and understanding (2 for presentation).

The kind of understanding you are expected to show would include direct participation by the citizenship in legislative and possibly executive decision-making; the lack of professional politicians, thus specialised posts being filled by lot or appointment of experts (e.g. military officials).

Illustrative knowledge could be used to link this system to ancient Athenian style democracy or in modern politics to the use of referendums, initiatives and town hall style democracy. Good answers will relate the ideas of certain theorists such as Aristotle, Plato and Rousseau.

Question 1 (b)

Twelve out of 15 marks are for analysis and evaluation (3 for presentation).

To achieve these the focus must be on direct points of comparison. Candidates who only describe the features of both systems will perform badly, achieving at best a D grade.

Consider the following points of comparison:

+ How far are the citizens involved in the decision-making process?
+ Is there any role for professional politicians/representatives?
+ How is the Executive chosen?
+ Does representative democracy overcome the practical obstacles of direct democracy?
+ Are the citizens capable of political input beyond choosing their representative?

Remember, the focus is upon the differences, although some credit will be given for discussing the extent of these. However, answers that focus upon the benefits and drawbacks of the two systems will perform badly.

Unit F856

Relax and prepare

Look at the following exam-style questions for unit F856. Discuss with your colleagues how you would go about answering them or try writing essay plans for as many as you can.

- Discuss the view that in theory and in practice democracy is an essentially contestable concept.
- Examine the view that elections are the most important characteristic of a modern democracy.
- Discuss which model of representation best suits the needs of a representative democracy.
- How relevant is direct democracy to modern politics?
- How far can the UK be described as a liberal democracy?
- Discuss the view that the democracy is the 'worst form of government'.

Refresh your memory

When revising for unit F856, it is important that you apply what you have learnt in F854 to practical examples of the operation of democracy. Once again copy out the table below and fill in the relevant sections.

Content	Issues and arguments	Practical examples
Defining democracy in practice		
Key characteristics of democracy in practice		
Direct democracy in practice		
Representative democracy in practice		
Models of democracy in practice		
Liberal democracy n practice		
Democracy vs dictatorship in practice		
Advantages and disadvantages of democracy in practice		

Case studies on democracy in practice

Each of the following events could be used as examples in a variety of democracy in practice essays. For each write a brief summary of the event and suggest the possible impact/relevance to the different aspects of democracy you have studied.

✓ The 2001 and 2005 Labour general election victories.

✓ The Zimbabwe presidential and parliamentary elections in 2008.

✓ The use of referendums in the UK since 1997, including devolution for Scotland and Wales, the Good Friday Agreement and the failure to hold referendums over recent EU treaties (e.g. Maastricht and Lisbon).

✓ The fall of the Berlin Wall in 1989.

✓ The crushing of pro-democracy protests in China in 1990 (Tiananmen Square) and Burma 2007.

Get the result !

This is the type of essay question that you may have to answer for unit F856 in your exam.

Examine whether in theory and in practice there is more to modern democracy than just majority rule.

Exam tips

You will improve your chances of securing a high mark if you plan your answer to this question before you write the essay. The essay should be organised into three parts.

Introduction

Outline the meaning of majority rule and put it into the context of modern democracy (i.e. representative-style protective/liberal democracy as practised in the UK).

Key themes

+ The background to the importance of majority rule (note literal definition of democracy and views of Aristotle).

+ Consider its role in specific elections and referendums (however, UK general election results tend to point to the rule of the largest minority), and how it operates in a representative system (i.e. democratic accountability as opposed to direct rule – see Schumpeter and 'the rule of the politician').

+ Note the dangers in excessive use of majority rule (i.e. de Tocqueville's tyranny of the majority – Northern Ireland pre-power sharing provides useful evidence for this).

+ Other important features of modern democracy are those such as constitutional safeguards to protect minorities (see Montesquieu and US separation of powers or in the UK, A. V. Dicey and parliamentary checks and balances allied to the rule of law), political pluralism (Dahl and importance of multi-party politics and sectional interest groups – relate to operation in UK) and representative institutions (note J. S. Mill and necessity of government by the wisest with evidence of parliamentary legislation sometimes against public opinion, e.g. vote over invasion of Iraq in 2003 and reducing the age of homosexual consent in 2000).

Conclusion

The importance of majority rule but the dangers of unfettered majority rule reflected in modern protective/liberal style of democracy.

If your essay only just deals with majority rule and does not consider other important features then you will gain at maximum a D grade mark.

People in a defined territory who have agreed to invest sovereign power in a body to govern them are living in a political and legal state. This power invested in the state is exercised on behalf of the citizens through public institutions with the purpose of creating and maintaining order and stability. It is the legitimate power to act on behalf of the citizens and it allows the state to coerce citizens to obey the law and punish those who don't. In return the citizens have an obligation to adhere to the demands of the state. Such a nation state is a political community which is bound by a sense of citizenship and nationality, with a common language, religion, ethnicity, history and traditions.

A major question now is whether sovereignty is diminishing the more nations become involved in international organisations. As the world has become increasingly globalised, changes have occurred that have had a significant impact on the cultural, social, economic, political, ethnic compositions of societies in various parts of the world. These have been brought about by new technologies such as satellite communications, the internet, mobile phones, computerised financial trading.

The changes are also seen as spreading the idea of liberal democracy and capitalism. Globalisation is also seen as more responsive to the needs of consumers, so undermining the authority of local elected officials.

The trouble is that multinationals undermine democratic accountability, leaving populations vulnerable to international unaccountable capitalist organisations. Supranational organisations are now also so powerful that they can impose their jurisdiction on other states, as in the case of international federations such as the World Trade Organisation. The dominance of national sovereignty in the 20th century has now given way to governments that are operating on a supranational level.

However, international arrangements can create order and stability between states, such as the EU, the International Monetary Fund and the World Bank. Also the United Nations has inspired agreements to peacefully solve international disputes, recognise national sovereignty, self-determination, human rights and freedom.

These pressures and changes have left many people wondering/revisiting the question about what a state is in practice.

Conservatives believe it should play a minimal part in the lives of its citizens. Apart from having a police force, a legal system and some military force to maintain order, everything else should be left up to the individual. There should be minimal government in the markets and limited tax. The government should not be involved in the redistribution of wealth. Others believe that government and business can cooperate in partnership agreements that drive the economy forward and modernise it. This is the Third Way associated with New Labour. Social democrats however take the view that there should be some intervention to carry out social restructuring. The aim is to restructure and redress injustices and imbalances through involvement in the market. This is economic policy to regulate capitalism and achieve full employment. The more extreme case for government involvement is that all economic activity should be controlled by the state (China and North Korea).

There are movements towards forms of federalism in certain parts of the world, most specifically Europe and Britain. The devolvement of power to Scotland, Wales and Northern Ireland and the attempt to set up assemblies in English regions all point to some diluted form of federalism in this country. This is also occurring in some European countries, such as Spain, and already exists in others – Germany and Switzerland. It raises fears among some that this undermines national sovereignty. The EU view is that the EU and member states share power. The EU deals with what affects Europe and the national governments handle domestic affairs. Federalism of course is common throughout the world, in different forms, the United States being the most notable example.

Globalisation is seen as threatening the sovereignty of the nation state. People are now consuming more and have a higher standard of life, but at a cost to their traditional ways of life and culture. Nation states are also making political and economic decisions under pressure from international organisations which have invested in them. Such decisions and events in one country could have serious implications for international trade and finance.

It may be that globalisation has accelerated the transition of certain nations from rule by dictatorship to government by liberal democracy.

The sovereignty of nations linked to the global economy may be affected in having to meet the needs and interests of the international community as well as their own population. Being part of an international organisation or regional ones such as the UK and the EU is also exerting strains on the sovereignty of nations. If the legal sovereignty of a state doesn't coincide with international law or with the notion of fairness, freedom and human rights, this could be challenged by the international community. If force is used within a nation to impose political will, its sovereignty can be threatened by pressures such as political and economic boycotts and the threat of invasion.

These are some of the issues covered in this chapter, in which the following are the key themes.

- The nature and theories of the state
- The characteristics of sovereignty and its relationship to government
- Globalisation – the different forms it takes; international interdependency; global citizenship and world government
- The different types of states in theory and in practice
- The development of devolution and regionalisation in Britain and Europe
- How federalism works and how might a federal Europe affect Britain
- The impact of globalisation on the political, economic and cultural facets of a nation state

In covering these themes the chapter is broken down into the following topics.

The chapter finishes with an exam café feature on page 76.

Mosta Bridge, destroyed during ethnic cleansing in the collapse of Yugoslavia during the Balkans conflict and rebuilt after the war

Ethnic cleansing

The use of threat, terror or force to expel or kill those belonging to ethnic minority groups, for example the expulsion of the Greek population of Northern Cyprus in 1974.

What is the state?

It is important to make the distinction between the state, the nation and what is known as the nation state. Broadly, a state is a political association that has sovereign jurisdiction within a defined territorial area. The state will exercise its authority through institutions. As we will see, there are five key features of the state. It has sovereignty – it therefore exercises absolute and unrestricted power, as it is above all other organisations and groups in that society. The institutions are public – these bodies make and reinforce collective decisions and are funded by the public. It has legitimation – decisions are usually accepted as binding on all citizens, as they are seen to be in the best interests of society as a whole. It has domination – the state possesses coercive power to make sure that laws are obeyed and those that break the laws are punished. It has territorial association – it exercises its power within a geographically defined area and in international matters it is treated as an autonomous area.

Nations, on the other hand, are somewhat more complex to describe. They are usually a collection of political, cultural and psychological factors. On the cultural side what binds groups of people together are: a common language, a common religion and a common history and set of traditions.

Politically, a nation is merely a group of people that consider themselves to be a political community. In other words, they have some form of civic consciousness, an example of which could be the Palestinians.

Psychologically, a nation is distinguished by the fact that a group of people have shared loyalties and, perhaps, a form of patriotism.

There is often a distinction made between nations that are bound by cultural issues and those that are bound by political ones. Examples of countries that have formed their own national identity as a result of a common cultural heritage and language include the English, the Greeks, the Germans and the Russians. However, some countries are bound together politically despite the fact that there may be enormous political and ethnic divisions within that nation. They are bound together by shared citizenship, such as the British as opposed to the English, the Americans and the South Africans.

The nation state is another form of political organisation. It is an autonomous political community and it has both features of citizenship and nationality bound together. The nation state has possibly never really existed in a pure form. There is always an ethnic and cultural mix. The nation state is based on concepts of loyalty, allegiance and unity.

Most modern states consider themselves to be nation states, as they are bound together in some way by cultural and political unity. They have self-government and there is a sense of citizenship. This may, perhaps, explain why, for example, many believe that a more integrated European Union will never replace the concept of the nation state as a super state, because there will simply be too many different cultures, ethnic groups, political opinions, regional identities and traditions.

The creation of a true nation state has brought with it the most horrific of violent acts. Greater Germany in the 1930s and 1940s attempted to create a true nation state effectively through **ethnic cleansing**. This was repeated in the Balkans in the aftermath of the collapse of Yugoslavia and the creation of several new states.

Perspectives on the state

There are many rival theories of the state and no generally accepted definition or explanation of either its nature or its relevance. The following table outlines the key perspectives on the state.

Perspective	Explanation	Key thinkers
Liberal	The state is a neutral arbiter. It arbitrates between competing interests and groups and effectively guarantees social order. Liberals view the state as a necessary evil.	Hobbes
Marxist	Essentially they view the state as a means by which class oppression is achieved. The ruling class allows relative autonomy in order to maintain stability in a system that supports unequal class power.	Marx, Engels, Gramsci and Nicos Poulantzas
Democratic socialist	The general view is that the state exists for the common good. The state is able to step in and deal with injustices within the class system.	Rousseau and Fourier
Conservative	They favour a strong state that is able to protect society from disorder. The state provides much needed authority and discipline.	Burke
New Right	The view is that the state has its own interests, separate from society as a whole. In protecting these interests the state often interferes and impedes economic performance. New Right theorists believe that the state is non-legitimate.	Samuel Britten and William Niskanen
Feminist	Essentially they view the state as a patriarchal state, which aims to exclude women or at least subordinate women, particularly in the political system.	Greer and Firestone
Anarchist	The state is a form of legalised oppression that is run by the ruling elite, whose sole aim is to protect their property and their privileges.	Bakunin and Kropotkin
Pluralists	Their view is essentially a liberal one, where the state is considered to be an honest broker that mediates various interests, promotes compromise and attempts to take a longer-term view.	Dahl
Neo-pluralists	This theory argues that the modern state is more complex and less responsive than classical pluralists lead us to believe. They still accept that the state acts as an arbiter, but qualify this by saying that some groups are better organised and more powerful and have therefore greater advantage than other groups (such as business). These groups dictate to the government or to the state in a number of areas, particularly economics.	Galbraith and Lindblom
Elitists	They believe that behind any liberal democracy is a ruling elite. Political power always lies in their hands and equality and democracy do not really exist. Modern elitists, whilst accepting that there is a distribution of power, still point out that political power is in the hands of the few.	Mosca, Pareto, Michels, C. Wright Mills and Schumpeter

Discussions about politics have always centred on the state. Not only are there different perspectives on the nature of state power, as we have seen above, but the other key issue is that of political obligation.

Hobbes and Locke provided a major justification for the existence of the state in what has become known as social contract theory. Without a state there would be unending civil war. People therefore enter into an agreement known as a social contract. In exchange for giving up part of their liberty they create a sovereign body that ensures an orderly and stable existence. Individuals then obey that sovereign body in order to protect them from chaos and disorder. In other words, the creation of the state has much to do with human nature and need, and seeks to offset an inherently aggressive nature.

DISCUSSION POINT ?

Which perspective on the power of the state is more persuasive and why?

Learning objectives

- Sovereignty
- Features of the state
- Relationship with the government

Feudalism

A system of organising and governing society based on the possession of land and service to the monarch.

Monarchical-based sovereignty

In his book *The Six Books of the Commonwealth* Jean Bodin argued the case for a sovereign that made laws, but was not bound by them. Law was the command of the sovereign and subjects should be required to obey them. The sovereign was not a despot as they were constrained by a higher law in the form of the will of God and natural law. Thomas Hobbes believed that sovereignty was based on power rather than authority. He saw sovereignty as the monopoly of coercive power and believed that it should be held by a single ruler. Although Hobbes preferred monarchs, he was happy to accept that the 'sovereign' could be a democratic assembly or a group of oligarchs.

Functionalist

The functionalism perspective is built upon twin emphases: application of the scientific method to the objective social world and use of an analogy between the individual organism and society.

Sovereignty

Sovereignty simply means absolute and unlimited power. It developed in the 16th and 17th centuries as a major result of the emergence of the modern state in Europe. Prior to this rulers had acknowledged that there was a higher form of authority – God, or at least the papacy.

As **feudalism** disappeared transnational institutions, such as the Holy Roman Empire and the Catholic Church, were replaced by centralised monarchs. In England this saw the emergence of the strong Tudor monarchs. For the very first time, secular kings and queens now had supreme power.

It is, however, unclear what this absolute power consists of and, as we will see, it can refer to legal authority and to political power.

The first principle of the British constitution is that the parliament in Westminster is the supreme law-making body in Britain. It has absolute power over every citizen, including the monarch. A. V. Dicey wrote: 'Parliament has the right to make or unmake any law whatever; and, further, that no person or body is recognised by the law of England as having the right to set aside the legislation of Parliament.'

The term sovereignty actually means legal supremacy. This means that parliament can:

- create legislation that cannot be overturned by any other authority
- legislate on any subject or issue that it chooses
- ensure that no current parliament can create legislation that will hinder the first two points, as far as a future government is concerned.

Does parliament still retain sovereignty? Possibly not, but the third point above does mean that if it has lost parliamentary sovereignty it can take it back if it needs to at a future date. As far as the parliamentary sovereignty debate is concerned, the principal focus is on the devolved governments of Scotland and Wales and Britain's membership of the EU. In both cases the creation of legislation has been passed on to these bodies. It has also meant that the power to legislate on any issue has been removed. However, parliament can get the powers back by the third principle. No decision to create or join an organisation is irreversible. If parliament wished it could:

- abolish the devolved parliaments and take their powers back to Westminster
- leave the EU and repeal any EU law it wants to remove.

Equally, decisions made on other issues can be repealed, such as the right to abortions, the return of capital punishment or the use of referendums to consult the electorate. Because parliament can repeal any Act, regardless of its source, it retains parliamentary sovereignty.

The biggest issue regarding parliamentary sovereignty is not the creation of a Scottish parliament or EU membership; it is the dominance of the executive. Centralised power has been approved by parliament, making any institution that is not constitutionally protected vulnerable.

Features of the state

A **functionalist** would view the role and purpose of the state as maintaining social order and would actually define the state as the institutions that achieve this. In fact this is a·view that has been adopted by modern-day Marxists, such as Ralf Dahrendorf, who see the state as a way in which the class conflict is managed, to ensure the continued existence of the capitalist system. Within the set of institutions functionalists would also include the church, trade unions, the family and the media.

On the other hand, an organisational view of the state would only include recognisably public institutions and those that are funded at public expense. This is a far clearer description of the state, as it separates the state from ordinary civil society. So it would include government institutions, the military, the courts, and other identifiable bodies.

This leads us to examine what may be the key features of the state. We have already seen that the state is considered sovereign and that it has absolute and restricted power over all organisations and groups in society. As we will see, there are particular perspectives even on this aspect of the state. These are the other key features.

- The state institutions are public and not private. Public bodies are responsible for both making and enforcing decisions. These are collective decisions, whilst groups such as families or private businesses deal with individual interests. The problem is that with the creation of agencies to replace government department responsibilities and the privatisation of certain aspects of government activity, this clear division is now far more blurred in Britain.

- The state is an exercise in legitimation. Any decision that the state makes is deemed to be binding on all members of society. The assumption is that the decisions are made in the public interest and that the state is responsible for the permanent interests of society.

- The state is an instrument of domination. It can use coercion to make sure that individuals in society comply with laws and that those who break laws are punished. Max Weber called this legitimate violence and that the state had a monopoly in this respect.

- The state is also a territorial association. The state's jurisdiction is limited to its geographical borders. It can require anyone living within those borders to comply with its instructions, whether they are citizens or not. To all intents and purposes the state is an autonomous entity on the international stage. Recently this too has been put into sharp focus by the Americans seizing foreign nationals around the world and then subjecting them to American law by extraditing them to a secure facility at Guantanamo Bay.

Relationship with the government

The state itself obviously incorporates the government, including the parliament, the judiciary and any regional institutions. But there is a difference between the state and the government, even though many will choose to interchange either term. The following are the key differences between the state and government.

- The state is more extensive than government and government is only a part of the state. The state includes all public institutions.

- The state is permanent and governments are temporary. Systems of government can also change, but the state continues.

- The state's authority is brought into operation through the government. The government perpetuates the state and makes and implements state policy.

- The state is impersonal in its authority. State officials are supposed to be neutral (e.g. the civil service). This should enable the state not to become political and ally with the government.

- The state represents the permanent interests of society and acts for the common good. Governments cater for partisan interests (following policies favoured by the electorate).

 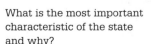

Learning objectives

- Organic and social contract theory
- Pluralist state
- Capitalist state
- Leviathan state
- Patriarchal state

Organic and social contract theory

Organic theory likens the state to a living creature. It takes a holistic view of all of the components of the state, claiming that it cannot be understood by simply looking at its constituent parts, but by looking at it as a total organisation or organism, which helps explain the functions of the parts and how they relate to one another. Theorists contend that like organic life the state is actually quite difficult to understand. They are also of the opinion that the organism will flourish if it is not meddled with.

There are two key alternatives to contract theory as a basis of political obligation.

- Teleological – a term from the Greek meaning 'purpose', this theory suggests that it is the duty of citizens to respect the state and obey it on the basis of the benefits that the state offers the individual. Political obligation therefore derives from common interest (rather like Rousseau's general will). This also links to utilitarianism which suggests that citizens obey government on the basis of 'the greatest happiness for the greatest number'.

- Natural duty – political obligation is seen as a natural duty, whereby citizens are bound to obey on moral grounds, such as Socrates not challenging the laws of Athens on the basis of the debt of gratitude he owed Athens. This approach is closely associated with conservative theorists (such as Burke) who believe that society is held together by mutual obligations and sets of responsibilities.

Social contract theory aims to explain why government is important and what is meant by political obligation. The expectation is that regardless of how long the social contract has been in effect, all subsequent generations are expected to accept and abide by the contract, as if they had entered into the contract themselves. Hobbes and Locke see this as being based on tacit rather than active consent. More recently, John Rawls has also suggested that this is a valuable way of examining the nature of the state.

Social contract theory has three essential elements.

- The state of nature – effectively a state of war, a stateless society, where in Hobbes's words life would be 'solitary, poor, nasty, brutish and short'.

- This state of nature is transformed by individuals' desires to escape from it. They recognise that a sovereign power, whose power will from them be absolute, will safeguard them, secure order and ensure stability.

- In entering into the social contract citizens will undertake to obey and to respect the state. This is in return for their protection and that of their property. The only condition placed upon this is that the sovereign power could be overthrown if the terms of the social contract were violated.

Pluralist state

The views of the pluralists are derived from liberalism. The fundamental belief is that the state is a referee or neutral arbiter. This has definitely meant that the theorists have viewed the state and government as very different entities. They believe that the state can be largely ignored because its role as an arbiter can be affected by the government.

Pluralist theory dates back to Thomas Hobbes. They looked at political obligation and argued, as we have seen, that the state was created by a social contract and this is the fundamental root behind their willingness to obey and to respect the state. Hobbes's view was that stability and order could only be achieved by an unlimited and absolute state, that citizens only had the choice between this absolutism and anarchy. Locke preferred the view of the limited state. He believed that the state should focus only on life, liberty and property. He made a clear distinction between what was the domain of the state and what should remain in the hands of individual citizens.

There have been further clarifications and theories, which are broadly pluralist, such as John Schwarzmantel in 1994, who said that the state is 'a servant of society and not its master'. He believed that the state should absorb pressure, that it should be subordinate to government and that the most important aspect is a meaningful and effective democratic process. Competition means that the government remains sensitive to public opinion and that in this respect the state changes direction in accordance with public opinion.

Charles Lindblom and John Kenneth Galbraith, as neo-pluralists, suggested that the state has its own sectional interests and that there is a state elite (such as judges and senior civil servants). They believe that it is a powerful interest group in its own right.

Capitalist state

Although Marx himself did not develop a full theory about the state, in the *Communist Manifesto* (1848) he wrote: 'The executive of the modern state is but a committee for managing the common affairs of the whole Bourgeoisie'.

By this he meant that the state is reliant on the dominant economic class. Lenin went on to say that the state was: 'An instrumental for the oppression of the exploited class.'

Later Marx described the state as being parasitic and that it would support the interests of any class in order to ensure its continued existence. Marx was not completely negative about the state. He believed that it could be used as a 'revolutionary dictatorship of the proletariat'. In other words, to be used as the transition was made from capitalism to communism. Ultimately, Marx believed that if antagonisms between classes disappeared then the state would also disappear, implying that a communist society would be stateless. It would no longer have a reason to exist.

Ralph Miliband (1969) saw the state simply as an instrument of the ruling class. He believed that the elite of the state came from the privileged and those with property. The state would therefore favour capitalism.

Nicos Poulantzas (1968) suggested that although the state had a degree of autonomy, its sole function was to ensure that capitalist society ran smoothly and therefore benefited the capitalist class, even though concessions were made from time to time to the working class.

Bob Jessop (1982) viewed the state as a dynamic entity that could change to reflect the balance of power at any time and its nature reflects whatever struggle is going on in society.

Leviathan state

The concept of the Leviathan state was originally suggested by Thomas Hobbes. He depicted it as a self-serving entity that only wants to expand and become more powerful. In this respect his view of the state is that of a radical individualist, or liberal.

Broadly, this view has been taken up by those who would seek to reduce state intervention, particularly in the economic and social spheres (such as the New Right). Samuel Britten argues that state power increases when the electorate demands increased spending or generous government policy, as politicians outbid one another to gain the votes. They typify this as a demand-side pressure. On the supply side, the state enlarges itself by over-bloated budgets, which suggests that parts of the state, including government, are motivated by self-interests and that the state is self-seeking.

Patriarchal state

The patriarchal state obviously has close associations with feminist theories. Liberal feminists, such as Friedan, tend to accept a pluralist view of the state. They believe that if a woman does not have legal and political equality then the state is biased in favour of men. But they believe that the state is essentially neutral and that over time inequality can be overcome by reform. This suggests that they believe that all groups, including women, have equal access to state power.

Radical feminists, such as Firestone, take a different view. They see the state as exercising a monopoly of legitimate violence, which imposes male domination in all aspects of life. They also associate the state as being an institution of male power, merely a tool that men use to help protect their own interests and ensure that patriarchy continues.

DISCUSSION POINT ?

Why might none of these theories give a full picture of the actual nature of the state?

The meaning of sovereignty

Sir William Blackstone, writing in the 18th century, said: 'There is and must be in every state a supreme, irresistible, absolute, and uncontrolled authority, in which the right of sovereignty resides.'

By this he did not mean that sovereignty resides with a monarch, but with 'the Queen in parliament'. This statement is quite a modern one, as it saw the monarch standing alongside parliament, bound by a law that they both had to respect, so that neither one had absolute or uncontrolled authority.

An alternative view, of course, is that power can be divided but still be sovereign, as in the concept of the separation of powers.

Many theorists have written on the concept of sovereignty, including Bodin, Hobbes, Rousseau and Hegel. What remains, however, is that sovereignty can either be a supreme legal authority or it can be unchallenged political power.

Learning objectives

- The meaning of sovereignty
- Jean Bodin's theory
- Thomas Hobbes's theory
- Albert Venn Dicey's theory

Jean Bodin's theory on sovereignty

Bodin, writing in the 16th century, tried to make the distinction between legal and political sovereignty. In his definition of the sovereign the ruler was beyond human law, so law was no more than just a command from the sovereign. Subjects were expected to obey. Sovereignty was absolute, exercised in the public sphere and did not fade away if the sovereign who held that sovereignty died, because it was not any individual's personal property.

Thomas Hobbes's theory on sovereignty

Writing in the *Leviathan* in the 17th century, Hobbes suggested that sovereignty is the monopoly of coercive power held in the hands of an absolute ruler. Hobbes actually supported the monarchy as the better form of government but he did accept that an elite group or even a democratic assembly would work just as well, providing it was unchallengeable.

Albert Venn Dicey's theory on sovereignty

Dicey identified both legal and political sovereignty. He saw parliamentary supremacy, or sovereignty, and the rule of law as being the mainstays of Britain's unwritten constitution. He tried to address the issue that current legislation could clash with legislation that had been created by a previous parliament. In English law current law supersedes any previous law. However in modern Britain there are problems with this, with the adoption of the European Communities Act (1972) and the Human Rights Act (1998), both of which are derived from external sources, the former from the EU and the latter from the European Court of Human Rights.

Undoubtedly the subject of sovereignty is one of the most hotly debated concepts in both politics and international law. It cuts to the very core of concepts of the state and government, as well as independence and democracy.

As a term it simply means supreme power, but in practice interpretations of sovereignty have often strayed very far from this. John Austin, for example, writing in the 19th century, believed that parliament is the supreme power in the state and has sovereignty. Parliament enacts laws that all citizens are bound to obey, but it is not bound by those laws itself and can change those laws at will.

Although Austin's view may well have accorded with the British political system at the time, it did not necessarily match what was going on in America. The US Constitution sets out the laws of the Federal Union and it did not give the national legislature supreme powers; it restricted them. Added to this the US Supreme Court from 1803 (Marbury vs Madison) established the right to declare laws unconstitutional through judicial review. This did not mean that the judiciary suddenly gained sovereignty; instead it perhaps gave sovereignty to the Constitution.

The situation in the United States became all the more complicated when not only the US Congress but also individual states and special conventions could propose changes to the Constitution. This could then imply that sovereignty in the US lay not with the Constitution but with the states themselves or the citizens of those states.

In reality, of course, sovereignty does not rest with the individual citizen. Instead their sovereignty is exercised on their behalf by national government and federal and state authorities.

A further complication has been the theories that have been put forward by a wide range of different individuals, including Leon Duguit, Hugo Krabbe and Harold Laski. They all suggested pluralistic sovereignty. The suggestion was that sovereignty is actually exercised by a wide range of different types of groups; some are religious, others social, some are economic and others are political. This goes a long way to explain how sovereignty in different states can actually reside with different types of groups. For example, sovereignty in states such as Iran lies with religious groups. In Saudi Arabia it could be argued that it is an economic group or a social group (hereditary ruling family) that has sovereignty. In Britain it is a political group (being the political party in power). The concept suggests that over time sovereignty can shift from one group to another or to an alliance of groups.

The growth of democracy has brought about enormous changes to our understanding of absolute, unlimited sovereignty. In fact democracy swept away this type of sovereignty, as it began to place limitations on the power of monarchs and on the disproportionate power of ruling classes.

With increasing interdependency between states, sovereignty is also under threat and under greater limitation. A monarch or a ruling class that has absolute and unlimited sovereignty could easily act as a rogue state operating outside generally accepted levels of behaviour and acceptability. In effect by joining organisations such as the European Union, the World Trade Organisation or the North Atlantic Treaty Organisation, states further chose to limit whatever sovereignty remains, in order to accord with a more general consensus on the world stage.

As we will see, there are many more aspects of sovereignty to be considered and over the years there have been attempts to understand how the internal affairs of state operate and where supreme power lies within it.

DISCUSSION POINT ?

Discuss where sovereignty ultimately lies in the modern state.

Internal and external sovereignty

Internal sovereignty relates to both the internal affairs of the state and the location of the supreme power. Internal sovereignty therefore refers to the final authority that has the right to make decisions that are binding on all citizens, groups and institutions.

In the past this power was held in the hands of an absolute monarch. In effect the absolute monarch was the state and sovereignty was indivisible. Rousseau suggested that the rule of the monarch should be replaced by what he called the general will, or popular sovereignty. In other words that sovereignty should lie in the hands of the citizens. Sovereignty can also lie in the hands of the legislature, such as the British parliament, as John Austin suggested.

Rousseau's theory on sovereignty

Rousseau's theory arguably influenced liberal, socialist, anarchist and even fascist thought. He believed that sovereignty ultimately lay with the people, which he described as the general will. But (and this is the link certainly to dictatorships) that the general will was indivisible and that a legislator should be used to articulate the general will.

Regardless of where internal sovereignty may lie, the general consensus of opinion is that it should lie with one distinct body. But critics say that this just harks back to absolutism and that there should be checks and balances. Liberal democratic principles argue that power should be distributed, so that not one single body can claim sovereignty. Rousseau actually suggested that even though he believed that sovereignty should lie in the hands of the people it should be initially formulated by a legislator or lawgiver.

We see this to some extent when a country is controlled by a dictator or a totalitarian regime, and even in Britain when a political party has an overwhelming majority (Lord Hailsham referred to this as an 'elective dictatorship', albeit of the narrow majority held by the Labour government of the 1970s).

In countries with a federal structure, internal sovereignty is even more difficult to locate because in effect there are two levels of government. Neither one of the levels of government has sovereignty. It is those countries' constitutions that lay out precisely what power each level of government may have. In the United States certain powers, duties and functions are allocated either to the president, to Congress or the Supreme Court, all of which exercise checks, balances and even vetoes over one another.

The British parliament is the single and unchallenged authority. However, whilst we have a unitary system where internally no other source can challenge the authority of parliament, legal sovereignty has actually been compromised by membership of the European Union. Parliament can only claim its internal sovereignty by virtue of the fact that it can withdraw from the European Union if it so wishes.

External sovereignty relates to a state's independence in relation to other states; in effect, the fact that other states recognise it as being independent. It is at the heart of national independence and self-government, hence the enormous difficulties that revolve around sovereignty when we consider an independent Palestinian state in a land that is claimed by Israel and to which the claim for a Palestinian state impacts on Israel's sovereignty.

Learning objectives

- Internal and external sovereignty
- Jean-Jacques Rousseau's theory
- Legal and political sovereignty
- J. S. Mill's theory

War broke out over this issue when Yugoslavia fragmented into separate states, such as Croatia, Slovenia and Bosnia, all of which pronounced their own sovereignty. Serbia denied their external sovereignty and attempted to retain these countries within the federation by force.

Legal and political sovereignty

Legal sovereignty (sometimes referred to as *de jure*) refers to the supreme legal authority that is the unchallengeable right to demand compliance. In the past, law was little more than the command of the monarch, however legal sovereignty tends to be based on the belief that final authority can be found in the laws of the state. Sovereignty is therefore based on the right to require an individual to comply, as stated in law.

Political sovereignty (de facto), on the other hand, does not have a basis in law but in power. Political sovereignty rests on the ability to be able to demand obedience because that power has the sole access to coercive force.

However, legal and political sovereignty are often indivisible because legal sovereignty without political sovereignty is toothless. An individual or group that breaches the law must have a reasonable expectation that they will be punished and that they cannot simply ignore the legal judgement. The two concepts are equally indivisible, as it is those that have political sovereignty that create the laws that underpin legal sovereignty.

Ruling by political sovereignty alone is possible, as was seen during Hitler's rule in Germany and Pol Pot's rule in Cambodia. They used political sovereignty to coerce and repress groups and individuals without legal foundation. In the case of Germany, the Reichstag passed an Enabling Bill which gave Hitler the right to rule without recourse to parliamentary approval.

As we have already seen, John Austin suggested that sovereignty in Britain did not lie with either the monarch or the citizens. Instead he suggested that there was parliamentary sovereignty. This is significant, as it is an underlying principle of the British constitution. Not all theorists obviously agree. What Austin had done was to link sovereignty to democracy and to constitutionalism.

It would appear that once a body such as a legislature has legal sovereignty it cannot be challenged. It was believed that the British parliament had this legal sovereignty, but judicial independence means that parliament can be challenged if there is a breach of natural justice. Equally, appeals can be made against legislation, either via the European Court of Justice or the European Court of Human Rights. It is now questionable if the British parliament is any longer fully sovereign. The same can be said of the US Congress; its legislative powers are limited by the constitution and interpretations of that constitution are constantly being made.

The skulls of some of the victims of Pol Pot's reign in Cambodia

DISCUSSION POINT ?

Of internal, external, legal and political sovereignty, which is the most significant?

J. S. Mill's theory

In many ways, John Stuart Mill's theory of sovereignty accords with that of Dicey. Mill said 'Parliament can do anything except turn a man into a woman.' He believed that Westminster had unchallengeable legal power; it can make, change or revoke any laws that it chooses. The main reason for this is that it lacks a written or codified constitution that specifically defines the powers of each institution.

What is globalisation?

Globalisation is a particularly difficult concept to define. It implies a greater degree of interconnectivity between states and the fact that events and decisions that take place in different parts of the world can have a direct and almost immediate effect on other nations.

National and state borders have become more open. No national economy is immune from the impact of the global economy. The interconnectivity has been driven by Internet communications, multinational companies, international production and the flow of financial capital. Information, products and marketing produced in one part of the world now flows out to other nations, creating similar patterns of consumption and business practices. Part of this has been referred to as cultural globalisation, with shared telecommunication, information and technology.

Equally, political globalisation is underway, as seen in organisations such as the European Union or the United Nations.

In the face of national governments' inabilities to avoid the impacts of globalisation, many have chosen to openly embrace it. But this has caused the creation of a significant but disparate anti-globalisation movement. To some extent this has replaced the traditional left versus right divisions, which saw capitalism facing socialism. The division has now been reworked into a pro- and anti-globalisation debate.

Critics of globalism maintain that multinational organisations manipulate consumer tastes and that through marketing they are irreversibly changing popular culture and lifestyles of national populations. Some countries, such as China and Iran, have tried to hold back the flood of information and marketing messages, but the concept of a virtual state, which suggests a borderless world, has undoubtedly eroded the ability of national governments to either control their citizens or to prevent external influence.

In 2000 the then French Foreign Minister, Hubert Vedrine, denounced the United States as being the driving force of globalisation. He described the country as a hyper-power that promoted uniformity and unilateralism. Vedrine was concerned that France was beginning to lose its national identity. Added to this, he believed France was also being adversely affected by the European Union, but he saw globalisation as the greatest threat.

The concept of hyper-globalism suggests that cultural and economic patterns within a nation change irrevocably with the arrival of new technologies, specifically satellite communication, the Internet, mobile phones and computerised financial trading.

Theorists who were writing well before the globalisation process truly began still have much to say that is relevant to the issue. Karl Marx, for example, recognised that capitalism was an international phenomenon and globalisation can be seen as simply an extension of capitalism. Lenin and J. A. Hobson also highlighted the links between capitalism and imperialism. Indeed many have described globalisation as a form of cultural, if not economic imperialism.

Globalisation and democracy

Fukuyama sees capitalism as a driving force in the triumph of liberal democracy. The collapse of communism and the US foreign policy using neo-conservatism values are aggressively expanding democracy in the Middle East. Noreena Hertz argues that multinational companies

Learning objectives

- What is globalisation?
- Globalisation and democracy
- Different forms of globalisation
- International interdependency
- Supranationalism and intergovernmentalism
- Global citizenship and world government
- Kant on world government

are responsive to the needs of the global consumer, thereby undermining elected officials – she sees this as beneficial as consumer control is more responsive than traditional democratic control. Chomsky's critique of US foreign policy focuses on their intention of expanding alien values to foreign countries thus leading to cultural hegemony. There has been resistance to this by Vietnam, Iraq and Afghanistan. Klein sees the rise of multinationals as negative in undermining democratic accountability, leaving populations vulnerable to whims of international unaccountable capitalist corporations.

Different forms of globalisation

Broadly, as we have seen, there are three distinct types of globalisation, the first being economic. National economies are now part of a far broader global economy. The Organisation for Economic Cooperation and Development (OECD) defined economic globalisation as: 'A shift from a world of distinct national economies to a global economy in which production is internationalised and financial capital flows freely and instantly between countries.' ("Globalization: What Challenges and Opportunities for Governments?" 1995, Secretary General of the Public Management Service, OECD.)

This has meant that national governments have found it more difficult to control their own economies and many have had to restructure their economies as a free market. Economic globalisation was accelerated after the collapse of the Soviet Union and indeed economic globalisation was one of the key factors that precipitated the collapse.

Although globalisation is obviously a very powerful phenomenon, the bulk of economic activity still takes place within national boundaries. This suggests that globalisation is not as dominant as it may first appear.

Hirst and Thompson (1999) suggested that globalisation has a number of major advantages.

* It makes labour more flexible – production is carried out where there are available skill sets and a cheaper workforce.

* Trade unions are weakened – production can be shifted away from areas with strong trade union representation.

* Business regulations are less controlling – the overwhelming need is to attract international businesses.

Cultural globalisation, which is sometimes referred to as 'McDonaldisation', suggests that products and services offered across the world are becoming less dissimilar, as consumption patterns, tastes and interests adopt the same features. This is driven by global marketing, access to the Internet, and the operation of multinational businesses that seek to sell standardised products across the world.

Political globalisation is particularly evident in the importance of various international organisations, including the EU, the World Bank, the International Monetary Fund, the OECD, the World Trade Organisation and the United Nations. On the one hand they provide support to states without a loss of national sovereignty. But on the other hand they can impose their will on nation states. These organisations are often referred to as supranational bodies and some see these as the building blocks of internationalism and a future world government. However, political globalisation has, so far, had a far lesser impact than economic and cultural globalisation.

International interdependency

With geographical distance and territorial boundaries becoming less significant, we can see that there is an increasing level of systemic interdependency. It spreads from the local, regional, national, international and global levels.

This interdependency can be typified in the following ways.

- **Economic interdependency** – there has been a drift towards industrialisation taking place in lesser developed countries, such as China and India. These have become the industrial powerhouses of the world, providing products for sale in a global market, but in cooperation with multinational organisations based in other countries.

- **Cultural interdependency** – primarily through the mass media, products and services are marketed worldwide, creating homogenous demand for similar ranges of products and services, regardless of the actual nature of a nation's culture. For example, the Chinese now consume 60 per cent more beef than they did five years ago.

- **Political interdependency** – the involvement of supranational bodies' impacts on the ability of individual nation states to follow their own preferred sets of policies by their ability to impose their will. They can set conditions on assistance, finances and support. In extreme cases they can even impose their will militarily. In Europe there is considerable debate as to the sovereignty of member states and whether their governments are now subordinate to the European Parliament and the European Commission.

Supranationalism and intergovernmentalism

A supranational body is an organisation that can impose its jurisdiction over a number of states. Throughout the 20th century national sovereignty was seen as being the most important consideration. But in this new century governments are beginning to operate on a supranational level. Supranational organisations are not new concepts. They were effectively how many of the ancient empires, such as Rome and Persia, used to operate. Equally, the British Empire, a collection of different cultures, nationalities and ethnic groups, was held together by Britain's political domination and the ultimate sanction of Britain being able to use force.

We see this process continue, even though to a very large extent imperial colonies no longer exist. The Soviet Union held numerous former independent or semi-autonomous states in line until the Soviet Union collapsed in 1991. We now see the Chinese using precisely the same forms of subordination to control Tibet.

In the modern day, however, most supranational organisations are ones that countries join voluntarily rather than as a result of force. In effect they are international federations. The most common is intergovernmentalism. These are treaties or alliances largely based on the desire to cooperate in economic development. Typical examples include the World Trade Organisation with the goal of creating a situation where tariffs and economic protectionism are either reduced or removed. A similar organisation exists that encompasses the US, Canada and Mexico, known as the North American Free Trade Agreement.

In the aftermath of the Second World War two organisations were created. The western allies created the North Atlantic Treaty Organisation in 1949 and the eastern allies, led by the Soviet Union, created the Warsaw Pact in 1955.

Supranational organisations are, however, relatively weak and only able to achieve fairly limited aims. Some aim to promote specific common ends for their member countries, such as the

Organisation of African Unity or the Organisation of Petroleum Exporting Countries. Other organisations are merely forums for consultation and negotiation, such as the Commonwealth of Nations, which has many member countries that were all former British colonies around the world. This organisation also proved to be fairly toothless, as it failed to exert any pressure on South Africa during the apartheid period and continues to fail to exert any meaningful pressure on Robert Mugabe's Zimbabwe.

Global citizenship and world government

In many respects the concepts behind world government accord with social contract theory. Just as a sovereign state is created in order to ensure order and stability within a limited territorial zone, world government can be seen as a way to ensure that there is no further conflict between states by creating a supreme world power.

There have been tentative attempts to move in this direction. The League of Nations was formed in 1919, in the aftermath of the devastating First World War. Another opportunity presented itself in 1944 at Bretton Woods, consisting of 44 states that were fighting the Germans and the Japanese in the Second World War. The hope was to create a cooperative post-war international trade and monetary system. Out of this was born the International Monetary Fund, the World Bank and the General Agreement on Tariffs and Trade. The system collapsed 30 years later. Once again, in the 1990s, the World Trade Organisation was seen as the vanguard of economic globalisation. Tariffs and barriers to trade were dismantled. The United Nations had been created at the end of the Second World War. The charter demanded high standards of conduct from its members, an undertaking not to use force, an agreement to peacefully solve international disputes, recognition of national sovereignty, self-determination, human rights and freedoms. It has developed to become an important part of international politics.

Important decisions need to be carried by a two-thirds majority, but the Security Council has five members that have permanent veto powers, which can effectively block decisions made by the United Nations. However, when it suits a state to ignore the United Nations the organisation seems toothless to prevent them. Such was the case in 2003 when the US and Britain chose to take action to remove Saddam Hussein in Iraq. Only on two occasions has the United Nations actually used military force: once in Korea (1950) and again in Afghanistan (2001). One of the major problems with the United Nations was that throughout the Cold War (1945–89) the United States and the Soviet Union were implacably opposed to one another and the United Nations was paralysed and unable to take decisive action. Effectively they could veto one another and did.

The prospects for a world government and the concept of global citizenship are still as remote as they were decades ago. There is a possibility that the United Nations could form the building block of a world government, but at present neither politicians nor significant numbers of the world population find the prospect either meaningful or attractive. As long as nationalism remains an important driving concept then the prospect of world citizenship is nothing more than a dream for those who want it.

DISCUSSION POINT **?**

What are the prospects for world government?

Immanuel Kant on world government

Kant, writing in the 18th century, believed that there should be a league of nations of autonomous republics. They would combine and create a permanent treaty in order to avoid war. Kant, however, believed that all countries should be republican states, in other words countries that had representative government and guaranteed the political freedom of their citizens. He was writing at the time of the French Revolution and initially applauded the republican government, but was later dismayed by the execution of the king and the reign of terror.

The night watchman

The night watchman, or minimalist state, derives its explanation from classical liberal theory. It spreads from the local, regional and national to international and global levels.

The state is there to constrain human behaviour, essentially to prevent individuals from trampling on the rights and liberties of others. It provides peace, social order and is essentially there as a protective safety net. It was Locke who coined the term 'night watchman' because the state is only there when needed.

Firstly, the state has to ensure domestic order. It then makes sure that any voluntary agreements entered into by its citizens are adhered to. Finally, it provides the citizens with a degree of protection from outside influence and attack.

In an idealised form the night watchman state would simply have a police force, a legal system and some form of military force. Everything else is left to the individual, including moral, cultural, economic and social relationships and activities.

The New Right effectively supports the concept of the night watchman state. They are drawn towards a truly free and unimpeded market. The theorist Robert Nozick, writing in the 1970s, had views not dissimilar to Locke. He believed that property rights were of vital importance and that wealth, as long as it had been legally obtained, should be protected. He supported minimal government and taxation and seemed opposed to any form of welfare or redistribution.

Other theorists also see state intervention as being negative, as it impacts on productivity, efficiency and competition. These theorists include Friedrich Hayek and Milton Friedman.

The New Right points to countries such as Singapore and Malaysia as being examples of minimal states. Government activity is restricted to controlling inflation, ensuring that businesses do not attain monopolies and that they do not collude to fix prices. Thatcher and Reagan economic policies in the 1980s and 1990s were designed to roll back the frontiers of the state through monetarism, privatisation (UK) and deregulation.

The developmental state

Whilst the minimalist state might be ideal for countries that have already developed a complex economy, there is a period during which industrialisation is underway that a more hands-on government approach needs to be adopted. This does not necessarily mean replacing the free market with a more socialist approach. What it does mean, however, is that the government becomes more directly involved with partnership agreements with businesses, in order to drive the economy forward and to modernise it.

The most common examples often cited were in the United States and Britain in the 19th century and after the Second World War in both Germany and Japan, which had been virtually flattened by allied bombing and were starting again from a very low base of production. More modern examples could include private funding initiatives, as encouraged by the British government. These encourage private businesses to invest in essentially public works, such as new hospitals, road infrastructure and flagship projects, such as the 2012 Olympic Village. In this respect the developmental state could be referred to as a partnership state, where workable relationships are encouraged between the state, business and the trade union movement.

Learning objectives

- The night watchman
- The developmental state
- The welfare state
- The collectivist state
- The totalitarian state

Asian Tiger economies

The 'Asian tigers' have attracted attention largely due to their high, long-term growth rates. Many of the tigers have maintained growth rates of 8–10 per cent over a number of years. They include Malaysia, the Republic of South Korea, Taiwan, Hong Kong, and Singapore. There is general agreement that high savings have permitted very high levels of investment in the tiger economies. There is no consensus as to whether the low share of GDP spent by the governments has been a significant factor in growth, or whether social stability and cohesion has been important.

Germany brought Nazism to Europe in the 1930s and 1940s at the barrel of a gun.

DISCUSSION POINT (?)

To what extent could most modern-day states be described as being welfare states?

The welfare state

Whilst a developmental state may use interventionism in order to boost economic growth, a welfare, or social democratic state, would use intervention to bring about a form of social restructuring. They would seek to more reasonably distribute rewards, encourage fairness and equality.

Often a country will adopt both developmental and social democratic approaches simultaneously, such as in Austria and Sweden. In the aftermath of the Second World War Britain, certainly with the creation of the welfare state, went partway through interventionism, but actually failed to channel resources and priorities into rebuilding British industry and infrastructure.

A social democratic state appeals to modern-day liberals and to democratic socialists (e.g. Rawls). The state is actively involved in the market, trying to restructure and deal with injustices and imbalances. Central to this approach is Keynesianism and social welfare.

The role of this type of economic policy is to try to regulate capitalism with the ultimate goal of full employment. This is achieved through fiscal policy, in other words government spending and taxation. In effect the state is seen as enabling individuals. The state provides a necessary safety net, allowing individuals to climb out of poverty with support and become empowered.

The collectivist state

A collectivist state puts all economic activity into state control. This has largely been exemplified by the Chinese post-war economy, as well as the Soviet Union and its satellite states until the late 1980s. They are often referred to as command economies, where all economic activity is directed from a centralised source.

There is little in the way of private property and in particular the means of production are held by the state for the citizens for their mutual benefit. This approach goes far further than the concept of the dictatorship of the proletariat suggested by Marx and by Engels. They did recognise that state control was essential, but believed that state ownership would only be a temporary measure. However, in China and the Soviet Union state control became a permanent state of affairs and over time became increasingly inefficient and over-bureaucratic. This is now more closely regarded as statism, which is the belief that only state intervention can bring about economic and social development. Economic reforms in China are lessening state control over the economy; compared to this is the decline of collectivist states such as North Korea and Cuba.

The totalitarian state

Having described the Soviet Union as having a collectivist approach, we can see that, particularly during Stalin's reign, the Soviet Union showed many of the signs of being a totalitarian state. The reason behind this is that state intervention permeates not only the economy, but virtually every other activity within the country. This extends to education, culture, family life and religion. It is also exemplified by the German state from 1933 to 1945. A more modern example that has often been used was Iraq under Saddam Hussein.

The state manipulates and controls every aspect of life. It has highly developed intelligence and surveillance systems, a large paramilitary police force and an overbearing ideological approach, which aims to draw the bulk of the population into support for the state whilst marginalising and persecuting dissenting groups or ethnic and cultural minorities.

Devolution in Britain

In 1998 a legislative framework was created which set out the devolution arrangements for Scotland, Wales and Northern Ireland. What is significant about this form of devolution, which transfers power from the centre (Westminster) to sub-national units (Scottish Parliament, National Assembly for Wales and Northern Ireland Assembly), is that it is **asymmetrical**.

There are different levels of devolved responsibility and no common pattern to the devolution. All three devolved areas have different forms of devolution. The Scottish Parliament is developed from the Westminster model. It can pass Acts and the executive can make secondary legislation in areas that are not reserved for Westminster. It uses a committee system and the parliament has the right to vary the standard rate of income tax.

In Wales there is no separate executive and legislature, although the assembly has begun to move towards this. The assembly can make secondary legislation, but primary legislation for Wales is still reserved for Westminster.

In Northern Ireland it is slightly more complicated. The assembly can make both primary and delegated legislation, but not in 'accepted' or 'reserved' areas. Power sharing in the executive was essential in order to overcome the perpetual Unionist majority. What was also significant was the surprising ability of the two extremes of Ulster politics in the form of Ian Paisley (now replaced by Peter Robinson) and Martin McGuinness to cooperate effectively for the mutual benefit of the community.

In England, however, devolved arrangements stalled after a rejection through a referendum in the north-east in 2004. Consequently the only devolved assembly in England is the Greater London Authority and the Office of the Mayor for London, however there has been a proliferation of locally elected mayors in many towns and cities, including Hartlepool and Mansfield.

Regional development agencies, which are in fact quangos, were developed shortly after the Labour Party election victory in 1997. These were designed to promote economic development in regions. Confusingly, they were variously called regional chambers or regional assemblies, but at present they have not been developed any further.

The Greater London Authority was created by legislation in 1999 and with it the Office of the Mayor for London. The Greater London Authority provides strategic direction for the capital. The London Mayor works in conjunction with the London Assembly, making proposals and carrying out initiatives for the benefit of the capital. Transport was a controversial topic in the recent mayoral contest between Ken Livingstone and Boris Johnson. Debate focused on the implementation of the congestion charge and proposals to extend its range and cost.

Asymmetrical devolution is not new to Britain. In fact for 50 years from 1922 there was a devolution settlement that gave devolved powers to the assembly at Stormont for Northern Ireland. The problem with asymmetrical devolution has not necessarily been the relative powers of the different assemblies, but the fact that English affairs are debated and voted upon by MPs from the devolved regions, whilst Westminster MPs cannot vote on certain issues that affect Scotland, Wales or Northern Ireland. This is known as the **West Lothian question**.

Other countries have also used asymmetrical devolution. In Spain, Catalonia and the Basque regions have considerably more autonomy than other provinces in Spain. In the United States there are also examples of asymmetrical devolution; Washington DC does not have the level of autonomy that most of the other states have. It is under a form of direct rule from the federal government.

Learning objectives

- Devolution in Britain
- Regional devolution in Britain and the EU

Asymmetrical devolution

This is a constitutional arrangement under which some of the constituent units within the system have more extensive powers than others relative to the central government.

SNP 2008

In 2008 an SNP minority executive was elected with the purpose of using devolution as a stepping stone to full independence via a referendum on the issue. It has already transformed the name of the Scottish Executive to the Scottish Government, implying greater authority.

Richard Report 2004

The Richard Report called for the Welsh Assembly to be given law-making powers in devolved areas such as health and education by 2011. It also wants to increase the number of AMs from 60 to 80 because of the extra responsibilities which would come with additional powers. The report went far further than political observers had expected.

West Lothian question

This was a phrase used by Labour MP Tam Dalyell in 1977 when he said 'for how long will English constituencies and English honourable members tolerate at least 119 honourable members from Scotland, Wales and Northern Ireland exercising an important, and probably often decisive, effect on British politics while they themselves have no say in the same matters in Scotland, Wales and Northern Ireland?'

Actually, the West Lothian question as a term was coined by Enoch Powell MP in his response to the speech.

Regional devolution in Britain and the EU

In November 2004 the government's plan for regional devolution received an overwhelming 78 per cent 'no' vote in a referendum in the north-east of England. It seemed that the project was dead in the water. It had been condemned as a project by a number of groups, including the Confederation of British Industry (CBI).

In Germany there are 16 Länder of equal constitutional status, in Britain there is a range of asymmetrically empowered devolved bodies. The Länder have a highly formalised and structured constitutional order. The main but not only division of power in German federalism is between federal level legislation and administration of that legislation in the Länder. The German Länder has formal access to the federal legislative process in Germany via the Bundesrat. Conflict in the interpretation of division of powers in Germany is subject to authoritative and independent adjudication by the constitutional court. It is unlikely, for a number of reasons, that this type of system will ever be adopted in Britain.

- Coordination will be technical and politically uncontroversial, but there would be competition for resources both between the devolved units and the centre and among the various devolved units.
- The role of UK-level authorities in European Union decision-making would be challenged and reassessed as the Scottish parliament and executive realise the commitments which have been made to allow them access to European decision-making processes.
- The role of local government in Scotland may well be challenged and reassessed as a result of the establishment of the Scottish parliament and executive authorities.

There are 17 devolved regional assemblies which cover all of the Spanish state.

- There is a difference between having devolved power to parts of the state as opposed to having devolved power to the entire state even though the power is asymmetrical.
- Since the Spanish system is not federal there is no transfer of sovereignty.
- The transfer of power is still evolving and being negotiated between each region and the centre, it is not a static situation. Some states consider themselves highly autonomous, such as Catalonia, with a strong political, economic and cultural identity (including own language). Also the Basque region has caused considerable problems for the Madrid government as the separatist movement ETA has resorted to terrorism to press for its demands for full secession from Spain.

As far as Britain is concerned, there are perhaps six key tests that would determine any future form of regional devolution.

- Firstly, any regional devolution needs to be able to give the regional assemblies sufficient power and funding to make a difference.
- Secondly, accountability is vital as any new structure in the region needs to be open to democratic scrutiny.
- Thirdly, there must be subsidiarity. Devolution must mean that powers are drawn down from the centre and not up from local government.
- Fourthly, each region must be able to have the capacity to adapt its own specific form of devolution to match its needs and preferences.
- Fifthly, there needs to be transparency in any of the devolved arrangements so that they are open to scrutiny.
- Finally, there needs to be full stakeholder participation, building on the strengths of existing stakeholders, such as local government.

DISCUSSION POINT ?

What are the key arguments for and against regional devolution in England?

What is federalism?

Federalism is a political system that divides power between two tiers of government. In the United States, Australia, Canada and India this means there is a federal government (national government) and state governments (sub-national governments). As far as definitions of federalism are concerned, the British view differs from that of the European view.

- **British interpretation** – the creation of a European supranational super state where major policy is decided at European level and local matters are dealt with by Westminster (and the devolved governments in Scotland, etc.).

- **European interpretation** – the constitutional sharing of powers between the EU and the member states where the EU deals with certain policy areas affecting Europe as a whole and national governments handle purely domestic affairs.

The following table outlines the characteristics of the EU which are common in a federal system and the characteristics that do not make it a proper federal system.

Federal features	Non-federal features
EU treaties define the powers held by different layers of government	Member states have their own identity and political systems
EU law supersedes national law	European citizens see themselves as nationals of their member state, not as Europeans
The EU has authority to pursue policies on trade, monetary issues and agriculture	All EU institutions, apart from the parliament, get their authority from national governments
The EU has its own budget and currency	The EU does not have authority in areas such as tax, foreign policy or health
EU citizens are directly represented in the European Parliament	
The European Commission negotiates trade deals on behalf of the member states	

What would be the main features of a federal system if Europe did adopt this system?

- It would have different types of institutions to deal with specific issues. The power to deal with them would be held at the lowest possible level; this is known as subsidiarity.

- It would need to be fully democratic with each level of government having a direct relationship with the electorate.

- Power would be dispersed, but coordinated. It would protect the rights of the individual against powerful institutions.

Federalism and co-federalism

Around a third of the world population lives in a state that has some kind of federal structure. None of the federal structures are the same, but they all do share the concept that sovereignty is divided between central and peripheral institutions.

Learning objectives

- What is federalism?
- Federalism and co-federalism
- A federal Europe?

It may in fact be better to describe many of the structures as being somewhere between a unitary state, where all institutions are centralised, and a confederation, in which all power is with peripheral institutions.

Federalism is therefore something of a compromise between the two and it attempts to retain a degree of national unity whilst allowing for regional diversities.

There are four examples of federalism.

- There is German federalism, which is a cooperative type based on shared sovereignty.

- The federal system of the United States of America is a type of dual federalism with divided sovereignty based on two independent levels of decision-making.

- Swiss federalism is a heterogeneous federation of a cooperative type where multilingual and multicultural diversity is accommodated.

- The Canadian system is the first federation to combine federal and parliamentary systems in order to accommodate and reconcile territorial diversity within a fundamentally multilingual and multicultural society.

The most developed form of international federation is, of course, the European Union, although it is a difficult organisation to categorise. It began as a confederation of independent states, using intergovernmental procedures. The sovereignty of each of the states was guaranteed, but in recent years, following the Single European Act (1986) and the Maastricht Treaty (1983), national vetoes are now more limited (with the rise of QMV). EU law is now binding on all members states and the power of the central EU bodies has increased to the detriment of national governments.

A prime example is the failed EU constitution which was intended to formalise the federal structure of the EU, but was rejected and replaced by the Lisbon Treaty. Critics maintain that the treaty is identical to the constitution with the notable omission of the word 'constitution'.

Federalism has tended to be adopted by a number of states for different reasons.

- Some were former colonies, like the United States, and they did not wish to establish a strong national government. They wanted to reserve some powers for the states.

- Others created federations out of smaller, more vulnerable states, such as those in Germany. They saw it as a process by which they could mutually protect one another.

- Another factor is geographical size and the fact that due to the size there is a wide range of cultural and ethnic groups within the territorial region. In India the 25 self-governing states were primarily defined on the basis of language. In Nigeria the 19 states were formed on the basis of tribal and religious customs. In Canada, as there were English- and French-speaking regions, it was based on language and cultural differences.

Federalism has certainly worked for a number of countries. In the United States the system began with what could be described as dual federalism, where there were very definite and separate power bases at both federal and state level. This moved to cooperative federalism, where the federal government assisted the states, usually financially, making the states more dependent on federal funds. Finally, America seems to have moved to a form of coercive federalism, where the federal government has passed laws that control the power of the states and impose restrictions on them.

Federalism does work, as it diffuses government power and imposes a network of checks and balances. It is also seen as a way in which unity and coherence can be maintained. For the

United States it provided a system by which successive waves of immigration and expansion could be brought into a single system without entirely overwhelming existing states.

A federal Europe?

How might federalism affect Britain? Britain had one of the most centralised political systems in Europe. In the past few years, there have been steps towards federalism, with the creation of the devolved governments and assemblies. In a federal Europe regional authorities would take much of the power from Westminster. This would bring the electorate closer to the decision-makers and reduce the role of Westminster and Whitehall.

Those that favour federalism believe that if the EU follows the federalist direction it will mean more democracy. They believe that the EU suffers because it does not control key policy areas, such as foreign affairs. The environment is another key area and federalists believe that both policy areas can no longer be effectively dealt with at national level. It may mean major changes for the EU; federalists believe that the European Commission should become an elected body and accountable to the European Parliament. The Council of Ministers should meet and vote in public (this is soon to happen). Also, every part of EU activity should be subject to the jurisdiction of the European Court of Justice.

Impacts on British sovereignty

The Factortame case was a landmark constitutional case which confirmed the primacy of European Union law over British law. The case first came to prominence when a Spanish fishing company called Factortame appealed against restrictions imposed on them by the British government using the Merchant Shipping Act 1988. Factortame's argument was that they were permitted to fish under the law of the European Economic Community (which became the EU in 1992). The case reached the High Court, which obtained an injunction from the European Court of Justice (ECJ) to temporarily suspend the Secretary of State for Transport from enforcing the particular part of the Act. In March 1989, this was overturned by the Court of Appeal on the basis that the constitution did not give any court the right to suspend Acts of Parliament, and this was confirmed by the House of Lords. The House of Lords ruling that they did not have the power to suspend Acts of Parliament was then referred to the European Court of Justice in 1990, as was legally required. The ECJ in June 1990 ruled that national courts could strike down laws which contravened EU law. Consequently, the House of Lords ruled in favour of Factortame, which in effect meant that the Merchant Fishing Act 1988 was also struck down.

Another prime example of the sovereignty of Britain being directly threatened by the EU was when the BSE crisis hit Britain in 1996. Unilaterally, the EU banned British beef imports, despite BSE being rife (but largely unreported) in other EU countries such as France and Spain.

DISCUSSION POINT ?

What might be the advantages of a truly federal Europe?

Learning objectives

- Organic and social contract theory
- Pluralist state
- Capitalist state
- Leviathan state
- Patriarchal state

Multinationals and corporations

To a large extent, the actions of multinationals and international corporations have fuelled and driven the process of globalisation across the world. These private business entities constantly seek new markets and opportunities in which to sell their products and services. Clearly, as far as economies of scale and production efficiencies are concerned, it is desirable for them to sell identical products into as many markets as possible without modification.

Globally, products and services such as Coca Cola, McDonald's, Hertz car rental and a host of other global brands are sold almost without modification or concern for the specific cultural differences in international markets. The brands are instantly recognisable, whether the marketing is being targeted at customers in the Far East, the Middle East or central Europe.

As we have seen, this process, which is often referred to as 'McDonaldisation', is a growing one, as through the power of global brands and marketing these vast business entities seek to create unparalleled demand in markets around the world.

Economic, cultural and political impacts

The economic impact of globalisation has led not only to the internationalisation of production, but also to the free flow of capital between countries. In 2008 Britain has seen gradually increasing oil and energy costs, which have had an impact on petrol prices. This has very little to do with the levels of oil and energy production, but more to do with the demand for energy products globally. Most products and raw materials are susceptible to changes in supply and demand. Put simply, increased demand without increased supply drives the price up. Increased demand from developing nations, such as China and India, is the main cause of the high prices.

Cultural impacts, as we have seen, largely revolve around creating a demand for products and services that were until relatively recently not as freely available in particular markets. Globalisation opens up markets to information, new products and services, and marketing through enhanced media. This creates a demand for products and services that are seen to replicate the affluent image of western society. A key impact is that traditional foods, clothes and lifestyles are sacrificed in order to copy what is perceived to be a better and more desirable way of life.

Political impacts make it far more difficult for countries to adopt an entirely neutral or independent position on national matters and certainly on regional issues. There is considerable pressure from international organisations to which the state may owe allegiance, as these international organisations may have contributed to the state's stability and economic development. It is more difficult for states to operate outside the influence of these organisations. Those that do may find themselves subject to worldwide condemnation, sanctions and possibly military action.

Impact of globalisation

The growth of globalisation does not necessarily mean that regional or national issues and importance are subordinate. But what it does mean is that events that take place, even in a particular region of a state, may have a global impact. Gradually, national economies have been brought into an international economy, tied together by multinational organisations, the growing importance of international trade and the movement of capital.

To begin with, globalisation began as a result of the Cold War period. The United States and the Soviet Union in particular were determined to extend their influence to as many parts of the world as possible. Since the collapse of the Soviet Union this process has, if anything, accelerated. Initially it was an attempt to bring particular countries and regions into a sphere of influence, rather than to adopt the system that had been used before, that of conquest and domination through the creation of a more identifiable empire.

Francis Fukuyama argues that globalisation has also accelerated the spread of liberal democracy. It has brought western liberal political views to a number of countries, notably those that were former Soviet Union satellite states in Eastern Europe and Central Asia. More controversially post 9/11 the Bush Administration adopted a neo-conservative approach to foreign policy in aggressively exporting liberal democracy to the Middle East in the form of invading Afghanistan and Iraq. Calls were also made to undertake a similar course of action in Iran and North Korea, however with the scale of losses, particularly in Iraq, the mood for such action has cooled. Even Fukuyama has changed his former neo-conservative attitudes in recognising that there are limits to the extent to which liberal democracy can be imposed upon an uncooperative nation.

Impacts on sovereignty

Globalisation has also had a marked impact on the functioning of nation states and indeed the politics of countries. A considerable argument has arisen regarding the relevance of national governments. This is based on the fact that national economies are now no longer separate entities and are part of a far larger global economy. Information, finance and culture are transmitted across the globe, almost without restraint or control.

Countries no longer have the ability to manage their own economies or make decisions that are beneficial solely to their own country and not in the best interests of competing nations. Agreements on tariffs, trade barriers and business systems mean that in order to continue to compete countries have to apply and enforce internationally recognised standards of practice. In effect rather than being a sovereign nation state countries have become competition states, but have to cope not with the threat of military or political force, but with the economic force of the competition. With nationality being replaced by increased social integration, any sense of individuality and sovereignty are gradually being eroded.

If we return to our original investigation into the nature of sovereignty, we can now see that each of the key determinants or descriptions of a sovereign state perhaps no longer hold true. External sovereignty is related to a state's capacity to act as an independent and autonomous entity. To some extent countries can still do this, but not without regard to the consequences if this is seen to be against broader interests. A prime example of this is Iran's nuclear programme which they insist on continuing against worldwide condemnation and belief that it is a nuclear weapons programme.

Internal sovereignty is also under threat. This referred to the notion of a supreme power and authority within the state that could make decisions that were binding on all within that state. Certainly the membership of international or regional organisations put this question into doubt. This is certainly the case for Britain with regard to their involvement with the EU and NATO.

Legal sovereignty referred to the unchallengeable right to demand compliance. Again, if this is seen to be in variance with international law or more generally held concepts of fairness, freedom or human rights then this is often challenged by the international community.

Political sovereignty refers to unlimited political power and a monopoly of coercive force. Once again this is in doubt, as countries are roundly condemned and face a raft of actions against them if they are seen to unreasonably use coercive force to impose their political power. Two prime examples in recent history have been in Zimbabwe and Chinese action in Tibet.

DISCUSSION POINT ?

To what extent do you believe that national sovereignty is now an outmoded concept?

Exam Café

Relax, refresh, result!

Relax and prepare

Here are several unit F854 essay questions of the type that could occur in your exam. How would you go about answering them?

- Discuss the main characteristics of the nation state.

- Evaluate the different models on the role of the state.

- To what extent are political and legal sovereignty mutually compatible?

- Compare and contrast internal and external sovereignty.

- Discuss the view that the nation state is in decline.

- Evaluate the claim that globalisation has a negative impact on democracy.

Refresh your memory

The following are key issues that are covered in unit F854. Think about what is meant by each of them.

✓ The definition of sovereignty.

✓ The different forms of sovereignty – internal, external, political and legal.

✓ The definition of the state and the meaning of the nation state.

✓ The characteristics of the nation state.

✓ The different models on the role of the state.

✓ The debate over the decline of the nation state.

✓ The meaning of globalisation in its political, economic and cultural forms.

✓ The theories on the impact of globalisation.

Are you able to explain these *and* deploy the ideas of relevant political thinkers to illustrate your arguments?

Key relevant political thinkers

For each of the following key issues in the left-hand column summarise the views of the political theorists listed in the right-hand column.

Key issue	Relevant theorists
Sovereignty definition	Bodin, A. V. Dicey
Internal/external	Rousseau, Austin, J. S. Mill
Political/legal	Bodin, Hobbes, A. V. Dicey
The state and nation definition	Hegel, Gellner, Meinecke, Weber
Characteristics	Hobbes, Weber
Role	Hobbes, Locke, Nozick, Rawls, Marquand, Marx, Hegel
Globalisation definition	Freedman, Ohmae, Scholte
Political, cultural and economic forms	Marx, Hobson
Impact on democracy	Fukuyama, Klein, Held, Hertz, Chomsky

Get the result !

In the exam you will be asked a certain style question for unit F854 similar to this one. Sample answer extracts to the question are given in the exam tips.

Analyse the differing views on the role of the state.

Exam tips

Consider the following extracts from Sally's answer to the above question. Is it well focused and does it show good understanding and analysis of theories on the role of the state? How well does it use the ideas of particular theorists? At what level would you award this if the rest of the essay continued in a similar theme?

A state is defined as a political entity with a geographical territory set within borders which has some sort of internal government.

The first role of the state is adopted by conservatives such as Burke. They believe the state is a natural organic part of society in which since the state created society and its citizens, they have a natural duty to obey the state. They see the state as the 'wisdom of the ages' (Burke) and the state's authority lies within traditional means such as convention and tradition, very much like the system of British government. There is a belief that without the state, society would fail, causing life to be 'nasty, short and brutish' (Hobbes).

Examiner says:

Sally has started out by giving a limited definition of the state which at least shows she has some understanding of the concept. Her description of the conservative 'role' is more concerned with a conservative general model of the state. If she had developed her good understanding to analyse how this translated to a law and order style role then her knowledge could have been used more appropriately. There were signs that she could have done this by referring to Hobbes. Her overall use of political theory was appropriate and varied.

The second view on the role of the state is offered by social contract theorists. This has been proposed through the ages by people like Socrates, Hobbes, Locke and Rousseau. Bentham takes his ideas on utilitarianism from this view ('the greatest happiness of the greatest number'). Here there is the idea that in the state there is a contract between the people and the government and the state is seen as necessary. The idea of the authority of the state is different here from Weber's view that 'legitimacy is power cloaked in authority'. The other idea of how the state gains authority is Rousseau's when he advocated, 'The strongest should never be strong enough to be master, he must transform power into authority and obedience into duty.' The word transform gives a much more positive view on the authority of the state. There are links with conservative organic theory in both seeing the necessity of a role for the state.

Examiner says:

Once again Sally has not really addressed the role of the state. She is right to argue that social contract theory has a positive outlook on the state and this is linked to the purpose of the state, but this is not really the role. Sally's answer went on to look at what she called an oppressive role advocated by Marxists and anarchists. As her answer only implicitly dealt with the role of the state, her overall grade was going to suffer. There was no mention of the standard theories of the minimal, developmental, social democratic and totalitarian roles of the state. Overall her answer gained a D/C borderline mark mainly based upon some good understanding and knowledge on the state but lacking appropriate application to the role of the state.

Do you agree with this mark?

Unit F856

Relax and prepare

Here are several unit F856 essay questions that you could be asked in your exam. Discuss with your colleagues how you would go about answering them or try writing essay plans for as many as you can.

- Discuss which model on the role of the state is the most applicable to the UK.

- Assess the impact of globalisation on British politics.

- To what extent has devolution and membership of the EU undermined parliamentary sovereignty in the UK?

- Discuss the impact of multinational organisations on the concept of external sovereignty.

- Discuss the likelihood of a fully federal European Union.

Refresh your memory

Case studies on the state, nation, sovereignty and globalisation

✓ The creation of the European Union and its development post-Maastricht.

✓ The creation of devolved assemblies and parliaments in Scotland, Wales and Northern Ireland.

✓ The creation of an SNP government in Scotland and proposals for a referendum on independence.

✓ UN attempts at intervention in international disputes and crises (both successful and unsuccessful).

✓ The role of the World Trade Organisation and the G8 nations in attempting to resolve issues of international trade.

✓ The influence of multinational companies in using Third World labour.

✓ Changes to the welfare state in the UK post-1979.

Get the result!

The following is the type of essay question that you will have to answer for unit F856 in your exam. There are tips below on how to answer it.

Discuss the implications of globalisation for the nation state in theory and in practice.

Exam tips

These are the issues you need to think about in answering the above question.

✦ What is meant by globalisation and what are its cultural, economic and political features?

✦ How has the nature and role of the nation state changed?

✦ In what ways do globalists argue that there have been positive benefits of globalisation?

✦ How do anti-globalists criticise the advent of globalisation?

✦ What impact have multinational organisations had upon the nation state (e.g. consider EU, WTO, IMF and UN)?

✦ Does the nation state have any future and what are the prospects for world government?

Remember when considering these issues to be prepared to examine the views of political thinkers (e.g. Soros, Chomsky, Klein, Herz and Fukuyama would all be relevant). If you do not consider the theory and its application in practice, the best you can achieve is a D grade!

In a liberal democracy a government must have the authority and therefore the legitimacy to govern. Having political legitimacy gives a government the authority and therefore the right to exercise power. There are different views as to how power is acquired.

One theory is that it is acquired from below, that is, from the citizens through consent. In return those exercising the power are accountable to those who granted them the power. Another view is that it is acquired naturally from above by the people best able to exercise it, namely those who have the appropriate wisdom, experience and social standing, and who respect the authority of the institutions of state: monarchy, aristocracy and church.

Power, authority and legitimacy to govern in a democratic system is acquired by a political party winning a fair and free general election. Voting a political party into government is an expression of the electorate's consent for that party to govern. Power can also be acquired by a dictatorship. But this is achieved through other means, for example by using plebiscites, mass rallies or suppressing opposition parties in elections. In a liberal democracy a government without authority will eventually collapse; in authoritarian regimes this is less likely as they depend less on the consent of the people, and perhaps more on the charisma of its leader, for example. In a democratic state seizing power by force isn't legitimate because it isn't authorised by the citizens.

In Britain the executive of a government has power through various sources: royal prerogatives, the leader of the executive (prime minister), emergency powers, patronage. These powers are fused with those of the legislature, unlike in the United States where they are separate.

Authority is said to be natural and necessary as the basis of society. Having it involves establishing order and stability through setting the necessary parameters to achieve this. Some say there would be violence and injustice without it. Others believe it is needed to prevent the emergence of authoritarian rule. The collapse of authority could lead to dictatorship and loss of individual liberties. Marxists saw it as necessary for order but were opposed to 'iniquitous authority' in the sense of imposing the will of another on others. Anarchists saw it as exploiting and oppressing citizens.

In a liberal democracy crises of legitimacy can occur when there is conflict between economic and political ideals, as might be the case when forces within the state pursue goals that are at odds with the government, as was the case in Britain in 1974 when the trade unions confronted the Conservative government of the time and challenged its authority. Voter apathy in recent times raises the question about a political party's legitimacy to govern after winning an election in which the turnout is so low that victory was achieved by less than 25 per cent of the potential vote.

These are some of the issues covered in this chapter, in which the following are the key themes.

- The meaning and interpretation of power, authority and legitimacy
- The exercise of power and authority from different perspectives
- The meaning of legitimacy and its interrelationships with power and authority
- The meaning of consent and how it is obtained in a democracy and in a dictatorship
- The way in which power operates through decision-making, setting agendas and thought control and coercion

- Where political power is located in Britain

- How governments gain authority and have it undermined

- How the legitimation of power is undermined by electoral apathy, the growth of an underclass, protest movements and loss of public confidence

In covering these themes the chapter is broken down into the following topics.

The chapter finishes with an exam café feature on page 106.

Use of naked power

In 2006, military leaders in Thailand staged a coup, suspended the constitution and declared martial law. Army chief Sonthi Boonyaratglin and the military leadership formed a council for political reform and ousted the prime minister, Thaksin Shinawatra. The coup leaders abolished the cabinet and parliament, but promised that power would be returned to the people. Some 15 months later the generals lived up to their word.

Grand Palace guard, Thailand

The meaning of power, authority and legitimacy

Broadly, power is the ability to achieve a desired effect even if there is opposition. As we will see, power can be shared, limited, delegated, conferred and may be on the basis of either some form of consent or coercion.

There is a distinction between power and influence. Power implies the ability to make and enforce decisions that are binding on others. Influence, on the other hand, is simply the ability to affect the decision-making processes of others by using external pressure. Power, however, can be exercised either through influence or some kind of control.

Unlike the two other key concepts that we will be investigating in this section (authority and legitimacy) power seldom exists without it being exercised. As a result power is at the very centre of politics. Every institution in government exercises some kind of power, whether it is economic, social, legislative or judicial.

It is important to understand the relationship between power, authority and legitimacy. Power without authority is often referred to as naked power, as exercised by an unrestrained individual or group. Ultimately, naked power is actually weaker than power that is accepted. Naked power is often not associated with legitimate power. In other words, a power that has been acquired through a recognised process and is exercised within known and accepted limits.

An important consideration is whether power is either deliberate or intentional. For example, a government could use its power to ensure the equality of same-sex relationships, but in exercising that power the government could be accused of hastening the demise of family life.

An intentionalist's view of power recognises that power is always linked to an identifiable group, such as a party or a corporation. A structuralist's view of power sees it as simply a feature of the social system.

There is, however, no broadly accepted definition of the term power. Steven Lukes (1974) believed that there were three different aspects (or faces as he called them) of power.

- The ability to influence decision-making. This decision-making power is the most public of the three faces and is the way in which governments want to be seen. It refers to the power of governments to make policy decisions after widespread consultation.

- The ability to shape a political agenda and prevent unwanted decisions being made. Essentially, this is non-decision-making power that gives governments the ability to control the agenda in debates and make certain issues unacceptable for discussion.

- The ability to manipulate an individual's perceptions and preferences and in effect his or her thought control. This is ideological power (and probably most important face of power). It is the ability to influence people's thoughts and make them want things opposed to what would actually benefit them.

Authority is a form of power; more precisely legitimate power. As we have seen, power is the ability to influence behaviour. Authority confers the right to do that.

Authority does not need to incorporate any form of manipulation or coercion. Individuals accept the authority and therefore obey. Authority is often based upon the notion of the 'right to rule'. As we will see, there have been a large number of different theories written on the nature of authority; the primary work is that of Max Weber and his attempts to define various forms of authority.

What he meant by this was being able to exercise power over another group by getting them to do exactly what they want them to do, even though they would not have chosen that option had they the choice.

Herbert Marcuse (1964) suggested that totalitarian societies work in this way. They used coercion, terror and brutality to mould the beliefs and thoughts of their citizens.

There was an all the more pervasive method used by even liberal democracies in the modern day. They manipulated needs and Marcuse called this: 'A comfortable, smooth, reasonable, democratic unfreedom.' (*One Dimensional Man*, 1964, Beacon)

He believed that indoctrination and psychological control produced a society that lacked any credible or even vocal opposition. There would be little conflict, but this did not mean that the people were necessarily content, or that they had any degree of power. Understandably, this has been a theme that has been attractive to Marxists, as it helps explain why people accept the situation; simply because they are not in a position to know their own minds.

Engels called this false consciousness, where the proletariat, being an exploited class, are deluded by bourgeois ideas, and are prevented from appreciating that they are being exploited.

Lenin suggested that only minor progress could ever be made whilst bourgeois ideology was dominant. All they could hope to do was improve their conditions within the same capitalist system. This has been used to criticise social democratic welfare reforms as a way of masking the continued exploitation of the proletariat.

DISCUSSION POINT ?

Why might true power be a combination of a number of different factors?

Media manipulation and elections

How much effect does the media actually have on voting behaviour? The following table outlines some possibilities.

Question	Probable answer
How significant is party bias in the media?	The majority of voters read the national press. Most of the tabloids support a particular party. Traditionally, most were pro-Conservative, now many are openly pro-Labour.
How reliable is media support for a party?	Some suggest that before the 1997 election Tony Blair negotiated press support for the Labour Party in return for promises of greater press freedoms. The press did support the party and subsequently have continued to support it.
How biased are television and radio broadcasts?	Public broadcasts should be neutral, but the two main parties have far more airtime during election campaigns. The agenda is often set by the media and the government of the day gets far more coverage.
How likely are voters to be influenced by media bias?	There is a greater impact due to party de-alignment and electoral volatility. The media can influence floating (undecided) voters. There may be long-term media influence, but it is hard to isolate the effects.
How do the parties respond to media bias?	New Labour abandoned socialist policies after constant criticism. Parties have employed spin-doctors to manage the media. Parties are prepared to attack the media if they sense inaccuracies or bias.

Post-modernists have also looked at this radical view of power. Michel Foucault analysed the link between power and knowledge. He was of the opinion that belief systems gained power as more people accept particular views associated with the system and they become common knowledge. Belief systems define authority. Within the belief system, or discourse as he called them, ideas become right or wrong, normal or deviant. Some thoughts and actions become unacceptable. The belief system defines how the world is seen; this is a subtle form of power and very difficult to resist.

Learning objectives

- Executive dominance in Britain
- Fusion of powers
- Lack of constitutional checks on the executive
- Operation of the royal prerogative
- EU power, authority and accountability

The Houses of Parliament

Executive dominance in Britain

There are many reasons why it is believed that the executive dominates parliamentary business in Britain. This has often been referred to as the decline of assemblies' debate. Whatever the model of assembly, they have always been seen as the way in which responsible and representative government is delivered. However, gradually the power of assemblies, and in Britain the House of Commons, is said to have been in decline, as a result of increased power and dominance by the executive.

There are several reasons for this, as outlined below.

- The disciplined parties – which require loyalty to the government of the day; it is parties rather than assemblies that have become the main agents of representation.

- The growth of big government – where power has been redistributed from parliament to the executive, as seen in the size and the status of bureaucracies and the fact that most policy initiatives come from the executive and not from parliament. Equally, government policy has become more complex, requiring professionals to handle it rather than amateurs (regular politicians).

- The lack of leadership – which tends to be provided by parties and the main focus of leaders has been on the executive rather than the assembly itself.

- The impact of interest groups – these groups often bypass parliament and deal directly with the executive or the bureaucracy of the executive.

Britain's prime ministers derive their power from a number of different sources, as described in the following table. This is an ideal example of executive dominance in Britain.

Source of power	Description and explanation
Royal prerogatives	In the past it was the duty of the monarch to appoint ministers and declare war or sign peace agreements. Over the centuries this power has been transferred to the prime minister. This is why Tony Blair did not have to seek parliamentary approval to go to war against Iraq to end the professed threat to Britain from weapons of mass destruction.
Leader of the executive	As the 'first amongst equals', the prime minister is the first and final decision-maker in the cabinet and in the country. The prime minister provides leadership and initiates policy. The prime minister is expected to take the initiative and ensure the support of the cabinet. Margaret Thatcher took the decision to send the British military taskforce to liberate the Falkland Islands in 1982 after the Argentinean invasion.
Leader of a political party	As the leader of a political party, the prime minister, or would-be prime minister, has enormous power in the creation of party policies and the final content of the party manifesto. The party leader will be the individual who will become the prime minister and transform the policies into legislation (if the party is elected). Many of the electorate votes on the basis of the character and image of the party leader. This reinforces the party leader's view that his or her policy approach is correct, acceptable to the electorate and that a mandate has been given. In a sense the electorate has approved the individual views of the party leader. In this respect particular favourite or priority policies of a party leader are likely to be first to be legislated on if they are successful in winning the election. It is undoubtedly the case that Tony Blair and his closest advisors were instrumental in putting together the manifestos for the three elections won by the Labour Party since 1997.

Emergency powers	An Act of parliament may give the prime minister extra powers to handle a crisis situation. In any case, the prime minister is expected to show immediately that they have an emergency under control. In the first few weeks of his prime ministerial career Gordon Brown acted decisively on widespread flooding in England, a new foot and mouth epidemic, a Glasgow airport terrorist scare and the panic in the money markets over Northern Rock.
Patronage	The prime minister has the power to make a wide range of appointments, including ministers, life peers, judges and diplomats. It is, therefore, possible for the prime minister to surround himself with allies and supporters. In March 2006, Tony Blair became embroiled in a scandal over the appointments for peerage of specific Labour Party campaign contributors. Four men who secretly donated money to the governing party – health entrepreneur Chai Patel, businessman Sir David Garrard, stockbroker Barry Townsley, and Indian food magnate Gulam Noon – were later nominated for peerage by the prime minister. The Lords Appointments Commission blocked the four appointments, and Blair denied having nominated the men in return for the loans. The seldom-used Honours Act of 1925 considers imprisonment for up to two years or an unrestricted fine for anyone found guilty of accepting 'any gift, money or valuable consideration as an inducement or reward for procuring or assisting or endeavouring to procure the grant of a dignity or title of honour.'

The table above outlines what is often referred to as being the formal powers of the prime minister, especially with regard to royal prerogative powers. It is important to note that the degree of authority a prime minister enjoys (which varies from to PM to PM and also within the period of office of each PM) is affected by party and cabinet support (note the problems of John Major and more recently Gordon Brown), the size of the government majority (compare Blair pre-2005 and post-2005) and the extent of public approval (witness Brown up to October 2007 and the decision to delay a general election in comparison to events afterwards, or Blair pre- and post-Iraq).

Fusion of powers

The term fusion of power has been attributed to Walter Bagehot, who wrote about government and economics in the 19th century.

The fusion of powers is seen as the opposite of separation of powers, where the executive and legislative branches are brought together. It is said to be particularly obvious in parliamentary-democracies.

In Britain the executive, comprising of the prime minister and the cabinet, are part of the legislature. Taking the separation of powers concept to its logical conclusion this should never be the case. In effect someone in the executive should never be part of the legislature, but within a fusion of powers this is essential. The legislature effectively chooses the leader of the executive and that individual still operates as part of the legislature.

There is also in Britain a fusion between the legislature and the judiciary, as the House of Lords is effectively the court of last resort in Britain (the Law Lords form the highest (or final) court of appeal in the UK). However, under the terms of the Constitution Reform Act (2005) this will cease to be the case from 2009.

The decoupling of the role of the Lord Chancellor failed to remove the post, but it is now rebranded as Secretary of State for Justice. The post has lost its role of Speaker of the House of Lords and the control of the day-to-day running of the judiciary, although it still inputs into the appointments of senior members of the judiciary.

The US Constitution expressly forbids any fusion of power, but this makes it difficult for the legislature to ever remove the executive. Attempts to impeach presidents have overall been unsuccessful, with the exception of Nixon's forced resignation prior to the completion of the full impeachment process. Note also the failure to successfully impeach Bill Clinton in 1998 on the grounds of abuse of power and obstruction of justice.

Lack of constitutional checks on the executive

Every British government between 1835 and 1874 fell as a result of votes in the House of Commons and not at a general election. At that time Britain was governed by parliament, but things soon changed. Increasingly, governing Britain was the responsibility of the cabinet. In effect, power had begun to shift from the legislature to the executive. By the 1970s there had been another shift, this time power had moved from the cabinet to the prime minister, even further distancing the legislature from the decision-making processes.

In 1976 Lord Hailsham described a situation where the party with a majority could effectively rule Britain as if it were a dictatorship (Hailsham was actually referring to the then Labour government which had a small majority but was able through party discipline to undertake extensive reform – this has often been misinterpreted to relate to the power of governments with large majorities). This was called an elective dictatorship, where by virtue of a majority the government can dominate all areas of politics and policy-making. It can control debates, bypass parliament and introduce and pass legislation. The problem remains that an executive-dominated parliament which retains control has no vested interest in changing the current system, so electoral reform may not be on the agenda.

Operation of the royal prerogative

The royal prerogative is a number of powers or privileges that used to be performed by the monarch, but are now carried out in the name of the monarch by the prime minister and the cabinet. This means that the authority of the prime minister and cabinet comes directly from the monarch and not from parliament. These powers give the right to declare war or to sign a peace treaty, send troops to fight in a conflict, appoint ministers, give honours to individuals, raise funds to pay for soldiers, appoint judges and maintain law and order.

These powers are applicable to individuals (e.g. the prime minister or a minister of state) and collectively (the cabinet as a whole).

The use of the royal prerogative is illustrated in the following cases.

- In 1982 Margaret Thatcher sent troops to the Falkland Islands to liberate it from Argentinian invaders.
- In the early 1990s John Major negotiated the terms of the Maastricht Treaty (which passed the right of the British government to make policy in certain areas of the EU).
- In 2001 Tony Blair decided on the date of the election and then changed his cabinet after winning the election.
- In 2003 Tony Blair sent troops to Iraq to remove the dictator Saddam Hussein

In reality, many of the prerogative powers lies with the prime minister, including the right to dissolve parliament to call an election or to appoint ministers. This has caused problems when it involves sending troops abroad to fight a war. It was not constitutionally necessary to gain the support of the House of Commons in the case of the Falklands war in 1982, nor was it necessary in the case of the Iraq war in 2003. But there were grave doubts about sending troops in both cases and many MPs disagreed with the decisions, believing other alternatives were available. As a result of the controversies, it is likely that a prime minister in a similar situation in the future will at least give the House of Commons a chance to comment before the decision to send troops to war.

Gordon Brown expressed his desire to limit and provide parliamentary scrutiny of many of the royal prerogative powers, including parliamentary approval before troops are deployed abroad in a combat role.

EU power, authority and accountability

The Lisbon Treaty which came into force in January 2009 had significant implications as far as the power and authority of EU was concerned, as illustrated in the following table.

Issue	Implications
A two-and-a-half-year Council President, rather than 6 months. The president would be elected by the European Council	A more permanent representative for the EU on the world stage with great continuity and impact
A high representative for Foreign Affairs and Security Policy	Effectively a new foreign secretary for the EU
Council decisions to be made by qualified majority voting (QMV), coming into affect from 2014–17	This means decisions can be taken if supported by 55% of member states and covering 65% of EU population. Previously many decisions required unanimity
Commissioners to be cut from 27 to 15, by 2014	'Unelected and faceless bureaucrats' reduced in number with the promise of greater accountability
MEPs to be limited to 750. Parliament's power would be enhanced by extending the co-decision procedure to new areas of policy	This will mean eventual losses of MEPs for member states as the EU continues to enlarge, but it should prevent the European Parliament from becoming too unwieldy
A strengthening of national parliaments' decision-making	This will mean a strengthening of EU accountability
An exit clause for nation states	There were no clear procedures in the past
Petitions are now possible	They have to be considered if they receive a million signatures
QMV to be extended to 40 policy areas	This should increase democratic decision-making
Opt in/Opt out provisions for Britain in certain areas	Allows Britain to retain power in key areas such as policing

When we consider the authority of the EU, perhaps the first question to tackle is not necessarily whether the EU has authority, but whether it is even publicly accepted in the first place. In Britain, the legitimacy and popularity of the EU hinges on whether the British have a European identity. The Eurobarometer survey features a series of measures of European identity. Reported levels of European identity vary over time. It is rather telling that research carried out by the University of Strathclyde found the following.

- When respondents are asked about European identity immediately after questions about the EU, then European identity appears rarer overall, and especially weak among anti-EU respondents.

- However, if the European identity measures are located prior to, or a long way after, the EU questions, then European identity is relatively strong, even among respondents who are EU-sceptic, anti-immigration and supporters of extreme right parties.

- This suggests that European identity is more fragile and volatile than attitudes to the EU and that European identity is perhaps a separate issue from the popularity of the EU.

The EU Commission, for example, is only indirectly accountable to the electorate via the European Parliament. The former French prime minister Édith Cresson was a European commissioner. She became a target for fraud allegations. This led to the resignation of the Santer Commission in 1999. The inquiry found that Cresson had 'failed to act in response to known, serious and continuing irregularities over several years'. She was found guilty of not reporting failures in a youth training programme from which huge sums of money went missing. In July 2006, the European Court of Justice declared that Cresson had acted in breach of her obligations as a commissioner.

There are constant calls for increased accountability to the citizens of Europe within more democratic European institutions. Currently, citizens are ill-equipped for well-informed assessment of their representatives. There are few formal mechanisms for withdrawing and replacing representatives. Neither the European Parliament nor national parliaments appoint commissioners or civil servants of comitology (this refers to the committee system which oversees the acts implemented by the European Commission). The European Parliament can only dismiss the entire Commission en bloc; this is an unlikely event as it has grave consequences for the legitimacy of the EU itself.

With the hierarchical order of multilevel governance in the EU, there is another challenge for democratic theory and conceptions of accountability and transparency. Political accountability is more difficult to ascertain and to place, because it is impossible to determine the constraints on policies. The unresolved questions are who should be accountable and by what standards should they be judged and what sanctions can be brought against them.

DISCUSSION POINT ?

To what extent is the executive dominance in Britain a major challenge to parliamentary democracy?

How governments gain authority

Governments gain authority three different ways.

In liberal democracies the most accepted means of achieving authority is by electoral consent. Marxists in particular, however, would contend that ideological hegemony is the main driving force behind government authority. Other theorists would argue that authority is gained due to the general submission, or respect, given to government; this is known as deferential authority. Here the tendency is to respect or follow orders or guidance of individuals or institutions, even when it is contrary to an individual's own opinion. This also relates to traditional respect for institutions such as the monarchy.

Deference and obedience to authority permeates a wide range of relationships. Traditionally, it was argued that females defer to males, the poor to the rich, the rural to the urban, and the less educated to the educated. Deference to authority can be viewed as an act of submission and as Stanley Elkins said, deference 'was a social reality, not a myth'.

In 1999 Ronald Inglehart found that: 'The same publics that are becoming increasingly critical of hierarchical authority are also becoming increasingly resistant to authoritarian government, more interested in public life, and more apt to play an active role in politics.' ('Post modernism erodes respect for authority but increases support for democracy', *Critical Citizens: Global Support for Democratic Governance*' P. Norris (ed.), 1999, Oxford University Press.)

This was an optimistic view, but the opposite can also be true because increased deference and withdrawal from democratic processes can lead to a rise in authoritarian governments.

Elections should be fair, competitive and free. Fairness should be reflected in the fact that more votes should mean more seats (MPs in parliament). Competitive means that the voters should be able to choose between the competing political parties and make a reasoned decision on who to vote for. Free implies that citizens have the right to make statements about policy (freedom of speech), the right to cast a secret vote and the freedom of the press to express views and opinions. Beyond this, elections have the following functions.

Learning objectives

- How governments gain authority
- How government authority can be undermined

Milgram on authority

In the 1960s Stanley Milgram performed a series of experiments to see how likely it was that individuals would obey authority, even in the knowledge that someone would suffer as a result. He found that most people would obey orders to punish someone when instructed to do so. To establish this, a participant in the experiments was ordered to administer a large voltage to other individuals who pretended they were experiencing a severe electric shock. Milgram believed that obedience to authority was widespread and that at least 65 per cent of the population were obedient.

Function	Explanation
Representation	The electorate is too large a group to govern itself, therefore it elects a smaller (but representative) group (the government) to act or speak on behalf of its interests.
Choosing governments	General elections in Britain create the legislature, but not the executive. The elections choose which party makes up the majority of the legislature and then the executive is selected from it.
Influencing policy	Voters choose parties on the basis of the policy announcements made. Victory is seen as an endorsement of the policies, defeat a reason to rethink policies.
Participation	For the majority of people elections are their only contribution to the political process.
Accountability	As the government has to call a general election at least every five years, it can be held accountable for its performance. Individual MPs can be held accountable for their own performance at constituency level.
Legitimacy	By voting people endorse the electoral system, giving it their approval and support. A winning party can rightly claim legitimacy, as it represents the wishes of the people.
Education	Electioneering aims to educate the people on major issues, options and debates. Ideally, this should make their voting decision an educated vote.
Recruitment of talented individuals	Parties should select talented people to stand as candidates. If elected they are trained and groomed to be effective politicians and part of the governing elite.

As to whether British elections achieve these functions is another question. It could be argued that they do not as there is relatively low turnout rates and disproportionate results.

As we have already seen, ideological hegemony suggests that there is an ideological manipulation at work even within liberal democracies. Liberal democracies are dominated by bourgeois ideologies as far as Marxists are concerned. The ruling class and therefore their ruling ideas dominate all life and exclude external viewpoints. The net result of this continuous process is to convince those who are subject to inequality and exploitation that in some way they are not as exploited or as put upon as some may lead them to believe.

In effect, the ruling ideology manipulates most individuals' views of society and life. They do not see the world as it is, but as they think it is, or more precisely what society tells them it is. This is the root of government authority; it is unchallenged as it is seen to be correct and legitimate. But Marxists would argue that legitimacy is actually just a social construct.

How government authority can be undermined through public and parliamentary accountability

One of the key issues that brought government authority into question was the second war against Iraq. One of the fundamental reasons for this second attempt to remove Saddam Hussein's regime was the supposed imminent deployment of weapons of mass destruction. Intelligence agencies presented a dossier that seemed to imply, albeit with very thin evidence, that the Iraqi regime had the ability to deploy these weapons. It is argued that this was the primary reason for Britain becoming involved in the invasion.

Subsequently, the existence of these weapons has been questioned. In the aftermath, the Butler Report was charged with investigating the failures of British intelligence and the government's decision to act on that intelligence. Crucial to this was who was responsible for the way in which the intelligence was effectively sold to parliament and the public in order to justify Britain's involvement. The Butler Report concluded that there was a collective responsibility and that there was no overt evidence to suggest that either the government or the prime minister had not acted in good faith.

However, the impact on Blair's public approval rating and the unity of his government and backbenchers diminished his overall authority as prime minister. Also both Blair and Brown have resisted calls for a full inquiry into the events surrounding the decision to invade Iraq until all British troops have withdrawn from Iraq.

The government's ability to wage war without deferring to parliament dates back to the royal prerogative. It gives the executive power to carry out many of the acts that contribute to foreign policy, including waging war and signing treaties. Government can make decisions without effective accountability and it is impossible for parliament to act and hold government to account, as there is a lack of transparency and freedom of information.

It is now argued that there should be a culture shift that places parliament at the heart of bringing the prime minister and the executive to account for their actions. Decisions made at an international level affect the British public and parliament should be an essential part of the line of accountability.

What is the legitimation crisis?

Orthodox Marxists dismiss legitimacy as being bogus; however modern Marxists accept that capitalism is adept at maintaining control by securing political support. Maintaining political support is not always easy, as there are times when political stability is difficult.

The neo-Marxist Jurgen Habermas identified that liberal democracies face crises that undermine legitimacy. The root of the problem is the friction between capitalist economies and democratic political systems. The democratic process itself is based on the assumption that political parties have to effectively outbid one another to gain power (or indeed they are under the influence of pressure groups once in power). This means that governments have to continually increase their public spending and become increasingly involved in all aspects of economic and social life. The government finds it hard to balance the demands: on the one hand increased public spending is desirable, yet it is a disincentive to private enterprises, as taxes will have to rise to meet the spending needs. If the government borrows instead of taxing then this adversely affects inflation.

The Habermas model

Habermas (1975) argued that liberal democracies cannot keep up the balancing act forever. There is a major underlying and unavoidable problem in that the liberal democracies either have to risk the economic collapse of the system, or resist democratic pressures. However, the electoral systems work in the liberal democracies' favour. Policy can be adjusted by different parties taking power and following their own brand of balancing – from free market through to interventionist.

In the 1970s, escalating fuel prices and trade union action led to challenges to the authority of the governments of the time. Faced with such challenges, in February 1974 the prime minister of the time, Edward Heath, called an election to decide 'who rules Britain': the elected government or the trade unions. Unfortunately for Heath, the British public decided it was not to be him!

We have seen this process in action in Britain. Under Margaret Thatcher in the 1980s, the Conservative government systematically set about changing peoples' reliance on government to meet their expectations and demands to a reliance on doing things for themselves. The people rather than the government were now responsible for savings, medical insurance, private pensions and home ownership. Prior to that, it could be argued that the welfare state provided many of these support mechanisms.

Since coming to power in 1997 New Labour has considerably increased public spending in health and education, resulting in a rise in overall government spending as a proportion of GDP; this has led to rises in indirect taxation and National Insurance contributions. However, their Third Way approach did not return to the state interventionist approach of the 1960s and 1970s, so nationalisation was not restored, instead it continued with a public–private sector partnership approach, seeking to introduce private-sector style methods into public sector organisations.

Electoral apathy and the growth of the underclass

There was great concern about the massive decline in the voting turnout at the 2001 general election. Until 1997 the percentage of eligible voters casting their votes had been relatively stable, at between 72 and 83.9 per cent. In 2001 turnout tumbled to 59.4 per cent. The fear was that a

Learning objectives

- What is the legitimation crisis?
- The Habermas model
- Electoral apathy and the growth of the underclass
- Anti-capitalist protest movements
- Declining public confidence

Abolition of Third World debt

An estimated 3 billion people watched Live 8 concerts in 2005. They came together with one message – make poverty history. Concerts in 10 cities, including London, Philadelphia, Paris, Berlin, Johannesburg, Rome and Moscow, were attended by hundreds of thousands of people. In Johannesburg the biggest cheer of the night was for former leader Nelson Mandela. He told the crowd that the G8 leaders had a 'historic opportunity to open the door to hope and the possibility of a better future for all'. The G8 conference agreed to write off $40 billion to 18 of the poorest countries.

Disruption at G8 summits

The G8 annual summits are subject to extensive lobbying by advocacy groups and street demonstrations by activists. During the 31st G8 summit in Scotland, 250,000 people took to the streets of Edinburgh as part of the Make Poverty History campaign. The largest and most violent demonstration occurred at the 27th G8 summit in Genoa. Since then and in the aftermath of the September 11, 2001 attacks on the United States, which occurred months apart in the same year, the G8 have held their meetings at remote locations. The 7 July 2005 London bombings were timed to coincide with the 31st G8 summit in Scotland.

continuation of this trend would make it difficult for governments to claim to have a mandate to follow policy programmes.

There were suggestions that this was a temporary blip and that the opinion polls were to blame. Throughout the duration of the parliament 1997 to 2001, the government had a clear lead in opinion polls over the Conservatives. A 'poll of polls' of the opinion polls in the last six months of the parliament gave Labour an average twelve-point lead. Many voters believed the result was a foregone conclusion and decided not to vote.

It was suggested that this was the case in 2005, when the turnout was 61.3 per cent, despite Labour not having a commanding lead. On average they were just five points ahead. As a result, the turnout increased modestly, so it is argued that a closer contest in the future will result in a far higher turnout. It is important to note that Labour only secured the positive approval of 23 per cent of the overall electorate when taking into account those who did not vote.

Anti-capitalist protest movements

There are many different anti-capitalist movements, many of which oppose one another far more than they oppose capitalism itself. Some of the groups characterising themselves as anti-capitalist actually only want reform in certain areas of capitalism, or the abolition of certain aspects of capitalism.

The anti-capitalist movement is part of a larger anti-globalisation trend, brought into sharper focus since the war in Iraq. The Stop the War Coalition is a British anti-war group set up in 2001. The Coalition held a series of protests in November 2003 climaxing in a march protesting against what it claimed was the aggressive foreign policy of George W. Bush, and against the continued US detention of prisoners in Guantanamo Bay. The group, however, has been criticised over its association with the right-wing Muslim Association of Britain.

The anti-capitalist groups include socialists, anarchists, eco-feminists, religious fundamentalists, and in the past even included fascists.

Socialists are implacably opposed to capitalism as they generally favour collective or government control of the economy. Anarchists simply want a total abolition of the state, eco-feminists view capitalism as a patriarchal construction and as Maria Mies (1993) said, capitalism is 'based on the colonisation of women, nature, and other peoples'. Religious fundamentalists either criticise or reject capitalism on the grounds of the use of capital and the lending of capital with interest. In the 1920s and the 1930s fascism was an implacable opponent of capitalism, as they believed that private corporations and private individuals should subordinate their own interests to the national interest. In Italy and Germany during this period the fascists entered into a practical alliance with industry leading to companies such as Krupps and IG Farben having a greater influence.

Declining public confidence

Successive perceived failures by British governments in handling a wide range of problems, from food safety to fraud, from oil prices to corporate profits and from education and the so-called credit crunch, has seen a gradual decline in public confidence in government. Confidence has been further undermined by the failure of decision-makers in government to be held to account for decisions they have made.

At the core of the matter, however, is a government's ability to deliver promises and to have the capacity to respond to issues as they arise. However, in November 2007 the government was forced to admit a fundamental breach in faith between the state and citizens when the personal details of 7.25 million families claiming child benefit were lost.

Tax rises, red tape, security leaks compromising the national identity card scheme, lingering doubts about the death of Dr David Kelly and the Hutton Enquiry, the discovery that illegal immigrants were being employed as security guards by government departments, and a host of other scandals and supposed mismanagement has done nothing to improve public confidence in the government's ability to manage.

In response to these problems, Blair launched in 2006 the Power Commission to investigate the declining confidence in politics and the state of democracy in Britain. It made a series of recommendations including calls for greater parliamentary scrutiny, more locally based democratic initiatives, amendments to UK elections and changes to party funding. As such these recommendations have yet to be implemented.

DISCUSSION POINT ?

Is there a legitimation crisis?

ExamCafé
Relax, refresh, result!

Relax and prepare

Here are several F854 essay questions of the type that could occur in your exam. How would you go about answering them?

- Evaluate the different models of political power.

- To what extent is political power based on coercion?

- Compare and contrast power and authority.

- Discuss the view that legal rational authority is the only legitimate form of authority in a democracy.

- Evaluate the ways in which governments gain consent.

- Discuss the relationship between power, authority and legitimacy.

Refresh your memory

The following are key points for revision.

Political power

For each of the following issues listed in the table try and write a summary of the issue and outline the view of a relevant political theorist.

Issue	Explanation	Views of a relevant theorist
What is meant by political power?		
What is meant by power as decision-making?		
What is meant by power as agenda setting?		
What is meant by power as thought control?		
What is meant by coercive power?		

Repeat the same exercise for the topics of authority and legitimacy.

Ideological perspectives on power, authority and legitimacy

For each of the following ideological perspectives, summarise their views on the different topics.

Theory	Views on power	Views on authority	Views on legitimacy
Liberal/pluralist			
Conservative/elitist			
Socialist			
Marxist			

Key relevant political thinkers

Below are examples of some of the central theorists related to this topic. Try and write a summary of the views of each.

Power
S. Lukes
R. Dahl
E. E. Schattschneider
P. Bachrach and M. Baratz
H. Marcuse

Authority
M. Weber
R. Scruton
H. Arendt
W. Reich

Legitimacy and consent
D. Beetham
J. J. Rousseau
J. Locke
K. Marx
A. Gramsci
J. Habermas

Get the result!

The following essay question is of the type that could occur in your exam for unit F854. How would you go about answering it?

Analyse whether power and authority are essentially the same thing.

Exam tips

Consider the following issues when answering this question.

✦ Define what is meant by power and authority.

✦ How far can authority be seen as a subsection of power – that is, legitimate power?

✦ What other types of power are there?

✦ Are there any types of authority that do not conform to traditional notions of power (note the distinction between 'in authority' and 'an authority' – is the latter a form of power)?

Don't forget to use relevant theory. Weber, Lukes, Beetham, Bachrach and Baratz, for instance, could be useful here.

Remember also that there is no need to relate to modern politics – that is the task you must do for unit F856!

Relax and prepare

The following questions are of the type that could occur in your exam for unit F856. Discuss with yo colleagues how you would go about answering them.

- How far is the UK still governed by an elite?
- Discuss the view that in theory and in practice the executive branch of government is too powe in the UK.
- Discuss the ways in which modern governments gain and maintain their authority.
- Discuss which model of authority best typifies the basis of prime ministerial authority in the UK.
- Is there a legitimation crisis in modern democracy?

Refresh your memory

The following are key points to revise for your exam.

Using the theory you have learnt for this unit, in F856 think of practical examples for the following topics.

Issue	Practical example
Models of political power	
Location of power in modern societies	
Models of authority	
How authority is gained/manufactured by modern governments	
Evidence for and against a legitimation crisis in modern politics	

Case studies on power, authority and legitimacy

Each of the following could be used as practical examples to illustrate your arguments in this unit. Find out about each and think about how it could be relevant to the topic area.

✓ The comparison of the extent of authority held by recent UK prime ministers and the way their authority can change (e.g. compare Tony Blair as prime minister in 1997 and after the Iraq war in 2003).

✓ The repression of Tibetan nationalist protests by the Chinese authorities in 2008.

✓ The complaints made by Richard Branson over the power exerted by Rupert Murdoch's News International Corporation on the British media 2007.

✓ The succession of Gordon Brown as prime minister in 2007 without an electoral mandate.

✓ The statistical evidence on the socio-economic backgrounds of senior figures in British politics, civil service, industry, media and the judiciary – does it suggest a ruling elite?

✓ The reduction in the size of the welfare state by New Right inspired governments in the 1980s and 1990s – did this solve the supposed legitimation crisis of the 1970s?

Get the result !

This essay question is of the type that could occur in your exam for unit F856.

Examine how authority is bestowed upon modern governments in theory and in practice.

Exam tips

Below is one way of potentially answering this question in the appropriate style. Do you follow the structure suggested and is there anything else you would like to add?

Relevant issue	Theory	Practical application
Introduction – What is meant by authority?	Basis upon perception of Heywood's 'right to rule', thus being legitimate power Note distinction over 'in authority and being 'an authority'	Acceptance of government authority in modern democracy
Liberal theories on how authority is bestowed upon democratic government	Weber's concept of legal rational authority Beetham's three forms of legitimate power – keeping to established rules, sharing same values as citizenship, achieving explicit consent of citizenship	Authority based upon constitutional position – e.g. role of judiciary and civil service Electoral consent through the ballot box – note size of majority may impact upon extent of authority – contrast 1997 with 2005 (or 1992) election results (note Brown government lacks electoral authority) Note decline in government authority when at odds with public attitudes – e.g. impact of Iraq war on authority of Blair government
Conservative theories on how authority is bestowed	Weber's notion of traditional authority Hobbes' concept of divine authority of monarchy	Traditional authority exercised by the British monarchy – is this in decline?
Marxist critique of authority in democracies	Manufacturing of authority through bourgeois hegemony – Gramsci	Role of the media in enforcing authority of ruling elite
How authority is achieved in dictatorships	Weber's charismatic authority Reich – fascist personality tendencies amongst the masses	Cult of the individual in totalitarian states– e.g. Stalin and Hitler Note role of charisma in democratic process – e.g. Blair and Thatcher charismatic politicians versus 'dour' image of Major and Brown
Conclusion	Importance of constitutional means of bestowing authority in democracies but variations in extent of authority can be based upon other factors	Good opportunity to end on Brown versus Blair comparison

Remember that to get above a D grade you will have to have dealt with the theory and practice aspects of the question.

Living in a society means that there are limits to the amount of liberty or freedom you can expect to have, given that an excessive amount could infringe on other peoples' liberties. So arrangements are made to avoid this. The individual however needs to be free to exercise their rights. The liberties citizens have in a state are the rights they are permitted to and can exercise freely. These rights in many cases are protected by law: examples are the right to be free of slavery, the right to free expression, the right to be free from torture. These rights are guaranteed in Britain by the common law and by the European Convention on Human Rights and the Human Rights Act.

Citizens of a state have moral and legal rights. The latter are enshrined in the state's legal code. Moral rights are those that are independent of legal ones, in that you may have a moral right but not a legal one, as in the case of black South Africans who had a moral right to participate in the elections of the state but no legal right to do so.

Human rights are guaranteed to enable individuals to live a minimally good life. These rights cover all human beings everywhere irrespective of legal rights, which may not cover all the moral injustices perpetrated against citizens under certain forms of government.

There is no universal agreement on what human rights consist of. Marxists see them as merely a bourgeois device to protect themselves, socialists say that social rights need to be added, and conservatives see them as encroaching on the values of society. Also there are parts of the world where extending the rights to, for example, protect homosexuality is rejected.

These are cases of where human rights are meant to eradicate some of the inequalities in societies. And the question is raised whether certain rights should be extended to animals so that they are treated with the same consideration as humans and whether we should treat animals not as ends for human purposes but as ends in themselves, just as humans are treated.

In a state such as Britain, a citizen has the liberty or freedom to act according to their will. But what this means varies according to your viewpoint. Socialists equate liberty with equality in that it depends on the equal distribution of wealth; for them there is no liberty in a state in which wealth is unequally distributed or shared. However the implication here is that this would involve increasing one person's liberty at the expense of someone else's.

Liberty is being free to actively participate in politics or being free from interference or coercion. There is the belief that individuals should be free to do what they want as long as it doesn't interfere with the freedom of others or cause harm.

There is conflict between those who think freedom is essential in economics and that there should be no interference in economic activities; others have the view that you should interfere if there is a threat to individuals' jobs or conditions of work. They would say that the freedom to change conditions of work or sack people is an excessive use of freedom and encroaches on the freedom of others.

There are disputes about rights connected to freedoms. For example, the right to free education is disputed by the New Right who reject it as a right but maintain that it is something individuals should do for themselves.

In liberal democracies there is a principle of equal liberty but you can't avoid inequalities.

Attempts have been made to overcome the notion that inequalities in society is a natural state by asserting that every human has equal moral worth, an egalitarian notion. The welfare state was an attempt to apply equality. Conservatives believe that natural inequalities arise out of the individual's talents and skills. However, homelessness and poverty can be said to be morally wrong. Modern conservatives now favour an equal opportunities approach that helps those confronted by obstacles to realise their personal development and are helped to overcome them. Another way is to introduce a system of positive discrimination. Others favour legislating against discrimination and getting rid of institutionalised inequality and encouraging the promotion of equal civil rights and liberties. Marxists support social equality by abolishing private ownership.

In search of social justice or fairness, that is, treating people equally well who deserve it, could mean an obligation to distribute wealth according to need/or according to just deserts, a reward or punishment. The differences in abilities leads to inequalities, for example the differences between men and women. However, there are moral issues here about how far this should go. The question arises as to whether it leads to social injustice and human suffering.

These are some of the issues covered in this chapter, in which the following are the key themes.

- The definition of rights
- The meaning of liberty
- The moral and political aspects of the abuse of liberty and political tolerance
- The meaning of equality and the different political views of it
- Theories of social justice
- The protection of rights in Britain and Europe
- Threats to the exercise of rights
- The various threats to civil liberties in Britain and Europe
- The various ways in which equality can be promoted
- Theories of social justice and the future of the welfare state

In covering these themes the chapter is broken down into the following topics.

The chapter finishes with an exam café feature on page 144.

Learning objectives

- Origins and definition of rights
- Legal and moral rights
- Natural rights – including Locke and Jefferson's attempts to codify these and 'God given rights' and themes in classical liberalism
- Human rights – secular form of rights and attempts to codify these
- Animal rights – Singer and Regan

Civil rights

The fundamental freedoms that are guaranteed by law.

Freedoms

The freedoms guaranteed to individuals, such as the freedom of speech.

Human rights

The rights that are guaranteed in the European Convention on Human Rights and the Human Rights Act.

Obligation

The things that a citizen ought to do, such as pay taxes.

Origins and definition of rights

The judiciary is seen as the ultimate protector of the **civil rights** of citizens. The judiciary's position and role in this was substantially reinforced when the Human Rights Act (2000) was passed. For many this was a major turning point in law and politics; from now on the judiciary would be far more active in the defence of rights.

A citizen is an individual who is formally recognised by a state as a member of that state. Within it the citizen automatically has certain rights and duties. Rights and duties are very closely linked. If an individual has the freedom to state their own opinions then everyone else has a duty to respect this right. Governments should protect the rights of citizens and punish those who fail to respect the rights of others.

In recent years we have come to accept that **human rights** are the way to express the rights of a citizen. Simply, this means equality of treatment. There are fundamental **freedoms**, guaranteed by law, such as the right to a fair trial, freedom from slavery, freedom of expression and freedom from torture. In Britain most human or civil rights are guaranteed in common law and the European Convention on Human Rights, as well as the Human Rights Act.

Along with these human and civil rights, citizens of Britain are expected to make their contribution to the state in the form of duties. This idea began in the 1980s, when the Conservatives were keen to point out that in accepting the rights of citizens, there was a price or **obligation** to be made by citizens, in the form of duties towards the state and to other citizens. This has certainly been a point of view that has been continued by the Labour governments since 1997. In the past the Labour Party would have stressed that the state would provide for citizens and that individuals would not be expected to provide for themselves. Typical duties of citizens now expected by the state are to:

- vote
- assist in law and order
- work
- provide for themselves in old age
- help the community
- be involved in social and political issues
- do voluntary work
- support charities
- take personal responsibility for one's actions (and that of the family and, perhaps, the community).

Legal and moral rights

The distinction drawn between moral rights and legal rights as two separate categories of rights is of fundamental importance to understanding the basis and potential application of rights. Legal rights refer to all those rights found within existing legal codes. A legal right is a right that enjoys the recognition and protection of the law. Questions as to its existence can be resolved by simply locating the relevant legal instrument or piece of legislation. A legal right cannot be said to exist prior to its passing into law and the limits of its validity are set by the jurisdiction of the body which passed the relevant legislation.

Moral rights are rights that exist prior to and independently from their legal counterparts. The existence and validity of a moral right is not deemed to be dependent upon the actions of jurists and legislators.

Many argued that the black majority in apartheid South Africa possessed a moral right to full political participation in that country's political system. There was no such legal right. Many believed that the approach in South Africa was morally unacceptable, as the regime denied fundamental moral rights, such as the right not to be discriminated against on grounds of colour and right to political participation. This particular line of opposition and protest was pursued because of a belief in the existence and validity of moral rights. A belief that fundamental rights which may or may not have received legal recognition elsewhere, remained valid and morally compelling even in a country whose legal systems had not recognised these rights.

A rights-based opposition to apartheid South Africa would not have worked as it could not be legitimately argued that the legal political rights of non-white South Africans were being violated under apartheid, since no such legal rights existed. The systematic denial of such rights did, however, constitute a gross violation of those peoples' fundamental moral rights. The lack of protection of these moral rights led Jeremy Bentham in the 19th century to describe their existence as 'nonsense on stilts'.

Natural rights – including Locke and Jefferson's attempts to codify these and 'God given rights' and themes in classical liberalism

Natural rights are moral rights that people would have no matter what their legal rights were and even if there were no government and no laws. Locke's views on natural rights suggest:

- a liberty right to equal liberty (in Locke's terms, a 'power') that permits one to dispose of one's person and possessions as one chooses

- a claim right not to be harmed in one's life, health, liberty, or possessions that generate corresponding duties for others not to cause such harms

- because these rights are morally enforceable, they generate further liberty rights (in Locke's terms, 'powers') of self-defence and punishment against transgressors.

According to Thomas Jefferson (*Rights of British America*, 1774): 'A free people [claim] their rights as derived from the laws of nature and not as the gift of their chief magistrate.'

Four years earlier, Thomas Jefferson wrote:

> Under the law of nature, all men are born free, everyone comes into the world with a right to his own person, which includes the liberty of moving and using it at his own will. This is what is called personal liberty, and is given him by the Author of nature, because necessary for his own sustenance.

These were attempts to codify the concept of natural rights. The Declaration of Independence launched the principle that every individual possesses certain unalienable rights. According to Jefferson: '[T]he majority, oppressing an individual is guilty of a crime … and by acting on the law of the strongest breaks up the foundations of society.'

Unalienable rights from God were also suggested in the Declaration of Independence: '. . . endowed by their Creator with certain unalienable rights . . .'

God-given rights are sometimes called natural rights, those possessed by man under the laws of nature. The writers of the Declaration of Independence would claim that man has no power to alienate (to dispose of, by surrender, barter or gift) his God-given rights.

Liberal rights tend to be based on the equal right of every person to his or her own person and proceed from a foundation of radical equality. Such rights are known as 'innate' or 'connate' rights as they come from birth. 'Acquired' or 'adventitious' rights are those that result from some act or condition of a person so they may be 'unequal' precisely because the acts or conditions of individual persons and may differ or be unequal.

Classical liberal rights tend to be negative, in the sense that they accept the dominant influence of John Stuart Mill's 'harm principle'. Following Mill, liberal rights are there to protect people from harm, they rarely try to construct solutions. They might try to protect certain groups from unnecessary police harassment, but would do little to empower that group.

Human rights – secular form of rights and attempts to codify these

Human rights are rights that attach to human beings and function as moral guarantees in support of the enjoyment of a minimally good life. Human rights are themselves derivative of the concept of a right.

When we considered moral and legal rights it should become clear that human rights cannot be reduced to, or exclusively identified with, legal rights. The legal positivist's account of justified law excludes the possibility of condemning such systems as apartheid from a rights perspective. It might be tempting to draw the conclusion that human rights are best identified as moral rights. After all, apartheid was founded upon the denial of fundamental human rights. Human rights certainly share an essential quality of moral rights. Their valid existence is not deemed to be conditional upon their being legally recognised. Human rights are supposed to apply to all human beings everywhere, regardless of whether they have received legal recognition.

There remain numerous countries that exclude formal legal recognition to fundamental human rights. Supporters of human rights in these countries insist that the rights remain valid regardless, as fundamental moral rights. The universality of human rights as moral rights lends greater moral force to human rights. However, legal rights are not subject to disputes as to their existence and validity in quite the way moral rights often tend to be. Human rights are better thought of as both moral rights and legal rights. Human rights originate as moral rights and their legitimacy is necessarily dependent upon the legitimacy of the concept of moral rights. A principal aim of advocates of human rights is for these rights to receive universal legal recognition. This was the fundamental goal of the opponents of apartheid. The legitimacy claims of human rights are tied to their status as moral rights; practically, however, they are largely dependent upon their developing into legal rights. In those cases where specific human rights do not enjoy legal recognition, such as in the example of apartheid on page 113, moral rights must be prioritised with the intention that defending the moral claims of such rights as a necessary prerequisite for the eventual legal recognition of the rights in question.

It is important to emphasise the lack of consensus as to what human rights consist of – Marxists see them as protecting bourgeois freedoms, socialists argue social rights need to be included (e.g. right to work and free health care), whereas conservatives see them as potentially encroaching upon the values of decent society (note criticisms of Human Rights Act as a charter for 'complainants and criminals'). There are also issues of morality over whether there is a universal right protecting homosexuality or a woman's right to abortion (note protected in US since Roe vs Wade 1973 on the woman's right to privacy) – many areas of the globe reject such rights.

Animal rights – Singer and Regan

Peter Singer (1993) has been influential in the debate concerning animals and ethics. Singer attacks the views of those who wish to give the interests of animals less weight than the interests of human beings. Singer concludes that we must instead extend a principle of equal consideration of interests to animals as well, in which human beings give equal weight in their moral deliberations to all those affected by their actions.

Singer defends this principle with two arguments. The first is a version of the Argument from Marginal Cases; the second is the Sophisticated Inegalitarian Argument. The attempt to grant all and only human beings a full and equal moral status does not work. We must either conclude that not all human beings are equal, or we must conclude that not only human beings are equal.

Tom Regan's *The Case for Animal Rights* (1983) is one of the most influential works on the topic of animals and ethics. He argues for the claim that animals have rights in just the same way that human beings do. Regan believes it is a mistake to claim that animals have an indirect moral status or an unequal status, and to then imply that animals cannot have any rights. According to Regan, the conclusion is that animals have the same moral status as human beings; furthermore, that moral status is grounded on rights, not on utilitarian principles. Regan concludes that humans need to alter the ways in which they treat animals. When animals are raised for food, regardless of how they are treated and how they are killed, humans are using them as a means to their ends and not treating them as ends in themselves. Consequently, humans should not raise animals for food. Likewise, when humans experiment on animals in order to advance human science, they are using animals merely as a means to their ends.

Contrast these views with less radical calls for welfare that seeks to limit human abuse of animals and to regulate human usage of animals in testing. This leads us to the merits of animal experimentation and the impact upon human activity such as forced vegetarianism or ethical treatment of animals in farming.

Peter Singer on animal liberation

In *Animal Liberation* (1975) Singer argued that animal welfare is based on the fact that animals are sentient and capable of suffering. He believed that they were equal to humans and that placing the interest of humans above animals displayed speciesism. Animal welfare simply emphasised treating animals with respect and to minimise their suffering, therefore they oppose issues like factory farming but do not insist on vegetarianism. Animal rights, however, is more radical.

Tom Regan on animal rights

In *The Case for Animal Rights* (1983) Regan argued that all creatures qualify for rights and the right to life is the most fundamental of these. He recognised that humans are capable of rational thought and moral autonomy, unlike animals, so giving animals free speech, freedom of worship and the right to education would be ridiculous. Regan notes that there were marginal cases, such as humans with mental disabilities. They had limited reason and an inability to enjoy autonomy. On the basis that if rights are given on the grounds of rational and moral capacity rather than life then why should these humans not be subjected to scientific examination like animals.

DISCUSSION POINT ?

Are animal and human rights equal?

Learning objectives

- The meaning of liberty
- Berlin's negative and positive connotations
- John Stuart Mill on liberty

The meaning of liberty

Our understanding of liberty revolves around whether an individual has the ability to act according to their own will. As such, liberty is synonymous with the term freedom.

Freedom is invariably perceived as being morally good and lack of freedom, typified by slavery, oppression or imprisonment, as morally bad.

Freedom or liberty suggests the extent to which an individual is a free agent in their lives, with the ability to have choice and privileges without restriction. As we will see in the next spread there is a perceived danger when we consider the difference between liberty and licence, as licence implies the abuse of freedom. Rousseau distinguishes between individual freedom consisting of a person's ability to do what they want only restricted by their strength and desires and what he perceived as a more virtuous form, civil liberty, which was gained through participation in the law-making process in a civil society ('civil liberty is the obedience to laws one proscribes to oneself').

There have been various attempts to try to pinpoint the exact nature of liberty or freedom. For a socialist liberty is equated with equality. They connect freedom with equal distribution of wealth and that there can be no liberty whilst unequal ownership exists. They connect freedom and material wealth. R. H. Tawney dismissed the inequality of individual political liberty as it did not take into account the ability of the wealthy to utilise their privileges – 'the freedom of the pike is death to the minnows'.

A classical liberal would argue that wealth cannot be evenly distributed without force and this means that certain individuals' liberties will be infringed and reduced by having their property taken from them so that it can be redistributed. Thus attempts by Locke to codify his conception of natural rights included the concept of property.

This is also apparent in conservative ideas such as that of Benjamin Constant, who, writing in the 19th century, identified 'the liberty of the ancients'. By this he was referring to direct and collective participation in politics. He contrasted this with 'liberty of the moderns', by which he meant independence from government and from the encroachment of other individuals and institutions.

Berlin's negative and positive connotations

Another such attempt to identify the key issues of liberty was carried out by Isaiah Berlin in an essay 'Two Concepts of Liberty', written in 1958. He identified positive and negative liberties or freedoms. By this he simply meant that positive freedom meant being free to do something and negative meant being free from something. Negative liberty was based around the freedoms all are born with and at best the state can only protect these, for example freedom of speech, but positive liberty involves the state actively seeking to remove the obstacles that prevent all from maximising their use of liberty, for example the state legislating to remove poverty (via benefits) or ignorance (via education). The latter form of freedom is very much a classical liberal idea whereas positive liberty was taken up by modern liberals such as T. H. Green as well as democratic socialists such as Tawney and Crosland.

It was clear that Berlin was actually rather suspicious of positive liberty because it could lead to a situation where government could force individuals into particular ways of life, on the basis that the government believed that it was the best course of action and that everyone should desire that way of life, whether or not they did. His problem was that he believed that positive liberty could lead to some form of totalitarianism.

But those who believe that positive liberty is a good thing point to the fact that there is an enormous gulf between a government's good intentions of providing positive liberty and a government then making the presumption that they should make decisions for their citizens.

Democratic governments, supporters argue, are not in a position to impose their will, as they would simply be voted out of office. Supporters of positive liberty see it as guaranteeing equal rights, a defence against discrimination and access to education and employment.

On the other side of Berlin's argument was the concept of negative liberty. This meant that an individual's liberty was subject to the authority of government or institutions. An individual would be considered free only to the extent that no one interferes with what they are doing.

Hobbes, for example, said: 'A free man is he that is not hindered to do what he hath the will to do.'

Berlin expanded on his ideas of negative liberty. The first concept was that negative liberty actually defines a zone of freedom in which people are able to be or act without interference by other people.

Hobbes was aware of this concept of freedom and referred to it as the 'silence of the laws'.

Berlin's second point concerned restriction on the freedom to act. By this he meant that sometimes negative liberty is imposed not due to incapacity of the individual, but by the threat or fear of punishment. However, a common argument which supports negative liberty is that unless governments step in to legislate and to control them, some individuals will undoubtedly take away the liberty of others.

John Stuart Mill on liberty

In 1859 John Stuart Mill provided a more straightforward way of defining liberty. He recognised the difference between liberty as a freedom to act and liberty in the absence of coercion. He simply applied what he termed the harm principle.

He believed that liberty should only be constrained at the point at which an individual may do harm to others. Beyond that freedom becomes excessive. The major problem is in defining what is construed as harm.

Mill obviously meant it to mean physical harm and he was firmly of the opinion that individuals should be able to write, think and say whatever they wished and also to carry out harmful actions as long as they were self-regarding. In other words, that the individual was still exercising control over their own lives – 'Over his own mind and body the individual is sovereign.'

In more modern times harm has been taken to involve far broader issues, including psychological, moral and spiritual ones. Equally, they include economic and social issues.

A prime example is any form of censorship on television. Would violence or blasphemy be regarded as harmful on the grounds that it corrupts and is offensive to certain individuals? Clearly some do believe this and at this point the harm principle would come into play.

John Stuart Mill on liberty

Mill's work was an important development of liberalism. In *On Liberty* (1859) he suggested that there was only one justifiable reason for restricting an individual's freedom and that was to prevent that individual from harming others. Beyond that there were no other justifications for restriction.

Isaiah Berlin on freedom

Berlin is best described as a liberal pluralist. He believed that individuals will always disagree about the ultimate purposes of life. He suggested that positive liberty meant self-mastery and self-realisation and could ultimately lead to totalitarian ideas. He also coined the term negative liberty, which he described as being non-interference, which could guarantee freedom of choice and personal independence.

Mary Whitehouse's National Viewers and Listener's Association

Mary Whitehouse (1910–2001) waged a tireless crusade against the 'tide of filth' she saw engulfing British society. In the late 1930s she became involved in the Oxford Movement (later Moral Rearmament). She became convinced that television was responsible for inappropriate attitudes to sex. In 1964, she called a public meeting in Birmingham town hall which brought in supporters from across the country. At the meeting the Clean Up TV Campaign came into being, later evolving into the National Viewers' and Listeners' Association. She was awarded a CBE in 1980 and, even after stepping down as Chair of NVALA in the 1990s, she remained the figurehead of the movement. Since her death, on 23 November 2001, the organisation has renamed itself MediaWatch-UK.

DISCUSSION POINT ?

Compare and contrast the views of Berlin and Mill. To what extent do they agree?

The Crucible

Arthur Miller was an American playwright who wrote *The Crucible* in 1953 during the McCarthy period when Americans were accusing each other of pro-communist beliefs. Many of Miller's friends were being attacked as communists and in 1956 Miller himself was brought before the House of Un-American Activities Committee where he was found guilty of beliefs in communism (this was reversed in 1957). The play is set against the backdrop of the witch hunts of the Salem witch trials in the late 17th century. Miller brings out the absurdity of these incidents with the theme of truth and righteousness.

Neo-conservative crusades

The Christian Right holds to the assumption that moral absolutes exist. These include many of the oldest and deepest assumptions of western culture, including the fixity of sexual identities and gender roles, the preference towards capitalism, the importance of hard work, and the sanctity of unborn life. More importantly, not only do moral absolutes exist, they are clearly discernible to any who wish honestly to see them. For this reason, the neo-conservative Christian Right have been implacably opposed to abortion and to homosexual marriages on clear moral grounds.

Excessive liberty

Excessive liberty, or licence, is generally taken to mean the abuse of freedom. It is at this point when freedom becomes excessive. It may be an infringement of an individual's liberty to prevent them from leaving their home. If an individual has it in mind to murder his neighbour, only the removal of licence will prevent that person jumping over the garden fence and committing murder.

Libertarians aim to maximise individual freedoms and therefore minimise actions that are regarded as licence. Liberals extend this to the defence of private property and free-market capitalism. Right-wing libertarians believe that freedom is essential in the marketplace. Socialists, on the other hand, see certain actions that might be taken by employers, such as changing working conditions and setting wage levels, as licence because the freedom of the employer is at the expense of the freedom of the worker. Radical socialists and anarchists take the view that private property is licence, as it leads to the exploitation of the property-less. Pierre Joseph Proudhan famously remarked 'All property is theft.'

Moral and political dimensions to the abuse of liberty

It is often difficult to distinguish between what are perceived as rights and what are perceived as liberties. If we were to adopt this approach it is relatively easy to make a distinction between liberty and licence. Liberty would mean acting within an individual's rights and licence beyond an individual's rights and certainly abusing the rights of others.

The major problem with freedom and liberty is that it is usually the case that if someone gains more freedom another loses it. It is incredibly difficult to balance the situation so that everyone's rights are respected in every circumstance.

Obviously the different political ideologies cannot agree on even the most fundamental of rights. Socialists and liberals would believe that everyone has a right to education and to health care. The New Right would argue that this is not a right and that individuals themselves should be responsible for this. This often forms the focus of debate over welfare benefits – whilst the state attempts to develop positive liberty by eradicating inequality, this may encroach upon negative liberty through higher taxation.

As we will see, liberty and licence are inextricably linked to equality. In other words, equal rights for all. In this way liberty does not become licence when rights are violated but when liberty is not equally shared. Theoretically, in liberal democracies, there is a principle of equal liberty but the problem remains that it is almost impossible to ensure that one group in society does not have special privileges and that another group faces disadvantages.

Political toleration

Toleration means a willingness to accept the views and actions of others even if you disagree or disapprove. Toleration is not about indifference or permissiveness. Permissiveness suggests that individuals should be able to act as they wish and that society has a moral indifference to their behaviour. Toleration means actually disapproving of a particular point of view and the willingness not to try to impose your own views on others. Toleration does not necessarily mean not interfering, but it does not mean constraining, and could allow influence and persuasion. Voltaire is often quoted as saying 'I disagree with what you say… but I will defend to my death your right to say it.'

Negative tolerance is a passive acceptance of other values and beliefs, whereas positive toleration actually celebrates and applauds differences, believing them to encourage the enrichment of society. Mill celebrated the notion of individuality to encourage the development of ideas in society – he used this as a basis to disagree with a state-imposed curriculum in schools.

In liberal democratic systems religious worship, freedom of speech and freedom of association are all examples of toleration. Laws have been brought in to try to combat the worst examples of lack of toleration, usually exemplified in some form of discrimination (e.g. Racial and Religious Hatred Act 2006).

Just as liberty may need to be clearly defined and licence considered excessive, toleration could also become excessive, when it is extended to those who would do harm to others if not constrained. There is a difficulty here, as interfering with freedom of conscience or expression would violate an individual's rights.

Political toleration, however, is needed in order to ensure that a democracy continues to function. However, the problem arises when we consider whether toleration should be extended to the intolerant themselves. What would be the situation if a political party promised, if elected to power, to ban other political parties and ban the freedom of speech? This was effectively what happened in Germany in 1933. When Hitler came to power he banned other parties, manipulated elections and created a one-party state. As a result, post-war West Germany banned anti-constitutional parties and took other steps to protect itself from excessive toleration.

Thousands of people on the left of US politics found themselves prey to intolerance in the 1950s, when Senator McCarthy's Un-American Activities Committee sought to root out anyone who they believed sympathised with a single-party system, rather than the American liberal democratic one.

Fundamentalist Christians in the United States are often accused of showing extreme intolerance, although they would claim that they are simply trying to bind the country together with a common culture and set of beliefs, in order to ensure its continuance.

Political intolerance can also cut across territorial borders. In 1989 the British writer Salman Rushdie was the subject of a religious death sentence by the Iranian religious leader Ayatollah Khomeini. Rushdie had allegedly offended Islamic principles in his book *The Satanic Verses*. There was enormous debate and indignation on both sides of the argument as to whether Rushdie's rights had been violated and on the nature of tolerance.

John Locke on toleration

Locke believed that the state was there to protect life, liberty and property and had no right to get involved in 'the care of men's souls'. He believed in human rationality and that truth could only emerge if there were free competition amongst beliefs and ideas. Religious belief to him was always a matter of personal faith and should never be imposed. In public affairs there could be a case made to limit toleration. Interestingly, Locke did not extend toleration to Roman Catholics, as he believed they were a threat to national sovereignty as they owed allegiance to the Pope.

Rousseau on film censorship?

Rousseau argued that society needed protecting from external threats to its customs and values, including organised international religion (i.e. Catholicism). He advocated creating a body of citizens to be known as the Censorial Tribune to police society's morals. In Britain today we have the British Board of Film Classification (BBFC) to monitor issues relating to obscenity in films.

John Stuart Mill on tolerance

As far as Mill was concerned, toleration was a vital concern for both society and the individual. He believed there was a case for toleration because he viewed individuals as having the right to have their own personal autonomy and the freedom to exercise control over their own lives. He was concerned that democracy and the 'despotism of custom' would threaten this autonomy. He believed that public opinion in a society dominated by the majority would be the greatest danger. There would be a spread of conventional wisdom, which would force individuals to conform. Mill was in favour of individuality and eccentricity. He believed that truth could only come from freedom of argument, discussion and debate and that over time bad ideas would be replaced by good ones. He did not believe that democratic elections could necessarily establish the truth because there was no way of telling whether the majority were right or wrong. He even believed that if only one individual had a particular opinion compared to the rest of society then society should have no more right to impose their views on that individual than the individual had on them.

DISCUSSION POINT ?

Where should the boundaries of tolerance be constructed?

Learning objectives

- Equality
- Types of equality
- Conservative perspective
- Liberal perspective
- Socialist perspective
- Marxist perspective

Egalitarianism

This is a vague term, but it is the belief that all individuals are or ought to be equal in almost every respect.

Equality

Equality is another key concept at the heart of political ideologies. In the past political thinkers worked on the assumption that there would always be a hierarchy, which inevitably meant that some would be more equal than others. Plato argued that inequality was natural and thus attempts to promote political equality ran counter to the laws of nature. More modern political theorists take the view that everyone has equal moral worth.

There are differing attitudes towards equality, but by and large most political ideologies accept some form of **egalitarianism**. This encompasses political participation, opportunity and legal rights. The opening lines of the US Declaration of Independence are: 'We hold these truths to be self-evident, that all men are created equal…' (Jefferson).

Where there is considerable debate is at the point of where equality should be applied and not to whether equality does or does not exist. It can be applied to the distribution of wealth and income (also known as social justice). Some argue that there should be a more equal distribution of rewards and benefits.

There is a very crucial link between equality and welfare, as this is seen to be an important part of creating a stable and harmonious society. In fact there was a welfare consensus but this seems to have broken down and there are now disputes as to whether the welfare state is as attractive or effective as it was once thought.

Types of equality

Central to the understanding of equality is the question of equality in what respect, as conveyed through the different views in the table.

Type of equality	Explanation	Key quotes
Foundational equality	This is based on the assumption that everyone is born equal and that their lives are of equal moral value.	The American Declaration of Independence says: 'We hold these truths to be self-evident that all men are created equal, that they are endowed by their creator with certain unalienable rights, that among these are life, liberty and the pursuit of happiness.'
Formal equality	This is based on legal equality or equality before the law, meaning that individuals should all have equal rights and entitlements.	John Locke said: '[F]reedom of men under government is to have a standing rule to live by, common to every one of that society, and made by the legislative power erected in it; a liberty to follow my own will in all things, where the rule prescribes not; and not to be subject to the inconstant, uncertain, unknown, arbitrary will of another man.'
Equality of opportunity	This is the assumption that everyone should have equal life chances. There should be equal social treatment, otherwise this is non-legitimate, but there can be unequal distribution (which is legitimate) on the basis of talent, merit and work ethic.	Alexis de Tocqueville observed: 'Democracy and socialism have nothing in common but one word: equality. But notice the difference: while democracy seeks equality in liberty, socialism seeks equality in restraint and servitude.'

Type of equality	Explanation	Key quotes
Equality of outcome	This is where there is an equal distribution of rewards, or social equality.	Milton Friedman, in *Free to Choose: A Personal Statement* (1980, Penguin), suggested that a society that focuses on equality of outcome before freedom will achieve neither of these goals. In using force to achieve equality freedom will be damaged. He believed that inevitably using force to achieve equality, no matter the good intentions, would always be used by those to further their own interests.

Clearly, some of these different views of equality are not compatible. On the one hand rewarding individuals for their work and giving them an unequal distribution of wealth is incompatible with equality of outcome.

As we will see, broadly left-wing perspectives favour social equality, whilst right-wing theorists either oppose it or question its foundation. The following table outlines the key arguments for and against social or material equality.

For	Against
It strengthens social cohesion through common identity and shared interests.	It fails to reward individuals for their talents because it treats unequal individuals equally.
It promotes justice.	It removes incentives and encourages economic stagnation.
It encourages freedom and satisfies basic needs, taking people out of poverty.	It can only be achieved through social engineering and government intervention and infringes on individual liberties.
Legal and political equality need social equality to be effective.	It discourages diversity and vitality and replaces it with uniformity.

Conservative perspective

Conservatives believe that natural inequalities arise out of an individual's talents and skills. They are inevitable and morally right. Margaret Thatcher, for example, believed that there is a right to be unequal. However, unemployment, homelessness and poverty can be considered morally wrong.

Traditional conservative attitudes support Plato's ideas on natural inequality, adopting at best a paternalistic attitude to those born into social disadvantage. Burke argued that inequality served the purpose of society as some are born to rule and others to be ruled.

Modern conservatives, however, seem to favour what could be referred to as a meritocracy, in which successes and failures are individually achieved. Inequality provides individuals with an incentive to use whatever talents they may have. The major problem is that natural talent can rarely be separated from social influences. In other words, an individual may be talented but comes from a poor social background that makes it difficult or even impossible for them to be able to use their talents or have them recognised.

Equal opportunities simply provide a means by which obstacles that stand in the way of personal development and realisation are overcome, according to the conservatives.

In the United States, where both major parties could be considered to be moderately conservative or liberal to one degree or another, there has been a move towards embedding equal opportunity in society. Systems have been developed that actually discriminate in favour of disadvantaged groups, partly as compensation for past injustices. They are given

---

Antatole France

'The law, in its majestic equality, forbids rich and poor alike to sleep under bridges, to beg in the streets, and to steal their bread.'

Anatole France (1844–1924), born Anatole François Thibault, was a French author.

formal equality through positive discrimination, or affirmative action. It is in effect a reverse discrimination. The British Conservative Party has rejected compulsory positive discrimination in the selection of more female and ethnic minority candidates, instead its present leader, David Cameron, has tried to elevate the status of these groups of candidates through his voluntary A-List scheme. It is also important to appreciate that affirmative action campaigns in the United States have tended to come from the Democratic Party with Republican administrations often closing down the schemes.

Liberal perspective

Modern liberals limit some aspects of liberty to promote a more socially equal society. Equality suggests sameness and this is opposed to most liberal viewpoints. Classical liberals believed that equality was a levelling system; the levelling was always downward and therefore a denial of difference, diversity and autonomy. Some liberals are therefore anti-egalitarian because they see it as being a threat to culture and civilisation. Thus democracy was criticised by de Tocqueville as rule by the lowest common denominator.

In general, liberals will support equal opportunity, but not necessarily equal outcome. Most liberal democratic parties would not favour state intervention to enforce equality, but would move to take action against arbitrary discrimination on the basis that it is morally wrong.

Socialist perspective

Socialists believe that there should be greater social equality and that inequality reflects unequal structures and opportunities for individuals in life. Hierarchies, privileges and prejudices impede an individual's ability to reach their potential. They would therefore favour laws prohibiting discrimination, the rooting out of institutionalised inequality and the acquisition of equal civil rights and liberties. This would free individuals from class oppression and free them from any form of exploitation or economic inequality. Social democracy thus supports the idea of equality based upon social justice through addressing the needs of all in society.

Marxist perspective

Marxists, or fundamental socialists, are of the opinion that social equality is both desirable and possible. Marx drew a distinction between equality and common ownership. In order to achieve complete equality then private property would need to be abolished and this would ensure absolute social equality. Marx in response to the Gotha Programme summed up this perspective when he advocated, 'From each according to their ability to each according to their need.'

In China during the Cultural Revolution of the 1960s, wage differentials, privilege, hierarchy and competitive sports were all denounced or banned.

Statue of the Cultural Revolution in Tiananmen Square, China

DISCUSSION POINT ?

To what extent might equal opportunities ensure equality of outcome?

Needs, rights and deserts based theories on social justice

Social justice is a concept that has been discussed ever since Plato in *The Republic* argued that an ideal state would rest on four virtues.

- Wisdom
- Courage
- Moderation
- Justice

The addition of the word 'social' is to distinguish social justice from the concept of justice as applied in the law. Social justice is also used to refer to the overall fairness of a society in its division and distribution of reward and burden.

Thomas Aquinas (1225–74) wrote, 'Justice is a certain rectitude of mind whereby a man does what he ought to do in the circumstances confronting him.' As a Christian theologian, Aquinas believed that justice is a form of natural duty owed by one person to another and not enforced by any man-made law. The Christian view is that all people are equal and must treat each other with respect.

The term 'social justice' was first used in 1840 by a Sicilian priest, Luigi Taparelli d'Azeglio, and given prominence by Antonio Rosmini-Serbati in 1848. John Stuart Mill gave this definition 13 years later in *Utilitarianism*:

> Society should treat all equally well who have deserved equally well of it, that is, who have deserved equally well absolutely. This is the highest abstract standard of social and distributive justice; towards which all institutions, and the efforts of all virtuous citizens, should be made in the utmost degree to converge.

David Miller in a book called *Social Justice* (1976, Oxford University Press) attempted to identify contrasting principles of social justice. Essentially this meant:

- 'to each according to his needs'
- 'to each according to his rights'
- 'to each according to his deserts'.

Needs theory has major egalitarian implications and implies a moral obligation to distribute according to need and therefore supports a welfare system. Needs are difficult to define. Conservatives criticise it as too abstract. They also believe that it is ridiculous to suggest there should be universal human rights because people are brought up in different social conditions and have different needs. It also means that some have to forego benefits that they have earned to subsidise others.

Rights are moral entitlements but imply that they need to be earned. Rights-based theories are concerned with how these rights have been established. Robert Nozick (1974) suggested that they were justice preserving rules. There is a justification for inequality based upon talent and hard work – thus some deserve to achieve more in the sense of higher wages and a better lifestyle because they deserve it. This is seen as the liberal interpretation of social justice.

A desert is a reward or punishment, which reflects what an individual is either due or deserves. Justice is based on deserts, as is food for the hungry and wages for the worker. Traditional

Learning objectives

- Needs, rights and deserts based theories on social justice
- John Rawls on social justice
- John Rawls on equality

conservatives support this approach, as they see that it grounds justice in a natural order. Differences in natural ability between people are sometimes used to explain a particular pattern of social or natural inequality. Men earn higher wages than women and this is often explained by the fact that they have greater strength and capacity for manual work. However, even in non-physical work women still tend to earn less than men. Equally, there are very few jobs these days that require physical strength as machines tend to do most of the work. Even if it was the case that women are less capable of doing physical work than men, natural inequality would not really justify that women are paid less than men.

The ideas of natural inequality, and thus allocating resources based on natural order (i.e. some will deserve to starve and others prosper as that is the natural way of things – or chance in nature) relate to social Darwinism. This was taken up by Herbert Spencer in his justification of racial superiority along the lines of survival of the fittest. This view has been criticised, as it avoids moral judgements in excusing a lack of intervention to address poverty and global human suffering.

By the latter part of the 20th century, the concept of social justice became associated with the political philosopher John Rawls (1921–2002). He drew on the utilitarian views of Bentham and Mill, along with the social contract theories of Locke. Rawls, in *A Theory of Justice* (1971), proposed that every individual has sanctity of life that cannot be violated. It is based on justice and cannot be compromised, even by the welfare of society. In his view, justice seeks to ensure that it is never right for an individual to lose their freedom on account of the greater good of society as a whole.

His views are restated in *Political Liberalism* (1993), where society is seen as a cooperative system that is fair and passes on from generation to generation.

In his view, all societies have a basic structure of social, economic and political institutions (formal and informal). Rawls tested how well these elements fit together and work, and created a test of legitimacy on the theories of social contract. In order to determine whether any particular system of collectively enforced social arrangements is legitimate, Rawls claimed that you needed to look for the agreement of those who were subject to it.

John Rawls on social justice

One of the most discussed elements of Rawls' view of justice as fairness is the original position. The original position has often been compared to the state of nature or the pre-political condition of humanity. It is a model to help us understand something else, in this case the principles of (political or social) justice. The three-way distinction basic to social contract theories is:

- the original position
- the just social order whose basic structure is described by the two principles of justice
- the actual society.

Representative persons in the original position choose principles of justice that would govern the basic structure of a (just and fair) social order. Each person in the just social order has a representative in the original position. These representatives represent every human being who belongs to the political association of free and equal persons. There are three fundamental features of the representatives in the original position that reflect two moral powers. The first is that the representatives are rational in the sense that they wish to secure for those they represent the kind of goods that would enable them to work out their own conceptions of the good and then try to realise this good. This feature recognises that each person has a set of interests which are his or her own. These interests are linked to the person's moral power to form, revise, and pursue a conception of the good; in the case of persons with a comprehensive doctrine, the interests will be linked to the comprehensive doctrine.

The second fundamental feature of the representatives in the original position is summed up in the phrase 'the veil of ignorance'. The representatives, unlike persons in the ideal society and unlike ourselves in a less than ideal society, stand behind the veil of ignorance. They do not know the following about the persons they represent: their sex, race or social class.

A third feature of the representatives in the original position is that they possess a great deal of commonsense general knowledge about human psychology and sociology. The first and second features of the representatives in the original position correspond to the two moral powers. Our capacity to frame and pursue a conception of the good is reflected in the rationality of the representatives who choose for us in order to optimise our ability to investigate and pursue the good. Our capacity for a sense of justice is reflected in the operation of the veil of ignorance. The veil of ignorance is what makes their imaginary choices on our behalf fair.

Rawls offers the following principles:

1   Each person has an equal right to a fully adequate scheme of equal basic liberties which is compatible with a similar scheme of liberties for all.

2   Social and economic inequalities are to satisfy two conditions. First, they must be attached to offices and positions open to all under conditions of fair equality of opportunity; and second, they must be to the greatest benefit of the least advantaged members of society.

Rawls' modern social contract theories ideas are based upon a compromise between aspects of needs and rights based social justice. His ideas on the original position and the veil of ignorance emphasise advocating greater social equality. He asserts that inequality can be justified on merit as long as it is to the benefit of all, particularly the most dispossessed elements of society.

John Rawls on equality

Rawls argues that self-interested rational persons behind the veil of ignorance would choose two general principles of justice to structure society in the real world:

1   **The principle of equal liberty** – Each person has an equal right to the most extensive liberties compatible with similar liberties for all (egalitarian).

2   **The difference principle** – Social and economic inequalities should be arranged so that they are both (a) to the greatest benefit of the least advantaged persons, and (b) attached to offices and positions open to all under conditions of equality of opportunity.

The first principle is egalitarian, since it distributes extensive liberties equally to all persons.

(2b) is also quite egalitarian, since it distributes opportunities to be considered for offices and positions in an equal manner.

(2a) is not egalitarian but makes benefits for some (those with greater talents, training, etc.) proportionate to their contribution toward benefiting the least advantaged persons.

The first obviously echoes, without exactly duplicating, libertarianism in its commitment to extensive liberties.

What does the difference principle mean? It means that society may undertake projects that require giving some persons more power, income, status, etc. than others, for example paying senior managers more than assembly-line operatives, provided that the following conditions are met: (a) the project will make life better off for the people who are now worst off, for example by raising the living standards of everyone in the community and empowering the least advantaged persons to the extent consistent with their well-being, and (b) that access to the privileged positions is not blocked by discrimination according to irrelevant criteria.

In this way, Rawls can be seen as supporting egalitarianism and individualism.

The difference principle has elements of other familiar ethical theories. The socialist idea that responsibilities or burdens should be distributed according to ability and benefits according to need is partly contained within the difference principle. It can be assumed that the least advantaged have the greatest needs and that those who receive special powers (suggested by social inequalities) also have special responsibilities or burdens. However, the merit principle that the use of special skills should be rewarded is also included in the difference principle. What (2a) does not permit is a change in social and economic institutions that makes life better for those who are already well off but does nothing for those who are already disadvantaged, or makes their life worse.

Rawls' theory of justice was featured in his book *A Theory of Justice* (1971). Since then it has been much discussed, and attempts have been made to improve and clarify it, not least by Rawls himself. One of those attempts at improvement is that of Martha Nussbaum, who has reinterpreted Rawls' argument from the perspective of substantial freedom. For Nussbaum the liberties mentioned in the principle of equal liberty, if they are to be meaningful at all, are capabilities or substantial freedoms, real opportunities based on natural and developed potentialities as well as the presence of governmentally supported institutions, to engage in political deliberation and planning over one's own life. Likewise, the concern of the difference principle to raise up those who are least advantaged must be clarified in light of substantial freedoms. What is needed is a commitment by citizens and governments to a threshold of real opportunities below which no human being should fall if he or she is able to rise above it.

In all, Rawls' concept of social justice suggests the following.

- The historical inequities inasmuch as they affect current injustices should be corrected until the actual inequities no longer exist or have been negated.

- The redistribution of wealth, power and status is for the individual, community and societal good.

- It is the responsibility of the government to seek to ensure a basic quality of life for all its citizens.

DISCUSSION POINT

?

Why is social justice such a contentious issue?

Rights protection in Britain

The relationship between rights and duties and the expectations of the state regarding citizens has not always been absolutely clear. Precise duties of citizens were not, necessarily, written down in the form of a contract between citizens and the state. However, in the 1990s the Conservatives under John Major began this process. Although the attempt was criticised by many, it was a key step in establishing precisely what the rights and responsibilities of a citizen were; for the first time stating the obligations and promises made by both sides.

What developed became known as the Citizens' Charter. The government had been wrestling with several major social problems, including crime and homelessness. It came to the conclusion that it needed the full support of the people to be able to tackle the root causes of the issues. The government wanted citizens to become more involved in their country. The Citizens' Charter focused on the rights of citizens, clearly stating what the government should provide, the quality of that provision and how citizens would be guaranteed that level of service. It also extended to the expectations of citizens in regard to private businesses, setting down minimum standards of service and opening up the possibility of legal action against a business that was seen to be consistently ignoring the rights of consumers.

Conservative governments have focussed on the rights of citizens; the trend of Labour governments have been to focus on the duties of citizens. Certainly the adoption of the European Convention on Human Rights and bringing in EU legislation, such as the minimum wage bill, has extended citizens' rights. But the main policies have sought to outline the duties of citizens, as set out in the table.

Learning objectives

- Rights protection in Britain
- The European Court of Justice
- The European Court of Human Rights
- Judicial review
- The EU, rights and liberties

Rights protection	Role	Examples
The UK judiciary	The judiciary, or the courts, are supposed to be a major defender of citizens' rights. The key problem is that the judicial process may take months or even years, by which time the results of the problem in the first place may have had an enormous impact on the citizen and in any case incur huge costs. The judiciary will rule on the case by interpreting the law, finding that either the action was lawful or unlawful. If the citizen feels that the decision was wrong, they can appeal to the European Court of Human Rights. If the ECHR finds in their favour then the judgement of the British judge can be overturned. British courts are obliged to obey the decision of the ECHR. The government is only morally obliged, it is up to government of day whether to accept a ruling – note Major rejected ECHR ruling over the illegality of the shoot-to-kill policy after the shooting of IRA suspects in Gibraltar in 1988.	In 2000 a judge ruled that an operation to separate conjoined (physically joined together) twins was lawful, despite the fact that the parents of the children were opposed to the surgery. The judge in this case weighed up the rights of the two children (one of whom would die as a result of the operation), the rights of the parents and the professional opinions of the surgeons. Other good examples are the Belmarsh detainees and the consequent decision of the Law Lords.

Rights protection	Role	Examples
Parliament	Constituents can try to enlist the support of their MP in their redress of grievance. Whilst MPs do not have a wide range of powers, they can assist in a number of different ways.	MPs can write on behalf of the constituent, outlining the complaint. They can directly bring up the case in the House of Commons. Prime minister's question time or ministers' questions provide this opportunity to direct the prime minister or minister to the specific case and request that an investigation take place and a suitable outcome be reached. At the end of the parliamentary day the MP can bring up the case as an adjournment debate. The case can be referred to a parliamentary select committee or an ombudsman by the MP. Written questions to the prime minister or a minister is also an option.
Ombudsman	An ombudsman deals with complaints about specific organisations or institutions (such as the Inland Revenue). Ombudsmen can only publish in report form, criticisms cannot compel change. There has been an expansion in the number of ombudsmen concerning various aspects of maladministration, e.g. in parliament, local government and health etc.	They can deal with delays, misleading advice, refusal to answer questions and unfair treatment. In 2006 PCA criticism of the government's refusal to accept compensation claims from members of company pension schemes that went bankrupt after being supposedly endorsed by the government. Note the early departure of Elizabeth France as Information Commissioner following frustration over lack of government cooperation.
Media	Instead of resorting to official and legal redress of grievance, the help and support of the media is always an option open to the citizen. This is, of course, dependent on whether the media considers it to be an important enough case and an interesting one. It may also depend on the political bias of the newspaper or magazine in question. Some are openly critical of particular governments; others are openly hostile to all forms of government. It is important to appreciate that whilst the citizen's case may be given media coverage, it may also mean that the case becomes associated with a particular political view.	The campaign to increase the amount paid to pensioners or the campaign to reduce or cancel proposed increased in the fuel tax. The media also strongly backed the Snowdrop Campaign which called for a ban on handguns.
Administrative tribunals	These are government created, independent bodies that handle specific grievances. Independent lawyers chair administrative tribunals. They will also have two specialists (experts in the field covered by the tribunal), along with two other members (called lay people). The lay people have been chosen not for their specialist knowledge, but for their abilities to fairly judge a situation.	They tend to cover areas such as tax, pensions, compensation and similar matters. Largely, they deal with complaints against employers (such as unfair dismissal, equal opportunities and racial discrimination) or government departments (including public bodies and agencies). Note in 1997 the Labour Party lost an administrative tribunal case in Leeds over the policy of all-female candidate shortlists – which eventually led to a change in the law to allow them to reintroduce the policy for selection of candidates in 2005.

Rights protection	Role	Examples
Public inquiries	In some cases citizens can convince the government to launch a public inquiry into the actions of government or a public body. The major problem is that the government is not bound to implement the findings and recommendations of the inquiry.	A prime example was the Stephen Lawrence case. Sir William MacPherson carried out the inquiry into the case in 1997. It reported in February 1999. MacPherson's conclusions were not complimentary towards the police.
Local councillors	Local councillors have the power and the ability to take up cases on behalf of citizens with a grievance, but will restrict their investigations and work on their behalf to the local authority.	Typical examples include housing, planning and education.
Pressure groups	Pressure groups can either be approached to help with the publicity of a case or give support in pushing the case. In some instances new pressure groups have been specifically created to carry a redress of grievance case forward. Although a pressure group cannot actually redress the grievance, it can bring significant pressure to bear on the government, the public body or the source of the problem. In some cases public inquiries have been authorised or the case taken up by MPs or councillors as a result of the intensity of feeling.	A prime example took place in Bristol in 1999 when a pressure group, Bristol Heart Condition Action Group (BHCAG), was formed. Numerous infants with heart conditions had died in the period 1984 to 1995 at the Bristol Infirmary. The numbers of deaths far exceeded the national average for children with similar conditions. The parents of the children mounted a vigorous campaign for an inquiry. Ultimately it was granted and chaired by Professor Ian Kennedy. The report was finally completed in 2001 and suggested wide-ranging checks and balances within the NHS.

The European Court of Justice and the European Court of Human Rights

The European Court of Justice is the highest court in the EU. It sits in Luxembourg and deals with all matters relating to EU law. As the most senior court its judgements even overrides the House of Lords as the final court of appeal.

The European Court of Human Rights, a non-EU body, sits in Strasbourg. The European Convention on Human Rights (ECHR) established it. Those that believe that their rights under the convention have been violated can appeal to the court. However:

- the individual must have had their case heard by all domestic courts

- the case must be referred to the ECHR by the United Nation's Commission on Human Rights.

The UN commission makes the decision whether the case is one for the court. At all times attempts are made to reach a settlement of the case before the ECHR hears the case, as it tends to only deal with urgent and acute human rights situations.

Judicial review

A judicial review is a type of court proceeding in which a judge reviews the lawfulness of a decision or action made by a public body or a government minister. Judicial reviews are a challenge to the way in which a decision has been made, rather than the rights and wrongs of the conclusion reached. The review is not concerned with the conclusions of that process and whether those were 'right', as long as the right procedures have been followed. The court will not suggest what it thinks is the 'correct' decision. This may mean that the public body will be able to make the same decision again, so long as it does so in a lawful way. There are three grounds for leave of appeal decisions: *ultra vires* (beyond powers), perverse (lacks justice and not based upon facts), or there was procedural impropriety (not correct procedures adhered to).

Judicial reviews are not automatic; the citizen or organisation has to apply to the High Court. Some countries, such as Canada or Germany, have very strong systems of judicial review. In the US this is the job of the Supreme Court. They can actually declare that an Act of Congress, the equivalent of an Act of Parliament, is unconstitutional and thereby make it invalid. The scope of judicial review in Britain is limited by the principle of parliamentary sovereignty, which states that parliament is the supreme law-making body of Britain. Parliament has the power to pass any laws it chooses and cannot be restricted by the judiciary. However, parliamentary sovereignty has potentially been undermined in this respect by the Human Rights Act (2000). This has extended the scope of judicial reviews to enable judges to make a 'declaration of incompatibility' if a British law is in breach of the European Convention on Human Rights.

The EU, rights and liberties

The European Union has a longstanding commitment to protecting human rights and fundamental freedoms (largely arising from the case law developed by the European Court of Justice from the 1960s onwards). These rights are now integral to the EU Charter of Fundamental Rights. This is designed to be a clear statement of the rights common to all citizens of the member states under six headings: dignity, freedoms, equality, solidarity, citizens' rights, and justice. The charter does not challenge the governments of member states on domestic issues that are dealt with by national authorities (Article 51).

Since the Treaty of Rome in 1957, each successive EU treaty revision has sought to strengthen rights. The Amsterdam Treaty (1999) not only gave the European Court of Justice the power to ensure that all EU institutions respect fundamental rights, but also strengthened EU cooperation in justice and home affairs.

Article 6 of the Treaty on European Union states: 'The Union is founded on the principles of liberty, democracy, respect for human rights and fundamental freedoms, and the rule of law, principles that are common to the Member States.'

Specifically, the EU has been active in six areas to underpin their work on rights and liberties. The following table lists the six areas.

Heading	Activities
Dignity	Fight against trafficking in human beings
	Ban on trade in instruments of torture
Freedoms	Data protection
	Education
	Workers' rights: charter of fundamental social rights, free movement of workers
	Asylum policy
	Enterprise

Heading	Activities
Equality	Combating discrimination – a framework strategy for non-discrimination and equal opportunities for all, European Year of Equal Opportunities for All (2007), Action programme to combat discrimination (2001–06), Equal opportunities between men and women Combating racism, xenophobia and anti-Semitism Equality and non-discrimination in an enlarged European Union Social action for target groups
Solidarity	Protection of the environment Consumers Public health
Citizens' rights	Citizenship of the Union Free movement of European citizens within the EU Fundamental rights and citizenship (2007–13)
Justice	Recognition of decisions in criminal matters: strengthening mutual trust Procedural guarantees: Green Paper Green Paper on mutual recognition of non-custodial pre-trial supervision measures

The following table outlines the EU's concerns about rights and liberties in Britain.

Concern	Implications
Extending detention of terror suspects before charges	The EU was already concerned that suspects could be detained for 28 days before charges being made, they are even more concerned with the proposed 42-day limit (the proposal was dropped in October 2008). The 28-day limit was already the longest in the EU. The Human Rights Commissioner for the Council of Europe (COE), Thomas Hammarberg (formerly head of Amnesty International), said: 'I think that governments have tried to stretch and break the rules. The proposed British 42-day legislation was not in the spirit of the Human Rights convention.'
Secret evidence	The House of Lords Judicial Committee ruled in October 2007 that control orders based on secret evidence not disclosed to defendants was a violation of their rights and that orders confining suspects to their homes for 18 hours in 24 breached their right to liberty. Hammarberg commented: 'The defendant should be able to see all evidence. There should be well-founded grounds for any detention.'
Release without charge	Government figures released in 2007 indicated that over half of terror suspects arrested and held since September 2001 were later released without charge.
Restrictions on free speech	In July 2007, two men were tried separately and a group of five students tried together and were sentenced to prison terms ranging from two to nine years for possession of terrorism-related documents. These trials and others raise concerns over improper restrictions on free expression.
Deportations and threat of torture	The government has had mixed results over the deportation of foreign terrorism suspects on the basis of diplomatic assurances of humane treatment. The Special Immigration Appeals Commission (SIAC) tends now to allow suspects into court but the reasons for granting or not granting their appeals are kept secret.

DISCUSSION POINT ?

How effective are rights protection mechanisms in Britain and Europe?

Learning objectives

- Key threats to the exercise of rights
- ID cards
- Anti-terrorism legislation
- The Islamic community, threats and freedoms

Right to silence

The right to remain silent and not incriminate oneself by answering questions if arrested.

Authoritarian

A government that is determined that citizens should obey the authority of the state.

Key threats to the exercise of rights

During the Thatcher years (1979–90) there were grave doubts as to whether British citizens' rights and liberties were safe. It was felt that the government could damage these rights, as the rights themselves were not clearly defined. Specifically, government has affected rights in the following areas.

- Official Secrets Act – this was used by the government to silence the press and prevent them from criticising the government on the grounds that featuring a story would be damaging to the national security of the country (e.g. Spycatcher).

- The press faced the prospect of legal action from the rich or well placed if they ran a story that was against the interests of such an individual. There were cases when the media was threatened with a slander or libel case, for example Jeffrey Archer, the then Deputy Chairman of the Conservative Party, and Robert Maxwell, who was a media proprietor.

- The **right to silence** was removed for those who had been arrested for a crime.

- The government sought to ban radio and television programmes that they felt damaged the security of the nation, for example the government's attempts to silence Andrew Gilligan's claims that the Iraq weapons dossier was exaggerated in 2003.

- Sinn Fein representatives could not speak on television or radio. Sinn Fein is the Irish Republican Party.

- The police and security forces were given the right to listen into telephone conversations.

- Celebrities and members of the Royal family constantly found themselves subject to media intrusion (photographs, 'kiss and tell' stories and constant comments in the press).

- Citizens did not have the right to access information held on them by public bodies (such as hospitals, etc.).

New Labour seemed to bring new threats. The Labour Party had held the view that the fundamental goal of civil liberties was safeguarding individual or minority rights against state power. Much of this changed when the party took power in 1997; what was added were citizens' responsibilities and the well-being of the community.

The first key piece of legislation was the Crime and Disorder Act (1998). It was designed to tackle anti-social behaviour.

Criminologist David Wilson believed that this legislation showed that the Labour Party was **authoritarian**.

Wilson saw Blair's moral stance and focus on individual responsibility as simply a version of Thatcherism. At first, the Labour Party simply followed Blair's lead. For Wilson issues such as terrorism and ID cards, grave concerns for civil liberties, were always a possibility and solutions such as these would always come to the surface.

In 2005 a new package of terror measures was announced, the most radical for thirty or more years. The director of the civil rights group Liberty, Shami Chakrabati, said in 2007: 'Democracy is not just about elections every five years. It is also about fundamental rights and freedoms and the rule of law. If you dump the rights and freedoms and rule of law, democracy descends into mob rule.'

The Labour Party saw the judiciary as a block to their proposed changes and after the 2001 election they announced fundamental changes to the role of the Lord Chancellor. Labour gave the police more powers to arrest, to hold mandatory drug tests and DNA tests, as well as new dispersal orders (creating dispersal areas where police officers can break up troublemakers and forcibly take under-16s home). All of these damaged liberties.

The freedom of the police to enforce the law and protect citizens was also affected. Tony Butler, the former Chief Constable of Gloucestershire, argued that the mid-1990s witnessed the biggest ever reduction in volume crime, such as car theft and burglary. However, the current obsession with performance management means that violent crime and drug-related offending are not being defeated, and people are rightly concerned.

Despite the changes, the Labour Party claims to still support the notion of civil liberties. They maintain that the Human Rights Act and the Freedom of Information Act have both improved government's accountability.

Many people believe that there are innumerable threats to the exercise of rights by individuals. This spread seeks to identify some of the major issues, including identity cards, anti-terrorism legislation and the difficulties in balancing the perceived threat from individuals within the Islamic community, whilst safeguarding the rights of the majority of that community.

ID cards

Most police forces support the idea of ID cards and civil liberties groups are convinced that the cards will lead to enormous loss of privacy and worsen the harassment of ethnic minorities. The ID cards will include fingerprints, eye or facial scans, and the details will be added to a National Identity Register from 2008.

The first attempt to introduce the Identity Cards Bill failed, as it had not gone through all the parliamentary processes before the parliament was dissolved for the 2005 general election. The second bill did narrowly make it to the House of Commons in June 2005. The bill was amended several times at committee level, as well as by the House of Lords, which rejected it 12 times.

The Identity Cards Act (2006) is now law. A voluntary scheme is due to start in 2008 and those applying for passports will have their details put on the National Identity Register. From 2010 those applying for a passport will also receive an identity card.

The government and supporters of the scheme claim that ID cards will help prevent identity theft and fraud, whilst groups opposed to the scheme say that the security of Britain will not be improved. The key arguments for and against ID cards are listed in the table.

For	Against
Prevent illegal immigration	Loss of privacy
Prevent illegal working	Costly and impractical
Aid anti-terrorism	Worsen harassment of ethnic minorities
Tackle identity theft	Have little impact on anti-terrorism
Reduce benefit fraud and the abuse of public services	Have little effect on illegal working
Enhance the sense of community (shared citizenship and belonging)	Could lead to a 'creep' function (the card would be used for purposes not originally intended)

Many groups do not object to ID cards in principle, but question the way in which they will be implemented. For example, whilst the groups accept they should be compulsory to be effective, it should not be compulsory to carry them. Groups either side of the debate are listed in the table.

For	In the middle	Against
Financial Services Authority (believes the cards would help the disadvantaged, such as setting up a bank account) Police Federation (believes it will help identification and help prevent fraud)	Law Society (sceptical) Information Commissioner (strong concerns over the National Identity Register and its impact on individual privacy) Rethink (believes those with mental illnesses may run into problems) Scottish National Party (believes it is a matter for the devolved government)	NO2ID Liberty Stand Liberal Democrats Conservative Party

Anti-terrorism legislation

A wide range of offences is bundled together under the description of terrorism offences, from murder and arson to sabotage and harassment. The Terrorist Act (2000) and the Anti-Terrorism, Crime and Security Act (2001) give the police enormous powers. Critics suggest that the anti-terrorism legislation has enormous implications for civil rights and liberties. Liberty, for example, states that the legislation affects the right to protest, as the police have the powers to stop and search 'whether or not the constable has grounds for suspecting the presence of articles (which could be used in connection with terrorism)'.

Checks are built into the legislation. The Terrorism Act requires searches to be authorised by a senior officer and approved by the Home Secretary. In an annual report made by Lord Carlile (a Queen's Counsel and a member of the House of Lords) in 2003, the question of detention without trial was examined. Carlile suggested that suspects be kept in a 'separate, secure environment with greater freedom of association and activity'. After all they had not been convicted of a crime.

Unlike the Prevention of Terrorism Act (replaced by the Terrorism Act), the legislation had to be reviewed and approved by the House of Commons each year; the new Act does not.

New proposals for anti-terrorism measures were announced in August 2005. These were:

- new grounds for deporting and excluding people from Britain
- agreements with other countries to ensure that people can be deported without facing the prospect of torture
- amended human rights legislation to prevent legal obstacles to the new deportation rules
- the Home Secretary to automatically consider deportation of foreign nationals involved in extremist bookshops, websites, centres or organisations
- automatic refusal of asylum if a person has been involved in terrorism anywhere in the world
- to consider allowing police to hold suspects longer without charges
- using control orders (which restrict the behaviour and movement of an individual) against British terror suspects
- increasing the number of special judges hearing terror cases
- the use of biometric visas from designated countries.

Update

Legislation was agreed to extend detention to 28 days in 2005 (a compromise after the defeat of the government's proposal for 60 days) and the government had a narrow victory in the Commons in June 2008 for reserve powers for 42-day detention.

The Islamic community, threats and freedoms

In the wake of the 7 July and 21 July 2005 attacks on the London Underground, Britain developed a new model for counter-terrorism, which aside from expanding the list of criminal offences tied to terrorism and enhancing police powers, also emphasised community-policing principles and partnerships with Muslim groups. Community-policing principles aimed to facilitate information sharing, to build trust in cases of arrests and operations, and to mitigate the negative impact of enforcement on the Muslim community at large.

The counter-terrorism strategy is based on the assumption that socio-economic deprivation does not drive terrorist recruitment. Conspirators have come from all backgrounds and evidence that recruitment now has shifted to prisons and to youths involved in gangs or street-crime suggests that it is necessary to address persistent problems of inequality and discrimination affecting Muslims. The government has been at pains to stress terrorism as a product of Al Qaeda linked organisations and not linked to Islam as such.

Muslim representatives stress the need to mitigate the impact of strengthened counterterrorism enforcement on the Muslim community at large. Muslims are disproportionately impacted by terrorism and by counterterrorism policy because they live in inner cities, where attacks take place. They fear a backlash when terrorism happens and the counterterrorism operations and measures that may target them or their mosque. Complaints focus on 'stop-and-search' procedures carried out under Section 44 of the 2000 Terrorism Act. The Muslim Council of Britain has described the procedures as 'Islamophobic policing', and it has complained that they are damaging community relations and confidence in policing.

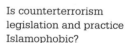

DISCUSSION POINT ?

Is counterterrorism legislation and practice Islamophobic?

Learning objectives

- Civil liberties under threat – the smoking ban
- Civil liberties under threat – press freedom
- Civil liberties under threat – encroachment of civil liberties

The cigarette ban in Britain has radically changed leisure activities.

Childhood obesity

There are other questions about civil liberty and health relating to tackling obesity, particularly amongst children, by imposing strict codes of school meals.

Civil liberties under threat – the smoking ban

Pope Urban VII's 13-day papal reign included the world's first known public smoking ban (1590), as he threatened to excommunicate anyone who 'took tobacco in the porch-way of or inside a church, whether it be by chewing it, smoking it with a pipe or sniffing it in powdered form through the nose'.

The introduction of a ban on smoking in public places in Scotland came into force in 2006 and in England, Northern Ireland and Wales in 2007.

Critics of smoking bans claim that the bans are misguided, and their argument is based on John Stuart Mill's harm principle, arguing that the damage to public health through passive smoking is insufficient to warrant government intervention. In *On Liberty*, Mill wrote: 'The only purpose for which power can be rightfully exercised over any member of a civilised community, against his will, is to prevent harm to others. His own good, either physical or moral, is not sufficient warrant.'

Critics of this view claim that it is only valid if it could be proved that passive smoking is entirely harmless. Other critics of the ban base their views on property rights; they draw a distinction between public and private property. This view is supported by some economists who suggest that private property rights and contractual freedom are capable of resolving conflicts between the preferences of smokers and those who want a smoke-free environment – without government intervention.

Costs and incomes from smoking

Tax is levied on tobacco in three ways: excise duty at a specific rate per 1000 cigarettes, an additional rate based on 20 per cent of the total retail price, plus VAT at 17.5 per cent of the final price – including the other taxes. Between 80 per cent and 90 per cent of the cost of a packet of cigarettes is tax.

The end result is that tobacco taxation, the amount levied in various ways by the government on every packet of cigarettes, cigars or smoking tobacco, comes to £12 billion per year, six times more than the £1.7 billion NHS bill run up by nicotine addicts.

With pubs closing and looking for alternatives to keep their core customers, they are likely to pump hundreds of thousands of tons of additional carbon dioxide into the atmosphere as a result of the smoking ban. Policy advisers predict that emissions from patio heaters in pubs and restaurants will increase from 22,200 tons of greenhouse gases a year to up to 282,000 tons – the equivalent of flying a jumbo jet 171 times around the earth. Heaters will be used for more than 237 days a year, when outdoor temperatures are lower than 15°C, says the report from Market Transformation. A further 80,000 tons of carbon dioxide will be produced next year by patio heaters in private gardens. There are proposals to extend the ban on smoking into private homes where children are present.

Civil liberties under threat – press freedom

Embassies were set on fire, there were riots and demonstrations across the globe, journalists went into hiding and all because of a series of second-rate cartoons inside the pages of a small Danish newspaper in 2006. *Jyllands-Posten* is a national newspaper with a circulation of 150,000 and the arts editor decided that publishing a page of cartoons of the prophet Mohammad would provoke a debate on multiculturalism. How wrong. Some 12 cartoons were published on 30 September on page 3 of the second section of the paper. One showed the prophet with a bomb as a head, another with either horns or half a halo growing out of his head.

The initial publication of the cartoons brought no response other than angry letters. Then in mid-October two of the artists received death threats, the menaces were widely reported and rekindled debate, prompting vicious, anti-Muslim comments on Danish talk shows; this came soon after a series of new, strict laws relating to marriage and citizenship, enforcing obligatory Danish lessons and clamping down on imams.

This was followed by a demonstration of 5000 Muslims in Copenhagen. A week later, diplomats from Islamic states complained to the Danish prime minister about the gross reaction to the cartoons, which threatens press freedom. A group of ultra-conservative Danish imams set off for a tour of Saudi Arabia and Egypt with a dossier of the cartoons and several other cartoons, unrelated to the *Jyllands-Posten* drawings, showing Mohammad with the face of a pig and as a paedophile. Saudi Arabia and Libya recalled their ambassadors from Copenhagen. Suddenly, Danish goods were being boycotted and its national flag burnt. The Danish prime minister expressed his regrets and admitted the caricatures had hurt the sensitivities of Muslims worldwide.

As other newspapers picked up on the story and reprinted some of the cartoons, an imam at the Omari mosque in Gaza City told 9000 worshippers that the people behind the drawings should have their heads cut off. 'If they want a war of religions, we are ready', Hassan Sharaf, an imam in Nablus, said in his sermon. In Ramallah, protesters burnt a Danish flag, chanting: 'Bin Laden our beloved, Denmark must be blown up.' In Pakistan, hundreds of activists from Islamic political parties set fire to French and Danish flags. Hundreds of Indonesian Muslims belonging to a hard-line political group went on a rampage in the lobby of a building housing the Danish embassy in Jakarta.

Clearly, questions of press freedom also dominate this story. In the aftermath of the controversy there was self-censorship of the British press in not showing the cartoons (this was replicated by a Channel 4 debate where in spite of a majority in a phone-in vote calling for the cartoons to be shown, the editors declined to do so). In France some right-wing newspapers published the cartoons and won cases in the French courts supporting their freedom of publication when legal attempts were made to prevent them showing the cartoons.

Civil liberties under threat – encroachment of civil liberties

There are many who believe that civil liberties are under threat by gradual encroachment or erosion of rights. Examples include the following.

- The legal definition of terrorism includes acts of civil disobedience that harm no one which potentially includes organising a mass emailing or faxing of an organisation.

- The outlawing of an organisation without proving wrongdoing, criminalising not only membership of that organisation but also that of organising protests in support of that organisation.

- The police, security agencies, Inland Revenue and Customs and Excise can monitor emails or phone calls, websites visited, and the location of a mobile phone whilst switched on, without the individual's knowledge and without a warrant of authorisation, or by effective oversight.

DISCUSSION POINT ?

To what extent are these examples true indications of the threats to civil liberties and not just panic or an over reaction?

- The detention of foreign nationals indefinitely without trial if the Home Secretary certifies they are 'suspected international terrorists'.

- Authorised officials working for local authorities or the Department for Work and Pensions can demand any information they deem relevant about a customer from banks, credit card companies, utility companies and phone companies without a warrant and without the customer being notified if they think the customer might be involved in benefit/tax fraud.

- The police can access confidential information held by the government or other public authorities without a warrant or any other oversight for the purposes of any criminal investigation. This information can even be shared with other polices forces overseas.

- In England and Wales, the Health Secretary can require confidential patient information to be handed over to any person or organisation specified.

- For various crimes a defendant has to prove his innocence, for example under the Terrorism Act 2000.

- The banning of peaceful protests that are unlicensed and the forceful ejection of Walter Wolfgang from the Labour Party Conference in Brighton in 2005 for daring to shout out 'nonsense' during a debate over Iraq – he was subsequently detained on suspected terrorist offences.

- The proliferation of CCTV cameras in UK (4.2 million in 2005, 20% of total global usage), making Britain the country with the most concentrated use of surveillance cameras in the world.

The human rights laws cannot override legislation passed by its national parliament even when it has been found to be incompatible with those human rights laws.

Attempts have been made to protect civil liberties through passage of the Human Rights Act 1998 and the Freedom of Information Act 2000. Also there are more ways in which an individual can access methods of redress of grievances (see previous spread).

Promoting equality through legislation

Certain legislation is in force in Britain which provides a legal framework for implementing equal opportunities in society. Legislation is seen as a vital plank in the protection and maintenance of rights and equality.

Equal opportunities, race relations and disability legislation

This covers a very broad area. The following table outlines some of the key legislation.

Legislation	Key coverage
The Equal Pay Act 1970 (EPA) (amended 1983)	Under this Act a person has a right to the same contractual pay and benefits as a person of the opposite sex in the same employment, providing: • the man and woman are doing like work • the work is rated as equivalent • the work is proved to be of equal value.
The Sex Discrimination Act (SDA) 1975 (amended 1986)	This applies to both sexes of any age, including children. It prohibits sex discrimination in: • employment • education • the provision of goods, services and facilities.
The Sex Discrimination (Gender Reassignment) Regulations 1999	These regulations have amended the Sex Discrimination Act to make it unlawful to treat a person less favourably because that person has undergone, intends to undergo or is undergoing gender reassignment.
The Employment Equality (Sexual Orientation) Regulations 2003	These regulations make it illegal to discriminate on the grounds of sexual orientation in employment or training.
Disability Discrimination Act (DDA) 1995 (came into effect 2004 and amended 2005)	This aims at ending the discrimination faced by many disabled people. It gave disabled people new rights in terms of employment and access to goods, facilities and services, education and public transport. The DDA requires 'reasonable adjustments' to be made by organisations supplying goods or services. Service providers should ensure, through making reasonable adjustments, that a person with a disability can gain access to the service or provision.
Race Relations Act 1976 and Race Relations (Amendment) Act 2000	This makes it unlawful to discriminate against anyone on grounds of race, colour, nationality (including citizenship), or ethnic or national origin. It applies to jobs, training, housing, education and the provision of goods, facilities and services.
Race Regulations 2003	These regulations incorporate the EU Race Directive into UK law. The Race Directive focuses on equal treatment between people, regardless of their racial or ethnic origin, and sets standards of protection for all EU member states. The regulations introduced a new definition of indirect discrimination on grounds of race or ethnic origin or national origin. There is also a new, statutory definition of harassment on grounds of race, ethnic or national origin.

Learning objectives

- Promoting equality through legislation
- Equal opportunities, race relations and disability legislation
- Positive discrimination – female shortlists and ethnic minorities in the police force
- Wealth redistribution – the welfare state and taxation

The Employment Equality (Religion or Belief) Regulations 2003	This offers protection for workers from discrimination and harassment at work on grounds of religion or belief. It covers all aspects of the employment relationship, including recruitment, pay, working conditions, training, promotion, dismissal and references.
Employment Equality (Age) Regulations 2006	These new regulations on age discrimination made ageism, age prejudice and age-based decisions in the workplace unlawful and covers direct and indirect discrimination, harassment and victimisation.

Positive discrimination – female shortlists and ethnic minorities in the police force

Political party selection

At the 2005 British general election, 98 Labour women MPs were returned compared with 17 Conservative women MPs, 10 from the Liberal Democrats and three from the Northern Ireland parties. The 128 women in the House of Commons constitute 20 per cent of all MPs. In a global ranking of parliaments based on the proportion of female members, Westminster is placed 47th, way behind the Welsh assembly, where 50 per cent of members are women and the Scottish parliament where the figure is 40 per cent. The Labour Party was the only political party to use all-female shortlists in the 2005 general election. The Sex Discrimination (Election Candidates) Act 2002 guarantees the legality of all-women shortlists until 2015.

Since 2005, the Conservatives have introduced the A-list – officially known as the priority list – containing high-flyers who the leader believes are essential to represent the country better. About 60 per cent of those on the list are female, reflecting David Cameron's view that the party needs more women MPs, and around 10 per cent are from ethnic minorities. The A-list is seen by party leaders as critical to persuading the public that the party is changing.

In the United States, positive discrimination or affirmative action is aimed at actively improving employment or educational opportunities for members of minority groups and for women. Affirmative action began as a government remedy to deal with the effects of long-standing discrimination against such groups. Policies, programmes, and procedures were introduced to give preference to minorities and women in accessing employment, higher education, government contracts, and other social benefits. The typical criteria for affirmative action are race, disability, gender, ethnic origin, and age.

Affirmative action was initiated by President Lyndon Johnson (1963–69) to improve opportunities for African-Americans; at the same time the legal basis for discrimination was being dismantled. By the late 1970s the use of racial quotas and minority set-asides led to court challenges against affirmative action as a form of 'reverse discrimination'. The first major challenge was Regents of the University of California vs Bakke (1978), in which the US Supreme Court ruled (5–4) that quotas may not be used to reserve places for minority applicants if white applicants are denied a chance to compete for those places.

The pros and cons of political parties adopting all-women shortlists are listed in the table.

Yes	No
Women are more than half the population, but less than 20 per cent of the House of Commons.	All-women shortlists are undemocratic and patronising, and lead men to question the merits of MPs chosen without open competition.
A heavily male legislature undervalues important issues such as child care, education, family health and equality at work.	The best women politicians have reached Parliament by showing they can stand up to men.
Leaving it to local party organisers to select women has been shown by experience not to work.	The Commons needs independent-minded MPs, not ones put there by party bosses.

The National Black Police Association favours setting quotas to increase the number of ethnic minority police officers; ten-year targets were set after the Macpherson report into the death of Stephen Lawrence in 1999, to make the police service more representative.

In 2007, chief constables in England and Wales discussed whether to boost the recruitment of black and Asian officers by 'affirmative action', but there were fears that it would require changes to employment law. Women would also be given priority in order to boost numbers. Critics branded the idea 'reverse discrimination' and suggested that the police should make itself more attractive to ethnic minorities. The Association of Chief Police Officers stated that raising the 3.7 per cent of officers from ethnic minorities to the Home Office's 7 per cent target by 2009 cannot be done without changing policy. The Metropolitan Police Commissioner at the time, Sir Ian Blair, said that recruitment from ethnic minorities in his force was close to 20 per cent but he admitted his force would not reach the 2009 target of 25 per cent black and Asian officers in the police workforce.

Wealth redistribution – the welfare state and taxation

The welfare state is a concept of government in which the state plays a key role in the protection and promotion of the economic and social well-being of its citizens. It is based on the principles of equality of opportunity, equitable distribution of wealth, and public responsibility for those unable to avail themselves of the minimal provisions for a good life. The general term can cover various forms of economic and social organisation.

A fundamental feature of the welfare state is some form of social insurance, a provision common to most advanced industrialised countries (e.g. National Insurance in Britain). Such insurance is usually financed by compulsory contributions and is intended to provide benefits to persons and families during periods of greatest need. It is widely recognised, however, that in practice these cash benefits fall considerably short of the levels intended.

The welfare state also usually includes public provision of basic education, health services and housing (in some cases at low cost or without charge). In these respects the welfare state is considerably more extensive in western European countries than in the US, featuring in many cases comprehensive health coverage and provision of state-subsidised education.

Anti-poverty programmes and the system of personal taxation may also be regarded as aspects of the welfare state. Personal taxation falls into this category insofar as its progressivity is used to achieve greater justice in income distribution (rather than merely to raise revenue) and also insofar as it is used to finance social insurance payments and other benefits not completely financed by compulsory contributions. In socialist countries the welfare state also covers employment and administration of consumer prices.

The modern use of the term is associated with the comprehensive measures of social insurance adopted in 1948 (introduced 1946) by Britain on the basis of the report on *Social Insurance and Allied Services* (1942) by Sir William (later Lord) Beveridge. In the 20th century, the earlier concept of the passive, laissez-faire state was gradually abandoned; almost all states have sought to provide at least some of the measures of social insurance associated with the welfare state. In the United States, the New Deal of Roosevelt, the Fair Deal of Truman, and a large part of the domestic programmes of later presidents were based on welfare state principles. In Britain the new liberal ideas of William Beveridge on tackling the '5 giants on the road to reconstruction' were taken on board by the socialist administration of Clement Attlee. This provided the basis of an all-party consensus upon the needs of the welfare state that lasted until the election of Margaret Thatcher in 1979.

In its complete form, the welfare state provides state aid for the individual in almost all phases of his life – 'from the cradle to the grave' – as exemplified in The Netherlands and in the social democratic governments of the Scandinavian countries. Many less developed countries have the establishment of some form of welfare state as their goal. The principal problems in the administration of a welfare state are: determining the desirable level of provision of services by the state; ensuring that the system of personal benefits and contributions meets the needs of individuals and families while at the same time offering sufficient incentives for productive work; ensuring efficiency in the operation of state monopolies and bureaucracies; and the equitable provision of resources to finance the services over and above the contributions of direct beneficiaries.

A statue of Roosevelt in Washington DC

DISCUSSION POINT ?

Is affirmative action just discrimination with a different name?

Social justice theories

Social justice is seen as a morally justifiable distribution of wealth and a greater commitment to equality. It tends to be embodied in social democracy with the idea of expanding the collective ownership of wealth, coupled with the acceptance that individuals need to be self-reliant and that market efficiency is vital for broader and sustained prosperity.

Marxists and socialists take the view that capitalism will never provide a just distribution of resources or rewards. The system itself is essentially riddled with inequalities and by simply taking inequality out of capitalism the system would fail to work because capitalism relies on incentives and inequalities at its heart. A form of rational distribution of rewards is needed to replace capitalism.

More modern-day socialists take the view that social justice can be achieved within capitalism. Typically they would involve themselves in setting minimum wages, granting trade union rights, using taxation to redistribute wealth, and create and enforce equal opportunity legislation. The distribution of rewards would still be largely governed by capitalism and by market forces. But the state itself would then intervene as necessary in order to ensure social justice. This became the basis for justifying interventionist welfare legislation by social democratic and liberal governments across Europe post-1945.

The main problem is to set what is an acceptable or reasonable just distribution. Absolute equality of rewards is probably not achievable and there will always be scarce resources that people will compete to obtain. In a socialist system a way forward could be to assign rewards according to the value of an individual's contribution. Socialists would argue that this incorporates incentives and has a natural justice about it.

The reality is, however, that social justice has generally come to mean distributive justice and the question is how much inequality can be tolerated in the society before the state has to step in. Welfare socialists seek to create a minimum standard of living, which implies redistribution of income from rich to poor. Above this base level there would be inequality. The state would ensure equality of opportunity through education and training.

Social democrats regard inequality as inevitable. Many moderate socialists accept the formula proposed by John Rawls (1972) for social justice, in which he proposed two principles of justice. Firstly, he suggested that all individuals should have equal right to basic liberties, as long as they are compatible with universal liberties. Secondly, he suggested that any social or economic inequalities must be reasonable in the sense that they are to everyone's advantage and that the benefits of greater social and economic advantage are only attached to positions in society that are open to all individuals.

Rawls accepts that inequalities are natural and in certain cases desirable, but that they need to be justified. The view is that a just society should provide freedom, equality of opportunity, it should dismantle barriers to individual advancement and it should protect the poorest members of society from being exploited by those that wish to enrich themselves.

The future of the welfare state

The British welfare state emerged in 1945, and the debate on how to reform it has never ceased. Debate about the inadequacies of the model began shortly after the Labour government implemented the Beveridge report on national insurance and created the NHS on 1 July 1948. Labour introduced what Professor David Gordon (Bristol University) dubbed 'truncated universalism'. By this he meant that the level of contributory benefits was too low to take people out of poverty.

Consequently, the first 25 years after the welfare state was introduced, the debate concerned how to increase its scope and abolish means-tested benefits. From the 1970s, the concern was how to trim it back.

Right-wing theory holds that excessive spending on the welfare state has weakened economic growth and reduced incentives. These New Right arguments, inspired by the writings of Keith Joseph and Theodore von Hayek, became the basis for the Thatcherite attempts to 'roll back' the state after 1979 with an emphasis on privatisation, withdrawal of government subsidies and opening up the public sector to free-market competition. Left-wing critics of the traditional welfare state however argue that it has paid too little attention to important groups like women and ethnic minorities, and to concerns of social justice in the household, workplace, and community.

Some argue that the strength of economic growth in the US, and its weakness in the Eurozone, stems from the generosity of the European welfare state. Other economists dispute whether welfare state spending has any correlation with economic growth. Peter Lindert (University of California) argued that there is no connection in the long term between high government spending and economic growth. He suggests that most welfare states have been designed in practice to avoid the labour disincentive effects.

Welfare states have proved difficult to dismantle politically whatever the economic arguments; Thatcher could only roll back the state to a limited extent on welfare reform, finding considerable resistance to any attempt to reform the NHS in particular. Bush found it difficult to reform the social security system, the heart of the US welfare state, which provides old-age pensions.

However, the British welfare state now has a greater emphasis on means testing and the involvement of the private sector (such as pension provision). When New Labour came to power in 1997 it was determined to make a clean break with Labour's past record as the party of 'tax and spend'. On the agenda was welfare reform. New Labour wanted benefit recipients to pull their weight, expressed as a 'rights and responsibilities' approach. Benefit recipients were to be encouraged into work and to retrain rather than remain on the dole. The emphasis was on a 'hand up not a hand out' approach. This has been particularly true in the area of those claiming incapacity benefits, with the government setting itself demanding targets aimed at reducing the figure of one million benefit claimants in 2005. This issue caused considerable difficulties for Tony Blair when in 1999 a rebellion by 66 Labour backbench MPs over reduction in benefits to single-parent mothers saw him only narrowly win the Commons vote.

Another part of the New Labour agenda was to tackle the 'social exclusion' of groups of the poor who lacked not just income but access to social institutions.

Many claim that Gordon Brown decided to introduce 'redistribution by stealth' by sharply increasing benefits to poor families in work paid through a system of tax credits.

However, Labour's plans have had their own problems and echo many previous debates. The first minister responsible for welfare reform, Frank Field, clashed with the then chancellor, Gordon Brown, over the extension of means-tested benefits. Brown believed that this approach was too expensive.

Labour's emphasis on people's responsibility to seek work harks back to the principles of the liberal welfare state that were only partially obscured by the Beveridge report. The means-tested (or tax credit) benefit system is the latest attempt to reconcile a desire for the state to ensure that everyone has a 'national minimum' income with the lack of resources to pay for a universal benefit. Probably the biggest challenge facing the UK welfare system is how to pay for retirement. So far the government has avoided making tough decisions – such as introducing a compulsory savings scheme, or substantially increasing state pensions, instead piloting only voluntary stakeholder pension schemes.

DISCUSSION POINT ?

Does the welfare state have a future in Britain?

Relax and prepare

Here are some sample essay questions for unit F854. How would you go about answering them?

- Compare and contrast the different types of rights.

- Discuss the different perspectives on the balance between rights and responsibilities.

- Discuss the view that 'we have a right to be unequal'.

- Compare and contrast the different types of equality.

- Discuss at which point liberty can be said to be transformed into licence.

- Discuss the extent to which society must show political toleration.

Refresh your memory

Look at the table below and use it to help you structure your revision for unit F854.

Topic	Key issues	Relevant theory
Rights – Definition	Understanding of term and historical role	Heywood
Typology	Consider moral and legal attitudes and how this links to natural, human and animal rights	Hohfeld, Bentham, Locke, Jefferson, Aquinas, Regan, Singer
Relationship between rights and responsibilities	Different ideological perspectives especially conservative, social contract theories, liberal and socialist	Plato, J. S. Mill, Burke, Rousseau, Hobbes, Locke, Marx, Rawls
Liberty – Definition	Understanding of term and literal translation	J. S. Mill and MacCallum
Distinction between positive and negative liberty	Ideological perspectives on the role of the state in promoting/protecting the two forms of liberty	Berlin, Hobbes, J. S. Mill, Green, Marx, Rousseau, Beveridge
Licence and toleration	Dangers of excessive liberty and the importance of political toleration	J. S. Mill, Nozick, Tawney, Milton, Locke, Falwell
Equality – Definition	Understanding of the term and historical importance	Heywood
Typology	Formal, opportunity, and outcome/wealth – including different ideological perspectives	Locke, France, Rousseau, Wollstonecroft, J. S. Mill, Young, Marx, Hayek
Social justice	Needs, rights and deserts based theories	Rawls, Marx, Maslow, Nozick, Locke, Hume, MacPherson, Burke, Spencer
Balance between liberty and equality	Compatibility of models of liberty and equality	J. S. Mill, Tawney, France, Marx

Get the result !

Here are some practice questions for unit F854. How would you go about answering them?

- How far has the balance between individual rights and national security changed since 9/11 in the UK?

- Do animals deserve the same amount of rights protection as humans both in theory and in practice?

- How effective has positive discrimination been in addressing inequality in the UK?

- Discuss the view that in theory and in practice individual liberty is more important than equality.

- Discuss the view that a welfare state is essential for the promotion of social justice in society.

- How far are civil liberties under threat in the UK?

Case studies on rights, liberty and equality

By using the theory you have learnt for F854 research the following topics and think about how they might be used in essays for unit F856.

✓ Anti-terrorism legislation post-2001 in the UK (amendments to the 2000 Terrorism Act through the Anti-Terrorism, Crime and Security Act 2001 [ATCSA], Prevention of Terrorism Act 2005, Terrorism Act 2006, and the proposed Terrorism Bill 2008).

✓ Anti-discriminatory legislation passed in the UK since the 1970s regarding gender, race, disability, sexuality and age (e.g. 1995 Disability Discrimination Act [came into effect 2004], the Employment Equality (Sexual Orientation) Regulations 2003 and the Employment Equality (Religion and Belief) Regulations 2003).

✓ The Labour Party's all-female shortlist policy versus the Conservative A-list scheme.

✓ Changes to the UK welfare state under successive Conservative and Labour administrations since 1979 (for instance the move away from 'hand out to hand up' culture impacting upon benefits claimants including the long-term disabled and lone parents, as well as introducing private-sector style organisation of public sector services in health and education).

✓ Recent legislation banning smoking in public places throughout the UK (e.g. England 2007), as well as government directives designed to tackle obesity particularly amongst children (e.g. £372 million pledged to tackle the issue in January 2008 through the introduction of strategic reduction targets and the introduction of traffic light labelling of food).

✓ The impact of the Human Rights Act and Freedom of Information Act upon civil liberties protection in the UK.

✓ The debate over the Danish cartoons depicting Mohammed and controversies surrounding Muslim women in the UK wearing the full veil.

The following are the type of essay questions that may occur in your exam for units F854 and F856. To improve your chances of achieving a high mark you should plan your essays before answering the questions. The suggestions below show you how this can be done.

Examine whether liberty and equality are compatible.

Exam tips

Introduction

Outline the meaning of equality and liberty – highlighting the flexibility of the two concepts. Introduce Berlin's distinction between negative and positive liberty.

Compare negative liberty with forms of equality

Highlight how only formal equality can be seen to be compatible, with opportunity and outcome requiring state action that inevitably limits liberty in its negative form.

Remember to use advocates of negative liberty such as Hobbes and Locke to highlight this. Note questioning as to whether formal equality is in fact any real sense of equality by theorists such as Anatole France and R. H. Tawney.

Compare positive liberty with forms of equality

Note greater potential for compatibility with equal opportunity and limited outcome, however complete equality of outcome as advocated by Marxist and other revolutionary socialists even exclude this form of liberty. Note that modern liberal thinkers such as J. S. Mill and T. H. Green and democratic socialists such as Tawney and Crosland highlight this compatibility, but note how Marx rejects the concept of individual liberty to advocate complete equality of outcome.

Conclusion

Liberty and equality are not ideal type concepts but can be viewed as a continuum with societies and theorists needing to strike a balance between the two.

Get the result !

This is the type of exam question you may be asked for unit F856.

Evaluate the extent to which rights are protected in the UK both in theory and practice.

Exam tips

To help plan this essay try and divide up rights protection in the UK into four areas: arguments for and against rights protection in the UK in theory and also in practice.

Effectiveness of UK rights protection	Theory	Practice
For	A.V. Dicey – traditional checks and balances in UK protection rights including the rule of law Bentham championing of legal rights above moral codes of rights	Common law principles protecting residual rights, e.g. right to free speech (dating back to Magna Carta 1215) Adherence to international treaty obligations on human rights such as UN Declaration of Human Rights and participation in the European Court of Human Rights Modern legislation protecting minority rights, e.g. Equal Pay Act, Race Relations Act and Disability Discrimination Act Human Rights Act 1998 – codifying into UK law certain articles of the European Convention of Human Rights
Against	Paine's advocacy of the universal 'rights of man' as a basis for the need for a written constitution The Founding Fathers' attitude towards written constitution and need for clear separation of powers, e.g. Madison and Jefferson and Montesquieu's belief in a formal separation of powers Hailsham's theory of UK as an 'elective dictatorship'	UK legislation often impinges upon residual rights, see impact of anti-terrorism legislation introduced as a result of IRA terrorism and 9/11 Lack of formal codified or entrenched Bill of Rights making rights legislation vulnerable to amendment and repeal – note Conservative Party attitudes towards the HRA Parliamentary sovereignty seen as above rule of law, limiting power of new Supreme Court and allowing derogation from articles of ECHR with executive and legislative approval, e.g. extension of detention of terror suspects to 28 days and potentially 42. Note also UK opt out of EU Declaration on Fundamental Human Rights

The law of a state encompasses the rules of society setting out the rights and responsibilities of the citizens so that they can live together peacefully and safely (as far as is possible). It tells people what is and isn't acceptable under the law. The rule of law is seen as a guarantee of citizens' liberty and not a restraint on it. It protects individuals from one another and society from the individual. In return the citizen has an obligation to behave in certain ways that does not violate the law.

However others have a different view of the law. Marxists see it as protecting certain members of society (private property owners) and sustaining social injustice. Feminists see it as biased in favour of men and multiculturalists claim it doesn't take into account the values and concerns of minorities.

The law is seen as aiming to help to bring about order in society. It does this by threatening to punish anyone who steps out of line from the accepted legal ways of behaving, and punishing them if they do. In the view of some punishment is justified simply because the individual being punished has committed a crime; in some cases the view is that the punishment should fit the crime. Others see punishment as being directed towards changing the behaviour of the offender so that they do not in future re-offend.

Laws are sometimes violated in the cause of a moral principle, as in acts of non-violent civil disobedience. Such acts are not directed at disrupting the order of society but rather at exerting pressure on those in power (government) to persuade them to make meaningful political, social and economic changes. The law in such cases is not being rejected wholly.

There are presently fears that the rule of law in Britain, under which all citizens in Britain are treated equally, is under threat from new legislation, particularly that directed at countering terrorist threats, which could infringe certain rights of citizens. The rule of law after all is directly linked to the implementation of citizens' rights. And this is crucial to prevent disorder in society.

In its role as interpreter of the rule of law, the judiciary is vital in protecting the citizen against abuse of their rights, in particular legislation on human rights, and for this reason it needs to operate as a separate power to that of the political executive (the government).

These are some of the issues covered in this chapter, in which the following are key themes.

- The function of law in helping to bring order to society and protecting the rights of citizens

- The way in which order comes about in society

- The various theories as to how punishment can be justified

- Interpretations of the different kinds of justice

- The theories as to what the obligation of citizens to the state means

- The theories and different forms of civil disobedience

- The significance of the rule of law in terms of sovereignty and the European Union

- The role of the judiciary in adjudicating on British common law and European Union legislation as it affects Britain

- Public attitudes on how law is enforced to maintain order in society

- Civil disobedience and terrorism as strategies to arouse political awareness and promote change in society

In covering these themes the chapter is broken down into the following topics.

The chapter finishes with an exam café feature on page 174.

Learning objectives

- What is law?
- Natural and positive law
- Key thinkers

What is law?

Law is essentially a group of rules that have been developed to make sure citizens know their rights and responsibilities. This aims to ensure people can live together safely and peacefully. Laws tell citizens what behaviour is acceptable, and what is not acceptable. Individuals talk about 'the law' when they talk about all the laws of the country, and also about the people who put them into force. Britain's laws come from a number of sources.

- Common law comes from basic ideas of justice, built up over many centuries based upon senior judicial rulings.
- Statutes are laws passed by parliament (e.g. Human Rights Act (1998) which incorporated the European Convention on Human Rights into British law).
- Courts have to decide how laws work in practice. They usually use earlier court decisions as a guide when they do this. These earlier decisions are called 'precedents'.
- Local authorities can have laws that apply in their area of authority – these are called bylaws or secondary legislation.
- Britain is a member of the European Union, so European laws and conventions are also part of the law. There are also international laws and conventions which determine the actions of governments and other bodies.

Natural and positive law

Natural law is a system of rights or justice held to be common to all humans and derived from nature rather than from the rules of society, or positive law. There have been several disagreements over the meaning of natural law and its relation to positive law. Positive law is law that has been laid down by a particular body or convention (i.e. by the sovereign or by a legislature). Positive law can also be an accumulation of customary rights.

St Augustine of Hippo (354–430) developed the idea of man having lived freely under natural law before his fall and subsequent bondage under sin and positive law. In the 12th century, Gratian, an Italian monk and father of the study of canon law, equated natural law with divine law – that is, with the revealed law of the Old and the New Testament, in particular the Christian version of the Golden Rule.

The Franciscan philosophers John Duns Scotus (1266–1308) and William of Ockham (c. 1285–1347/49) and the Spanish theologian Francisco Suárez (1548–1617), emphasised divine will instead of divine reason as the source of law. This 'voluntarism' influenced the Roman Catholic jurisprudence of the Counter-Reformation in the 16th and early 17th centuries, but the Thomistic doctrine was later revived and reinforced to become the main philosophical ground for the papal exposition of natural right in the social teaching of Pope Leo XIII (1810–1903) and his successors.

Hugo Grotius (1583–1645) claimed that nations were subject to natural law and his fellow Calvinist Johannes Althusius (1557–1638) had proceeded from theological doctrines of predestination to elaborate his theory of a universally binding law. Grotius insisted on the validity of the natural law 'even if we were to suppose…that God does not exist or is not concerned with human affairs'. Grotius and Hobbes stand together at the head of that 'school of natural law' that, in accordance with the tendencies of the Enlightenment, tried to construct a whole edifice of law by rational deduction from a hypothetical 'state of nature' and a 'social contract' of consent between rulers and subjects.

In France Charles-Louis de Secondat Montesquieu (1689–1755) argued that natural laws were pre-social and superior to those of religion and the state, and Jean-Jacques Rousseau (1712–78) postulated a savage who was virtuous in isolation and actuated by two principles 'prior to reason': self-preservation and compassion (innate repugnance to the sufferings of others).

The confidence in appeals to natural law displayed by 17th- and 18th-century writers such as Locke and the authors of the American Declaration of Independence evaporated in the early 19th century. The philosophy of Immanuel Kant (1724–1804), as well as the utilitarianism of Jeremy Bentham (1748–1832), served to weaken the belief that 'nature' could be the source of moral or legal norms. In the mid-20th century, however, there was a revival of interest in natural law, sparked by the widespread belief that the Nazi regime in Germany had been essentially lawless, even though it also had been the source of a significant amount of positive law. As in previous centuries, the need to challenge the unjust laws of particular states inspired the desire to invoke rules of right and justice held to be natural rather than merely conventional. However, the 19th century's scepticism about invoking nature as a source of moral and legal norms remained powerful, and contemporary writers almost invariably talked of human rights rather than natural rights.

Legal realism is defined as a belief that law is a product of human action. As a result, it is the result of the aims of different groups and individuals. Legal realists emphasise the importance of human will and the fallibility in the law making and interpretation processes. Oliver Wendell Holmes (1841–1935) set the tone for the movement in 1873 when he wrote:

> The life of the law has not been logic; it has been experience. The felt necessities of the time, the prevalent moral and political theories, intuitions of public policy avowed or unconscious, even with the prejudices which judges share with their fellow-men, have had a great deal more to do than the syllogism in determining the rules by which men should be governed. The law embodies the story of a nation's development through many centuries, and it cannot be dealt with as if it contained only the axioms and corollaries of a book of mathematics.

H. L. A. (Herbert) Hart's *The Concept of Law* (1961) attempted to explain law in relation to its purpose in society. Hart believed that law comes from 'the union of primary and secondary rules', each of which has a function. Primary rules aim to set out social behaviour and to regulate it (such as criminal law). Secondary rules actually set out the powers institutions have to make the primary rules (i.e. how the legislature makes the rules and how the judiciary enforces, adjudicates and validates them).

Hobbes on the state of nature

Thomas Hobbes (1588–1679), starting from the assumption of a savage 'state of nature' in which each man was at war with every other – rather than from the 'state of innocence' in which man had lived in the biblical Garden of Eden – defined the right of nature (*jus naturale*) to be 'the liberty each man hath to use his own power for the preservation of his own nature, that is to say, of life', and a law of nature (*lex naturalis*) as 'a precept of general rule found out by reason, by which a man is forbidden to do that which is destructive of his life'. He then enumerated the elementary rules on which peace and society could be established.

Hart on the concept of law

Herbert Hart in *The Concept of Law* (1961) produced a critique of John Austin's theory that law is the command of the sovereign backed by the threat of punishment. Hart made a distinction between primary and secondary legal rules, where a primary rule governs conduct and a secondary rule allows of the creation, alteration, or extinction of primary rules.

Locke on observing natural law

John Locke (1632–1704) departed from Hobbesian pessimism to the extent of describing the state of nature as a state of society, with free and equal men already observing the natural law.

Aquinas on natural law

St Thomas Aquinas (c. 1224/25–1274) maintained that though the eternal law of divine reason is unknowable to us in its perfection as it exists in God's mind, it is known to us in part not only by revelation but also by the operations of our reason. The law of nature, which is 'nothing else than the participation of the eternal law in the rational creature', thus comprises those precepts that humankind is able to formulate – namely, the preservation of one's own good, the fulfilment of 'those inclinations which nature has taught to all animals', and the pursuit of the knowledge of God. Human law must be the particular application of natural law.

Austin on positive law and morality

Austin was an English jurist who in his writings, especially *The Province of Jurisprudence Determined* (1832), advocated a definition of law as a species of command and sought to distinguish positive law from morality. He had little influence during his lifetime outside the circle of utilitarian supporters of Jeremy Bentham.

DISCUSSION POINT

What do you understand to be the differences between natural and positive law?

The rule of law

The rule of law is an aspect of the British constitution that has been particularly emphasised by the 19th century constitutional writer A. V. Dicey. It involves:

- the rights of individuals being determined by legal rules and not the arbitrary behaviour of authorities

- there being no punishment unless a court decides there has been a breach of law

- everyone, regardless of their position in society, being subject to the law.

Liberals tend to regard the rule of law not necessarily as a constraint, but as a way in which liberty can be guaranteed. In their view, without law to protect them an individual is under threat from other parts of society and society is under threat from that individual.

As we will see there are different ways in which the rule of law is enshrined within the political system of different countries. But broadly the view is that the rule of law ensures a government of laws and not a government of men.

In the United States the US Constitution expressly states the supremacy of the law. It is there to provide checks and balances and the Bill of Rights ensures the individual rights of American citizens. The US Constitution in its 5th and 14th amendments expressly forbids either federal or state government to deny an individual their property, liberty or life without 'due process of law'. This idea restricts the power of officials and makes concrete the rights of individuals. However, considerable power is put into the hands of judges who must interpret the law.

The importance of the rule of law

The British constitution has developed over the centuries. It is an uncodified constitutional system, it has laws that are derived from customs and traditions, and individuals have rights and duties as laid down in common law. As far as A. V. Dicey was concerned the rule of law had four key features.

- Firstly, he maintained that no individual should ever be punished unless they had breached the law. This was an important consideration, as it clearly stated that the rule of law binds governments to stick to the rules. The rule of law exists to limit a government's ability to act as it pleases without any restriction and to punish individuals because it objects to them. In other words, arbitrary government is unacceptable.

- Everyone should be equal before the law. Dicey called this equal subjection. The law should not respect anyone's rank or privilege, neither should it treat less fairly nor discriminate against an individual on the grounds of their gender, race or social background. As important, it should apply to both citizens and government officials.

- People should be under no illusion that if they break the law then they will have to submit to a punishment. The rule of law can only operate correctly if it is applied to all circumstances and at all times. There must be no selectivity about who should be punished and who should not be punished. If a law is broken then regardless of the circumstances or potential consequences that individual should be punished if appropriate.

- There should be within the rule of law absolute guarantees of an individual's rights and liberties. If an individual's rights are violated then they have the automatic right and access to the legal system to receive redress.

The British system of government is actually often at odds with the rule of law. The idea of the rule of law is challenged by the fact that there is parliamentary sovereignty and the legislature is not bound by external constraints. It can therefore do as it pleases. This is a particular problem, as parliament itself no longer really drives policy and legislation. This is now in the hands of the executive and parliament is controlled by the executive and by party discipline. This has often led to the British political system being described as an elective dictatorship.

Parliament has the role of determining civil liberty and not the courts, even though we have a Human Rights Act (1998). This has recently been brought into sharp focus by the extension of the detention of terror suspects from 28 to 42 days (June 2008).

As Britain has an uncodified constitution, it may mean that to ensure that the country has a meaningful rule of law that considerable constitutional change needs to take place. This could mean a Bill of Rights, a clear indication of the separation of powers between the executive and the legislature, and a codification of the constitution.

The rule of law has broader implications. It should aim to limit how laws are made and how laws are judged. It should also effectively rule out the prospect of there being cruel or inhuman punishment for a breach of the law. Issues such as retrospective legislation, which effectively criminalises an activity that took place in the past at a time when the activity was not illegal, are also unacceptable as far as the rule of law is concerned.

It is also important to ensure that the judiciary remains independent and outside government.

Critics of the rule of law suggest that it is nothing more than simply saying that everyone should obey the law. Marxists of course view the rule of law in an entirely different way. They see it not as ensuring liberty, but as a means of protecting the capitalist system by ensuring that property is protected. In Marxist views, law is there to ensure that individuals retain their private property, that social inequality remains and that the ruling class hold on to their domination of society.

Feminists would claim that there are inherent biases within the system that favour men, and multiculturalists suggest that the system only reflects the dominant cultural group and takes no account of the values or concerns of minorities.

Albert Venn Dicey

Dicey was a British jurist whose *An Introduction to the Study of the Law of the Constitution* (1885) is considered part of the British constitution, which is an amalgam of several written and unwritten authorities. Dicey taught law at the University of Oxford (1882–1909), where he was Vinerian Professor of English Law and a fellow of All Souls College, and served as principal of the Working Men's College, London (1899–1912).

DISCUSSION POINT ?

Are A. V. Dicey's criteria for the basis of the rule of law too idealistic?

Learning objectives

- Meaning and origins of order
- Conservatives on discipline and control
- Socialists and anarchists on natural theory

Thomas Hobbes on absolute government

Hobbes believed that absolute government was the only way in which order could be maintained. He believed that humans had a 'perpetual and restless desire for power, that ceaseth only in death'.

Edmund Burke on organic society

As a founding father of Anglo-American conservative tradition, Burke saw society as an organic living entity. Each part of society is inextricably linked to one another and in a delicate state of balance. He believed that the glue that holds society together is the traditional institutions that establish culture, tradition, custom and religion. These are the fabric of society. He would hold that social order is of vital importance, but a fragile concept.

Meaning and origins of order

Social contract theorists of the 17th century were concerned with order and social stability and looked for ways in which to describe how this could be achieved to prevent society from lapsing into chaos. Theorists such as Hobbes believed that without some form of stability and order then life would be 'solitary, poor, nasty, brutish and short'.

Order and its attainment is a key issue for many political theorists. For traditional conservatives the creation and maintenance of order requires obedience, discipline and control. On the other side of the political spectrum, anarchists believe that order has everything to do with balance and natural harmony. Theorists have no particular common ground as to how order can be established and once established how it can be maintained.

However, there are some areas of common ground.

- Order implies some kind of regularity or pattern. There should be some level of stability and predictability in behaviour.

- Social order should mean that some kind of continuity or permanence for society can be obtained.

- Social disorder is seen as being characterised by random and violent behaviour, by instability and rapid change.

- Obtaining order and the reason for desiring some kind of order is individual security. This implies freedom from violence, intimidation and a degree of comfort and stability for all individuals.

It is important to make a distinction between political and natural order.

- Political order is often seen as a form of social control that is imposed from above by both government and the law. It is therefore closely associated with authority, regulation and the requirement to adhere to a degree of discipline.

- Natural order derives from individuals and their voluntary adherence to certain codes of practice and behaviour. It implies a degree of equilibrium and social harmony that is naturally occurring in society.

Conservatives on discipline and control

Conservatives are broadly of the opinion that crime, social unrest, delinquency, anti-social and uncivilised behaviour are all as a result of individuals being naturally corrupt. Without some form of restraint there will undoubtedly be disorder. This harks back to the Christian doctrine of original sin, which characterises human beings as being self-centred and if left to themselves they will always follow actions that are to their own benefit, and at the expense of others.

Hobbes in particular was pessimistic about the way in which most individuals would behave.

Conservatives therefore view criminals as being essentially bad and, as such, they need to be treated accordingly. For them law and order are inextricably linked. Order needs to be enforced by law. They therefore stand at the forefront of increasing the powers of the police and the courts to meet out stiffer sentences to criminals. They are not particularly concerned with the root causes of anti-social behaviour, but focus instead on providing the means by which the police and courts can handle the consequences of criminality.

Law is a way of maintaining order, as it threatens punishment to the offender, whilst simultaneously reinforcing traditional beliefs and values. Order is also important on a psychological level. It aims to provide individuals with safety and security. It also tackles unconventional behaviour, from which most of society feels threatened. For example, conservatives are opposed to unchecked immigration without a system by which the immigrants are forced to assimilate into the host culture.

Socialists and anarchists on natural theory

In an anarchist society with no state as such there would be no formalised law and order. Marx believed that law and order would no longer be necessary as an apparatus once social equality had been established.

Socialist and liberal governments, however, have taken the view that social order can take the form of spontaneous harmony, which is regulated by the natural sense of individuals. They claim that disorder does not come from the individual but from society and that in some way there is a link between the ills of society and the level of criminality. Order is not achieved through threat of punishment, but by sweeping social reforms.

Marxists and many anarchists would claim that disorder is derived directly from economic inequality. Capitalism breeds social disorder through competitiveness and self-interest. If social solidarity and cooperative behaviour are fostered then social order would be easy to maintain. Anarchists believe that law is a major culprit for causing crime and disorder. They believe that law is just a way of protecting the wealthy from the poor and it is the use of naked power, an oppressive force and, as Leo Tolstoy said, 'organised violence'. He also said 'by blows, by deprivation of liberty and by murder punishment is used by law'.

The general belief is that order is a natural state. There is a natural order. Humans are rational with the ability to solve problems between one another by means other than violence. Common humanity is therefore behind social order, as individuals feel concern, sympathy and compassion towards one another.

Peter Kropotkin on liberty and fraternal care

A Russian, Kropotkin (1842–1921) was a strong supporter of anarchism and believed that order could only be obtained by liberty and fraternal care. He also suggested that crime was as a result of 'idleness, law and authority'.

William Godwin on sound reason and truth

An English political philosopher, Godwin (1756–1836) was a radical liberal rationalist with anarchist beliefs. He was an individualist and was of the opinion that 'sound reason and truth' was all that was required to prevent conflict in society that would lead to disorder.

Jean-Jacques Rousseau on original sin

Rousseau was of the opinion that human beings are born pure and do not have original sin, but rather it was society that corrupted them. In *The Social Contract* (1762) he wrote: 'Man is born free but is everywhere in chains.' In effect Rousseau was making a link between social deprivation and crime.

DISCUSSION POINT ?

Is order in society essentially positive or negative?

Retribution, deterrents and rehabilitation theories

The concept of retribution is a theory of punishment based on the idea of just deserts, or the punishment fitting the crime, and it suggests that the offender deserves the punishment because of the crime that has been committed. As such, the punishment should not be excessive. The Old Testament phrase 'an eye for an eye, tooth for a tooth' is the notion that for every wrong done there should be a compensating measure of justice. It is derived from the Code of Hammurabi (Hammurabi was King of Babylon, 1792–1750 BC) and can be found in Matthew 5:38. Mahatma Gandhi used the phrase 'An eye for an eye, and soon the whole world is blind' in reference to his Satyagraha philosophy of non-violent resistance.

Retributive theory emerged from the 17th and 18th centuries to replace what was effectively revenge. It permitted revenge to become a humanised approach to punishment, which is not excessive but is calibrated to match the seriousness of the crime. The criminal makes reparation to society by suffering a just punishment.

Retribution is also a way in which the state can act on behalf of society to show disapproval or censure of the crime. Censure is more than just the extraction of reparation; it suggests that a criminal should not have carried out the crime and just because they are now being punished does not wipe the slate clean. However, there is still a sense in that having suffered the punishment the individual can become a full member of society once again. Retribution theory focuses primarily on the past behaviours of an offender. The offender is not making direct reparation to the victim, but indirectly via the state.

The theory also suggests that it is the duty of the state to punish offenders, not on the basis of deterrents because retribution confirms the free will of the offender. A human has a choice of not committing the crime; it is their own moral responsibility and punishment is a recognition that a criminal act was chosen rather than simply being an impulse over which the offender had no control. These views accord with theories suggested by Kant and Hegel.

Deterrent theory links to the future behaviour of an offender; in other words, what punishment is needed to stop them doing it again. Deterrents therefore focus on the nature of the offender and are orientated towards the control of crime rather than due process. For this reason deterrent is often referred to as utilitarianism, such as that suggested by theorists like Jeremy Bentham and the fact that punishment benefits the interests of the maximum majority in society. Deterrents are also referred to as consequentialism.

One of the problems with deterrents is that if the gain for the crime is more than the pain of the punishment then the offender will undoubtedly offend again.

Rehabilitation and incapacitation place an emphasis on the state's role in reducing crime. They are seen as a way in which to move beyond deterrent theory. Rehabilitation focuses on attempting to change an offender's outlook on life so that they will not offend again in the future. This can be attempted in a number of different ways. Psychological intervention, such as therapy and education, can be focused on changing an offender's personality (such as making them less aggressive). Education and training could also be used, so that the offender now has minimal life skills.

Kant on punishment

Kant believed that it is wrong to punish people for utilitarian reasons. Legal punishment must always be a response to guilt. If the motive in punishing someone is to deter others, or to protect society, or to set an example, then the person punished is wronged; their humanity has not been respected. Punishment must always be in response to guilt. Guilt is a necessary condition for punishment, but that the guilty must be punished otherwise justice and equality, the foundations for the law, will not have been served. Equality is the principle that must be used in punishment.

There is always, however, a tension between retribution and rehabilitation. The focus of both of these concepts is entirely different. On the one hand retribution demands an appropriate level of punishment, whilst rehabilitation may focus on re-education. Individuals may also face circumstances when they may only be released on completion of a rehabilitation programme and this does not strictly accord with retribution theory.

Incapacitation is removing an individual from society through being in prison and hence protecting the public. It does not necessarily tackle the issue of reoffending and neither does it necessarily imply that there should be a definite sentence or tariff for a particular crime; it is merely removing that individual as a danger to the rest of society.

Victims and criminals

The most important form of punishment in modern society is seen as the deprivation of an individual's liberty or resources. This can take the form of either imprisonment or other restrictions on their freedom. Restrictions are often measured in terms of time or money, which raises the concept of tariff; in other words, a calculation as to how much time or punishment needs to be metered out to match a particular crime.

There is enormous inequality and diversity in society. Inequalities on the one hand produce different motives to commit crime. On the other hand, however, fines also are relative. The question often posed is whether the same fine should be imposed for a particular crime on both the rich and poor offender, given that the punishment will have a different impact on each, producing a greater or less effect on their respective resources.

The same can be said for age and background, perhaps taking into account previous offences. As we have seen, retributive punishment is a censure on behalf of society, but attitudes differ between different societies. In Britain, for example, car vandalism might attract a community sentence or a fine, but for the same offence in Singapore an offender would suffer six strokes of the cane, four months in prison and a fine.

There is a distinct problem in multicultural societies, where there is no fundamental consensus about the seriousness of most forms of criminality. Retribution still remains an important doctrine; not only does society have to exact a punishment on the individual on behalf of the victim, but it also needs to appear to be a just desert for the crime and be an acceptable level of punishment as far as the victim, or victims, are concerned.

There is no general consensus on the effectiveness or desirability of rehabilitation. A more modern view of rehabilitation is known as restorative justice. This aims to give offenders an insight into the impact of their crimes and then to force them to make amends. This usually also involves meeting their victims.

Rehabilitation theory also suggests some form of personal engineering, or re-education. It seeks to change human nature, effectively absolving the offenders from moral responsibility and blaming society for the root of their wrongdoing. However, humans do have free will. Individuals act as independent agents. Some contend that they should be held morally responsible for their own actions and, as a result, this provides a clear justification for punishment.

Hegel on punishment

Crime is one of the three forms of wrongdoing Hegel identifies, the other two being civil wrong and fraud. Crime concerns a threefold negation of right – the right of the victim, law and society. For Hegel, punishment aims to overturn the negations of right, so in the first case it serves to restore the victim to his or her proper place as a right-bearing individual, since they were treated by the criminal as a being without rights. The whole system of right itself must also be addressed through punishment. The threats to the system created by crime must be overturned so that right is rehabilitated to its proper place in society; otherwise in the absence of punitive action wrong is effectively treated as if right. But punishment must be retributive rather than vengeful. Hegel sees retributive punishment as objective, universal and mediated, whereas revenge is subjective, particular and immediate.

DISCUSSION POINT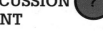

On what grounds can punishment be justified?

Learning objectives

- What is justice?
- Procedural and substantive justice

Judicial activism

Judicial activism suggests that judges are more willing to get involved in situations beyond making legal decisions. It also implies that they are willing to influence government policy. Those who believe that judicial activism is a good thing believe that the courts should take an active role in cases involving immigration, citizens' rights, asylum and other sensitive issues. Judicial activists are seen to be 'doing the right thing' rather than simply following the exact letter of the law.

Patrick Devlin on enforcing morality

Devlin (1905–92) was firmly of the opinion that law had no business getting involved in an individual's private acts that harmed no one else. He believed that law should be based on the moral values of the average citizen, which he referred to as consensus laws. Non-consensus laws were those that were viewed as being unjust and created widespread disobedience.

What is justice?

Justice implies moral correctness, fairness or rightness. Justice, however, is actually deeper than this, as it implies a moral judgement being passed, one that can dispense both rewards and punishments. It also implies that individuals receive what they are due.

Some focus on this distributive aspect and precisely what rewards and penalties that justice actually addresses. Justice can be applied to the distribution of almost anything and some argue that the same principle of distribution should be applied to every case. It is not however as straightforward as this because on the one hand an equal distribution of wealth or income might be achievable through social engineering. But can there ever be an equal distribution of friendship or loyalty?

Michael Walzer suggested that there is no universal theory of justice and believed that there should be complex equality; in other words different rules should apply to the different areas of justice.

Justice is, however, a much used term in law, or legal justice, which is primarily concerned with the way in which it compensates individuals for damage and injury and punishes those who have done wrong. Justice therefore needs, in this respect, a set of clear rules that need to be just and morally correct.

As we will see, there are two ways of approaching this.

- One way is procedural justice, which focuses on how rules are made and how they are applied.
- The other way is substantive justice, which looks at whether the rules themselves are just.

Society and individuals recognise that law is binding, and accept their obligation to obey it but only because they feel that it is just. In this respect justice needs to have legitimacy. If the law does not appear to be just, or the way that law is administered seems to be unjust, then many would argue that individuals have a moral justification for breaking those rules. Locke suggested the concept of the right to break the law if that law no longer protects the natural rights of citizenship (i.e. to withdraw consent from being governed).

Procedural and substantive justice

Procedural justice is often referred to as formal justice. These are the ways in which outcomes are actually decided. Legal systems need to have a set of established rules that aim to ensure a just outcome. The rules that govern the way in which the legal system works have to be seen as being fair and in effect this refers to the administration side of law.

Law should not discriminate on any grounds, it needs to be impartial and therefore the judges need to be unbiased and independent. This is not, however, always the case, as in the United States, for example, the US Supreme Court is seen as being a political entity. Vacancies filled by presidential nominations are vetted by the Senate, often leading to appointments reflecting the ideological perspectives of the presidents – note that the US Supreme Court has moved to the right after two recent appointments of right-wing constructionists by President Bush, replacing two liberal justices, which may have an impact upon moral issues such as amending the Roe vs Wade ruling on abortion. In addition they are accused of a degree of bias on the grounds of their age, gender and colour. In Britain, judges are sometimes seen to be biased and political when they are involved in judicial activism.

Judicial activism has increased in Britain for a number of reasons.

- The tendency of governments to legislate over newer and broader areas, such as restrictive legislations on asylum seekers.

- The greater willingness of citizens to use the courts. In the past the courts were seen as protecting the status quo and were also distrusted.

- The development of international agreements and conventions, such as the European Convention on Human Rights. This has encouraged the view that government decisions should be questioned.

- Judges have been seen by the media and pressure groups as having greater confidence to tackle policy issues. The more courts are used the greater the willingness for judges to get involved, thus encouraging more cases to be taken before the courts.

In their book *Freedom Under Thatcher* (1990), K. Ewing and C. Gearty asked whether it is reasonable, justifiable or legitimate to make a political decision on a minority right by a group of men that are unrepresentative of society and have been appointed by the prime minister. They believed that judicial preference should be used to handle problematic ethical, social and political questions.

In most societies the legal system uses a jury, which is also seen as part of procedural justice, the idea being that the defendant is being effectively judged by impartial members of society. The juries are randomly selected and therefore reflect the standard of justice that is common in society.

The legal system also needs to have a distinctive hierarchy, which allows miscarriages of justice and mistakes to be referred to other courts in order to be rectified. This process is in the hands of judges who determine whether or not there are grounds for an appeal.

Procedural justice suggests that individuals are innocent until proven guilty. There is a presumption of innocence. Just because an individual has been accused of a crime does not mean that they are necessarily guilty. The burden of truth rests on the prosecution. For this reason courts are not told of an individual's previous criminal record, as it is felt that this would unreasonably influence a jury and that they may reach a verdict that is not based on the facts in front of them but on the past misdemeanours of the defendant.

Procedural justice also applies to dealings with the police. The police are required to tell the accused person about the charges and about their rights. This is considered to be under threat in Britain, with terrorist legislation restricting the accused's rights despite the Human Rights Act.

Whilst a legal system may have a set of procedural rules, this does not necessarily mean that the rules are just. Neither does it imply that the procedures are fair or impartial.

Substantive justice refers to an acceptable outcome of the legal proceedings. It is subjective and as Patrick Devlin suggested, law should enforce morality based on the moral values of the average citizen. In other words, justice should be dispensed in relation to what is generally held to be a reasonable punishment or reward and that these levels are consistent and reflect the current opinion of the population. Devlin suggested, however, that if there were no consensus for a law then breaking it was justified. By prosecuting and enforcing that law it would bring the legal process and the judiciary into disrepute. A prime example was the widespread non-payment of Poll Tax in the 1990s on the grounds that most people believed that it was socially unjust.

Substantive justice

This example helps illustrate the concept of procedural or formal justice in contrast to substantive justice. If, in truth, a person has killed another person, substantive justice requires that the killer be punished according to law. However, if the killer is illegally tortured by the police to confess to his crime and, as a result of the confession, the police find conclusive evidence (i.e. evidence proving guilt beyond reasonable doubt), such as the weapon, the body of the victim, etc., for the court to convict the killer (which results in substantive justice), there is no procedural justice because the process of finding guilt has violated the basic rights of the killer. A good recent example is that of the Appeal Court decision in June 2008 to block the extradition of Abu Qatada to Jordan on the grounds that any evidence that may be used against him could have come from witnesses who have been tortured.

DISCUSSION POINT ?

Which is more significant, procedural or substantive justice?

What is obligation?

Obligation implies a requirement or duty for individuals in society to behave in a particular way. Generally, however, it is taken that there are two distinctly different forms of obligation.

- **Moral obligation** – This is conduct that is thought to be rightful, the most important of which is a political obligation, which suggests the duty of a citizen to acknowledge state authority and to obey the laws. In this respect obligation is a key part of citizenship, suggesting the balance between rights and obligations.

- **Legal obligation** – This is the requirement to observe laws that are enforceable through courts and may have penalties if not observed. There is an element of coercion in a legal obligation. The laws may not necessarily be right but they are obeyed as disobedience would lead to punishment.

Political obligation is an important concept, as it looks at the obligations on a moral basis of political rule. Social contract theorists would suggest that citizens are obliged to accept the authority of the state in return for the benefits they receive. Plato suggested that citizens make a promise to obey the state by actually choosing to remain in that state. Hobbes and Locke, on the other hand, suggested that it was based on a state's ability to ensure order and stability. Rousseau suggested that it was based on the state's ability to reflect the general will or collective good.

For conservatives obligation is not just a contract but an integral part of any stable society. They believe that obligation is a natural duty and that an individual's values and identity are largely based on those held by society in general.

Anarchists, however, reject political obligation as a concept and instead believe that personal autonomy is far more significant.

Natural duty

According to natural duty theories, political obligation is grounded not in a morally significant transaction that takes place between citizens and polity, but:

- in the importance of advancing some impartial moral good, such as utility or justice
- in a moral duty owed by all persons to all others regardless of their transactional history.

A utilitarian spin on political obligation is forward rather than backward looking, deriving political obligation from the future goods to be produced by obedience, rather than from what citizens have done in the past or what has been done for them. Utilitarianism suggests that actions that maximise utility are morally required. Utility is maximised by acts that produce more happiness and well-being than any alternative course of action that is open to the agent. The duty to obey the law is derived from this since as obedience produces more happiness than disobedience, one must obey.

Teleological theory

This is a theory of morality that derives duty or moral obligation from what is good or desirable as an end to be achieved. The theory suggests that citizens have a duty to respect the state and obey it because it provides them with enormous benefits. This assumes that the state acts in the public interest (such as Rousseau's general will).

Teleological theory is closely linked to utilitarianism, as citizens have an obligation to government because government tries to cater for the requirements of the greatest number of citizens.

Social contract

Social contract theories suggest that there are rational and moral grounds to obey the state. Political obligation is therefore founded on voluntary commitment and individual choice.

What social contract theory does not take into account is the fact that society itself shapes the views and beliefs of individuals and encourages them to take on duties and responsibilities, so in many respects it is not a voluntary commitment. The individuals have in fact been socialised into accepting political obligation.

Social duty

Socialists and social democrats favour social duty as an approach. Socialists consider cooperation and community as being at the heart of an effective society. Social duty for them is an expression of an individual's commitment.

Liberals would suggest that individuals have a broad range of rights, which are protected by the state. In return they should willingly have an obligation towards the community and a duty to provide support for those who are less able to do that for themselves.

In some respects social duty even features in an anarchist's view. Although they reject any concept of political authority or obligation, they recognise the importance of a cooperative, respectful and sociable community that has a sense of social responsibility towards one another. This can be seen in the writings of Kropotkin, Bakunin and Proudhon.

Hobbes on absolute obligation

Hobbes suggested that citizens have an absolute obligation to obey political authority, regardless of the behaviour of the government. He believed that whilst citizens had an obligation the state did not have an obligation. He believed that having any type of state was better than not having a state and that any form of protest could bring about the collapse of authority and a return to anarchy.

Locke on two treatises on civil government

Locke believed that political obligation was based on a social contract, where citizens sacrificed part of their liberty to have order and stability. The second element was trust, in which the state undertook to protect the natural rights of its citizens. He therefore implied that obedience was conditional.

Joseph de Maistre on subordination to the master

De Maistre (1753–1821) was implacably opposed to political obligation, seeing it as dangerous. He believed that politics was based on complete subordination to 'the master' and was of the opinion that society would collapse if it were not bound together.

Marx on obligation as class oppression

Marx believed that there should be no social contract and that the function of the state was to protect individual rights and not the interests of the ruling class. Political obligation was part of the delusion to try to ensure that the proletariat remained exploited in the capitalist system.

Social contract thinkers

John Locke's political theory was founded on social contract theory. Unlike Hobbes, he believed that human nature was based on reason and tolerance. He believed that human nature allowed men to be selfish. In a natural state all people were equal and independent, and everyone had a natural right to defend his 'life, health, liberty, or possessions'. The right to defend was not enough, so to resolve conflict, civil societies were created.

Jean-Jacques Rousseau stated in *The Social Contract* (1762):

'[The social contract] can be reduced to the following terms. Each of us puts his person and all his power in common under the supreme direction of the general will; and in a body we receive each member as an indivisible part of the whole.'

The form of social contract described by John Rawls in *A Theory of Justice* can be called the 'fictive assembly'. Rawls does not use 'assembly', but it is implicit in his model. Natural persons are removed from their real physical existence, and converted into rational beings that can debate, discuss, agree and contract. The non-physical beings agree a social contract – for Rawls that is essentially his minimum principles of justice.

DISCUSSION POINT ?

Is the expectation of political obligation reasonable in a liberal democracy?

Civil disobedience

Socrates

Socrates held that it is wrong to harm another person no matter what injury they may have inflicted upon you; and by harm, he means to damage somebody's character – to make them less capable of virtuous action [*Crito* 47–49]. By extension it is therefore not permissible to engage in an act of civil disobedience if the result would be to inflict harm upon any man or group of men.

Hobbes

Hobbes certainly does not preclude dissent. He emphasises that any decision made by the sovereign must be fair and just. But once a decision has been made it is binding, and active civil disobedience thereafter is prohibited. An individual may be in fundamental disagreement with the decision; believe it wrong; that it against the best interests of the commonwealth; nevertheless, the individual has a contractual obligation to obey, or face the consequences of the punishment power exercised by the sovereign.

Joseph de Maistre

He believed that any adherence to politics means that the individual willingly subordinates to a master. He believed that society was organic and that it would collapse if not held together by the 'throne and the altar'. He was a huge critic of the French Revolution.

Civil disobedience

Civil disobedience is often referred to as passive resistance. This is a refusal to obey the demands or commands of a government or an occupying power, without resorting to violence or active measures of opposition; its usual purpose is to force concessions from the government or occupying power. Civil disobedience has been a major tactic and philosophy of nationalist movements in Africa and India, in the civil rights movement of African-Americans and of labour and anti-war movements in many countries.

Civil disobedience is a symbolic or ritualistic violation of the law, rather than a rejection of the system as a whole. The civil disobedient, finding legitimate avenues of change blocked or non-existent, sees themselves as obligated by a higher, extra-legal principle to break some specific law. It is because civil disobedience is a crime, however, and known by actor and public alike to be punishable that the act serves as a protest. By submitting to punishment, the civil disobedient hopes to set a moral example that will provoke the majority or the government into effecting meaningful political, social, or economic change. Under the imperative of setting a moral example, the major spokesmen of civil disobedience insist that the illegal actions be non-violent.

A variety of criticisms has been directed against the philosophy and practice of civil disobedience. The radical critique of the philosophy of civil disobedience condemns its acceptance of the existing political structure; conservative schools of thought, on the other hand, see the logical extension of civil disobedience as anarchy and the right of the individual to break any law he chooses, at any time. Activists themselves are divided in interpreting civil disobedience either as a total philosophy of social change or as merely a tactic to be employed when the movement lacks other means. On a pragmatic level, the efficacy of civil disobedience hinges on the adherence of the opposition to a certain morality to which an appeal can ultimately be made.

The philosophical roots of civil disobedience lie with Cicero, St Thomas Aquinas, John Locke, Thomas Jefferson and Henry David Thoreau, all of whom sought to justify conduct by virtue of its harmony with some antecedent superhuman moral law.

The principle of civil disobedience has achieved some standing in international law through the war crime trials after the Second World War, which affirmed the principle that an individual may, under certain circumstances, be held accountable for failure to break the laws of his country.

Criminal and political disobedience

Disobedience is often part of a political process. Fundamentally, protestors may believe that particular laws or policies are unacceptable. In these cases disobedience is not driven by greed or self-interest and is not criminal in the ordinary sense, but instead it is political disobedience.

Disobedience tends to be met with repression or a backlash. The state will claim that the laws and policies are legitimate and however justified the political disobedience has been it may well be criminalised and certainly oppressed.

Rawls and Mill were of the opinion that political disobedience could be directed against democratic laws on the grounds that there should be limits to the authority of democratic governments.

As the assumption is that laws and policies reflect the majority view, it is a relatively small step for the state to take the line that disobedience should be criminalised and repressed until such a point that there is an overwhelming majority that feel the laws and policies need to be radically changed to decriminalise any disobedience. To some extent this was the process that took place when the poll tax was introduced.

Thoreau's civil disobedience

Civil Disobedience (1849) is an essay by Henry David Thoreau. It argued that people should not permit governments to overrule their consciences, and that people have a duty to avoid allowing such acquiescence to enable the government to make them the agents of injustice.

Gandhi on civil disobedience

The man who most clearly formulated the concept of civil disobedience for the modern world was Mahatma Gandhi. Drawing from eastern and western thought, Gandhi developed the philosophy of **satyagraha**. First in the Transvaal of South Africa in 1906 and later in India, Gandhi led his people in satyagrahas to obtain equal rights and freedom. Gandhi rated Thoreau very highly as a great writer, poet, philosopher and practical individual. Above all, he saw Thoreau as a man who was prepared to practise what he preached. Gandhi believed that Thoreau was one of the most moral individuals produced by the USA, prepared to suffer imprisonment for the sake of his beliefs. In doing this, his essay *On the Duty of Civil Disobedience* (1849), was 'sanctified by suffering'. Gandhi maintained that the essay's core message was as important now as the day it was written.

Martin Luther King on civil disobedience

Inspired by Gandhi's example, the civil rights movement of the African-Americans from the 1950s to the 1970s adopted the tactics and philosophy of civil disobedience, perhaps best expressed by Martin Luther King, Jr. Later, the tactics of civil disobedience were employed by a variety of protest groups. King had read Thoreau's essay *On the Duty of Civil Disobedience* (1849) when he was a student. It was instrumental in drawing King towards the notion of non-violent resistance. King was impressed by Thoreau's stance against taxes and the spread of slavery into Mexico, willing to accept imprisonment as a result. King read and reread the essay, becoming more convinced that it was wrong to cooperate with evil. King believed that it was as morally wrong to cooperate with evil as it was morally right to cooperate with good. Never before had King read a piece that contained such passion and eloquence. King came to recognise himself and his followers as being the natural heirs to Thoreau through the use of non-violent protest and refusal to cooperate. He saw Thoreau's ideas as being alive within the civil rights movement. Thoreau's approach could be seen in the sit-ins, the Mississippi freedom ride, and the non-violent protests in Albany, Georgia and in the Montgomery, Alabama bus boycott. All of these activities were natural progressions of Thoreau's approach in which evil was being resisted and that a moral individual would not 'patiently adjust to injustice'.

Satyagraha

Gandhi used this term to describe non-violent resistance. To Gandhi, this meant truth-force, love-force or soul-force. He believed that violence was not an acceptable response to dealing with an opponent; rather, he believed that they should be slowly made to see the error of their ways through sympathy and patience. Gandhi recognised that truth as seen by one side would be seen as an error by their opponents. Hence, he maintained that to move them from the state of being in error, it was necessary to be patient and be prepared to suffer. Truth was borne out of self-suffering, rather than inflicting suffering on the opponent.

DISCUSSION POINT ?

At what point should political disobedience become criminal?

The rule of law and parliamentary sovereignty

The rule of law determines the relationship between the state and its citizens. It ensures that actions by the state are both responsible and limited (obey the law and recognise citizens' legal rights). All citizens, including the monarch, the executive, judiciary and legislature are under the law. They must all obey the law and everyone is equal under the law. If anyone has acted outside their authority then they can be held accountable for their actions in court. This is illustrated by the fact that there have been prosecutions of members of the Royal Family and leading politicians (e.g. Princess Anne fined by magistrates for failing to control her pet dogs in a public place and more politically Tony Blair's questioning under oath during the Scotland Yard investigation in the 'loans for peerages' affair 2007).

The rule of law states that the judiciary is independent and is free from interference. Citizens are entitled to a fair trial and should not be imprisoned without regard to legal processes – this relates back to habeas corpus which dates from the Magna Carta 1215. Citizens have the right to take the government or a local authority to court if they feel they have not been treated properly.

Despite this, some argue that the rule of law is under threat. Governments have legislated to restrict the rights of asylum seekers, for example restricting their rights to the legal process or the right to protest, which does not relate to foreigners.

Parliamentary sovereignty, in theory, means that the rule of law is vulnerable, as citizens' rights are withdrawn by parliament. With the exception of cases such as asylum seekers, any government that attempted to restrict citizens' rights would find itself opposed at every turn by civil rights groups such as Charter 88 and Liberty, and any proposals they made would be considered anti-democratic and illegitimate. Despite this recent anti-terror legislation has had a dramatic effect on rights and liberties.

The first principle of the British constitution is that the parliament in Westminster is the supreme law-making body in Britain. It has absolute power over every citizen, including the monarch.

The term sovereignty actually means legal supremacy. This means that parliament can:

- create legislation that cannot be overturned by any other authority

- legislate on any subject or issue that it chooses

- ensure that no current parliament can create legislation that will hinder the first two points, as far as a future government is concerned.

Does parliament still retain sovereignty? Possibly not, but the third point above does mean that if it has lost parliamentary sovereignty it can take it back if it needs to at a future date. As far as the parliamentary sovereignty debate is concerned, the principal focus is on the devolved governments of Scotland and Wales and Britain's membership of the EU. In both cases the creation of legislation has been passed on to these bodies. It has also meant that the power to legislate on any issue has been removed. However, parliament can get the powers back by the third principle. No decision to create or join an organisation is irreversible. If parliament wished it could:

- abolish the devolved parliaments and take their powers back to Westminster

- leave the EU and repeal any EU law it wants to remove.

Equally, decisions made on other issues can be repealed, such as the right to abortions, the return of capital punishment or the use of referendums to consult the electorate. Because parliament can repeal any Act, regardless of its source, it retains parliamentary sovereignty.

The biggest issue regarding parliamentary sovereignty is not the creation of a Scottish parliament or EU membership; it is the dominance of the executive. Centralised power has been approved by parliament, making any institution that is not constitutionally protected vulnerable.

The Human Rights Act and the application of the rule of law

Lord Woolf in a speech to the Royal Academy linked the Human Rights Act, judicial reviews and the rule of law and warned that there could be a major confrontation between judges and the executive. He believed that judicial reviews had proved to be extremely effective in handling contentious issues. He maintained that the Human Rights Act would protect the interests of individuals, which can often be ignored when governments try to handle increasingly complex global political and economic issues. Woolf believed that the Human Rights Act would be tested to the full when public opinion had been stirred up by the media against particular individuals and minorities. It would then be the role of the courts to ensure that those that are under attack are protected by the rule of law. Woolf saw the Human Rights Act as essential in preventing discrimination and ensuring the dignity of the individual.

Whether this is entirely possible is dependent on the following factors.

- Judges need to be sufficiently competent to consider issues under the guise of a judicial review that are affected under the HRA. Judges are not experts in areas of policy, but experts in law. When there is an issue that could be incompatible under the HRA it will need to be passed back to parliament for review and reform.

- Constitutionally, the separation of powers applies as equally to the judiciary as it does to the executive. If judges involve themselves in substantive decisions they may be involving themselves in political matters, albeit on the basis that they are trying to decide on a point of law. The judiciary may well be seen as exceeding their constitutional powers. What is also significant to remember is the fact that judges are unaccountable and they are unelected. A good recent example is the judicial review over the government's decision to close the SFO investigation into BAE defence contracts with Saudi Arabia. Also recent criticism of the role of the Attorney General being a political appointment despite him supposedly giving impartial legal advice to the government and the issue of the advice given over the legality of the Iraq War in 2003.

The rule of law is still generally seen as being directly applicable to the implementation of rights. The rule of law can also be indirectly related to the protection of rights, as it is associated with development, which in turn brings better performance in human rights. The rule of law remains integral to democracy and attempts to democratise without the application of the legal system could lead to social disorder.

British courts have been committed to upholding human rights and the rule of law, but in a democracy parliament and civil society also need to play their role to ensure that the rule of law is not eroded and that human rights protection continues to be built into the system.

DISCUSSION POINT ?

Is the rule of law in Britain under threat?

Learning objectives

- Common law
- Human Rights Act and the EU law
- Socio-economic background of judges
- Fusion and separation of powers
- Impact of the Constitutional Reform Act 2005

Common law

Common laws are usually principles that have developed and been applied in British courts. Where the law is unclear, it is the role of judges to interpret or clarify the rules. Over time this has meant that the major rights of citizens have been accepted. New rulings always take precedence over earlier decisions and they become the guidelines to which other judges work and may make changes to the common law in the future. Sometimes ministers may decide that they need to clarify or amend common law by passing legislation. When this happens and an Act of Parliament comes into existence, it becomes a statute law. In the National Health Service, for example, there is a common law duty of confidentiality. This means that information about a patient cannot normally be disclosed without the patient's consent.

Human Rights Act and the EU law

The 1998 Human Rights Act incorporated many of the provisions of the European Convention on Human Rights (1950). Britain had already signed the convention, but before the Human Rights Act the British government was not compelled to alter legislation to fit in with the convention. The Human Rights Act changed several aspects in that:

- tribunals would hear cases brought under the convention
- judges could declare British law incompatible with the convention, but did not have the power to overturn the legislation
- parliament could amend the legislation to make it compatible
- if it failed to do so the case could be referred to the European Court of Human Rights (ECHR) in Strasbourg.

After October 2000, all British legislation (both Westminster and the devolved assemblies) had to be given a compatibility declaration from the ECHR. There were considerable constitutional complications, which required new interpretations of British legislation. Many believed that the simplest way forward would have been to draw up a Bill of Rights. It is important to remember that the ECHR is a separate entity from the EU.

When Britain joined the EEC (later the EU), radical changes had to be made to the British constitution. In effect, membership meant that Britain was accepting that European law would take precedence over British law and its constitution.

European law comes into existence as parts of treaties (such as the Treaty of Rome) and legislation in the form of regulations and directives.

Before Britain joined the EU, the British parliament was sovereign in all matters. Membership means that the EU now has powers to bind British citizens. Unlike countries such as the Republic of Ireland (who have to hold a referendum before making a constitutional change – in 2008 Ireland rejected the Lisbon Treaty via a referendum), Britain, without a written constitution, can just incorporate changes caused by EU legislation.

The process of accepting the precedence of the EU began in 1973 when Britain joined the EEC. The subsequent treaties establishing the EU and legislation from the European Commission and European Parliament, along with judgements made by the European Court of Justice, have all become parts of the British constitution, as has Britain's membership of NATO.

Socio-economic background of judges

Senior judges are drawn from barristers (lawyers who present cases to judges). Becoming a barrister is a long and expensive business. Many of the barristers need an additional income in their early years, in order to survive financially. This means that huge numbers of the population are excluded from becoming barristers, let alone senior judges. As a result, the bulk of senior judges come from very privileged backgrounds. Although there are increasing numbers of women who reach the ranks of the senior judiciary, the numbers of ethnic minorities are still very low. The following table outlines the latest available Annual Diversity Statistics (April 2007).

Post	Total	Female		Ethnic minority	
		Number	%	Number	%
Lords of Appeal in Ordinary	12	1	8.3	0	0
Heads of Division	4	0	0	0	0
Lord Justices of Appeal	37	3	8.1	0	0
High Court Judges	108	10	9.3	1	0.9

Source: Crown copyright

As we can see, the judiciary is still predominantly white and male. Equally, the ages of the judges tends to be high (understandable in some respects, as the senior judges have to be established and experienced barristers). Most of them attended public school and the majority went to either Oxford or Cambridge universities. The average age of a senior judge is at least 60 years old, with the most senior judges well above the average. Note that under CRA there is now a statutory obligation upon the Independent Appointments Commission to encourage greater diversity amongst senior members of the judiciary, but in their first batch of appointments all were white and only one had not attended private school.

Fusion and separation of powers

Just as the apparent separation of powers between the judiciary and the executive existed in theory, but not in practice, so too did the relationship between the judiciary and parliament (legislature).

Ideally, they should be separate so that they can independently check on the actions of one another. In theory, the process should be that:

- parliament can remove a judge who is seen to be corrupt or has committed a criminal offence
- judges can highlight incompatibility if a law passed by parliament violates one of the conventions of the European Convention on Human Rights. They are now also responsible for the observance of EU law in the UK
- parliament alone makes the laws
- judges implement and enforce the laws
- parliament votes to fund judges
- judges are subject to being dismissed by parliament.

Parliament has always had a large number of practising, or former, legal experts serving as MPs. Despite this, the House of Commons in particular has never really closely scrutinised the judiciary. Some believe that the fact that the Blairs (both lawyers) were close friends of Lord Irvine (who was the Lord Chancellor between 1997 and 2003) could have speeded up the changes that were made in the Constitutional Reform Act (2005).

Impact of the Constitutional Reform Act 2005

The main concern of the judiciary is that decisions made by the executive adversely affect judges' ability to perform their role 'without fear or favour'.

The Lord Chief Justice of England and Wales, Lord Woolf, speaking in 2005 stressed the importance to both the judiciary and to the general public of an independent judiciary. In his view judges, by enforcing law regardless of the social or economic status or the gender and connections an individual may have, illustrates the fairness of the British justice system. Judges in essence uphold the rule of law.

The **Constitutional Reform Act** came as much as a surprise to Lord Woolf as it was to many others. Woolf was adamant that neither government nor public bodies should ever be in a position where they are able to influence the decisions of the judiciary. For him the judiciary operated like a watchdog, to prevent government or public bodies from abusing their power and therefore to protect the public.

In consultation with the judiciary, the executive had established the following.

Constitutional Reform Act

This received Royal Assent in March 2005 and covered four areas: judicial independence, reform of the Lord Chancellor, the establishment of a Supreme Court and the creation of the Judicial Appointments Commission.

- The government should not have control over the appointment of judges (but they could have an input).

- The creation of an Independent Appointments Commission to appoint junior judges and advise the Minister of Justice on appointments to the senior judiciary.

- The government should not be able to remove a judge, unless the Lord Chief Justice agreed.

- The creation of the post of the Lord Chief Justice who handles the day-to-day affairs of the judiciary.

- The government should not be able to pick a judge to hear a particular case – this is a statutory duty of independence where interference with specific cases by ministers becomes a criminal offence.

- The government should have no input over the use of judges and where they sit as a means of disciplining the judge.

- The creation of a Supreme Court made up of new Supreme Court justices (formerly Law Lords), removing the Appeal Court function of the House of Lords. Note powers of new Supreme Court have remained those formerly enjoyed by the Law Lords.

- The decoupling of the role of the Lord Chancellor – title still remains as a ceremonial one but now commonly referred to as Minister of Justice. There is no longer an obligation to sit in the House of Lords as the former function of Speaker of the House of Lords has been removed and now resides in a position in a person elected by the peers themselves. Also day-to-day running of judiciary now handled by the Lord Chief Justice.

Until the changes in the role of the Lord Chancellor, the theoretical separation of powers between the judiciary and the executive were not separated in practice. The appointment of judges was down to an unelected (and unaccountable) individual. Added to this, the Lord Chancellor was a member of cabinet committees that discussed political issues. This was too close a relationship between the judiciary and the executive to ensure that the judiciary remained independent. Despite this, the last three Lord Chancellors were all keen not to be unduly influenced by the executive. Lords MacKay, Irvine and Falconer seemed all to be of the opinion that it was better to change a system that had ensured independence, rather than try to change one that was failing, so it was a good time to consider reform. Note that Falconer was the first to use the new title of Lord Chancellor, with his successor Jack Straw taking up the mantle of Secretary of State for Justice. Now the focus on legal separation has turned to the position of the Attorney General and his supposed impartial advice to the government (witness Iraq 2003).

DISCUSSION POINT ?

What is the role of the judiciary in Britain?

Attitudes to law enforcement

According to a report, *The Public and the Police*, carried out for Civitas in May 2007, the police and law enforcement, in terms of its popularity and support by the public, is at an all-time low in Britain. Complaints have risen, particularly from the law-abiding middle classes who no longer see the police as being on their side. The view is that law enforcement criminalises trivial offences, it concentrates on easy-to-handle offences, such as road traffic offences, and is slow to respond and unwilling to deal with real crime.

In their defence, the police and law enforcement find themselves overwhelmed with government initiatives and this has left fewer to deal directly with public situations. There is also an enormous burden of paperwork, which has been a growing concern.

There is a strong call for a return to traditional policing, with high visibility policing being the key call.

ASBOs

Anti-social youths are often the targets of ASBOs.

Anti-social behaviour is a relatively wide legal definition and falls under the Crime and Disorder Act (1998). It is generally defined as behaviour that is likely to cause harassment, harm or distress. It therefore includes graffiti, abusive and intimidating language, excessive noise, littering, drunken behaviour and drug dealing.

The number of ASBOs issued by December 2006 was 12,675 throughout England. Many offenders consider ASBOs to be a badge of honour and there is a high level of non-compliance, suggesting that they are ineffective. ASBOs are usually imposed for terms of between two and five years.

In May 2008 figures were released by the Home Office that suggest that there was a sharp drop in the number of ASBOs issued, as the government turned to different remedies. Jacqui Smith, the Home Secretary, believed that ASBOs proved to society that no one should be expected to put up with anti-social behaviour without the government acting upon it.

Ed Balls, the Children's Minister, had already admitted that ASBOs had been a failure. The focus now seems to be on harassing the harassers, as it was termed, notably in the Essex-based Operation Leopard, which targeted known offenders, visiting their homes regularly and filming The Home Secretary, speaking of Operation Leopard, stressed that those involved in anti-social behaviour would find themselves in an impossible situation. There was nowhere for them to go. They were the ones that would now be harassed because the tables had turned.

There are divided views on ASBOs, particularly from civil liberties groups who believe that they were targeting more vulnerable groups in society, such as the mentally ill, addicts and victims of violence. There was a concern that ASBOs were dragging the young into the criminal justice system without addressing the root causes. It also extended the likelihood of being in prison for non-imprisonable offences, such as begging. A beggar could be issued an ASBO and could be imprisoned for breaching the ASBO, even though begging is not a crime.

Supporters of ASBOs suggest the scheme has given the police more power to reduce problems.

Zero tolerance

Zero tolerance is a form of policing that refuses to overlook any crime or anti-social behaviour. It was first introduced in the United States in the 1970s as a means of clamping down on mugging and prostitution, particularly in New York.

Since then it has been applied to a broad range of situations, including verbal and physical abuse in the NHS, bullying in schools and religious intolerance. In September 2007 the government launched a zero tolerance criminal justice drive, which would see the police targeting low-level crime in every community. New technology would also be a vital plank with handheld fingerprinting machines being issued to police officers and new referral centres for assaults being set up in most areas.

In Merseyside, US-style zero tolerance was adopted by the police in 2005 and since then violent crime has fallen by 38 per cent and robberies by 23 per cent. The key criticisms, however, are that it not only tackles burglars and drug dealers but also children playing sport on streets and those that drop litter. It is a controversial tactic and critics suggest that it would not suit racially sensitive areas, such as London, although the new mayor, Boris Johnson, as a part of his election campaign, set out his intention to bring zero tolerance to the capital.

Prison population

There are over 80,000 people in Britain's prisons and conservative estimates suggest that by 2012 this will reach 100,000. There are varying views on jailing individuals rather than focusing on rehabilitation strategies. The chairman of the Prison Officers' Association in May 2005 observed that a prisoner often appears when a prison space is available. He queried to what extent the police are only executing warrants dependent on prison and police cell places.

The views of others, such as the Liberal Democrats, are reflected in comments made by David Haworth, the Liberal Democrat Justice spokesman: 'The punishment should fit the crime and not be based on ever-decreasing availability of prison cells.'

As far as the Ministry of Justice is concerned, a spokesman commented: 'We will always provide enough prison spaces for serious offenders, those who should be behind bars: the most dangerous, the seriously persistent offenders, the most violent.'

In January 2007 the government faced the prospect of no additional spaces in British prisons (the figure had just risen to 80,000). The then Home Secretary, John Reid, sought to influence the sentencing policy of magistrates and the judiciary by writing an open letter reminding them of other potential sentences beyond custodial ones. This caused significant criticism from members of the judiciary and public outcry when a convicted paedophile in Wales was given a suspended sentence and in his summation the judge implied he would have given a custodial sentence but was responding to the plea from the Home Secretary.

In the United States in 2007 there were an estimated 1.5 million people in state and federal prisons, costing the country £13.44 billion per year. According to American critics of the prison system there is no evidence to suggest that keeping individuals in prison longer makes society any safer.

In the US, as in Britain, many thousands of people are sent to prison for crimes that actually pose little danger to society. A prime example was a woman in Florida who received a two-year term for throwing a cup of coffee at a car.

DISCUSSION POINT ?

Is zero tolerance a solution to the low levels of trust and support for law enforcement?

Civil disobedience in action

There are innumerable examples of civil disobedience in action in Britain, ranging from widespread public acts to individual acts based on deeply held personal grounds. This is also a feature of the choice of many pressure groups to now use direct action as a strategy.

One government initiative, believed to cost £5.6 billion, will undoubtedly cause a civil disobedience campaign to be launched. The introduction of biometric ID cards has brought promises of civil disobedience from a number of individuals, including the Liberal Democrat peer Baroness Williams, who explained in November 2007 that she would be prepared to go to prison rather than submit to having an ID card, which she believes was fundamentally against civil liberties.

The Countryside Alliance and more specifically the pro-hunt lobby, which tends to dominate this broad-based group, routinely engage in civil disobedience by continuing to launch hunting events, particularly on Boxing Day each year. The pro-hunt lobby had threatened civil disobedience across the country and have been true to their word. This has left police forces in a quandary as to how to handle the situation without widespread arrests.

Mass demonstrations closed Hillgrove Cat Farm in Witney, Oxfordshire, where cats were bred for scientific research. The RSPCA (animal welfare group) were forced to go in and rescue 800 abandoned cats on the day Hillgrove closed (August 1999). The cost of policing the demonstrations was estimated by Thames Valley Police to be not far short of £3 million. At one time an exclusion zone was declared around Witney.

A more sinister example of civil disobedience/direct action involved the exhumation of the body of Gladys Hammond, in 2006, whose family owned a guinea pig farm in Staffordshire, by animal rights extremists where guinea pigs were bred for research. This was only the final stage in a long-running campaign against the farm, with other tactics including spreading rumours amongst the local community that the owner was a convicted paedophile and also threats of arson.

In October 2007, police were called to a comprehensive school in Abertillery, in South Wales, where pupils had walked out of class and set fire to their black school blazers in a protest against new rules requiring them to wear uniforms. The pupils put their new blazers in a pile and set fire to them in front of the school. The protest came the day after Michael Gove, the Shadow Schools Secretary, during a speech at the Tory conference, promised to reintroduce blazers at all secondary schools. The decision to reintroduce the blazers was made by the school council and had been popular with parents, despite the blazers costing an average of £34. Pauline Thomas, the head teacher, said that the pupils congregated in the bus bay at about 11 am and set fire to the blazers. She said she called the emergency services 'to get the group under control'. The pupils ran off when the police arrived.

Fathers 4 Justice is a British-based civil rights movement, focusing on the inherent bias of the family court system against men. They have been involved in a number of civil disobedience campaigns and actions, but have distanced themselves from more extremist splinter groups that have plotted to become involved in political activities. The group formally disbanded in January 2006 after a linked splinter group were allegedly involved in a plot to kidnap the prime minister's son Leo Blair.

Groups such as Fathers 4 Justice and environmentalists view small crimes such as the disruption of roads and public spaces as a justified aspect of civil disobedience, particularly when they are protesting against greater crimes, such as legal injustice, environmental damage or war. Civil disobedience often means a breach of normal or legal boundaries and a typical law enforcement way of dealing with this is to treat it as trespass.

More militant resistance organisations advocate civil disobedience instead of peaceful demonstrations. They believe that personal risk and responsibility are key elements. Many groups have a core membership that is prepared to engage in direct action without concern for their own security or any fear of arrest and imprisonment. A good example is the work of the Animal Liberation Front and its involvement in direct action attempts to close the Huntington Life Sciences laboratory in Oxford.

Terrorists and freedom fighters

Terrorism is most commonly defined as an act of violence carried out against civilians with the intention of creating terror or fear. The action may be directed at causing injury, death, disruption to normal life or destruction of facilities of the state under attack, or all of these.

One of the justifications of terrorism rests on the distinction between military and non-military targets and that some non-combatants are not innocent and therefore legitimate targets of violence, such as Israeli settlers in the occupied territories of Palestine and white South Africans during apartheid.

There is another distinction. Whilst international law often prohibits violence, it may accept it as morally excusable in certain cases, as that of an attack on a dictator oppressing his people, provided an effort has been made to protect innocent people as much as possible. International courts have recognised assassinations as proportional political acts. However, the argument for killing non-innocent civilians is still taken to be unacceptable. Sometimes an attempt at assassinating the leader of a nation engaged in a conflict may be directed at disabling or destabilising the state to force its military forces to cease fighting. Acts such as these that are acceptable under international law of course may not be acceptable under the law of a particular nation.

The argument for a violent attack on civilians is even more tenuous in the case of terrorists targeting people in Britain for that country's involvement in the Iraq war. Many view this as punitive as it threatens people regardless of whether they had any involvement in causing the grievance. The point can also be made that targeting UN or humanitarian personnel for complicity in the war implies that such individuals are exposed to terrorist harm in spite of their intention to help bring about peace and aid. Such attacks may simply be motivated on the grounds of the attackers' religious affiliations, nationality or political beliefs.

Ted Honderich (2003), the political philosopher, suggests that Palestinian terrorism against Israel was a moral right, aiming to free the Palestinians from Israeli domination. Terrorism is therefore justifiable in circumstances when it had a decent probability of success at a cost that was acceptable.

The arguments against the use of terrorism against Israel are broad.

- Under international law, Palestinians, for example, do not face grave and imminent peril. They are not experiencing genocide or threat to their survival. Occupation is an insufficient threat.

- The killing of civilians is a disproportionate response.

- The killing of civilians is too remote from the political end that is sought by the terrorists and in fact all it has succeeded in doing is increasing Israel's will to continue to dominate Palestinian lives.

- In the case of the Palestinians, it is not clear that the terrorists actually express the will of the people. There are no clear lines of political authority; some attacks are made by secret militant groups.

DISCUSSION POINT ?

Is civil disobedience an acceptable tactic in a liberal democracy?

Unit F854

Relax and prepare

Here are some practice exam questions for unit F854. How would you go about answering them?

- Compare and contrast natural and positive theories of law.
- Discuss the need for order in society.
- Compare and contrast substantive and procedural forms of justice.
- To what extent should citizens be obliged to obey the state.
- Critically examine the arguments in favour of civil disobedience.

 ## Refresh your memory

The following are key points for revision for unit F854.

To help organise your revision, look at the following table. Do you understand each of the concepts and can you explain the relevant issues and illustrate them with reference to the ideas of political thinkers?

Concept	Relevant issues	Relevant political theorists
Definition of law	Understanding of term and the concept of the rule of law	Heywood and Dicey
Natural and positive theories of law	Focus on the role morality plays in determining the law	Plato, Aristotle, Locke Jefferson, Austin, Hart, Hobbes
Definition of order	Understanding of term and historical role	Hobbes
Ideological perspectives on order	Conservative attitudes on the benefit of order versus more critical liberal, socialist and anarchist attitudes	Hobbes, de Maistre, Burke, Devlin, Marx, Rousseau, Kropotkin, Godwin
Theories of punishment	Retribution, restorative, deterrent and rehabilitation theories	Hobbes, Adam Smith, Bentham, Hart, Rawls
Definition of justice	Understanding of term and historical role	Walzer
Procedural and substantive forms of justice	Focus upon application and outcome in determining justice	Rawls and Devlin
Definition of obligation	Understanding of term and historical role	Hart
Theories justifying obligation	Social contract versus natural duty theories	Plato, Hobbes, Locke, Rousseau, Rawls, Burke, Kropotkin
Definition of civil disobedience	Understanding of term and historical role – distinction with law breaking for personal gain	Heywood
Justifications for civil disobedience	Violation of unjust laws, breach of 'lesser laws' to make overt political statements and lack of alternative forms of protest	Locke, Gandhi, Thoreau, Martin Luther King

Get the result !

The following is the type of essay question that may occur in your exam for unit F854. How would you go about answering it?

Discuss the different justifications for punishment by the state.

Exam tips

To answer this question think about how to compare the four justifications discussed in this unit. Look at the following table and complete where appropriate.

Justification	Basis for punishment	Attitude towards the criminal	Attitude towards society and the victim	Relevant theory
Retribution	Old Testament notion of 'eye for an eye'	Criminal seen as evil and the crime a moral sin	Encourages a sense of satisfaction that justice seen to be done and improve moral fibre of society	Hobbes, Adam Smith
Deterrence		Severe punishment to deter the criminal and potential others		Bentham
Restorative	Right the wrongs perpetrated by criminal		Make good damage done by criminal	
Rehabilitation		Educate the criminal to encourage future compliance with the law		Rawls

Unit F856

Relax and prepare

Here are some practice exam questions for unit F856. Discuss with your colleagues how you would go about answering them or try writing essay plans for as many as you can.

- Discuss the view that in theory the UK judiciary is meant to be independent but in practice it is not.

- Discuss how far obligation to the state should extend in modern society.

- Assess which model justifying punishment is the most effective at dealing with crime in the UK.

- Discuss the effectiveness of civil disobedience campaigns in the UK.

- Can terrorism ever be justified?

Refresh your memory

Case studies on law, order, justice and obligation

Think about the following events and issues, and consider how what you have learned in unit F854 could be added to what you have learnt for unit F856.

- ✓ The impact of the Constitutional Reform Act 2005 upon the operation of the judiciary in the UK.

- ✓ The statistics on the gender, ethnicity and socio-economic profile of British judges (see Ministry of Justice website for most up-to-date statistics).

- ✓ The rising prison population in the UK (61,000 in 1997 to 80,000 in 2007).

- ✓ The government initiatives to tackle law and order issues (e.g. ASBOs, zero tolerance initiatives, ID card and national DNA database proposals).

- ✓ The pressure group civil disobedience campaigns (e.g. non-payment of poll tax campaign in the late 1980s, Greenpeace protests against Shell over the Brent Spa episode in1995–96 and blockade of oil refineries by Fuel Lobby 2000).

- ✓ A comparison of the use of economic and terror tactics by the ANC in their campaign to abolish apartheid in South Africa with terror campaign used by Al Qaeda against western foreign policy in the Middle East.

Get the result!

This may be the type of essay question that you have to answer for unit F856 in your exam. To improve your chance of achieving a high mark you should plan your essay before you start writing it.

Discuss the effectiveness of the rule of law in upholding the liberty of citizens both in theory and in practice.

Exam tips

Think about the following essay plan. Does it use the relevant theory from unit F854 and does it provide effective application to modern politics?

Introduction

This defines the concept of the rule of law (A. V. Dicey is useful here).

Outline the operation of the rule of law in the UK

This relates to the role of the courts through judicial review and tribunals in upholding rights and liberties through application of common law, statute law (Berlin's positive notion that liberty can be enhanced through legislation by removing obstacles to freedom – see views of T. H. Green) and increasingly international conventions protecting rights and liberties (e.g. EU and ECHR).

Case study examples are important – you could include challenges to government anti-terrorism legislation such as the Law Lords overruling of the detention of suspected terrorists in Belmarsh prison only on the approval of the Home Secretary (2004) and legal protection for certain civil liberties such as homosexuality and abortion.

Outline limitations of the effectiveness of the rule of law

This may include:

+ the subservience of the rule of law to parliamentary sovereignty in the UK (this could include comparison with states with entrenched constitutional safeguards),

+ the lack of a complete separation of powers potentially allowing executive influence over the judiciary (note that reward would be given for some rebuttal of this through examining the impact of the 2005 Constitutional Reform Act), and even

+ questions as to the impartiality of the process based upon the dominance of upper middle class, white male judges.

It would also be relevant to highlight those theorists such as Hobbes and Mill who see law in a negative sense in limiting individual liberty as opposed to protecting it – thus adopting a more libertarian approach in limiting the areas by which the rule of law should apply (e.g. the debate over the legality of cannabis or perceived infringement to civil liberties of the UK smoking bans).

Conclusion

The crucial concept of a Bill of Rights in the UK armoury of upholding civil rights and liberties, potentially growing in importance, yet in the UK it is less effective than in other western states where there exists entrenched Bills of Rights and complete separation of powers.

British conservatives traditionally supported the old order of society, in which the aristocracy and monarchy formed the ruling elite. They have always fought to protect traditional values and social order, even when confronted by the radical social changes that characterised the industrial revolution of the 19th century. However they are quite different from French conservative nationalists and American religious conservatives, and are not as extreme as those conservatives in Argentina and Iran. Their core values are a belief in the natural inequalities of life, the importance of the individual, property ownership, pragmatism, tradition, preservation and a pessimistic view of human nature.

Thatcherism ushered in a more radical and ideological version of conservatism in the 1980s. This was a brand of conservatism that became known as the New Right. It retained the basic principles of authority, discipline and order but infused it with paternalistic state interventionism allied to a commitment to free-market economics. They had moved a long way from their traditional commitment to the order imposed by aristocracy and monarchy.

For much of the 19th century the political map of Europe was characterised by numerous small states and frequently marked by rivalry and conflict. The nationalist movements that emerged in the midst of this were to reshape Europe. German nationalism in particular shifted from being liberal democratic in character to being conservative. A succession of wars in the second half of the century persuaded Germans that their 39 separate states would be more secure and orderly under a single independent state with an elected parliament but with executive power in the hands of an emperor. The appeal of creating a single state out of many smaller ones spread to other parts of Europe and beyond – to Italy, Russia and South America.

The spread of nationalism continued into the 20th century but experienced a serious loss of credibility through the excesses of Italian, German and Spanish fascism. Later, indigenous nationalist movements in Europe's declining colonial empires, in Africa and Asia in particular, ushered in a transformation of many of those societies into new independent states. In certain cases, nationalism in the new emerging nations combined with powerful political ideologies or fundamentalist religious convictions, as in the case of China and Iran.

Nationalists in general believe in the state as the most natural form in which citizens can determine how they will be governed, and that sovereignty and independence are crucial for this. However the globalisation of the world through the creation of supranational organisations and the suspicion that certain powers are engaged in economic imperialism threatens the independence, traditions and cultures of many smaller nations.

These are some of the issues covered in this chapter, in which the following are key themes.

- The origins, core principles and values of conservatism

- Whether conservatism is now ideological or opposed to ideology

- The nature of nationalism and the values of self-determination, oneness and independence

- The key thinkers and the types of conservatism and nationalism

- How conservatism and nationalism differ in regard to human nature, the role of the state, reform and organicism

- The trends of modern conservatism

- The ideology of the Conservative Party since 1990 and the impacts on its ideology

In covering these themes the chapter is broken down into the following topics.

The chapter finishes with an exam café feature on page 202.

Origins and development of conservatism

Conservatism is one of the most difficult ideologies to define, as it is in essence a reactionary movement. It is often seen as the antithesis of individualist liberalism which became prominent after a series of liberal-inspired 18th and 19th century revolutions. Conservatives favour an interrelated, organic society. However, by the 1980s in Britain when collectivist-style socialism was popular, the Conservative Party under Margaret Thatcher abruptly turned towards individualism.

It is important to note that the Conservative Party in Britain is not the same as conservatism; rather conservatism is an international ideology with different elements. French conservatives are nationalist; Americans have a strong religious theme whilst British conservatives are often portrayed as being quite liberal.

Conservatism can trace its roots back to the late 18th century, with one of the first statements of conservative principles written by Edmund Burke in 1790 (see the section on 'Key conservative thinkers' on page 186) as a response to those in Britain who supported the French Revolution in 1789.

Later, by the 19th century, as industrialisation got underway in Britain and there was a growth in the popularity of liberalism, socialism and nationalism, all of which at the very least were in favour of sweeping reforms, conservatism stood alone in order to protect the traditional social order.

Over the years, conservative ideas have developed and adapted. In Britain conservatism has generally been exemplified by the concept of change in order to conserve, in other words making adjustments rather than sweeping reforms to maintain traditional structures and social order. In the United States conservative ideas only really began to be labelled as such from the 1960s, with southern Democrats being associated with conservative views such as racial segregation, along with the bulk of the Republican Party.

In other parts of the world, political movements have displayed conservative tendencies by trying to resist change and to hang onto traditional ways of life. In countries such as Iran and Argentina conservatives have been able to mobilise support for the defence of traditional values, as well as nationalism.

Conservatives do not tend to tie themselves down to fixed sets of ideas. Margaret Thatcher and Ronald Reagan are associated with radical and ideological forms of conservatism, which as we will see are often referred to as the New Right. This was a challenge to traditional conservative views. It did not abandon basic principles on authority, discipline and order, but it was clearly influenced by classical liberal economic ideas, as they were strong advocates of the free market.

Conservatism has moved significantly on from the 19th century defence of the aristocracy and the monarchy through to a support for paternalistic state intervention allied to championing the free market. It has, however, as we will see, aroused enormous ideological debate that has at times threatened to overwhelm conservatism.

Core principles and values of conservatism

As we have seen, the key theme of conservatism is to conserve tradition. This does not necessarily mean that conservatives actually resist change. Over the years there have been different interpretations and practice of the core principles, as they have adapted to each new challenge. The key values are examined in the following table.

Core value	Explanation
Human nature	Conservatives are rather more pessimistic about basic human nature than many ideologies. Some conservatives take the Roman Catholic view of original sin and believe that however hard individuals try they cannot achieve perfection. Some conservatives also believe that individuals are not driven by reason but by their basic drives and appetites. Individuals cannot be trusted with government, as they will use it solely for self-interest. They also believe that human nature is not constant and that it is ever changing and therefore there should not be a fixed view of human nature. Sometimes individuals will desire individualism whilst at other times they will look for a paternalistic government. Many conservatives see people as being largely self-seeking and that government is absolutely necessary to control them. This in a nutshell is paternalism, and the conservatives can provide that firm government. In 1984 Margaret Thatcher said 'there are individuals and there are families. There is no such thing as society.'
Belief in order	Conservatives believe that the most basic needs for humans are order and security. They therefore believe that humans are prepared to give up freedom and rights in favour of security, hence they support strong government. They traditionally strongly support law and order, rather than civil liberties.
Support for tradition and preservation	This is closely related to the desire to ensure order. By protecting traditional institutions and values the accumulated wisdom of the past can be used. As Burke said 'no generation should ever be so rash as to consider itself superior to its predecessors'. Conservatives favour continuity between the past and the present and avoid radical reforms and changes. Ideologies, governments and fads may come and go but in order to give people security something has to endure. Having said this, British conservatives in the 1980s embarked on privatisation, monetarism, a rejection of the dependency culture (welfare state) and even attacked the Church of England, the civil service and the city of London.
Natural inequality	In the past conservatives accepted that society was naturally divided by hierarchies. This was natural and inevitable. However, they have adapted to change in society, particularly since the 1980s, and now view people as individuals rather than part of a hierarchical structure. Redistribution of resources is seen as unnatural and conservatives believe that inequality is a positive aspect of competition.
Pragmatism	Conservatives take a flexible approach. They try to understand what is best, most acceptable and what will preserve a stable society. They reject strongly held ideologies and dogmatic decision-making. A conservative should engage with people and come up with solutions that reflect the traditions of the community. This was particularly evident in 1951 when the conservatives did not roll back the Labour Party's nationalisation programme, the creation of the welfare state and new powers for local government.
Individualism	Conservatives believe that the state should restrict choices for individuals as little as possible. They also strongly support privacy. The private life has nothing to do with the state and religion, property, family expenditure and the running of private businesses should not be interfered with by government. They believe that individualism works well in a stable environment, with morality, law and order and tradition as a backbone.
Sanctity of property	Originally, conservatives in Britain were wary of the property-owning middle class as they believed that they would use their economic power in the political sphere. By the late 19th century conservatives believed that they needed to incorporate the interests of property owners in their policies. Conservatives are resistant to common ownership of property and high property taxes. Law and order focuses on protecting property and broadening property ownership, such as requiring councils to give preferential terms to tenants in purchasing council-owned property (Thatcher referred to this as the creation of a 'property-owning democracy'). This is on the basis of giving individuals a stake in society and promoting responsibility.

DISCUSSION POINT ?

How far do the values of conservatism add up to a coherent ideology?

Learning objectives

● Reactionary

● Authoritarian

● Paternalistic

● One nation

● Libertarian

● The New Right

Reactionary

It was the French Revolution that prompted the reactionary right conservatives to leap to the defence of the old European order. They defended traditional religious authority against radical scepticism and liberal secularism. They supported the established monarchies against the republicans and rejected any attempt to dislodge patriarchal authority.

The most significant theorist of the time was Joseph de Maistre. He believed that authority needed defending to preserve order and that there should be obedience to tradition and religiously sanctified rulers.

In many respects there is little to distinguish this from authoritarian conservatism, however the differences lie in reaction rather than viewpoint.

Authoritarian

We have seen that de Maistre was reactionary and unprepared to accept reform, even though the traditional French state had been overthrown in 1789. Even after the French Revolution conservatives remained solidly behind hierarchical values and autocratic rule, despite pressure from other ideologies and movements.

Conservative authoritarianism was alive and dominant in Germany, where although there was constitutional development there was authoritarianism under Bismarck who was determined to protect the authority of the German Kaiser. In Russia Tsar Nicholas I and his successors held back constitutional government and parliament, refusing to relinquish any power. By 1864 authoritarianism had even been granted the seal of approval from the Pope.

Conservative authoritarians though are not averse to sweeping aside existing governments. Napoleon Bonaparte is one such example, as is Juan Peron who was elected as the President of Argentina three times but whose enemies regarded him as a dictator.

Paternalistic

This tradition can be traced back to Edmund Burke and is a rather more flexible and successful strand of conservatism. At the centre of the beliefs are tradition, property, authority and order, and policies are developed purely to handle specific circumstances.

Paternalism literally means acting in a fatherly manner, exercising power and authority over others with the intention of providing a beneficial outcome and protecting them from harm.

As we will see, one of the key paternalistic forms of conservatism is 'one nation conservatism'; however, Christian democratic parties, particularly those in Europe since 1945, could also be considered to be paternalistic in nature.

One nation

Benjamin Disraeli was undoubtedly the founding father of the conservative paternalistic tradition. He had already established many of his views before he became prime minister for the first time in 1868. He identified that there were two nations in Britain: the rich and the poor.

Disraeli believed that something had to be done about the growing social inequality, as he feared that unless action was taken there could be revolution. Reform was therefore the key. It would be difficult for the wealthy and the privileged, but he believed they had an obligation and a responsibility to do something, and ultimately it would be in their interests. The belief was that society was inherently hierarchical, inherently unequal and that the wealthy and the powerful should take on the responsibilities as the price for their privileges. In effect it was based on a kind of feudal image of obligation.

Libertarian

Understandably, libertarian conservatives are heavily influenced by classical liberal ideas. They believe that traditional conservative ideas on authority and duty are entirely compatible with liberal economics. Key theorists include Edmund Burke and Adam Smith, both supporters of economic liberalism. The libertarians believe that the free market is both fair and efficient, and that it could be defended on the grounds of tradition, just as the church or the monarchy could. They have a pessimistic view of human nature and believe a strong state is needed to ensure order and authority, and see the free market as being a way in which to ensure social discipline, as it regulates economic and social activity.

The New Right

The New Right tradition developed during the 1970s. It was originally used as a term to describe a junction of beliefs between the free market theories of Adam Smith and traditional conservatism based on the defence of order, authority and discipline.

Some describe the new right as neo-conservatives; others might describe them as neo-liberals. However, they stand for lower taxation, control on immigration, a reduction in economic and social intervention by government and the rolling back of permissive social values.

There are in fact two competing strands of the New Right, as can be seen in the following table.

Liberal New Right *Hayek and Nozick*	Conservative New Right *Strauss and Kristol*
They favour classical liberalism.	They are essentially traditional conservatives.
They believe that the focus should always be on the individual and not on society.	They view society as a whole rather than as a collection of individuals.
They are essentially radical and reformist.	They represent traditionalism.
They support libertarianism.	They are essentially authoritarian.
They are strong supporters of economic dynamism.	They place social order as their highest priority.
They encourage and support self-interest and private enterprise.	They stand for traditional Christian moral values.
They seek to provide equal opportunities for all.	They believe in a natural hierarchy.
They are against state intervention and argue for a minimalist state.	They favour a strong state.
They take an international view in terms of involvement.	They are inward-looking nationalists.
They are in favour of economic globalisation.	They are against globalisation.

Disraeli and conservatism

Rather than Britain consisting of two nations it would be one nation, with a commitment to pre-industrial, hierarchical and paternalistic values. In effect one nation conservatism is the conservative version of the welfare state.

Wider social support as a result of the new relationships would bring working-class votes for the Conservative Party, as voting rights were extended. This scenario was realised in the 1960s with full employment, welfare provision and a balance or moderation of views among the population.

In later years this has been referred to as 'compassionate conservatism' and a means by which to improve the conditions of the poor so that they do not pose a threat to the established order.

DISCUSSION POINT ?

Which tradition would you most closely associate with the modern Conservative Party?

Hayek and Thatcher

With the rise of conservative governments in Britain and in the US in the 1980s, Hayek became a key theorist and influence. Margaret Thatcher (prime minister 1979–90) according to John Ranelagh in *Thatcher's People: An Insider's Account of the Politics, the Power, and the Personalities* (1991), just after she became leader of the Conservative Party, pulled out a copy of Friedrich Hayek's *The Constitution of Liberty* from her briefcase. Brandishing it so that all of the cabinet could see it, she told them that she was a firm believer of Hayek's views and she slammed the book onto the table.

Taxation is theft

Robert Nozick's book *Anarchy, State and Utopia* (1974) is much misunderstood by its admirers. Many believe that it provided philosophical support for the policies of Ronald Reagan and Margaret Thatcher, but its criticism of social conservatism is at least as devastating as its criticism of the redistributive welfare state. Nozick argued that everyone should be allowed to do what he liked with his own property. Nozick saw progressive taxation for any purpose other than the maintenance of a minimal **'night watchman' state** as a form of voluntary slavery.

To what extent is conservatism ideological?

A political ideology is a comprehensive set of beliefs about the political world or a belief system that society can be improved by following certain doctrines.

Given that an ideology tends to have fixed principles that are both clear and interrelated and that there should be clear, specific goals, added to which there should be a consistent belief system and a series of theories and assumptions about humans and the nature of society, then probably conservatism is not ideological.

Traditional conservatism, as far as theorists such as Michael Oakeshott is concerned, should not have any real sense of direction. However, there was a vision of society where there were free individuals, broader ownership of shares and industry, and a personal responsibility for welfare in the New Right conservatism of Thatcher and Keith Joseph.

Traditional conservatives avoid the creation of fixed principles and have tended to be implacably opposed to parties and movements that have these. Conservatives adapt to change and reflect the dominant political environment of the time. When the conservatives' main opponents in the 19th century were the liberals they had an essentially organic view of society. They wanted individuals to have a sense of responsibility. When their key opponents in the 20th century were the socialists the conservatives switched to individualism and free markets, to offset the collectivist views of socialists.

The New Right, however, does have fixed ideas. Central to these is monetarism and the belief that by controlling public spending and currency the whole economy can be manipulated. They had inflexible views towards the welfare state and taxation, both of which they saw as challenges to economic prosperity. They believed that society would be far more prosperous if there was less government regulation. In this respect, perhaps traditional conservatives with a more flexible approach are less ideological than their modern-day counterparts.

Underlying conservative ideology is the preference of order over liberty, the belief that tradition and existing institutions are more desirable and reliable than the unknowns of radical change. However, the New Right is a radical movement and it has, at times, rejected traditional values.

Opposition to ideology

As we have seen, conservatism is adaptable and perfectly prepared to respond by adjusting itself to match the dominant political landscape at a particular time. At heart conservatives are opposed to radical change, yet their unwillingness to create immovable ideologies is far more entrenched.

- Most ideologies have some idealised form of society and the focus is on achieving that vision. Conservatives see this as being a major danger to tradition, as some visionary image of the future is contrived and somewhat artificial. It also undermines social stability. On the one hand, conservatives do not oppose social improvement; they believe it should be pursued but only within the context of traditions and the desires of individuals, rather than basing it on a set of vague visionary principles. This was the view of Oakeshott.

- We have already seen that Burke had grave reservations about the impact of the French Revolution and the way in which radical change swept aside traditional institutions and values. Conservatives therefore view ideology as being radical in its very nature. Burke referred to the revolutionaries as 'tearing away the decent draperies of life'. They favour gradual reform, which sustains a sense of continuity.

Night watchman state
This is a state whose only role is to protect its citizens' rights. In other words government is limited to courts.

- Conservatives are also wary of ideology in the sense that it could bring about some kind of authoritarian or totalitarian system. Conservatives have supported this view by pointing out that certain ideologies do engender a radical pursuit of political goals. They have seen this in communism, fascism and radical feminism. They see these views as being essentially tyrannical and ruthless. Conservatives see political correctness as being akin to the revolutionary and tyrannical rule of the Jacobins under Robespierre in France. They also see that any revolutionary change could bring anarchy, as it will inevitably dismantle traditional authority and social order.

- Conservatives also view ideology with a degree of suspicion on the basis that it is mostly based on a fixed view of human nature. They do not have a fixed view of human nature; they believe that it is changeable and irrational. Further, they actually believe that ideological views are not often based on human nature; they simply influence human nature. This implies that ideologies are manipulative and they create societies that are doomed to failure as they are artificial. The view of Karl Popper was that the communist regimes inspired by Marxism were not natural, as equality and state or common ownership was imposed and therefore they were doomed to failure.

Bizarrely, conservatives are not only suspicious of fixed political principles, but also of politics itself. They believe that it should be limited. Lord Hailsham, a prominent British conservative, said (in Hogg, Q. (1947) *The Case for Conservatism*, Penguin): 'The man who puts politics before his family is not fit to be called a civilised human being.'

Conservatives favour judging current options with what has happened in the past. They believe that politicians should learn and mimic policies and approaches that worked for past generations. Somewhat unfairly, the 19th century writer G. K. Chesterton described this as being 'the democracy of the dead'.

This reflects the view that rather than being ideological conservatives are backward looking. But they would claim that many great things have been achieved in the past and by studying and copying the ways in which these events unfolded and were handled informs us of how we should deal with situations in the future. Burke referred to each generation as 'life renters' who have a duty to form a partnership between 'those who are living, those who are dead and those yet to be born'.

None of this necessarily explains the blend of modern-day conservatism or Margaret Thatcher's contention that she was a classical liberal. Thatcher and her supporters were opposed to policies that appeared to drain society of its dynamism and reduce economic freedom.

The New Right can be described as having a form of ideology. There has been an emphasis on personal morality and they strongly support a return to basic values, such as traditional education, patriotism and the family. They are strong supporters of using prison sentencing as a deterrent, they take a hard line on crime, and they favour greater powers for the police. As we will see, they are deeply committed to protecting national sovereignty and the unity of Great Britain. As a result, they have opposed greater European integration and devolution. Essentially, the New Right sees Britain as a nation state and fundamentally resists any attempts to undermine its independence. They see diversity as a threat to the community and wish to limit immigration but also ensure that the immigrants that remain in Britain adhere to British values.

DISCUSSION POINT ?

Is conservatism ideological?

Learning objectives

- Thomas Hobbes
- Edmund Burke
- Benjamin Disraeli
- Michael Oakeshott
- Friedrich Hayek

Thomas Hobbes (1588–1679)

Hobbes was the son of a vicar and an Oxford graduate. In 1608 he became the private tutor to Charles Stuart, the exiled Prince of Wales.

Hobbes was writing at a time of great upheaval, a time of civil war in Britain, and by 1640 he fled to Paris in fear of persecution as a result of his writing. He returned to England in 1651, the same year in which his tour de force, *Leviathan*, was published.

With the restoration of the monarchy in 1660 and his former pupil on the throne, Hobbes enjoyed a new prominence in Britain. Six years later he would again face danger when the House of Commons legislated against atheism and profanity and appeared to be hell bent on investigating Hobbes.

Hobbes saw absolutist government as the antidote to anarchy and disorder – he described life outside of an ordered society as, 'nasty, short and brutish'. He believed that citizens should have total obligation to the state and he supported authoritarianism. In Hobbes's view, humans were selfish and greedy and they craved power. He believed that individuals should be prepared to sacrifice liberty in order to have social order.

Edmund Burke (1729–97)

Burke was born in 1729 and he too lived through a turbulent period of British and world history: the American War of Independence in 1776 and the French Revolution 13 years later.

Burke became a Whig politician, sympathetic towards American independence, but critical of the French Revolution. He supported the sanctity of property and supported the American colonists in their campaign for 'no tax without representation'. He also supported the right of property-owning Irish Catholics to be given the vote. He was, however, implacably opposed to the idea that tradition and history should be swept aside as they were the cornerstones of all wisdom. He saw that the French were trying to replace this with what he considered abstract ideas of liberty, equality and fraternity. He blamed the French monarchy for what had happened and felt they had failed to make vital changes in order to preserve their position. However, he continued to uphold the right of the French aristocracy, church and monarchy to have their traditional interests preserved and displayed his contempt for democracy and egalitarianism by describing the expansion of the franchise by the new National Assembly as the 'rule of hairdressers and candle-makers'.

Overall, Burke, although he became a member of parliament for Bristol in the 1770s, had a very dim view of government. He saw that it could prevent evil, but he believed it was rare that it would promote good. Burke was broadly in favour of parliamentary reform, and he was in favour of limiting the power of the monarch.

Although Burke never provided a comprehensive view of his beliefs, we can say that his key principles revolved around natural law. He believed that man should be in harmony with his environment and that he had a natural impulse towards self-restraint. This meant that man should have a respect for traditional institutions, customs and values, yet it was acceptable to make reforms in order to deal with specific tensions and issues.

Benjamin Disraeli (1804–81)

Benjamin Disraeli was to become what many regard as the great Tory prime minister. He believed that by the 1860s society effectively consisted of three classes. There was the working class, that should not exercise power in a direct way, but their interests should be represented. The second class were the wealth creators, capitalists and commercial individuals. They could not be trusted with power because they were driven by self-interest. The third class were the landed and aristocratic individuals, who had always enjoyed privileges. They had to accept responsibility if they were to continue to enjoy these privileges. These were, in effect, the ruling class.

Disraeli's greatest contribution to conservatism was his belief in the organic nature of society. He was a strong advocate of pursuing policies that united the nation to create a one nation. (This is a quote from his novel *Sybil*: 'Two nations between whom there is no intercourse and no sympathy; who are as ignorant of each other's habits, thoughts, and feelings, as if they were dwellers in different zones, or inhabitants of different planets: the rich and the poor.') He believed that government should not rule in the interests of only one class but in the interests of all classes. Unity and the avoidance of social conflict were the key considerations. He believed that there needed to be constitutional unity, the maintenance of tradition, the encouragement of patriotism and the availability of welfare for the poor.

A great many conservatives still follow Disraeli's principles. Admittedly they are updated. These include Kenneth Clarke and Michael Heseltine.

Michael Oakeshott (1901–90)

Michael Oakeshott was a civil servant who became a leading member of the Fabian Society and was a close friend of George Bernard Shaw.

Most significantly, Oakeshott suggested that conservatism should not have fixed goals. In his book *On Being Conservative* (1962) he drew the analogy of the state as like being a ship in a sea. The ship has no origin and no destination. The role of the government or the captain that commands the ship is simply to keep the ship moving and to look after the passengers. In this respect he believed that conservatives should be pragmatic, they should value tradition, but they should also take notice of the demands of people. He used the term 'intimations' and by this he meant the government should be consistently aware of what people want and run the state in line with this.

Oakeshott believed that if the government had fixed principles and theories then this would be impossible. Central to his beliefs was that government should govern by doing what is right for the citizens, not what they think is right for the citizens.

Many have seen Oakeshott's views as encompassing both traditional and New Right conservatism. He is in accordance with traditional conservatives in that he does not favour ideology but favours pragmatism. He also is associated with the New Right and limited government, and the desire to give freedom to citizens and pull back from regulating and legislating.

Friedrich Hayek (1899–1992)

Hayek was an enormous influence on Margaret Thatcher and Keith Joseph. He was concerned about the dangers of socialism. As far as he was concerned, individualism was the big loser in socialism and that socialism was merely one step on the road to totalitarianism. He saw the power of the state and trade unions as being the ways in which totalitarianism would come into existence. Hayek pointed at the Soviet Union as the prime culprit, but believed that other countries could replicate this disastrous set of circumstances.

Hayek supported traditionalism, individualism, market order and constitutionalism. He would become an enormous influence on the conservative New Right.

> **DISCUSSION POINT** ?
>
> How much have the key conservative thinkers influenced modern-day conservatism?

Learning objectives

- Origins and development
- Self-determination
- Organic society
- Independence

Origins and development

The term nationalism was first used in 1789. Originally, the term nation simply described a group of people who shared a birthplace. It was a breed of people or a racial group and did not necessarily have any political overtones.

Nationalism, however, grew during the 19th century as a political movement. It can be said to represent the desire for the world to be divided up into distinct nations with the nation as the only legitimate and appropriate type of political rule.

Before the birth of the nationalist ideology individuals were simply subjects of a ruler; there was no particular patriotism or national identity. The French Revolution changed this for the people of France; instead of simply being subjects of a monarch they became citizens of the country.

Much of Europe was a patchwork of small states, often under the control of larger empires. The Napoleonic wars were instrumental in bringing these small states together to form single nations each with a national identity, particularly in Italy and Germany. This was replicated in Latin America, where new nations such as Peru and Venezuela were created after a successful revolution against the Spanish Empire. There were further nationalist movements across Russia, Austria and Turkey. By 1871, what had been 39 tiny German states was now one nation.

Nationalism began to stand for cohesion, order, stability, and was indeed a popular movement. Each nation looked to its past glories and its strengths, and viewed other countries with a degree of xenophobia.

Nationalism continued to spread in the 20th century. In the aftermath of the First World War, new nations were created out of a defeated Germany and Austria, as well as parts of Russia. These included Hungary and Poland.

However, extreme right-wing nationalism created tensions in the 1920s and 1930s, in particular in Germany where fascism became a powerful force in the form of the Nazi Party, whose ambitions to spread its ideology to other nations led to the Second World War. In the second half of the 20th century the decline of the western colonial powers in various parts of the world and the spread of nationalism among indigenous peoples led to the emergence of new nations, as in Africa and Asia.

In some parts of the world nationalism combined with political and religious beliefs, as in the case with Marxism in China and Vietnam and with Islamic fundamentalism in Iran.

Self-determination

The principle of self-determination is one that underlies many of the priorities of democratic politics. In effect this simply means that people have the right to determine how they are governed. Nationalists would claim that the nation is the most natural unit upon which to base self-determination. However, this has not always been particularly easy, due to circumstance and history.

Many different parts of the world have been compelled to be subjects of a foreign power. In many of these areas the desire grew among the people to have their own sovereign state and independence, as was the case in India, America and Vietnam. Sovereignty is an important aspect of being a nation and should be at the heart of self-determination and independence. However, there are regions of countries which have a degree of self-determination but no sovereignty, such as Catalonia in Spain and Quebec in Canada.

Other groups of people have sought self-determination to free themselves from oppression by a small minority that controls the government and military power, such as the black majority in South

Creation of the state of Israel

The creation of Israel was the culmination of the Zionist movement's goal (Zionism is an international political movement that originally supported the re-establishment of a homeland for the Jewish People in Palestine) of establishing a homeland for Jews scattered all over the world following the Diaspora. After the Holocaust, pressure grew for the international recognition of a Jewish state, and in 1948 Israel was created. For Jewish people it marked the end of millennia of dispersion, the failure of anti-Semitic groups, political organisations and religious factions. It established a safe haven, a country where the Jewish people could organise their own defence and establish their own state.

Africa which was freed from the oppression of the apartheid system of government controlled by the white minority, and the people of Tibet who were absorbed by force into China in 1951.

Other national groups of people have been in the position of not having a country of their own yet sharing a common ancestry and identity. This is particularly true of the Jews who created the state of Israel and achieved self-determination in Israel.

Equally nationalist movements have emerged in order to protect sovereignty and self-determination. Israel again is a prime example, as are Poland and South Korea.

Organic society

The organic society is basically the concept of oneness, a notion that binds individuals together, and is stronger than individual identity. The German philosopher Georg Wilhelm Friedrich Hegel (1770–1831) believed that this was an expression of the universal will, something that bound individuals together, seeing themselves as a single entity. Johann Gottfried von Herder (1744–1803), also a German philosopher, believed that the world consisted of national cultures and collectively they represented an organic whole.

The German term Volksgemeinschaft (national community) describes the factors that bring people together so that they consider themselves as a separate community, or as having a shared identity. These factors could include institutions, history, language and national symbols.

An even more radical form of nationalism was used by Mussolini and his fascists in Italy to create the idea that individual interests had to be sacrificed in favour of the nation.

Independence

For most nationalists independence is a key objective, but in Britain we have clear nationalist groups in Scotland, Wales, England and Northern Ireland. Although there are factions within each area of Great Britain that support some kind of independence, the most overwhelming concern is the protection of culture and ways of life.

Whilst some Welsh nationalists want independence, most are more concerned with retaining their culture and language. Northern Ireland is more complicated, as there are strong unionist groups that want nothing to do with independence. They also wish to defend their culture and their affinity to Britain. On the other hand there are the republicans who wish to sever links with Britain. Both groups could be considered nationalist.

There is a small movement in England advocating English nationalism (e.g. English Democrats), but an integral part of their nationalism is to retain the United Kingdom. The concept of British nationalism is frequently viewed by Welsh, Scottish and Irish nationalists as a front for English cultural and political dominance. In most other cases around the world, however, nationalist movements do want political independence. Some desire it because they are still dominated by an Imperial power; others believe it is necessary in order to ensure their self-preservation; and others desire independence to avoid the risk of being dominated by a supranational body, such as the European Union. In fact most nationalists in Europe are implacably opposed to the European Union on the grounds that the creeping influence of the supranational organisation is undermining independence.

Countries that have come to rely on supranational bodies, such as the World Trade Organisation, the International Monetary Fund and the World Bank, also view their independence as being threatened by these bodies. In return for financial aid they have to surrender a degree of economic freedom. Such countries include Tanzania, Indonesia and Argentina. Many of the nationalists in these countries believe the United States is behind the apparent threat to independence and view this as a form of economic imperialism.

Stormont parliament building in Belfast, Northern Ireland, where peace talks took place to resolve the conflict with the Republican nationalist movement, the IRA

DISCUSSION POINT

Why might English nationalism be a less significant force in British politics than Scottish or Welsh nationalism?

The Welsh Assembly debating chamber

Liberal nationalism

Liberalism aims to secure the rights of individuals so that they can be free. A logical extension to this is that every nation should be free. The liberal nationalists link the freedom of nations with the freedom of individuals.

Liberal nationalists contend that a nation has to have the right to freedom from other nations and states. Notable examples include the Young Italy Movement of Giuseppe Mazzini (1860s Italy), which sought to bring together the different states in Italy that were then controlled by a number of other countries. Another example is the Scottish nationalists that emerged in the latter part of the 20th century and believed that if democracy were to be fully established in Scotland then self-determination was a priority.

Conservative nationalism

Conservatives were somewhat suspicious of liberal nationalism, as they believed that it would sweep away traditional authority and undermine order. They also feared that in countries that had a multinational population there would be civil war when the imperial power relinquished control.

Conservative nationalists base their ideas on the fact that a nation is a cultural idea, binding people together with a common sense of history and tradition. They believe that nationalism could unify the people of a society and ensure order. This would prevent social conflict and allow for the development of the nation so that it could achieve its destiny; this required national unity.

Conservative nationalism in Britain today is represented politically by the UKIP (United Kingdom Independence Party), which believes that British national identity is under threat by European integration.

Right-wing nationalism

Right-wing nationalism is an extreme version of conservative nationalism and is exemplified by these three different examples.

- **Imperialism** – This is the creation of an empire as part of a country's national interest and destiny. This reflects competition between nations for superiority and access to economic resources. Notable examples are Britain in the 19th century, Japan in the 1930s and the Soviet Union in the 20th century.

- **Expansionism** – This is an attempt by a country to spread its political control over neighbouring countries and to ensure that they have dominant influence in a region. Recent examples include China, Russia and Serbia.

- **Xenophobia** – A suspicion of foreigners and a desire to maintain a clear national identity. This would include attempts to ensure cultural uniformity and resist immigration. There have been notable examples in France, Austria and Holland.

Cultural nationalism

This is not necessarily related to independence as such, but more to do with ensuring that a distinctive culture is freed from a more dominant culture that threatens to overwhelm it. A prime example in Britain is Welsh nationalism.

The Welsh nationalists are more interested in limited autonomy than sovereignty. A more extreme version is known as Volkism, which is more radical and can often lead to conflict. It was particularly obvious in Germany in the 1930s to 1940s, where they believed in race superiority, a sense of historical destiny and used nationalism to justify expansionism. Zionism can also be described as Volkism, as it seeks to ensure that Israel remains in Jewish hands.

Post-colonial nationalism

Nationalism is a powerful tool when a country is trying to gain its independence, as it seeks to ensure that there is a directed and coherent opposition to the imperial power, based on social unity and national identity. Many newly independent states are actually authoritarian, as the boundaries of those states are often determined in an arbitrary way and, therefore, incorporate multicultural groups, such as different tribes or racial groups. Without an authoritarian government many of them have collapsed into civil war (such as Uganda or Ethiopia). Others have become one-party states, such as Zimbabwe or Tanzania. Others, as we will see, have become socialist states.

Socialist nationalism

Socialism and nationalism do not naturally fit together. Marxists view nationalism as a fake consciousness created by the ruling class in the interests of capitalism, to divert attention away from revolutionary activities. Having said this, there are examples of modern-day nationalists who are in fact socialists. This is particularly true of countries that had been former colonies, such as Zimbabwe or Vietnam.

Socialism is used in conjunction with nationalism to underpin independence and self-determination and to distance them from the former imperial and capitalist power. Socialism is used to create solidarity, national purpose and unity through justice. It is also seen as a blueprint for state-led rapid economic development.

Racial nationalism

In countries where nationalism is based on ethnic identity, racialism is obviously a key part of the equation. Hitler, for example, based his racist world view on theorists such as Nietzsche, Count Arthur de Gobineau and Houston Chamberlain. These theories rested on a hierarchy of races with German or Aryan people at the top of the hierarchy and Asians and Africans at the bottom. Also central was the purity of the nation's bloodline. Retaining purity would give strength of will.

Not all nationalism based on racialism has this necessarily sinister background. The Organisation for African Unity recognises that countries in Africa are based on ethnic groups, that they should all be treated equally and that there should be mutual respect and peace. Other ethnic groups that do not have this superiority element are those that seek to unite Arab peoples or the Slavic race.

The table on the right provides a summary of the characteristics of the various types of nationalists.

Type of nationalism	Characteristics	Examples
Liberal	Self-determination Democracy Liberty	Scotland and Ireland
Conservative	Preserve national interest Retain social unity Possibly imperialist	British conservatism and French Gaullism
Right wing	Xenophobic National superiority Totalitarian Expansionist	Italian fascism French National Front
Cultural	Protecting cultural tradition from other dominant culture	Welsh nationalism Hindus in India (against the influence of Muslims)
Post-colonial	Socialist or autocratic focusing on self-sufficiency and national unity	Tanzania and Nigeria
Socialist	One-party state Centralised Resistant to foreign investment	Zimbabwe and Cuba
Racial	Racial superiority and exclusivity Unifying the racial group in one state and therefore expansionist	Nazism and South Africa under apartheid

DISCUSSION POINT ?

Can Scottish nationalism be described in any other way than liberal nationalism?

Learning objectives

- Johann Gottfried von Herder
- Giuseppe Mazzini
- Charles de Gaulle
- Julius Nyerere

Johann Gottfried von Herder (1744–1803)

Von Herder was the forerunner of the German Romantic Movement. He was closely associated with other theorists such as Immanuel Kant and Johann Wolfgang von Goethe.

Von Herder became the leading figure of the Sturm und Drang (storm and stress movement), which focused on culture and language. At the time the area of Europe that we now know as Germany was a jigsaw of tiny states. He believed that culture was transmitted from one generation to the next through language and that nationality was a key component of language.

Herder was not directly concerned with politics, but more focused on cultural independence and how it should be freed from the domination of other cultures. To him nationalism was all about the restoration and preservation of culture, as well as state power.

Von Herder was a great lover of language. In 1784 he wrote:

> Has a nation anything dearer than the speech of its fathers? In its speech resides its whole thought domain, its tradition, history, religion, and basis of life, all its heart and soul. To deprive a people of its own speech is to deprive it of its one eternal good. As God tolerates all the different languages of the world, so also should a ruler not only tolerate but honour the various languages of his peoples. The best culture of a people cannot be expressed through a foreign language.

The 20th century fascists drew on Herder's beliefs, but distorted them, as he himself did not believe in racial distinctions or tyranny as ways of promoting nationalism. His thoughts have far more in common with Welsh nationalism, that focuses on history, culture and language.

Giuseppe Mazzini (1805–72)

Mazzini was also something of a romantic who saw nationalism expressed in social solidarity and underpinned by comradeship. In 1831 he was the founder of the Young Italy Movement, a revolutionary nationalist group.

Mazzini himself was a liberal republican who believed in self-determination and unity of freedom. He believed that Europe should be composed of just 12 nation states, built on dominant cultural groups. To him the underlying purpose of nationalism was social progress. In many respects dividing people into cultural groups was rather like the division of labour in capitalism. They could develop their own cultures and have liberty.

Mazzini was also a strong supporter of guerrilla warfare, where small secret groups would try to undermine repressive government by waging war against them. His influence led to Garibaldi's unification campaign that resulted in the final unification of the Italian state in 1871. He was ultimately to become an inspirational figure for nationalist movements across South America and Indo-China.

Charles de Gaulle (1890–1970)

After the ignominious collapse of the French in 1940, de Gaulle was one of the relative handful of Frenchmen who fled occupied Europe and who would become the self-proclaimed leader of the Free French forces.

De Gaulle was a French nationalist and would pursue policies that were solely in the national self-interest of France. In the years after the Second World War, France had insuperable difficulties in hanging onto their colonies in Algeria and Indo-China. Both were in rebellion; French military leaders appeared poised to topple the French civilian government. De Gaulle stepped in to form a new government. He rewrote the constitution, brought in the fifth French republic and gave himself sweeping presidential powers.

Throughout his political career, de Gaulle ruthlessly pursued national self-interest. France withdrew from NATO in 1966 and retained its own nuclear deterrent. De Gaulle stood in the way of Britain joining the European Community, because he felt that their membership would not be in the interests of the French. He also supported independence for French-speaking areas of Canada. Above all, de Gaulle wished to retain independent status, refusing to allow super powers to manipulate world affairs. To offset their influence, de Gaulle encouraged relationships with the Arab world, China and nationalist groups in Asia and Africa.

He resigned in 1968 after widespread unrest in France in response to his new proposals for changes to the French constitution.

De Gaulle's political group was known as the Union of Democrats of the Republic. It dissolved in 1976 and was replaced by Jacques Chirac's Rally for the Republic, a right-wing political party. The new movement was rather more pro-European than that of traditional Gaullists, and in fact some of the right of the party even denounced the group as not being true Gaullists in the spirit of the party's glory years of 1958 to 1976.

Statue of Charles de Gaulle

Julius Nyerere (1922–99)

Julius Nyerere became the first prime minister of an independent Tanganyika in 1961 and the first president of the renamed state of Tanzania in 1964. He was a major driving force behind the Organisation of African Unity (now known as the African Union).

Nyerere was born into and became leader of a country that had been artificially created as a former British colony and which was beset by deep divisions on tribal and linguistic lines.

Nyerere was determined to create an egalitarian socialist society based on cooperative agriculture. He collectivised farms, launched a mass literacy campaign and brought in free education. He focused on the country's abilities to become economically self-sufficient and not dependent on foreign aid and investment. He called his experiment family-hood, blending cooperation, racial and tribal harmony, and self-sacrifice.

Nyerere created a one-party state, but his policies largely failed. There were tensions between Tanzania and Uganda. In 1978 Uganda attempted to annex the Tanzanian province of Kagera. Nyerere responded by declaring war and ordering his troops into Uganda. Idi Amin's forces were defeated and he was deposed and expelled from his country, to live in exile for the rest of his life.

By the time Nyerere resigned in 1985, Tanzania was still one of the world's poorest countries. Industry and transport were underdeveloped and agriculture had barely moved beyond subsistence level. A third of the budget was still foreign aid, but Tanzania was far more politically stable than its neighbours and had one of the highest literacy rates in Africa.

DISCUSSION POINT ?

Is nationalism purely a right-wing ideology?

Conservatism and nationalism

Industrialisation in the 19th century hastened the decline of old-fashioned conservatism. It strengthened the middle class and created an industrial working class, with rather limited allegiance to traditional institutions. In Western Europe essentially liberal parties won repeated elections over conservative parties between 1830 and 1880. The progressive expansion of the franchise meant that the conservatives had to look for a new angle to secure the support of a broader electorate.

The chief sources of support, the rural workers, were in decline relative to other social groups and in any case there were too few of them to support an effective national party. Conservatives turned to nationalist sentiments, particularly in Germany, where the unification question had been the preoccupation of many parties since the middle of the 19th century. The Prussian chancellor, Otto von Bismarck, used nationalist sentiments to help create a united Germany under a Prussian monarch in 1871. His governments were essentially conservative and he used social welfare policies, such as national insurance schemes and the introduction of old-age pensions, to attract working-class support from the left-wing Social Democratic Party. Bismarck continued to protect landowners and the military classes using welfare measures to reduce the possibility of class conflict and to foster social cohesion.

By the end of the 19th century, most conservative parties in Europe had nationalist strategies. This brought them increased appeal in a period when patriotic feelings were running high and there was great international rivalry.

Human nature and the role of the state

Different political theories have developed alternative ideas about human nature. Each focuses on the assumptions they make about the natural state of humankind; in other words, how individuals would have behaved before there was society.

Socialists believe that humans are naturally sociable and cooperative. Conservatives tend to view individuals as being unreliable and driven by self-interest. Liberals view human nature as being essentially self-seeking and self-reliant, but they temper this with the belief that humans are essentially reasonable individuals and capable of personal development through education and training. Anarchists view humans as being essentially sociable and cooperative and that they are perfectly capable of sustaining order through collective effort.

Right-wing views, such as those of fascists, believe that humans are driven by their will and irrational drives and have a yearning for social belonging. The elite can become new men and strong leaders through their dedication to their race and their nation, whilst most other individuals are only capable of serving and obeying the elite. Nationalists such as von Herder believed that social belonging was both an essential part of both nationalism and of human nature.

David Cameron in 2008 gave his view on the role of the state, highlighting it as a major issue in British politics. He said that the Conservatives believed in bottom-up social responsibility, whereas the Labour Party favoured top-down state control. The Conservatives aimed to achieve this by collective provision, not supplied by the state, whereas Labour focused on state-delivered collective provision. Cameron stressed that society and the state were separate and that they would focus on enhancing the role of community groups, social enterprises and the voluntary sector, in order to create a stronger society.

Reform and organicism

Conservatives take the view that minor reforms and social engineering are necessary in order to safeguard traditional institutions and values. Socialists, for example, see sweeping reforms as being essential in order to create a more equal society. Liberals view reform in the context of ensuring that individual liberties are continued to be protected and supported.

Nationalists can take the view that major reforms may be necessary and may certainly be affected by the type of nationalism, such as right-wing nationalism restricting liberties and socialist nationalism focusing on equality of opportunity.

Organicism is almost the direct opposite to liberal pluralist democracies. Organicism is common to both conservatives and fascists; they believe that society is a single, evolving whole with a life of its own above the lives of individuals. Members of society are therefore interdependent.

Some theorists such as Hegel believed that organicism might be the answer to individual freedoms without undermining society's collective interests. In an organic society there is a strong social harmony and purpose running alongside individual fulfilment.

In terms of society itself, conservatives certainly see it as an organism that has an existence outside of the individual. Society binds people together by common morality, authority and tradition. Liberals simply see society as a collection of individuals, a voluntary or contractual arrangement made by humans who are essentially self-interested. Socialists begin by looking at society as exhibiting inequality with deep divisions. They see society in terms of the class struggle and aim to create a classless society.

Nationalists view society largely in terms of ethnic or cultural distinctions, with individuals in societies sharing beliefs and values, which are at the root of their national identity. They imply that multicultural societies are unstable.

Multiculturalists themselves view society as being a patchwork of different cultural identities and that the only common social bond is civic allegiance.

Feminists view society as being inherently patriarchal and make no distinction between public and private life. Society to them simply upholds male dominance.

Fascists view society as an organic whole and each individual's own existence only has meaning if it is dedicated to the common good; having said that, they limit membership to national or racial groups.

In Britain, for example, the New Right does not accept organic ideas and theories. They are more like libertarian conservatives who believe that society comprises self-reliant and self-seeking individuals.

Back in the early Victorian period, Jeremy Bentham put forward this view and it was echoed nearly 150 years later by Margaret Thatcher when she said: 'There is no such thing as society, only individuals and their families.'

The EU, immigration and the rise of British nationalism

Britain's quarterly accession monitoring figures support findings that eastern European migration into Britain is slowing down. The number of eastern European workers applying under the Worker Registration Scheme dropped to its lowest level since 2005, according to 2008 figures released by the Home Office. Between January and March 2008, 45,000 applications were lodged by nationals of the eight EU countries that joined in May 2004 (the so-called A8 nations). This was a 13 per cent decrease from the 52,000 applications lodged during the same period in 2007. The A8 nations are Estonia, Latvia, Lithuania, Poland, the Czech Republic, Hungary, Slovakia and Slovenia. Thousands of workers, mainly from Poland, Latvia and Lithuania, have come to Britain to work since their countries joined the EU; however, increased opportunities at home have led to many of these workers returning home.

During the first three months of 2008, 8205 applications were received from nationals of Bulgaria and Romania, compared to 10,420 received during the same period in 2007. The figures support a recent study by the Institute for Public Policy Research (ippr), which concluded that almost half of eastern European migrants who came to work in the UK since 2004 have already left.

Despite these figures, the perception that the country is being overrun with economic migrants and that by default the very nature and the culture of the British people are at threat, has led to a surge in support for the ultra-right nationalist groups, particularly in England. In the economically difficult 1970s, the National Front (another right-wing party) gained considerable support, but they made little electoral progress. The NF finally collapsed. There is no straightforward correlation between economic slumps and increased immigration and increased support for ultra-right groups in Britain. Their support has tended to be intermittent, geographically patchy and short-lasting, and has never really threatened the dominance of the main political parties.

Despite this appraisal of the situation, the BNP has continued to gain seats in east London and Stoke-on-Trent (it now holds 46 council seats in England). They had great success in the 2002 local elections in the North of England and a 4.9 per cent support in the Euro elections in 2004. For the first time ever in Britain, an openly racist party has gained the support of more than one in 20 British voters over several contests. In May 2008, the BNP's defeated mayoral candidate, Richard Barnbrook, won the party's first-ever seat on the Greater London Assembly. Final results from the GLA elections gave the BNP 5.33 per cent (130,714 Londoners) of the vote, enough to secure it a seat. According to the BNP itself, it had been 'propelled into the very centre of the government of our capital city'.

In April 2006, the YouGov carried out a poll to test overall electoral support for BNP policy and discovered that:

- 59 per cent supported a halt to all further immigration to the UK – one of the BNP's main pledges – when they were not told of the far-right group's association with the policy (this dropped to 48% when they were told)

- 52 per cent agreed that all immigrants should be denied the right to bring further members of their family into this country; when told about the BNP connection this fell to 43 per cent

- overall 55 per cent of people backed the BNP policies but when informed of the party's stance, this dropped to 49 per cent

- 37 per cent said they would seriously consider voting for the BNP's policies in an election, but identifying the BNP with the policies caused support to fall by 17 per cent

- 68 per cent refused to support the BNP view that non-white British citizens are less British than white ones, and 52 per cent were opposed to the BNP policy of encouraging immigrants and their families to leave Britain.

DISCUSSION POINT ?

How might the different theories on human nature tell us much about the nature of the theory itself?

New Right or neo-liberal?

Authoritarian conservatism, reflecting paternalistic and pragmatic views, dominated post-war politics until the 1970s. However, in the 1970s a more radical approach gained momentum, which would come to be known as the New Right. It is a broad term, but effectively it mixes elements of classical liberal economics (notably the free market theory of Adam Smith) and a traditional conservative view, focusing on discipline, authority and order. It is therefore possible to describe the New Right as being both neo-liberal and neo-conservative. These two strands were brought together in economic libertarianism and state and social authoritarianism. On the one hand it was traditional and reactionary, whilst on the other it was radical.

On the radical side the New Right sought to dismantle interventionist government policy and combat permissive social values. In this respect it dismisses tradition, however young or old that tradition may be. It is also reactionary, as it looks back to reconstruct a time when there was a solid economic basis to society and embedded morals. Simultaneously, traditional values are brought to the fore.

The following table seeks to identify the key differences between what could be described as the liberal New Right, or neo-liberals, and the conservative New Right, or neo-conservatives.

Learning objectives

- New Right or neo-liberal?
- Thatcher vs traditionalists
- Trends in modern conservatism

Neo-liberal	Neo-conservative
There is a focus on classical liberalism, specifically free market theory and an emphasis to dismantle economic and social intervention by government.	There is a focus on traditional conservatism, primarily social theory and its emphasis on order, authority and discipline.
There is a belief that society is made up of self-interested and self-sufficient individuals, who are referred to as atoms.	There is a primary focus on organicism, which is the belief that society operates as a single organism or entity and that it is greater than the sum of its parts.
There is a desire to change society through radical policy-making.	There is a desire to support and maintain traditional institutions and values.
The driving force behind policies is the support and maintenance of libertarianism.	There is a tendency towards authoritarianism and the imposition of policy, rather than by consensus.
Economic policy should support free enterprise and entrepreneurialship and this is a key goal.	The key goal is to sustain and foster social order, which could mean gradual or even radical reform.
Policy-making should ensure that individuals can fulfil their own self-interests and are able to be entrepreneurial without unnecessary limitations set upon them by government.	Policy should be focused on the maintenance of traditional values, which suggest a backward-thinking view towards a golden age of prosperity and social stability.
There is an inherent belief in equality of opportunity, not equality as such. Each individual should have an equal chance of achievement on the basis of their own skills.	There is a natural hierarchy which is inherently unequal. Inequality is a natural state and those with sufficient skills and contacts will always succeed.
State intervention should be rolled back and there should be a minimalist state that only involves itself in absolutely essential areas of society.	There should be a strong state that controls and directs all relevant and important areas of society.
The state should view itself in its international context and foster relations and business opportunities across the globe. It should welcome cultural and technological advances from worldwide sources.	Essentially the country should display insular nationalism, with a focus on the key skills and qualities of the nation.

Neo-liberal	Neo-conservative
There is an essential support for globalisation and a worldwide free-market economy, which offers opportunities across the world for entrepreneurial citizens.	Essentially anti-globalisation, seeing that the economic and social impact of other countries as fundamentally undesirable and disruptive and could bring about challenges to traditional values and social order.

Thatcher vs traditionalists

Margaret Thatcher's version of liberal conservatism, known as the New Right, swept away the power and influence of the one-nation conservatives in the party, who were ridiculed as Wets. She believed that people were naturally competitive, that private enterprise should be encouraged because it rewarded effort. There was a belief that high taxation meant that those who created wealth were penalised so that the less gifted could be subsidised. Her supporters were strong believers in the individual, yet just like the liberals of the Victorian era they believed in a strong state.

There were many key differences between the traditional conservative views and the New Right under Thatcher, as identified in the following table.

Thatcher's version of classical liberalism	Traditional conservative version
Radical change is a necessary step	Opposed to any form of radical change
The individual is paramount	The needs of all are more important
The freedom of the individual, particularly in business, is vital	Too much freedom is dangerous
Strongly opposed to the welfare state	Welfare state is necessary
Hostile towards trade unions and to 'unelected bodies, such as pressure groups'	Prepared to cooperate and listen to their views
Suspicious of local government	Supportive of local government and recognises their role

Trends in modern conservatism

In the United States conservatism, as exemplified by the Republican Party, is undoubtedly still a strong force. However, in Europe the conservatives face far stiffer opposition from social democratic and liberal parties.

By the late 1990s, the British conservatives had become very unpopular and the party had started to fragment. In the US neo-conservatism was particularly strong, but this has not been the trend in Europe. The relative failure of the neo-conservatives in Britain, for example, has led to the creation of an even further right-wing group, UKIP. These extreme right-wing conservatives propose lower taxation and public expenditure, freeing up opportunities for enterprise.

The golden era of the New Right in Britain ended effectively with the fall of Margaret Thatcher, but stuttered on under the leadership of John Major. In the US it was exemplified by Ronald Reagan and by the two Bush presidents.

The conservatives struggle with the apparent truth that a free market is inevitably a short-term fix, as it widens in inequality and social exclusion and means lower investments in industry. They are also faced with the problem that globalisation is sweeping away traditional values and cultures, making it almost impossible to defend them.

DISCUSSION POINT ?

Is David Cameron neo-conservative or neo-liberal?

Conservatives since 1990

Margaret Thatcher resigned in 1990, to be replaced by John Major. It was Major who put many Thatcherite policies into practice. Whilst Major took a moderate view on Europe, Eurosceptics, who were opposed to European integration, undermined his policies. Major's campaign 'back to basics' focused on the economy, education and policing. After his defeat in the 1997 election, Major was replaced by William Hague, who brought about massive party policy changes between 1997 and 2001.

- Party members were now allowed to vote for the leader.

- A written party constitution was created.

- A national membership scheme was brought in to increase income and membership.

- Party members could now become involved in policy-making through the policy forum.

The proposals were almost unanimously accepted under the banner 'The fresh future'. Despite democraticising the party, Hague still offered a right-wing electoral agenda, especially focusing upon his ill-fated 'days to save the pound' campaign in the 2001 election.

Direction of the party under Cameron

In 2007 Oliver Letwin claimed that David Cameron was winning the 'battle of ideas' against Gordon Brown with his vision of 'social responsibility'. 'Cameron Conservatism' contrasts 'provision theory' – under which the state provided services – directly with Mr Cameron's 'framework theory' in which services would be funded by the state but some would be run by the voluntary or private sector.

'Cameron Conservatives have recognised the profound consequences of having entered a post-Marxist era. Politics – once econocentric – must now become sociocentric. Instead of being about economics, politics in a post-Marxist age is about the whole way we live our lives; it is about society.'

The following table outlines the key ideas of 'Cameron Conservatism' and what they mean.

Key ideas	What it means
'A shift from an econocentric paradigm to a sociocentric paradigm.'	Labour has focused on free-market philosophy, but social policy will be the main battleground at the next election
'A shift in the theory of the state from a provision-based paradigm to a framework-based paradigm.'	Gordon Brown favours a top-down, 'big brother' approach. Cameron wants a localised, bottom-up approach with some services delivered by the voluntary and private sector
'Seek to identify externalities that participants in the free market are likely to neglect, and then seek to establish frameworks that will lead people and organisations to internalise those externalities'	Cameron's 'social responsibility' will encourage people to do their bit for society

Learning objectives

- Conservatives since 1990
- Direction of the party under Cameron
- Impact of New Labour and continuing links
- Policy announcements

Changing leadership

Hague's defeat at the 2001 election saw him replaced by Iain Duncan Smith. Smith never fought an election as he was replaced by Michael Howard because of his failure to raise the party's standing among the electorate. The party moved to an even more right-wing position in 2005, focusing upon so-called 'dog whistle politics' issues, including immigration, and extreme Euroscepticism. This stance led the Tory Party Chair, Theresa May, after the election defeat under Howard in 2005, to proclaim that the public saw the Tories as 'the nasty party'.

After the election defeat, Howard was replaced by David Cameron. The Conservatives under Cameron describe themselves as 'compassionate conservatives'. At times he has been described as a liberal conservative and he has failed to criticise Margaret Thatcher's policies.

Impact of New Labour and continuing links

In 2006, David Cameron vowed to never give in to the Tory right-wing. He said that the party would face 'irrelevance, defeat and failure' if it allowed itself to be swayed again by 'well-intentioned cheerleaders on the right'. He claimed that since the emergence of Tony Blair's New Labour Party, the Conservatives had been wrong to campaign so hard on right-wing issues such as immigration as they tried to differentiate themselves. He gave a veiled criticism of his predecessors William Hague, Iain Duncan-Smith and Michael Howard. He believed the Conservative Party had moved to the right when Labour had occupied the centre ground. Under their leadership the Conservatives had ignored areas of general agreement with the Labour Party and had instead focused on contentious areas based on Conservative values and principles, such as tax cuts, immigration and Europe.

Cameron has certainly responded to the challenge by distancing himself from the policies of Margaret Thatcher and rejecting many policies promoted by the right, including tax cuts. Cameron sees himself as the natural heir to Tony Blair, but many conservative traditionalists were angered by the fact that Cameron was instrumental in drawing up the last Conservative manifesto that he now criticises.

Cameron admitted that Blair grasped what Labour needed to do to win power, and that was to imitate Margaret Thatcher: 'A more middle class Britain wanted a middle class lifestyle based on a prosperous market economy. Tony Blair understood this – profoundly understood it . . . Tony Blair saw that the task of New Labour was to preserve the fruits of the Thatcher revolution.'

Cameron believed that in recent years the conservatives had made 'terrible strategic and political mistakes': 'Having defined ourselves for many years as the anti-socialist party, how were we to define ourselves once full-blooded socialism had disappeared from the political landscape?'

In Cameron's view, the conservatives now accept that they have very similar aspirations to New Labour, what is different are the ways in which they would seek to realise them. On the one hand, New Labour (in Cameron's eyes) put their faith in 'legislation, regulation and bureaucracy' and view action by the state as the way to deliver economic dynamism and social justice; the conservatives favour a different approach: 'We will respond to state failure by empowering individuals and civil society.'

Lord Tebbit, the former party chairman was one of the many dissenters.

Tebbit saw the centre ground as being difficult territory to operate in. The electorate is confused if the parties occupy the middle ground, as they find it impossible to recognise the differences between the parties. They cannot see the value of voting and so do not. With eighteen million people not bothering to vote, Tebbit saw this as dangerous, as this was the equivalent of the total number of voters for the two major parties.

Policy announcements

The Conservative Party leader David Cameron needed 'more policies, more quickly', according to former Chancellor Lord Lamont. Lamont believed that policies should be carefully considered and that there was a danger in releasing detailed plans too early. The opposition party would just steal the idea. However, he believed that Cameron desperately needed more content in his policies.

In response to the challenge, Cameron has aimed to remain continually in the media with a spate of policy announcements, his clear attention being to keep the Labour Party on the back-foot. The following table provides a list of these.

Policy announcement	Brief description
Environment	The work of rebranding the Conservative Party as a cleaner and greener option began the very moment Cameron became leader. He appointed environmentalist Zac Goldsmith to initiate a massive policy review, focused on delivering a fundamental rethink of Conservative policy on the environment. 'I want Britain to adopt micro-generation: small providers, including homes and businesses, producing energy for their own use, using a variety of methods from combined heat and power, to wind to solar photovoltaic power', David Cameron at a Greenpeace meeting in December 2007.
Taxation	'Conservatives believe in the benefits of low taxes. It is right that people keep more of what is theirs; it leads to better economic performance which benefits everyone. Taxation is the most pervasive intrusion by the state into the lives of citizens. It must reflect the reality of how people behave and what they see as fair. Taxes which encourage widespread (legal) avoidance or (illegal) evasion erode the state's legitimacy.'
Inheritance tax	The threshold for inheritance tax would rise from £300,000 to £1 million under a Conservative government, George Osborne told the party's conference in October 2007. But just days later in the pre-Budget report, Alistair Darling, the Chancellor, announced his own plans to allow couples to use the allowance of a partner – doubling the total to £700,000. The Conservatives accused Brown of shamelessly stealing their policy but Labour pointed to differences in how the money was raised for the scheme.
Social inclusiveness agenda	People who refuse to join a return-to-work programme will lose the right to claim out-of-work benefits until they do. People who refuse to accept reasonable job offers could lose the right to claim out-of-work benefits for three years. There will be time limits for out-of-work benefits – so people who claim for more than two years out of three will be required to join community work programmes.
Law and order	They would scrap the early release scheme, and build emergency prison places. They would double the sentencing powers of magistrates to 12 months and repeal any new restrictions on their ability to hand down suspended sentences. They would introduce 'honesty in sentencing' so that convicted criminals serve a minimum sentence handed down to them by the judge. They would ensure sufficient prison capacity to hold all those sentenced by the courts – and reform prison regimes to break the cycle of re-offending.
Terrorism/ID cards	A Conservative government will scrap the ID cards scheme, and use some of the savings to build more prison places, provide more drug rehab in prisons and create a new border police force.
Education	'Raising the bar, closing the gap' was the Conservative action plan to raise school standards, create more good school places and make opportunity more equal. In it, they set out their plans to address the educational under-performance which blights our nation's future through a long-term, supply-side revolution, along with a number of immediate measures.
Health service reform	Key policy announcements include: 'Phasing out Labour's process-driven targets; a national focus on the health outcomes we want the NHS to deliver; collecting information about the results of people's treatment in the NHS; publishing those results, so we can see where we are making progress and where we lag behind other countries; developing outcome measures which patients with chronic conditions themselves provide; giving patients a choice of provider so they can use published outcome information to get the care they want; introducing payment-by-results within the system.'
Forced marriages	'Our aim is that all those who come here to live will participate fully in British society, and that British society will be confident enough to allow diversity (as it always has) without losing its central values. One of those values is individual freedom over the key decisions in our lives. Choosing who to marry is one of those decisions, so there is no place in Britain for forced marriage.' Shadow Immigration Minister, Damian Green.

DISCUSSION POINT ?

Is David Cameron the Tory Party's Tony Blair?

ExamCafé

Relax, refresh, result!

Relax and prepare

Here are some exam practice questions for unit F854. How would you go about answering them?

- Discuss the extent to which conservatism can be regarded as ideological.

- Compare and contrast one-nation conservatism with New Right theories.

- Discuss the extent to which conservatism can be regarded as merely opposition to change.

- Compare and contrast different forms of nationalism.

- Discuss whether nationalism is more than just self-determination.

- Discuss the extent of similarity between conservatism and nationalism.

 Refresh your memory

To help your revision for unit F854, in the table below summarise the key ideas of the following political thinkers and explain how their ideas fit into the following themes.

Theme	Relevant political theorist	Key ideas
Authoritarian conservatism	Hobbes	
Paternalistic conservatism	Burke	
One-nation conservatism	Disraeli	
Neo-liberal conservatism	Hayek	
Neo-conservative conservatism	Strauss	
Liberal nationalism	Mazzini	
Cultural nationalism	Von Herder	
Conservative nationalism	De Gaulle	
Racial nationalism	Houston Chamberlain	
Socialist nationalism	Nyerere	

Get the result !

The following is an example of an exam essay question for unit F854.

Discuss the extent to which nationalism is more than just a right-wing ideology.

Exam tips

To improve your chance of achieving a high mark you should plan your essay before you start writing it. These are the issues you should consider.

Introduction

You should precisely define what is meant by nationalism.

Aspects of nationalism

You need to discuss what aspects of nationalism can be considered right wing (conservative, right wing and racialist nationalism).

You should also cover other aspects of nationalism (cultural, liberal, socialist and post-colonialist).

Use the ideas of relevant theorists

These will include right-wing nationalists, such as De Gaulle, Houston Chamberlain, Nietzsche, Mussolini and Hitler.

Other ideological traditions should be covered through theorists such as von Herder, Mazzini and Nyerere.

Conclusion

You should identify the elements that see an ideology as right-wing – patriotism, organicism, racial connotations and potential dislike/fear of outsiders/immigrants and external authority; but also highlight other ideological aspects – opposition to empire, belief in common identity and freedom and equality, and free citizenship.

Unit F856

Relax and prepare

The following are essay questions of the type that would occur in your exam for unit F856. Discuss with your colleagues how you would go about answering them or try writing essay plans for as many as you can.

- Examine the legacy of Margaret Thatcher on the modern Conservative Party?
- What if anything is meant by the term 'new conservatism'?
- Discuss the view that above all else the Conservative Party is pragmatic.
- Examine the impact on the future of the UK of the growth of nationalism in Scotland, Wales and Northern Ireland.
- Discuss the influence of right-wing nationalist parties in the UK.
- To what extent can the Conservative Party be described as a party of 'Little Englanders'?

Refresh your memory

Case studies on conservatism and nationalism

Think about the following events and issues, and consider how what you have learned in unit F854 could be added to the theory you have learnt for unit F856.

- ✓ The key principles of Thatcherism.
- ✓ The legacy of the Conservative Party defeat in 1997.
- ✓ David Cameron's election as Conservative leader in 2005.
- ✓ The redesign of the Conservative Party logo in 2006.
- ✓ David Cameron's social inclusiveness agenda.
- ✓ The creation of devolved assemblies in Scotland, Wales and Northern Ireland.
- ✓ The formation of an SNP-led executive in the Scottish Parliament in 2007.
- ✓ The UKIP successes in winning 12 seats in the European Parliament elections in 2004.
- ✓ The impact of the BNP becoming the second largest party in the Burnley local council in 2003 and increasing its number of seats to 100 after 2008 local council elections.

Get the result!

This is the type of essay question that you may have to answer for unit F856 in your exam. To improve your chance of achieving a high mark you should plan your essay before you start writing it.

Evaluate the extent to which contemporary conservatism can be regarded as ideological.

Exam tips

Consider how the following table adopts elements of F854 theory with the practical application also required for F856.

Key themes	Relevant theory	Practical evidence
The meaning of conservatism	Define ideology and identify key conservative themes	Changing nature of Conservative Party manifestos
One-nation conservative themes	Burke – 'partnership between those who are living, those who are dead, and those who are to be born' Disraeli – 'You shall have the estate, but you will do something for it; you shall feed the poor, endow the Church, you shall defend the land in case of war, and you shall execute justice and maintain the truth to the poor for nothing' – concept of 'noblesse oblige'	Cameron's agenda on environmental concerns and social inclusiveness
Neo-liberal themes	Hayek – belief in individualism and 'market order'. Duty of the state to defend freedom and prevent 'creeping collectivism' Nozick – saw welfarism and redistribution as 'theft' and violation of property rights	Tax-cutting agenda – note proposals to abolish income tax on all estates less than £1 million Giving autonomy to local schools and hospitals
Neo-conservative themes	Irving Kristol – 'A neo-conservative is a liberal mugged by reality' Leo Strauss – call for moral regeneration in US society after the counterculture years of the 1960s	UK – support for traditional nuclear families and marriage through tax credits Strong law and order themes, e.g. Cameron's proposals for mandatory prison sentences for those convicted of knife crimes US influence of Christian Right on Reagan and Bush Senior and Junior administrations
Evidence of influence of other ideologies	David Cameron – admitted that Tony Blair and the Third Way had grasped the necessity of preserving the middle class way of life and a prosperous economy	Support for Labour-led agenda on foundation schools and hospitals
Pragmatic/ populist themes	Oakeshott – conservatism as an endless voyage where the captain and crew must keep their passengers happy, 'conservatism must be a conversation, not an argument'	1950s acceptance by Macmillan of the mixed-market economy Rejection of ID card scheme Adoption of calls for referendums on Lisbon Treaty
Concluding comments	Multifaceted and chameleon-like qualities of conservatism making it highly durable and adaptable Ian Gilmour – 'the wise conservative travels light'	Note success of the Conservative Party in dominating 19th and 20th century UK government and key points of reinvention – 1951, 1979 and post-2005

Liberalism is founded on the idea that the ultimate goal of politics is to ensure that every individual in society is free and tolerant. In such a society each individual has rights and equality of opportunity, under which they should be free to say and write what they want, own property, and be protected by the rule of law. In return they should tolerate other individuals' beliefs, values and thoughts, though not acts of discrimination, violence and incitement to commit crime.

The Liberal Democrats are the party in British politics founded on liberal values. Though these values demand only limited government interference in peoples' lives, the Liberal Democrats support the intervention of the state to achieve social and economic equality (social justice) through the redistribution of wealth. Their commitment to state intervention in such a cause however does not extend to infringing peoples' liberty in cases such as ID cards and anti-terrorism legislation to imprison terror suspects.

Fundamentally, socialism is about changing society in order to create a more equitable and safer place in which citizens would be free to exercise their abilities and fulfil their aims in life. Some socialists insist that everyone has the same natural or potential abilities to be equal and therefore the aim of politics is to eradicate inequalities from society, however others share the liberal view that there are different abilities and therefore inequalities. For them inequalities can be justified if citizens have the same opportunities to make what they can of their abilities. For this to happen poverty and barriers to opportunity must be eradicated to create the minimum conditions in which people can live and use their abilities to the fullest degree. It is also crucial that no one enriches themselves by exploiting the poor.

The socialist idea that humans are social animals and are more inclined to achieving their aims collectively, through being part of a group, still survives. The NHS, the trade unions, the state education are examples. Nevertheless, European socialism has been moving away from the collectivist approach to society, convinced that it hampered enterprise, suppressed the instincts and hindered economic prospects. Also many are no longer convinced that private property and industry should be held in common ownership.

The Labour Party's (and the Conservative Party's) gravitation towards certain liberal values gave the impression of coveting these around which to formulate policies to expand their electoral appeal. Many in the Labour Party now see the creation of equality as a crucial aim, though the Liberal Democrats haven't discharged their belief in natural inequality and nor has the Labour Party disclaimed their belief in inequality being created by society. For liberals a free society is one in which there is freedom to be unequal whereas for socialists it is the means of achieving greater equality. Even so both agree that inequality is tolerable as long as it is for the general good.

The common ground between the Labour and Liberal Democratic parties on welfare in recent years led to overtures as to the possibility of them forming a 'progressive alliance'. More recently Gordon Brown has appointed the Liberal peer and legal expert Lord Carlile as an adviser on anti-terrorism legislation. Liberal ideas have also percolated into new Labour thinking with respect to greater autonomy for local state schools and hospitals.

The Conservative Party, unelectable as the party without compassion after years of Thatcherism, and in search of a new image, attempted to rebrand themselves as the compassionate conservatives under Iain Duncan Smith and then as the inclusive party under David Cameron.

Their opposition to ID cards and the 42-day detention legislation, which are Liberal Democrat policies, was part of this transformation.

The Liberal Democrats are now projecting a tougher image in their stances on certain issues. They have rejected the managerial approach of the other parties in favour of something more inspirational, through policies to empower the people, promote social mobility, protect the environment, defend liberty and radically reform the political system. As for crime they propose policies aimed at rehabilitation, neighbourhood involvement and making offenders face what they've done.

Labour's New Way strategy was aimed at confronting the challenges of globalisation by formulating policies to deal with the likely changes to the economy and society. It advocates a centrist approach directed at synthesising capitalist and socialist ideas.

These are some of the issues covered in this chapter, in which the following are key themes.

- The key thinkers, core values and types of liberalism and socialism
- A comparison of liberalism and socialism with respect to their views on human nature, the role of the state, reform, the role of the individual and the extent of equality
- Liberalism in British politics and how it influences the ideas of the political parties
- The triumph of liberal democracy and how relevant it will be to 21st century politics
- The Third Way and New Labour and the consensus between the political parties
- The comparison between the political parties

In covering these themes the chapter is broken down into the following topics.

The chapter finishes with an exam café feature on page 242.

Origins of liberalism

Liberalism is said to have grown out of the breakdown of feudalism in early modern Europe and became an influential feature in the so called Age of Enlightenment. Both the American and French revolutions had liberal overtones, challenging the power of the monarch and the privileges of the aristocracy and the church.

By the 19th century liberals favoured an industrialised economic society, free from interference. It has been a truly influential ideology, radical at times and at other times more conservative.

Early or classical liberals wanted little government interference, whilst modern ones see it as essential to deliver welfare and to regulate the economy. Liberal models have dominated politics since the 19th century.

By 2000 approximately two-thirds of the world's countries had significant liberal democratic features.

Individual liberty

Liberty is at the heart of liberalism, but views on liberty have differed over the years.

- **Political and revolutionary liberty** – This type of freedom is often referred to as self-determination; the ability of people to determine their own form of government.
- **Individual liberty** – This places individual liberty as the key priority, rejecting paternalistic government and regulation. Individuals are the best judges of their own interests.
- **Negative and positive liberty** (classifications used by Isaiah Berlin) – Negative liberty is what an individual can do without being obstructed by others and positive liberty is what an individual alone decides to do through the removal of obstacles to the achievement of self-mastery and participation in the decision-making process.

Tolerance

John Locke suggested: 'That every man may enjoy the same rights that are granted to others.'

Liberals support toleration of beliefs, values, faiths and thoughts and an individual's right to express them. It is summed up in Voltaire's words: 'I detest what you say, but I shall defend to the death your right to say it.'

There are, however, limits to tolerance, including discrimination, violence and incitement to crime. Liberals would look to assist individuals to reform their behaviour rather than punish them and they also have great tolerance about individual morality.

Equal rights

Liberals aim to afford individuals an equal right to reach their full potential and self-fulfilment. Some view inequality as unnatural. They would seek to end discrimination and ensure that individuals have equality of opportunity. Classical liberals however seek only foundational equality through the legal protection of individual rights (natural or human).

Equality of opportunity

Classical liberals would view equality of opportunity as freedom to fail or succeed, become rich or become poor. However in a free society not everyone has equality of opportunity. The liberals were therefore supporters of education and championed broader access to law, government and the army. Modern liberals such as T. H. Green believed that the only way to achieve self-mastery is by the state providing opportunities for self-fulfilment, such as the removal of poverty, ignorance and poor health.

Beveridge's welfare state, created after the Second World War, aimed to expand opportunity for all in education, health care and social security. Comprehensive education can be seen as a liberal measure, as was the outlawing of discrimination.

Pluralism

Theorists such as Alexis de Tocqueville believed that pluralism was essential for true democracy as a way of avoiding a majority tyranny. James Madison also called for 'a multiplicity of interests' to be represented in order to prevent the domination of majority opinion. It would ensure that there were a variety of groups which individuals could join to help them achieve their objectives. Collectively there would be a strong civil society that would stop the state from becoming too powerful.

Modern views of pluralism incorporate cultural and religious diversity, state toleration of beliefs, philosophies and religion, the ability to participate in groups, ensuring that groups have access to the political system and can influence policy, and ensuring that no one group becomes dominant.

Government by consent

Both Hobbes and Locke believed that government by consent was essential, with individuals coming together to agree and allow the government to have power over them, in order to achieve peace and security. As Locke wrote: 'And thus every man, by consenting with others to make one body politic under one government, puts himself under an obligation to everyone of that society and to submit to the determination of the majority.'

This is reflected in part of the US Constitution, written in 1787, nearly 100 years after Locke:

> We, the people of the United States, in order to form a more perfect union, establish justice, insure domestic tranquillity, provide for the common defense, promote the general welfare, and secure the blessings of liberty to ourselves and our posterity, do ordain and establish this constitution for the United States of America.

Liberals see government by consent as incorporating free elections and referendums and the ability for free speech (which is tolerated) that can challenge government.

Limited government and constitutionalism

Liberals believe that unless government is limited it will adversely affect freedom and citizens' private lives; it needs to be controlled. Government must not use arbitrary power. Power must not be concentrated in too few hands. Montesquieu called for a clear separation of powers within government to avoid the dangers of excessive state power. Democratic systems also need to be viewed carefully, as minorities may be at risk from the tyranny of the majority. Limiting the role of government and the engagement of citizens in the decision-making process is known as protective democracy.

Liberals favour government by consent through constitutionalism, which they see as a means by which the freedoms of individuals and groups can be guaranteed.

Justice

Justice is an important consideration for liberals. Firstly, they believe in legal justice, in as much as there should be equal application of the law to all. This is based on equal rights. Social justice is rather more difficult because on the one hand it often needs government intervention, however classical liberals are opposed to government intervention. Modern liberals now tend to accept that inequality is natural, but in a free society social justice is also required.

Some contemporary liberals, however, do not accept this and even though they support a free-market system, inequalities are not seen to be just. Deprivation means that there is always inequality and as a result some believe that income needs to be redistributed in order to balance society. Some inequalities just cannot be tolerated and this means that government intervention is needed. Not all modern liberals accept this viewpoint. They retain the view that inequalities can be justified because an individual's position is based on their own abilities and efforts.

John Rawls stated that an inequality is unjust except insofar as it is a necessary means of improving the position of the worst off. It is not enough to say that inequalities provide incentives; it has to be shown that this degree of inequality is necessary to achieve a higher level of welfare for the poorest group. That some inequality provides an incentive is not enough; it has to be shown that no less degree of inequality would do as much for the welfare of the poorest.

DISCUSSION POINT

To what extent are the core values of liberalism compatible?

Utilitarianism

The concept of utility had been developed in the late 18th century. It meant satisfaction or happiness. Jeremy Bentham argued that it was possible to work out how much utility an individual would receive from consuming goods and then calculate the total utility of society. For them it was for individuals to decide what gave them more or less utility.

The free-market economy would guarantee that individuals would be able to purchase whatever they wanted within their income and society's total utility would be maximised. Governments could add to utility through policy and should pursue the aim of 'the greatest good for the greatest number'.

The problem was that utilitarianism focused on consumption and not on other issues that could give satisfaction, such as education. It also meant that government could intervene and threaten the freedom of individuals.

Classical liberalism

The key elements in John Locke's political theory were natural rights, social contract, government by consent, and the right of revolution. Locke did not believe that the right to property was the only natural right (although he seemed to focus on this). The expression which Locke uses to identify natural rights was 'life, liberty, and estate'. (Note this expression is a familiar one as it appeared in a slightly different form in the US Declaration of Independence: 'life, liberty, and the pursuit of happiness'.) Locke defined political power as:

> the right of making laws with penalties of death, and all less penalties, for the regulating and preserving of property, and of employing the force of the community in the execution of such laws, and in the defence of the commonwealth from foreign injury, and all this only for the public good.

He believed that a power can arise only by consent and this must be the consent of each individual for himself.

John Stuart Mill was a key influence on the development of classical liberalism. To him individual freedom was most important. Classical liberals believe that freedom comes from natural rights and that freedom would maximise society's progress by encouraging creativity, self-fulfilment and innovation, essentially entrepreneurialship.

Central to freedom was tolerance, respecting others' freedoms. The law should allow people to choose their own beliefs and values and express them. There should be guarantees of civil liberty.

Classical liberals were not in favour of popular democracy. They believed universal suffrage was dangerous on the basis that it would bring about the tyranny of the majority, thus leading to society being governed by the lowest common denominator, or through dull conformity. They argued for a minimal state that was only involved in maintaining order and security, the protection of liberties and the prevention of monopolies. J. S. Mill did however advocate the expansion of the franchise to include educated women and members of the working class, albeit their views counterbalanced by plural voting so as not to swamp the ideas of the most educated sections of society.

Learning objectives

- Utilitarianism
- Classical liberalism
- Social Darwinism and libertarianism
- New liberalism
- Welfare liberalism
- Contemporary liberalism

The Manchester School, associated with the writings of Richard Cobden and John Bright, was a version of classical liberalism; they believed in free trade and adult suffrage, believing that free trade in particular would improve the overall conditions in society. They were far more working-class orientated than followers of Mill, who focused on the middle classes and the property owners.

Social Darwinism and libertarianism

In 1859 Charles Darwin's *On the Origins of the Species* was published. There was almost an immediate attempt to apply the theories to humans. This was spearheaded by Herbert Spencer, who believed that social justice allowed individuals to make whatever they could from their lives as long as they were dissuaded from affecting the freedom of others. He believed that individuals were unequal in abilities and motivation and coined the term 'survival of the fittest'. He believed that those who could adapt were most likely to succeed; some would fail, but he saw this as being the natural order.

Samuel Smiles argued that individuals could improve themselves through diligent activity and that people should not rely on charity or the state. He was strongly in favour of entrepreneurialism.

Social Darwinism and libertarianism came back into vogue in the 1980s with the New Right. They wished to remove state restrictions and taxation and believed that education, health care and law and order should be subject to market forces and handed over to the private sector. They wanted a deregulated society where only the most able and dynamic would excel. They believed that there had developed a dependency culture where too many people were relying on state aid. They wanted to remove this because those individuals contributed little to society and their burden held back progress.

The right-wing version of libertarianism is often referred to as anarcho-capitalism. Robert Nozick, an anarcho-capitalist, wanted the state to be dismantled with no welfare, tax, law and the responsibility of individuals' freedom placed upon themselves. This was the most extreme call for a minimalist state.

New liberalism

New liberalism came into existence in the 1870s. There were in fact two different strands: a philosophical and a practical approach. T. H. Green believed that individuals had a social obligation to consider the needs and the welfare of others and not just themselves. This was his interpretation of negative liberty. He also believed in positive liberty, the freedom of choice and opportunity and ultimately self-realisation or fulfilment.

New liberalism also tried to impact on the growing gulf in fortunes of the working class and those who had prospered through capitalism and industrialisation. There was high illiteracy, poor health and housing, and periods of high unemployment. New liberals believed that there was a social responsibility to focus on those who could not benefit from economic freedom. In order to progress all individuals had to be able to take advantage of their freedoms. The state would have to become involved in education, health care, welfare, housing and pensions. This would give greater equality of opportunity and the benefits of prosperity would be more widely spread. Practical moves to accomplish this were initiated at the beginning of the 20th century, with elementary education, pensions, state-sponsored insurance schemes, but it was not yet a welfare state.

Welfare liberalism

Following on from New Liberalism and the desire to spread prosperity, it was not a politician but a senior civil servant who began to frame welfare liberalism. After the Second World War, William Beveridge was given responsibility for devising a new social policy. He was a liberal who considered that poverty, unemployment and poor education were as dangerous to freedom as interventionist government. On balance he believed that trying to solve these problems through government involvement would aid liberty, not threaten it. His fundamental beliefs were:

> To my mind there are three things above all that every citizen of this country needs as conditions of a happy and useful life after war. He needs freedom from want and fear of want, freedom from idleness and fear of idleness enforced by unemployment, freedom from war and fear of war.
>
> Source: Crown copyright

Although the welfare state itself was a Labour or socialist triumph, it was inspired by Beveridge, a liberal.

Contemporary liberalism

Contemporary liberalism has failed to make much impact on the party political agenda in the UK. However, many of the core values of liberalism have been hijacked by social democrats. Modern liberals still believe in the decentralisation of power, constitutional protection against government power, the use of referendums, legal safeguards for individual rights, freedom of information and the protection of minority groups through legislation if necessary.

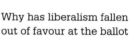

DISCUSSION POINT ?

Why has liberalism fallen out of favour at the ballot box?

213

John Locke (1632–1704)

Locke was writing about liberalism before the term liberal was coined. He believed that government had to be established by consent and it should respect the natural rights of citizens through natural laws. Authority could only come from the people; governments should be limited and be there to respect the key natural rights of life, liberty and property ownership. Thomas Jefferson later added the pursuit of happiness to this list. He developed the idea of the social contract, believing that government agrees to govern according to natural law and respect of individual rights, whilst citizens accept the authority of the government and undertake to obey the law. Locke did however argue that citizens had the right to withdraw their consent if the government was no longer upholding their natural rights. He used this to justify his support for the removal of the Catholic monarch, James II, in the Glorious Revolution of 1688.

Jeremy Bentham (1748–1832)

Bentham was the founder of utilitarianism. His views were radical and were behind many of the changes in law, government, economics and social administration. He developed a theory that humans are self-interested, utility maximisers and the idea that society should encourage free market, constitutional reform and political democracy to achieve general utility.

John Stuart Mill (1806–73)

Mill began as a utilitarian, his father James Mill having been a close associate of Bentham. He believed that individuals are in the best position to judge what is or is not in their own interests and no one has the right to believe they have a better idea of what is in the best interests of everybody. He broke from utilitarianism on the basis that it only focused on the pursuit of material possessions and that there were other goals, such as education and art, to take into consideration. He tried to define the limits of freedom, categorising them as self-regarding (where actions had no effect on others) and other-regarding (which did affect the freedom of others). Mill believed that individuals should be allowed a different number of election votes based on their education. He also championed women's rights. He recognised that a free society was inherently unjust and in later years believed that state intervention was preferable, rather than to tolerate these injustices. Mill is often seen as theorist who straddles classical and modern liberal ideals.

Herbert Spencer (1820–1903)

Spencer borrowed much from Darwin's *Origin of the Species* and suggested that individuals and societies are subject to the same laws of natural selection as animals in nature. He believed that government should uphold and defend natural rights; beyond this they should not be involved in society. A renewed interest in Spencer grew in the 1980s amongst conservatives and libertarians and his theories were applied by those who opposed the dependency culture.

Thomas Hill Green (1836–82)

Green believed that individuals should not simply be self-seeking, that they should also have an obligation towards others, in other words social responsibility without loss of personal liberty. He also believed in the organic society, viewing society as a living entity with an existence beyond the sum of the individuals within it. Green had enormous influence on new liberalism. He defined freedom in both the positive sense (that is, the ability to realise aspirations, or self-realisation) and the negative sense, (that is, there were external constraints to what you could do); this was similar to John Stuart Mill's view. A completely free society would fail most people. Government intervention was needed to promote positive liberty.

William Beveridge (1879–1963)

Beveridge believed that social justice was vital and that free-market capitalism could not provide this. He believed that inequality of opportunity bred inequality. On freedom he believed that legal and political rights were one side of the coin; poverty and unemployment made any attempts to achieve equal rights impossible. Beveridge was the architect of the British welfare state; a universal, publicly funded education, health care, pension and social security system that appeared to be more socialist than liberal.

John Rawls (1921–2002)

Rawls tried to address the issue of freedom and inequality. He realised that policies aimed at reducing inequality or preventing inequality would lead to loss of liberty. Redistribution of income through taxation would impinge on the liberties of tax payers to spend money that they had earned as they wished. Rawls believed that individuals should be as free as was possible and that freedom should be tolerated as long as it is not at the expense of the freedom of others. He believed that inequalities needed to be justified (justified if it increases the prosperity of society, unjustified if it makes the poorest poorer). Rawls called this the difference principle. His views were very much taken on board by Tony Blair and Bill Clinton.

John Gray (1948 to date)

Gray's views have switched from New Right to New Labour. He has argued that it is difficult to categorise or explain society in purely liberal terms. To him pluralism is post-liberal, in which society rejects liberal values, regimes and institutions. In his latest writings Gray criticises the free market. Gray is quite pessimistic about human behaviour and predicts that there may be wars in the future over natural resources.

> **DISCUSSION POINT** ?
>
> What makes each of the above theorists fundamentally liberal?

Origins of socialism

Socialism can trace its roots well into the past, in that individual thinkers were inspired to consider what society might be like without property ownership.

Some of the thinkers of the past advocated communism, which is a form of socialism where wealth is divided among citizens equally or according to individual need. Imaginary or hypothetical communist societies have been discussed by philosophers and other thinkers for many centuries (such as the ancient Greek philosopher Plato in his *Republic* and the English Renaissance scholar Thomas More in *Utopia*).

Communism was actually practised by small communities of Christians in the 1st and 2nd centuries (and indeed in some Roman Catholic monasteries). There were also short-lived communist communities established by radical Protestants, the Anabaptists in 1534, and later by the English group known as the Diggers in 1649.

Socialists were inspired by the social consequences of the industrial revolution. The growth of new industries and the rise of the factory system of manufacturing triggered the mass movement of people from rural areas to the industrial cities. The vast majority worked long hours for very low wages in harsh conditions.

Socialists focused on the injustices in the system and believed it was harmful to the human character, family life and the community in general. Socialists have a positive view of human nature, but also see it as malleable. Capitalism therefore distorts human nature, encouraging humanity to be selfish and greedy. Only within a socialist-style society will man's true nature flourish.

Workers laboured for many hours, doing boring and repetitive tasks. Socialists believed that under these conditions individuals would lose their initiative, compete with others to avoid penniless starvation and ultimately lose their regard for others. They believed that if factory workers were treated like animals they would behave like animals. And the root cause of the problems was the ownership of property.

Economic equality

Socialists maintain that everyone is born with equal rights and they reject the idea that society may have a natural order. They also believe in equality of opportunity and varying degrees of equality of outcome.

In order to achieve absolute equality, all individuals would have to receive the same reward, provided they use their best abilities to make a contribution. This eliminates incentives and it can be seen as unjust; however, socialists believe this is the foundation of social justice. On the one hand there are socialists who believe that all humans are born with the same potential, on the other hand there are those who recognise that individuals have different abilities, therefore inequality is inevitable and so there should be differential rewards. One way forward would be to ensure that everyone has the same opportunity to make what they can of their abilities, but in practice this means that welfare should be available to ensure that everyone has a minimum standard of living.

Class conflict

There are differing views on class conflict and its importance amongst socialists. Social democrats have virtually ignored class as a key consideration, believing that the breakdown of the class system and broader affluence has made this an irrelevance.

Democratic socialists seek to modify capitalism through state intervention and through welfare provision. Non-revolutionary socialists aim to create governments that operate primarily in the interests of the working class. For example, in certain cases production and distribution is often handled by the state itself, in order to fully control it.

Revolutionary socialists believe that capitalism is at the heart of class conflict. In order to eliminate class conflict capitalism needs to be replaced with a socialist system.

Social justice

For socialists social justice applies to the way in which the rewards from the economy are distributed. Marxists and revolutionary socialists claim that capitalism will never produce a fair distribution because it is inherently unequal and relies on incentives. Moderate socialists believe that it can be achieved through modification, such as minimum wage legislation, trade union rights, the use of taxation and welfare.

Fundamentally, however, there is the problem of what represents a fair distribution. Karl Marx said 'from each according to his abilities, to each according to his needs'. But this suggests that there is no limit to the funds or wealth available, whereas in fact there will always be scarcities. As a result, more modern socialists have reframed the debate as distributive justice and tackle the problem of how much inequality should actually be tolerated.

Provided everyone has a minimum standard of living, incentives need to be tolerated in order to encourage wealth creation. Provided the inequalities can be justified and everyone enjoys freedom, equality of opportunity, unrestricted opportunities for personal advancement and, above all, no one enriches themself by exploiting the poorest, then inequalities can be tolerated.

Collectivism and common ownership

Collectivism recognises that individuals much more prefer to strive to achieve their aims as part of a group, and that these groups are inevitably far more effective than individuals striving alone. Socialists believe that humans are social animals, but beyond this there are divisions.

Marxists, for example, believe that a centralised state is the most effective means of achieving collective action. Even socialists who believe in free-market capitalism take the view that some collectivism is desirable.

In the past thirty years or so, socialism in Europe has moved away from collectivism. The view was that it held back enterprise, suppressed instincts and did not allow economic prosperity.

Vestiges of collectivism still remain in Britain; a large number of workers are members of trade unions, there is a national health service, local government provides housing, state education is provided, and, although this is no longer the case, many large industries were nationalised.

Common ownership is a key part of collectivism and can be raced back to its roots in the Christian principles of pooling and sharing resources. Common ownership can be seen to be an alternative to private ownership.

Socialists believe that no one has the right to claim that property exclusively belongs to them, as it deprives others of its use. Property ownership means inequality and property owners can exploit those who do not own property. Common ownership would mean economic equality. Socialists view this as natural and providing the basis for creating a natural state of society. Common ownership of property would then serve the interests of the broader society, not just private owners.

Marxists hold that all property should be in common ownership. State socialists allow some elements of private ownership, but production and distribution would be in public hands and run by the state. Syndicalists believe that industry should be owned and run as a collective by the workforce. Worker cooperatives are owned by the workers and retail cooperatives by the consumers. Democratic socialists see key services, such as health, as being state owned and controlled and larger important industries as being state run. New Labour and social democrats believe that only welfare services should be publicly owned and state run. This dispute over the role of the state in controlling the means of distribution and exchange in society was polarised by the decision of Tony Blair to write out of Clause 4 of the Labour Party's Constitution the commitment to public ownership.

DISCUSSION POINT ?

Do all socialists hold the same fundamental views on how society should be organised?

Primitive and Utopian

Utopian socialists, such as the French aristocrat Henri de Saint-Simon, advocated the establishment of ideal communities that would serve as models for the rest of society. He announced the imminent arrival of a new age he called industrialism and believed it would be a system in which experts from science, technology, and industry would take the place of traditional political and economic leaders. They would direct the productive resources of society for the common good. The material needs of society would be met through rational central planning by enlightened civil servants. This would eliminate the main cause of disorder in industrial societies.

Later followers of Saint-Simon believed that his theories were inconsistent with private property.

Charles Fourier believed that modern industrial capitalism was the source of great misery and hardship because it forced people to do dull, unsatisfying work and to compete with each other for scarce jobs. He argued that people have a natural desire to work at interesting tasks and to live in harmony with others. His solution was to reorganise society into self-sufficient communities of people, called phalanges. In these communities most property would be communally owned. People would move from one type of work to another, as their tastes and interests changed.

Several phalanges based on Fourier's ideas were founded in the United States in the second quarter of the 19th century, though they were all short-lived.

In Britain Robert Owen, a factory owner, was one of the earliest socialists. He owned textile mills in Scotland, the most famous of which was his New Lanarkshire Mill, and they were reputed to be humane by the standards of others of the time, offering educational and welfare benefits to the workers and their families. Owen believed that capitalism produced harmful effects on human character and that these effects could be prevented through proper education, public control of industry, and communal living arrangements. Owen invested his own money in the creation of a socialist community, called New Harmony, in Indiana, but it was plagued by internal dissension, and dissolved after only three years.

Marxism and other revolutionary forms

Despite their theories being predominantly communist, Marx and Engels are probably the most important theorists of socialism. They believed that the fundamental force in history, the source of all historical change, is the struggle between economic classes and that each of these stages can be characterised by the opposition of classes in that stage. After each stage of struggle a new stage is characterised by different opposing classes. This process is known as dialectical materialism.

Marx and Engels believed that in ancient times masters were opposed to slaves. In the middle ages, the aristocracy was opposed to the peasants or serfs. In modern society, the bourgeoisie, or capitalist class, maintains its wealth and power by exploiting the labour of the proletariat, or working class. They believed this opposition to be unstable, because in the final stage of history the proletariat will rise up in revolution and seize the state and all means of production. They would establish a dictatorship of the proletariat. Eventually, as people lose the selfish attitudes produced by capitalism, the state would diminish and the citizens would live in harmony and

Statue of Karl Marx and Friedrich Engels in Berlin

cooperation in a classless society. Marx and Engels were influential in the labour movement in Europe, particularly in Germany.

In 1864 Karl Marx was paramount in the creation of the International Working Men's Association (also known as the First International). It was established in London by representatives from various countries and brought together a wide range of intellectuals, revolutionaries and reformers, amongst whom was the Russian anarchist Mikhail Bakunin.

Bakunin rejected Marx's claim that the dictatorship of the proletariat was necessary to a classless society. Marx and Bakunin clashed and this led to Bakunin's expulsion from the First International and to the organisation being dissolved in 1876.

Another form of socialism, syndicalism, called for direct action. Originating in France, the syndicalists called for a general strike that would bring the economy to a halt and cause the government to collapse. They wanted to replace the state with a federation of workers' cooperatives, organised by trade.

Syndicalism and anarchism were influential in Italy and Spain in the early 20th century, but were later destroyed by fascist governments.

Democratic socialism and social democracy

When Marx died in 1883 there was already a split between those who agreed with Marx that there was a need for violent revolution, and those who felt that the classless society could be brought about by peaceful means, through gradual political and economic changes. The reformists were championed by the German writer Eduard Bernstein.

In 1889 the Second International was formed, but by this time the split had widened. Within the Social Democratic Party (SDP) of Germany, the dominant organisation in the Second International, the split was evident between the orthodox Marxism and the revisionist wing. The party maintained its official rejection of the bourgeois state at the end of the 19th century. But the split and conflict between the party's orthodox and revisionist wing continued for many years. Eventually the revisionists won.

This split continued between the Marxist social-democratic parties throughout western and central Europe during the late 19th century. In each case the revisionists won.

The triumph of revisionism was illustrated by the behaviour of the national parties when the First World War broke out. Socialists had believed until then that the only war the proletariat should fight was the class war against the bourgeoisie. When world war came, however, most of them supported their own bourgeois states and abandoned their ideas of working-class solidarity.

However, orthodox Marxism did not disappear completely. It continued to be supported by an important minority within all the socialist parties. The most influential of the figures supporting orthodox Marxism was Lenin. He eventually led a coup that overthrew the provisional government of Russia after the Russian Revolution.

DISCUSSION POINT ?

How do the different forms of socialism compare to the core values of socialism?

Other socialist viewpoints contributed to the international labour movement towards the end of the 19th century. In Britain socialism developed along a non-Marxist social democratic route, being championed by Christian non-conformist style socialists and radical trade unionists. An intellectual form of revisionist socialism was promoted by the Fabian Society. This was a group of intellectuals and writers, including George Bernard Shaw and H. G. Wells. They believed that through their writings they could influence government policy and legislation toward a gradual and peaceful reform that would lead to socialism.

Charles Fourier (1772–1837)

Fourier's utopian socialism did not attract many followers and neither did it develop. But Karl Marx and Friedrich Engels owed much of their ideas to socialism based on Fourier's ideas. He regarded socialism as a way people could experience the community spirit, which he felt had been diminishing through capitalism. He believed that socialism was about social responsibility and social support and that industrialisation had deprived individuals of creativity and forced them to compete with one another. Fourier believed that in small, free communities life would be better. There would be a minimum standard of living, good education, housing and contentment. He felt that human nature could create this through community life. Fourier was not so concerned with class conflict but saw socialism as being about individuals in society getting along with one another.

Robert Owen (1771–1858)

Robert Owen had an enormous influence on British socialism. Described as being an ethical and Christian utopian socialist, his views were humanist. Agreeing with Fourier, he believed in social responsibility. Many of his enterprises were criticised for being too optimistic of human nature, particularly his beliefs that capitalists were capable of adopting a humanitarian approach to employees by providing education and welfare. He felt this could influence the employees to be more creative and enlightened.

At New Harmony in the United States, he set up an experimental enterprise. It was a cooperative where employees' production was collective. The employees were not exploited but shared the proceeds of their work to fulfil their needs. Owen believed that if the groups came together through the cooperative they would balance the power of the capitalist organisation. He believed that this would balance power within capitalism, rather than eradicate it.

Karl Marx (1818–83)

A scientific socialist, Marx combined the theories of several other liberal economists, such as Ricardo, Hegel, Engels and Blanqui. Marx was living in England during the industrial revolution and it was then that he experienced capitalism. Marx was a scientific socialist with many views on human nature. He believed that individuals worked because it gave their life meaning and a purpose. He believed capitalism alienated employees and that socialism was the inevitable outcome of capitalism, which came about as the result of a revolution.

Marx believed that capitalism, which was driven by profit, inevitably meant that workers would be exploited within the system. Marx claimed to have uncovered the fundamental laws of economics which he believed took precedence over political matters, making his ideas deterministic and dogmatic in their use by later inspired Marxists – Lenin, Mao etc. It is also important to note that Marx's revolutionary beliefs became an essential blueprint for revolutionaries throughout the 20th century.

Learning objectives

- Charles Fourier
- Robert Owen
- Karl Marx
- Eduard Bernstein
- Anthony Crosland
- Antony Wedgewood Benn
- Anthony Giddens

Eduard Bernstein (1850–1932)

Initially a Marxist sympathiser, Bernstein towards the end of the 19th century developed a form of socialism that would oppose classical Marxism. His development of socialism was termed revisionism by Marxists, but it eventually dominated European socialism. Bernstein disagreed with Marx about the revolution of the workforce and believed that socialist principles would develop through democracy. Within such a framework he believed that the workforce would respond and in return they would be fairly treated. Bernstein believed in the formation of elected democratic parties and reforms in the interests of the citizens, particularly the welfare systems, the rights of trade unions and equality of opportunity. The British Labour Party was heavily influenced by Bernstein's non-Marxist socialist theories.

Anthony Crosland (1918–77)

Following his writings in *The Future of Socialism* (1956), Crosland became known as a Labour revisionist. His theories on British socialism helped to bring about New Labour in the 1990s. He argued against claims that the only effective way for socialist objectives was through nationalisation. He believed that capitalism was an important factor. Crosland argued against centralised planning in the Labour Party during the 1950s and 1960s. He also believed that a class-based society was out of date. The working class was becoming richer, so government intervention was no longer required to ensure equality of opportunity. He believed that socialism was based on values rather than on institutions and that the Labour Party of the 1950s and 1960s had given too much importance to trade unions and taxation. He regarded socialism as the provision of social justice, equality of opportunity and social equality. He wanted an end to poverty, poor education and health care through the redirection of capitalist wealth. Many of the theories of Crosland were adopted by the German social democrats and by New Labour under Tony Blair.

Anthony Wedgwood Benn (1925 to date)

In his 1980 book *Arguments for Socialism*, Tony Benn disagreed with Anthony Crosland about capitalism. He believed that large-scale capitalism had prevented the even distribution of wealth and that capitalists would not accept higher taxes as a way of distributing income. He believed that all major industries should be publicly owned if Britain was to ever achieve economic equality.

Anthony Giddens (1938 to date)

Also known as Tony Blair's guru, Giddens has written a number of books on UK social and political theories. His theory of structuration broadly claims that human action is performed within the context of a pre-existing social structure. This structure is governed by a set of norms and/or laws which are distinct from those of other social structures. Social structures make social action possible, and at the same time social action creates those structures. According to Giddens, a social system can be understood by its structure, modality and interaction. Structure is the rules and resources governing and available to agents. The modality of a structural system is the means by which structures are translated into action and the interaction is the activity carried out by the agent acting within the social system. The agent is human action. The knowledge the agent has of their society informs their action. These actions reproduce social structures, which in turn enforce and maintain the dynamics of action. Giddens believes that the trust people have in social structure ensures social stability.

DISCUSSION POINT ?

To what extent might any of these key theorists still be relevant to the modern-day New Labour Party?

Human nature

The following table sets out the different ideological views of human nature.

Ideology	Attitude
Liberalism	Classical liberals believe that individuals are essentially self-interested and self-reliant. This is known as egotistical individualism. Modern liberals believe in developmental individualism, believing that humans will progress given the opportunity to do so.
Socialism	Socialists have a fairly optimistic view of human nature. They tend to take the line that humans are naturally cooperative and sociable and are therefore prepared to act for a collective good without being overwhelmed by self-interest.
Conservatism	Conservatives believe that humans tend to be driven by their own self-interests and desires rather than reason, and as such are somewhat unreliable. New Right theorists also believe in egotistical individualism.

Role of the state

The table below sets out the different ideological views of the role of the state in society.

Ideology	Attitude
Liberalism	Liberals see the state as being essentially a neutral referee or arbiter between the various competing groups and interests in society. To them the state aims to guarantee social order. Classical liberals would see the state as being a necessary evil and have a preference towards a night watchman or minimalist state. More modern liberals take the view that the state should be more proactive to promote equal opportunities and broaden freedom.
Socialism	Socialists do not have an all-encompassing view of the state. Marxists see the state as a key part of maintaining wealthy property owners' rule and a key actor in dampening down the possibility of class tensions. They see a major link between the state and the existing class system. Other socialists see it in a different way, with the state acting towards the common good and intervening where necessary.
Conservatism	Conservatives view the state as protecting society from disorder and is therefore linked to authority and discipline. They favour a strong state. Traditional conservatives believe there should be a balance between state involvement and the freedom of civil society. Neo-liberals believe that state involvement should be kept to a minimum and that current unnecessary involvement should be curtailed. They believe that a strong state impedes economic progress and creates its own problems, as it is bureaucratic and has its own self-interest at heart.

Learning objectives

- Human nature
- Role of the state
- Reform
- Role of the individual and the extent of equality

Note

This topic focuses on the similarities and differences between liberalism, socialism and conservativism on a number of fundamental core values and ideas.

Reform

The table lists the ideological differences towards the role of reform in society.

Ideology	Attitude
Liberalism	Reform liberalism is one of the more dominant forms of liberalism in the modern day. It recognises that there are deep economic and social problems in free-market economies. It views the state's function as creating reform programmes to modify the free-market system and reduce these inequalities. Unlike other forms of liberalism, reform liberalism believes that the state is there to provide the common good and accepts that regulation may be needed to create a more just society.
Socialism	Marxists and revolutionary socialists do not believe that a capitalist system can be changed enough by reform alone. It needs to be overthrown. Some socialists, referred to as reformists or revisionists, believe that over time enough reforms can be put into place so that capitalism will evolve into socialism. Some early socialists believed that socialism could be achieved not by revolution but by parliamentary means. As Rosa Luxemburg wrote: *People who pronounce themselves in favour of the method of legislative reform in place and in contradistinction to the conquest of political power and social revolution, do not really choose a more tranquil, calmer and slower road to the same goal, but a different goal. Our programme becomes not the realisation of socialism, but the reform of capitalism.* New Labour is often described as being revisionist rather than reformist, or at least neo-revisionist. In effect New Labour offers a reinterpretation of the balance between social justice and economic efficiency. Their reforms incorporate work-orientated welfare reforms and private sector investment in public services.
Conservatism	According to David Cameron: 'The modern Conservative Party stands for a simple principle when it comes to social reform and the role of the state: that there is such a thing as society, it is just not the same thing as the state.' (Conservative Party press release, 3 June 2008) Certainly modern-day conservatives are far less radical than they were in the 1980s. Enormous reforms were made then in order to reverse the decline, as they saw it, of Britain. They carried out a full programme of reform in order to revive the spirit of Britain and restore Britain's reputation in the world. Notable were home ownership, rights for council tenants, share ownership, sweeping educational reforms (including the national curriculum), radical trade union legislation, lower taxation, the use of American-style links between work and benefits, driving through privatisation, increasing competition and modernising the transport system.

Role of the individual and the extent of equality

This table outlines the different ideological views on the role of the individual and the extent of equality in society.

Ideology	Attitude
Liberalism	Liberals believe that everyone is born equal and are of equal worth. They believe in legal and political equality and equality of opportunity. They see that social equality could threaten freedoms and impede individuals. Classical liberals favour meritocracy and economic incentives. Modern liberals favour a form of social equality in order to achieve equal opportunities.
Socialism	Socialists favour social equality. However, recent practice, particularly in the case of social democracy, has seen a shift towards a more liberal view. This stresses equality of opportunity and social equality. For social democrats these are taken to be relative. In communist views this is more absolute. In either case whatever the form of social equality, socialists view it as being essential for social cohesion and fraternity. At its heart is justice and equity, as well as ensuring freedoms.
Conservatism	Traditional conservatives view society as being naturally hierarchical. As such, they believe that equality is unachievable and not necessarily desirable. The New Right believe in equality of opportunity based on strong individualist traits. They also believe that inequality has enormous economic benefits, as it makes individuals strive to achieve.

> **DISCUSSION POINT**
>
> Are modern-day social democratic views closer to liberalism or conservatism?

Liberalism and the Liberal Democrats

Although the Liberal Democrats have had mixed fortunes in their various guises since the 1920s, it has not been so much that the parties have enjoyed electoral success, rather it is that their ideologies have permeated other parties.

As far as the Liberal Democrats themselves are concerned, liberal ideologies still remain at the heart of their policies and ideas. They place individual liberty and tolerance at the top of their agenda. They also favour state intervention as the means by which social and economic equality can be achieved. This is based on the foundation of social justice and they therefore support the redistribution of income from the wealthy to the poor.

As we will see when we consider the triumph of liberal democracy on pages 230–31, liberal philosophies have become integral parts of New Labour, the New Right, neo-liberal Conservatives and the Welsh and Scottish nationalists.

Placing the Liberal Democrats to the left or the right of centre is comparatively difficult. Their former leader Charles Kennedy claimed that the Liberal Democrats were both social libertarians and liberal economists. Today's Liberal Democrats still focus on, in their own words: 'A fair, free and open society, in which we seek to balance the fundamental values of liberty, equality and community, and in which no one shall be enslaved by poverty, ignorance or conformity. We champion the freedom, dignity and well-being of individuals.' (preamble to the Liberal Democrat Constitution)

Liberalism and New Labour

Many commentators suggest that New Labour is no longer a socialist party. But there are still vestiges of socialism, as can be seen when we look at the question of whether the Labour Party is still socialist on pages 235–36. In this topic we will look at the impact and interchange between socialism and liberalism.

Both socialists and liberals see equal rights and equality of opportunity as being vital. But radical socialists do not believe that these can be achieved within a capitalist society. More broadly, however, socialists see the creation of equality as a key goal.

Just how close radical liberals are to radical socialists can be seen by comparing the two following quotes: 'From each according to what he chooses to do, to each according to what he makes for himself' and 'From each according to his abilities, to each according to his needs.'

It is difficult to tell the difference between these two statements, but the first was written by Robert Nozick, an extreme liberal, in 1974 and the second by Karl Marx in 1875. There is, however, a key difference. Liberals believe in natural inequality, whereas socialists believe that inequality is an artificial construct of society. Liberals see that a free society stresses the freedom to be unequal whereas socialists see society as providing the conditions for broader equality.

Looking at New Labour it is difficult to know whether there is any significant distinction between their view and that of the liberals. Writing in 1972 (*A Theory of Justice*, Harvard University Press), John Rawls said: 'All social values – liberty and opportunity, income and wealth, and the bases of self-respect – are to be distributed equally unless an unequal distribution of any, or all, of these values is to everyone's advantage.'

Learning objectives

- Liberalism and the Liberal Democrats
- Liberalism and New Labour
- Liberalism and the Conservatives

Liberal demands

The Liberal Democrats want Britain to have a written constitution and a bill of rights to guarantee civil liberties. They are opposed to the identity card and anti-terrorism laws, but many are in favour of decriminalisation of recreational drugs, local initiatives towards crime, progressive taxation, increased public spending, fair trade and sustainable development. They are pro-European and they believe that military action abroad should only be taken after a UN Security Council agreement.

In effect this brings the liberal and the socialist views of equality together. It makes a justification for inequality under certain circumstances and these circumstances are the general good.

Liberals have often held that socialism inevitably curtails freedom. Marx held that the working class believed they were free because they could sell their labour to whoever they pleased, but ultimately they had to sell their labour or starve, so to him this was not true freedom.

In order to redress inequalities and broaden opportunity, along with a redistribution of income, it was a Labour Party that brought in the welfare state. Most liberals and conservatives were aghast at this enormous level of state power and intervention. They believed that many would suffer from a loss of liberty, but in truth liberty had actually been extended.

There are welfare and economic links in Labour adopting liberal ideas through Beveridge and Keynes. The Labour Party in 1997 under Blair talked about re-creating a 'progressive alliance' in British politics (harking back to period 1906–14) even offering the Liberal Democrats seats in his cabinet, a proposal that was opposed by elements in his government and turned down by the Liberal Democrats themselves. Liberal Democrats did take up positions in a Cabinet Committee to develop constitutional reform and cooperated at a parliamentary level in major constitutional reform projects such as devolution, the Human Rights Act, House of Lords reform and the Constitutional Reform Act. Gordon Brown has also sought some Liberal Democrat input in advising his government by seconding the Liberal peer Lord Carlile to act as an independent assessor on anti-terrorism legislation. Beyond cooperation on the constitutional reform agenda there are also other liberal-leaning ideas relating to greater autonomy for local schools and hospitals, as well as the encouragement of internationalist-style policies. Prime examples are the pro-European Union stance and the doctrine of liberal interventionism to tackle humanitarian and political problems in the Third World.

Liberalism and the Conservatives

With the Conservative Party shift to the right under Thatcher and subsequent leaders prior to David Cameron, they have been perceived as a party that lacks any real degree of compassion. Margaret Thatcher may have been a neo-liberal and certainly property owners and middle-income families benefited from her reforms, but there were huge numbers of people, particularly amongst traditional working-class communities, who suffered directly or indirectly. More recently the Conservative Party has tried to respond by appearing to be more compassionate towards deprived groups within society. But this was already the domain of the Liberal Democrats and New Labour, so they have tried to find another way to appear different and distinctive.

There are some fundamental differences between conservatism and liberalism. Conservative individualism focuses on aspects of positive liberty, whereas liberal freedom is based on negative liberty. Conservatives maintain that their policies, such as driving down crime, protecting private property and reducing taxation, are all to do with creating a climate in which individuals can flourish. As far as liberals are concerned, providing that the state guarantees individuals' liberties, then there is nothing wrong with state involvement in society.

There is substantial agreement between conservatives and liberals over property rights. Locke, Jefferson and Paine all saw property rights as being a basic human right. Liberals thus see private property as an important part of individual aspiration. For the conservatives they view property ownership as helping to provide social stability. Those that own property have an interest in ensuring that order is maintained and are more responsible. Therefore, property protection should be a state priority.

Compassionate conservatism

Iain Duncan Smith put forward the idea of compassionate conservatism; David Cameron has focused on the inclusiveness agenda. The party has taken up the mantle of protectors of civil liberties in opposing ID cards, voting against 42-day detention legislation for terrorist suspects and even advocating a referendum on the Lisbon Treaty (albeit this may be more due to political opportunism). Cameron, whilst disliking the Human Rights Act, does instead propose a British bill of rights, although still subservient to parliamentary sovereignty.

DISCUSSION POINT ?

To what extent are both New Labour and the Conservative Party essentially liberal?

Liberal democracy, economic and social liberalism and tough liberalism

Sir Menzies Campbell, speaking at the Liberal Democrat spring conference in March 2006, summed up the key elements of liberal democracy and economic and social liberalism and how they could form the basis of Liberal Democrat policy in the coming years (the key points are in **bold**):

*I will draw on the many strands of our liberal democracy – social, economic, personal and political – to mark out distinctive territory in British politics. There is no conflict between economic and social liberalism. **You cannot deliver social justice without economic success – and discipline**. We can build a fairer Britain, not the means-tested, target-driven, over-centralised country run by Labour today. Our unity must not come at the price of clarity. We must be clear and consistent in all that we say and do. We are moving out of the comfort zone of opposition politics. We must make three-party politics a credible reality. Under New Labour, politics has become managerial, not inspirational. The Conservatives have taken the same course, shunning conviction and desperate only to emulate a value-free Downing Street. Britain does not need a third managerial party. It needs a distinctive liberal democratic party. I will lead this party with a clear vision of liberal democracy. To **empower people, and not the state**; to **promote social mobility**; to **nurture the aspirations of all individuals**; to shape events in the wider world; to **cherish our shared environment**; to **defend the cause of liberty**, and to promote the **radical reform of Britain's** tired **political system** – and that means fair votes for Westminster. To be the leader of the Liberal Democrats is to be the trustee of a great party, with so much to be proud of – but with so many dazzling achievements still to come.*

At the Liberal Party's Scottish spring conference in March 2004 Charles Kennedy had outlined his views on tough liberalism, specifically related to law and order issues (the key issues are in **bold**):

*For too long, all the time I've been in politics, when it comes to these sort of issues, okay these are Conservative issues. Labour has done their best to occupy that territory themselves, first with Jack Straw, now with David Blunkett, but I don't see any reason why those of the liberal tradition should not have something to say about this as well. What we are saying is the toughest of all, it's not just the crackdown, the knee-jerk, the thing that will get you a good tabloid headline. It's actually saying **too many people offend**, go in, come out, **reoffend**, go back in. How are you going to break that pattern? That means being **tough with people and saying that rehabilitation is a word that you've got to be prepared to use**, **neighbourhood involvement**, **making people confront the consequences** of their violence or their crimes, this is a tough option to take. Despite all the rhetoric, the fact is that Labour's approach to crime has failed. It has fed rather than diminished the climate of fear. It has led to a record prison population and record reoffending rates. It has been tough on crime, but soft on the causes of crime. H.G. Wells once said: 'Crime and bad lives are the measure of a state's failure, all crime in the end is the crime of the community.' Labour's crime has been to resort to the quick fix, with no long-term strategy to **bring local communities into the process** so that people can be **part of the solution rather than powerless victims**. And as I have set out today, the real liberal approach to law and order issues can be tough – very tough – without descending into populist illiberalism. That is the task we are setting ourselves. We are sure it can work.*

Tough liberalism can be found in the writings of Mark Oaten and Vince Cable in their contributions to *The Orange Book: Reclaiming Liberalism* published in 2004. They are seen as partly responsible for realigning the party from its centre-left image under Ashdown and Owen to a more centrist/centre-right stance, placing greater emphasis upon personal responsibility and free-market economics.

New themes for the Liberal Democrats

In preparation for the possibility of a snap election the Liberal Democrats created a policy guide which is constantly updated. The key themes include the following plans to:

- create a zero carbon Britain, tackle climate change, sustainable housing, taxing pollution, renewable energy

- introduce voting reform, increase devolution, increase open government, scrap ID cards and destroy the DNA database, and cap party spending

- abolish BERR, provide additional consumer protection, invest in the Post Office and Royal Mail

- devolve decision-making to local communities and councils, scrap council tax and replace it with local income tax, to build affordable homes

- cut basic rate of income tax but increase environmental taxes, cut quangos and bureaucracy

- invest in early learning, allow tailor-made education, cut class sizes, focus on primary skills, scrap tuition fees

- establish local health boards, fund personal care, introduce a patient contract, free the NHS from government intervention

- make EU more accountable, cut number of nuclear weapons

- establish community panels for anti-social behaviour, set up a 24-hour border force, bring back entry and exit controls

- introduce a citizen's pension, reform tax credit and new deal

- increase investment for public transport.

The 2006 leadership contest

Sir Menzies Campbell resigned as leader of the Liberal Democrats in October 2007. In a letter to party president, Simon Hughes, he said questions about his leadership were 'getting in the way of further progress by the party'. His critics accused him of lacking dynamism, a coded reference to his aged appearance, especially in contrast to the youthful leadership of Cameron.

In his letter of resignation, Sir Menzies said that when he took over in March 2006 he had sought to restore stability and purpose to the party, professionalism to its internal operations and to prepare it for a general election. He wrote: 'With the help of others, I believe that I have fulfilled these objectives, although I am convinced that the internal structures of the party need radical revision if we are to compete effectively against Labour and the Conservatives.'

The battle to replace Sir Menzies would be between Nick Clegg and Chris Huhne. In their opening remarks, both seemed remarkably similar:

Britain's political system is broken. First-past-the-post elections entrench a confrontational style of politics in which the Labour and Conservative parties compete for the votes of 800,000 swing voters in marginal constituencies dominated by the concerns of Middle England. (Huhne)

Our political system is broken. Go to the Houses of Parliament and you'll see what I mean. Far from being the 'mother of all parliaments' as the official tour guides will tell you, it is fast becoming a museum piece – a 19th-century home for our 21st-century political elite. [There is a need for] a wholesale commitment to constitutional reform. A written constitution. A fully elected House of Lords. Fewer MPs. And, crucially, electoral reform. (Clegg)

Both Clegg and Huhne were fairly new faces, only taking their seats in 2005. Huhne had stood against Sir Menzies Campbell and Simon Hughes for the leadership after Charles Kennedy's resignation. Huhne had come out in favour of green taxation, allowing for reductions in the income tax rate on the lowest paid. He thus aligned himself with both environmentalists and market liberals. He was opposed to the government's anti-terrorism legislation, and was in favour of the withdrawal of British troops from Iraq within a year. Huhne described himself as a 'social liberal'. He became the first member of the party to announce his candidacy in 2007, declaring his vision of a 'fairer and greener society'.

In his acceptance speech upon winning the leadership contest, Clegg declared himself to be 'a liberal by temperament, by instinct and by upbringing' and that he believed 'Britain [is] a place of tolerance and pluralism'. He declared his priorities as: defending civil liberties; devolving the running of public services to parents, pupils and patients; and protecting the environment. The campaign was largely uncontentious with Clegg and Huhne clashing over Trident but largely in agreement on many other issues.

Clegg's leadership has been overshadowed by the re-emergence of a more confident Cameron-led Conservative Party and was rocked by party divisions over his decision that his party abstain in the Commons vote on a referendum over the Lisbon Treaty in 2008, resulting in resignations from his frontbench team.

DISCUSSION POINT ?

How far has the Liberal Democrat Party strayed from classical liberalism?

Liberal democracy and Fukuyama

Liberalism has been an incredibly powerful ideological force. Many see liberalism as exemplifying the industrialised west and western civilisation. However, radical liberalism has faded away, being replaced with a form of conservative liberalism, which looks at maintaining institutions.

Modern liberals came to believe that government should deliver a wide range of welfare services and, as a result, both classical liberalism and modern liberalism have operated alongside one another.

The most important consideration with regard to liberalism is its dominance since the 19th century. Certainly the liberal model of representative government can be found in many countries, coupled with free-market economies.

Francis Fukuyama began to outline his view of the triumph of liberal democracy in 1989, although he extended his theory three years later. In *The End of History and the Last Man* (1992), Free Press, he said: 'We are witnessing the end of history as such: that is, the endpoint of mankind's ideological evolution and the universalisation of western liberal democracy as the final form of human government.'

Fukuyama argued that the success of liberal democracy was based upon three key elements, which are:

- dynamic capitalism
- support for liberal individualism
- the appeal of political pluralism giving real electoral alternatives.

It is important to remember the context in which he was writing; when Soviet-led communism was collapsing in Eastern Europe. Fukuyama's views have been extended by writers such as Philip Bobbitt (2002). He believed that liberalism had finally won what he called 'the long war' that had raged between 1914 and 1990 between liberal parliamentarianism, fascism and communism. He illustrated his point by suggesting that market reforms and democratic government had spread into Africa, Asia and South America. Indeed, by 2000 around 60 per cent of states across the globe had major liberal democratic characteristics.

Fukuyama was not the first to prophesise the end of ideological debate. This idea dates back ironically to Marx's use of the Hegelian dialectic, in which he argued history would end with the triumph of communism. Later theorists such as Daniel Bell and James Burnham also talked about the end of ideological conflict, resulting in politics driven by the need for competent administration rather than stark political choices.

Relevance to 21st century politics

Theorists such as Fukuyama proclaimed a new world order dominated by liberal democracy when they saw the final collapse of communism in Eastern Europe. Many of the former communist states quickly embraced democratic processes. The Cold War was over and there was peace.

Supporters of liberal democracy contend that in an increasingly complex and culturally diverse society the only way to retain political stability and order is to ensure that liberal democratic

Francis Fukuyama on the triumph of liberal democracy

In his first major work, *The End of History and the Last Man* (1992), Fukuyama suggested that western-style liberal democracy had been the winner of the Cold War and it marked the last ideological change. After the September 11 attacks in 2001 critics suggested that Islamic fundamentalism threatened the power of the west, but Fukuyama described them as being 'a series of rearguard actions' against the prevailing political philosophy of new globalism. Although Fukuyama was considered to be a major neo-conservative figure, he has in recent years distanced himself from this. He became an opponent of the allied invasion of Iraq and criticised neo-conservatives.

principles are upheld. Government has to ensure that democratic elections and factors such as freedom of speech can cope with pressures, which could otherwise destabilise society. They believe that eventually virtually all political systems will display these characteristics.

They also point to globalisation and the fact that it is primarily economic based. They view globalisation as being capable of delivering prosperity to all and therefore a complex network of liberal democratic countries must operate together to ensure its smooth operation.

There are, however, continued challenges to this so-called triumph. Capitalism is essentially unequal. There will always be opposing forces within capitalism based on property ownership. There is also the problem that globalisation challenges and destroys cultural differences and diversity. Traditional industries and ways of life are swept aside by globalisation. To some extent this has fuelled the many and often violent anti-globalisation and anti-capitalist rallies across the world.

Major challenges to liberal democracy have come from other parts of the globe. In Eastern Europe there is a strong nationalist tendency. They have focused on ethnic issues and authoritarianism as a means by which they can achieve their own security and strength. This is most aptly conveyed in Vladimir Putin's authoritarian-style democracy in Russia.

Further afield, fundamentalism poses a considerable challenge to liberal democracy. This has spread across the Middle East and into Asia and Africa. It is not only perceived as being anti-liberal democratic, but also anti-western. Fundamentalist Islam rejects western moral relativism and the focus upon the needs of the individual, instead advocating a single unquestionable source of moral authority, the Qur'an. This rejection of liberal toleration was pertinently revealed in the response to the publication of Danish cartoons depicting the prophet Mohammad in 2005.

In China there is another form of challenge. This vast, highly-populated country has moved towards creating a market economy, and is now openly expansionist and involving itself freely in the global markets. However, its market economy is not based on liberal democracy, but rather on a desire to ensure social stability.

Many believe that rather than the world becoming a liberal democratic one, there are in fact three strands of ideologies competing with liberalism. In the Middle East and in parts of Africa and Asia there is the political manifestation of Islamic fundamentalism; in Eastern Europe and in former parts of the Soviet Union there is authoritarian nationalism; and in China there is **Confucianism**.

Internally, aspects of liberal democracy have been criticised. The anti-capitalist movements in the West have been very vocal in their opposition to the spread of globalisation and its impact upon the Third World. Furthermore, extreme sections of the environmentalist movement are turning to increasingly illiberal options as a solution to global warming, such as the forced rationing of carbon entitlements for individual citizens.

Others see liberal democracies as being fundamentally flawed, as they provide through tolerance a forum for those who would otherwise sweep liberal democracy aside and remove the liberties of others. Critics believe that liberal democracy allows those with fanatical visions for society to threaten it from within. They take advantage of liberal institutions to pursue different ideological doctrines and to use freedom and democracy as a means to an end, whilst not pursuing democracy or defending it themselves. This makes liberal democracies vulnerable and lead critics to claim that liberal democracies should have minimal expectations of those who enjoy the benefits of democratic principles.

Post-modernists

Many now believe that liberalism and multiculturalism are incompatible. Multiculturalists believe that identity is based on religion, language, culture and ethnicity, all seemingly at threat from globalisation. Post-modernists also believe that liberalism is under threat and cannot possibly work in the longer term. Their view of liberalism is rather like other ideologies and claims that it is not accurate and does not reflect the true nature of society or humanity. Samuel Huntingdon sees liberal democracy as only suitable to western liberal values and is alien to large sections of the global population.

Statue of Confucius in the Temple of Confucius in Beijing

Confucianism

This ideology focuses on individual morality and ethics, along with the correct exercise of political power by government. In many respects social ethics and morals based on Confucianism are blended with Taoist and Buddhist concepts.

DISCUSSION POINT ?

Is liberal democracy the final form of politics?

The Third Way and New Labour

Learning objectives

- The Third Way and New Labour
- Post-Thatcherite consensus

The vision of those behind the Third Way is the need to move away from what they see as a pointless debate between left and right. In other words, this refers to the constant war of words between those who favour state intervention and those who are wedded to the free market.

Instead, the Third Way looks towards a new form of political philosophy that focuses on adapting economies and societies to the demands and pressures of globalisation. The concept emerged in the United States in the 1980s when a group called the Democratic Leadership Council was set up in response to concerns that the Democratic Party had drifted too far to the left. The feeling was that the party needed to be realigned into the centre of politics to appeal to a wider constituency.

This strategy culminated in 1992 when the Chairman of the DLC (Governor Bill Clinton) was elected as the US president campaigning as a 'New Democrat'. He stressed the themes of opportunity and responsibility and promoted programmes like welfare to work. Some of the slogans, along with specific policies, were adopted in the UK by Tony Blair as Labour became New Labour.

But what is the Third Way and how has it impacted on New Labour?

- It is a synthesis between capitalism and socialism, neither left nor right, but centrist in nature.

- It is used to describe any type of politics of the centre, for example the Macmillan government in the 1950s.

- It was created primarily in response to the triumph of the New Right and global capitalism.

- The Third Way combines New Right politics with traditional socialist values.

- It blends traditional socialist ideas of collectivism and devolution of power to communities, tackling social exclusion, devolution and regeneration.

- It retains the traditional socialist idea of equality of outcome (everyone receives the same benefit) and combines with the New Right view of equality of opportunity (everyone receives the same access to benefit) and seeks to create equality of opportunity to enable equality of outcome (through positive discrimination etc.)

- On responsibility and accountability it has a New Right emphasis on individual responsibility, but public bodies have an important role to play in people's lives (traditional socialist influence), but bodies must be accountable (New Right influence).

- The New Right would argue for a minimal state and traditional socialists for a larger state that plays a full role in people's lives, the Third Way argues that the state is important, but inefficient, so the private sector needs to be involved.

- On the economy, the New Right would favour the free market, the traditional socialist Keynesian economics and full state involvement, the Third Way sees regulation of the free market in the pursuit of equality.

Turning specifically to the Third Way and New Labour, we can see the following as examples of the influence.

- The modernisation of the Labour Party organisation and ideology since the mid-1980s is exemplified by the rewriting of Clause 4 in 1995.

- Constitutional reform was used to redress the balance between rights and responsibilities, and the location of power within the state. Labour's constitutional reform programme, including devolution, the Human Rights Act, Freedom of Information Act, reform of the House of Lords, and the Constitutional Reform Act, has been probably the most radical and long-lasting legacy of the Third Way ideas.

- The New Deal (1998) was introduced with the purpose of reducing unemployment by providing training, subsidised employment and voluntary work to the unemployed with benefits withdrawn from those who refused employment or a place on the scheme. This had New Right influence regarding the cutting of benefits to those who refuse work and traditional socialist influence in providing schemes to encourage the unemployed back into work.

- The National Health Service was reformed with New Right influence on the maintenance of the influence of the private sector (internal market, private finance initiatives) and traditional socialism influence as the NHS remains free at the point of entry.

- On the minimum wage there is traditional socialist policy (trying to help those less well-off in society) with increases in the basic wage: in 1999 it was £3.60 p/h; this rose to £5.73 p/h in 2008.

Post-Thatcherite consensus

Many believe that there is little difference between the centre parties (New Labour, Liberal Democrats and Conservatives) and feel that there is a post-war consensus and a post-Thatcherite consensus as exemplified in:

- pro-welfare
- collectivism
- pro-equality.

In the Thatcherite period, the key policies seemed to focus on the reverse of this, as they focused on:

- pro-enterprise
- individualism
- anti-dependency.

Returning to the Third Way, it can be seen as the expression of a broader strategy for Labour domination at the centre of the political spectrum. Many have called this an 'empty-vessel' strategy in that it can be expressed in different ways. Under this assumption, the Third Way is 'a device of accommodation' within the post-Thatcherite consensus.

Chantal Mouffe, amongst other left-wing critics, argue that such a 'neutering' of the political argument can have disastrous consequences for democracy. Supporters of New Labour and of post-Thatcherite policies suggest that the Third Way is an original and genuine set of ideas and values that can be applied to everyday politics and policies. They see a different political practice that goes beyond left and right.

In combination with the electoral rise of the Liberal Democrats and the appearance of the single-issue UKIP, the view has signalled a completely different political landscape for the 21st century.

The extent to which one can say 'Thatcherism' has a continuing influence on British political and economic life is not quite as clear as it may appear. Peter Mandelson in 2001 famously declared that 'we are all Thatcherites now'.

There may well be a post-Thatcherite consensus especially in regard to economic policy. In the 1980s, the Social Democratic Party suggested a 'tough and tender' approach in which Thatcherite reforms were coupled with extra welfare provision.

Neil Kinnock began the Labour Party's move to the right when he was leader between 1983 and 1992. His new-look party largely agreed with the economic policies of the Thatcher governments.

The New Labour governments of Tony Blair and Gordon Brown have often been described as 'neo-Thatcherite' by some, since many of their economic policies mimic those of Thatcher. Most of the major political parties are in agreement over the issues of:

- anti-trade union legislation
- privatisation
- general free-market approach.

None of the parties are committed to serious reform of the policies instituted by the Thatcher governments. Such a convergence of policy is one reason that the British electorate perceive few apparent differences in policy between the major political parties.

What challenges do Gordon Brown and his new deputy Harriet Harman face? Tony Blair had given the Labour Party what it wanted after 18 years in opposition – power. He delivered one overwhelming and two significant majorities. Brown is unlikely to be able to match that.

Brown faced a resurgent Conservative Party under a new leader. The left of the party, which had felt particularly sidelined during the Blair years, began to flex its muscles. Perhaps this is Brown's greatest challenge, and the extent to which he is able to manage the different issues of Iraq, British territorial integrity (Scottish calls for independence) and the British economy.

In July 2008, Gordon Brown urged Labour to 'have confidence' in policies which he said would 'persuade' voters to back the party at the next general election. Chancellor Alistair Darling told the BBC that Labour had to 'concentrate on getting the right policies to support people through what are undoubtedly difficult times' and 'articulate the reason for our existence in the first place'.

DISCUSSION POINT ?

We are all Thatcherites now. Discuss.

Modern Labour Party policies

Learning objectives

- Modern Labour Party policies
- The Labour left and party policy
- The rise of the new left
- Social democracy vs democratic socialism
- Radical socialists in the EU

As we have seen, there is a strong argument to suggest that many aspects of New Labour are in fact liberal and certainly New Labour has seized the centre ground of British politics. There has been a quantifiable shift to the right in the Liberal Democrats under Campbell and Clegg, but a marked shift to the centre ground in the Conservatives under Cameron.

The Labour Party has always been seen as a coalition of left and centre-left interests, with committed socialists never completely dominating the party. However, following the defeat of the Callaghan government in 1979, there was a marked shift to the left under the guidance of Tony Benn, which culminated in Michael Foot's leadership producing the 1983 election manifesto advocating mass nationalisation and other socialist measures. The subsequent failure of the party in the election resulted in the document being referred to by Labour politician Gerald Kaufmann, as 'the longest suicide note in history'. New Labour still retains vestiges of socialism, but at the same time there are a number of factors that lead us to suggest that New Labour has abandoned socialism. The key features are shown in the following table.

New Labour's pro-socialist credentials	New Labour's rejection of socialism
They are committed to reducing poverty, having a declared target of abolishing child poverty	Clause IV has been amended, which called for common ownership of the means of production
A social exclusion policy is used to create social equality	Individualism is rated as more important than collectivism as seen in granting greater autonomy to local schools and hospitals
They uphold the welfare state and all it represents; public commitment to the NHS	They accept that some economic inequality is tolerable – gap between wealthiest and poorest sections in the UK has risen since 1997
In the public interest regulation has been applied to large industry	They have failed to restore the powers of trade unions that were taken away during the Conservative governments prior to 1997
They signed the Social Chapter, extending employment rights	They have limited progressive taxation to redistribute income (e.g. cut income tax) and failed to restore the earnings link to state pensions
They appear to still support limited redistribution of income through a targeted tax credit system	They have not set aside funds to subsidise council housing, instead further relaxing regulations affecting the sale of social housing
Education is still seen as a major factor in ensuring equality of opportunity with significant increases in education budget, leading to a huge school rebuilding programme and the declared aim of 40 per cent of the population going to university	Higher education is no longer free given the introduction of tuition fees. LEA control over schools has diminished with the creation of city academies sponsored by private firms and individuals, and foundation schools

The Labour left and party policy

Since the mid-1980s the left in the Labour Party has been more than marginalised. When John Smith took over as leader of the Labour Party in 1992 he wanted all the wings of the party to come together to influence policy. However, after Tony Blair took over, the left in the party either had to decide to remain within the party or to leave. Those who remained have found it hard to reclaim what they see to be a socialist party that has been taken over by neo-conservatives.

Left-wingers remaining in the party obviously hope at one stage in the future they will be able to reclaim their party. They view their work as being ideological, as exemplified by organisations such as the Socialist Campaign Group. They have also at times decided to risk the wrath of the party hierarchy and the Whips by refusing to turn out and vote in favour of government legislation.

When Tony Blair stood down in June 2007, the left-wing candidate John McDonnell could not even raise the 45 nominations he needed to stand. Gordon Brown, by comparison, had 318 nominations. It was a huge vote from Labour MPs, strengthening Brown's neo-liberal approach. John McDonnell responded quickly to what many believed to be the death of the Labour left by saying that the party was in a stronger position to fight for socialist policies than it had been for years.

Many believe that had there been strong grassroots left support in the party then McDonnell would have got more than 45 nominations. There is a serious crisis for the left within the party and it now seems that many of the true Labour left have shifted their allegiance to smaller and more radical parties.

The rise of the new left

The Respect coalition was founded in the aftermath of the anti-war protests resulting from the September 11 2001 terrorist attacks. In a high-profile contest in Bethnal Green in 2005 during the general election, the Respect Party's George Galloway beat the Labour MP Oona King.

For some time the Respect Party has worked alongside the Socialist Workers Party (SWP), providing at times mutual support. But more recently there has been a rift between the two groups. The Socialist Workers Party is believed to be the largest far-left political party in Britain.

The SWP can trace its history back to the 1950s and it first put up candidates for election in the 1970s. The SWP is still essentially a revolutionary socialist movement that aims to overthrow capitalism, as it believes that reform will not bring about a new society based on collectivism and equality. They are implacably against globalisation and claim to be pro-peace, equality, justice and socialism.

The party has been and continues to be riven with internal disputes and disagreements over direction and priority. They have also been accused of deliberately infiltrating other groups in order to either undermine or adversely influence direction and policy. Some also claim that the party is fundamentally undemocratic, although this is fiercely denied.

In the 2005 general election Respect put up 26 candidates; the only successful candidate was George Galloway. However, in a Birmingham constituency another Respect candidate came second with 27.5 per cent of the vote. In the 2006 local elections Respect gained 15 councillors. They had even more success in 2007.

In September 2007 Galloway began the process of trying to reorganise the party, believing it to be infiltrated and unduly influenced by SWP members. There had been a major split between the SWP and Respect, but in 2008 an official Respect candidate stood on the left list platform as the London Mayor candidate.

Respect has been criticised by other smaller left-wing groups, such as the Socialist Party, the Alliance for Workers Liberty and Workers Power, claiming that the group is undemocratic and too London centred. At present the party's future fortunes lie primarily in the hands of George Galloway. His intention is not to stand for his current seat in the next general election, but to stand for the newly created and safe Labour seat of Poplar and Limehouse.

Social democracy vs democratic socialism

Democratic socialism does share some characteristics with social democracy inasmuch as it has a commitment to pursue change through the existing institutions. It does aim to reform or transform capitalism rather than just trying to mitigate the worst effects of it. Democratic socialism also aims to make longer term change to capitalism by replacing it with a society that is more based on collective control and equality rather than a society that is dominated by private capital and a social structure that is influenced by market forces.

Whilst democratic socialism can be seen as a radical version of social democracy, there are different versions of social democracy and not just one broad approach. Compensatory social democracy aims to offset many of the negative impacts of the free market. Countervailing social democracy looks at replacing the system rather than amending it and in doing so is a clearer form of socialism.

Since the Second World War, social democracy has tended to be based around a series of ideological features including a universal welfare state, Keynesian economics, trade unions, solidarity with the working class and corporatist arrangements. Approaches have varied, particularly in the case of the welfare state and corporatism. From the 1970s, these ideological and policy approaches have come under attack. The loyalty of the working class has diminished (although inequality is a still an important consideration), however class as a means of delineating economic and social divisions has become less important. Considerable numbers of middle-class voters have supported social democracy, but the decline in manufacturing has seen the traditional core support for social democracy shrink, and voters are more pragmatic and less partisan and loyal than before.

For the British Labour Party, making the switch to a cross-class approach took many years of bitter infighting and several electoral defeats. Building cross-class support has meant that the party has had to rethink its messages to the electorate, something that similar parties in Sweden and Holland did much earlier and with success.

There have also been policy crises. Many social democrats now see that state welfare supported by relatively high taxation has reached its limits. No longer are many voters prepared to pay for universal services beyond current levels. In any case, it is also perceived as encouraging a dependency culture and that current systems are unwieldy and undemocratic, and many people have opted out by funding their own pensions, insurances and private health care.

Radical socialists in the EU

The European United Left–Nordic Green Left is a socialist, eco-socialist and communist political group in the European Parliament. The group is in opposition to the current political structure of the EU, but is committed to Europe. Their three key ideas are:

- a change of institutions to make them 'fully democratic'

- a new model of development and ecology aimed at creating a 'social space' and breaking with neo-liberalism

- a policy of co-development and equitable cooperation.

Elements of the group could be described as being revolutionary whilst others are reformists. They would aim to abolish the Maastricht Treaty. Significantly, they choose to work inside rather than outside the EU institutions to influence decisions made regarding co-decisions. With the addition of two new MEPs from Ireland's Sinn Féin, and one from the Left Bloc of Portugal, the group now has 41 members from 17 member parties in 13 member states.

In EU member states there has been resurgence of interest in left-wing ideologies. The Polish Left (Polska Lewica) is a newly formed left-wing political party in Poland. Its formation was announced in September 2007 by the former prime minister Leszek Miller. He claimed that the party would be a 'true leftist' alternative to the centre-left coalition of the Left and Democrats (Lewica i Demokraci or LiD). Miller and many members had left the LiD because they felt it had taken a turn to the right. However, the left-wing vote in Poland has all-but collapsed (42% in 2001). The biggest problem for LiD is voters' perception that the left-wing in Poland is associated with the old Communist Party, and therefore there is reluctance to vote for them. The other major issue is that many Polish left-wing parties feature economic redistribution as part of their policies; even the Polish Peasant's Party, in government with Thatcherite-type conservatives, have always positioned themselves on the redistributionist left as the opposition to the Self-Defence and the League of Polish Families.

In Germany The Left (Die Linke) is also relatively new (June 2007). It was created by the merger of the Left Party/PDS (the former SED, once the governing party of East Germany before unification) and the Labour and Social Justice party, to form The Electoral Alternative (WASG). By the end of 2008 it had over 76,000 members, making it the fourth largest party in Germany. In the Bundestag it is also the fourth largest faction of the five parties, with 54 of the 614 seats. The majority of its membership and voting support comes from the former East Germany. On the international stage is it the largest party in the European United Left–Nordic Green Left group in the European Parliament.

Policy-wise, and therefore ideologically, it is difficult to assess The Left at this stage. They do not yet have a party programme as such, although some of the members are left-wing social democrats, others are Marxists. Nonetheless, it seems clear that they are in favour of:

- democratic socialism
- self-determination for workers
- redistribution of wealth
- end of privatisation
- higher minimum wages.

DISCUSSION POINT (?)

Is New Labour still socialist?

238

Comparing and contrasting Labour, Liberal Democrat and Conservative policies

The list of policies in the table are based on the 2005 election manifesto commitments of the three parties.

Issue	Labour	Conservative	Liberal Democrat
Asylum and immigration	Reduce asylum numbers by tougher rules on settlement and more deportations; electronic register of all crossing borders; skills-based points system for permanent immigrants	Annual refugee and immigrant quotas; bonds for temporary workers; compulsory health checks; offshore asylum processing centres; new border police; quit UN refugee convention	Back common EU asylum policy with fair sharing of asylum settlement; allow asylum seekers to work so they don't rely on benefits; quota for immigrant workers from outside EU
Health (devolved in Scotland, Wales and Northern Ireland)	Patients able to choose their NHS hospital; waiting times down to 18 weeks; 100 new hospital schemes; 2700 GMP premises to be improved; no 'cut price' hospital cleaning contracts (New foundation hospitals with limited local authority influence)	Patients able to choose hospital or take 50 per cent of NHS operation price to go private; matrons to keep hospitals MRSA-free; Whitehall targets scrapped; foundation status for all hospitals	£8 billion more on health; reduce diagnostic waiting lists for tests; free long-term care for elderly; free eye tests, drugs for long-term illnesses; ban smoking in public places (introduced in 2006 in Scotland and 2007 in England)
Crime – law and order (devolved in Scotland)	Dedicated policing teams for every area; record police numbers already; plans total of 25,000 community support officers; 1300 more prison places; double cash for drug treatment	40,000 extra police; 10-fold rise in drug rehab places; addicts to choose rehab or prison; end some early releases; 20,000 more prison places; judges to set minimum and maximum sentences	10,000 extra police; tackle drug dealers rather than cannabis users; out-of-hours school courses against yob culture; local communities decide sentences for low-level criminals
Education (devolved in Scotland, Wales and Northern Ireland)	Parents can select specialist schools; 200 new city academies; new powers to control truancy and disruption; university top-up fees up to £3000, with grants for poorest students	600,000 new school places to boost choice; allow good schools to expand and new ones created; heads able to expel disruptive pupils; no student fees but interest would be charged on loans	Cut class sizes for youngest children; ensure all children are taught by a qualified teacher in each subject; abolish 'unnecessary tests'; scrap university fees
Terrorism and Iraq	Stands by Iraq war – even if weapons intelligence was wrong, Saddam flouted UN resolutions; emphasis now changed to commitment in Afghanistan; want new powers for Justice Minister to detain terror suspects at home with an increase in potential detention to 42 days; £3.7billion more spend on defence	Still backs Iraq war but say Tony Blair lied over the intelligence; oppose 'internment without trial' and want wiretap evidence admitted; spend £2.7 billion more on defence, save regiments	Opposed Iraq war and demand Blair reveal when he promised to commit UK forces; would start phased withdrawal of troops after Iraqi polls; want only judges to imprison terror suspects

Issue	Labour	Conservative	Liberal Democrat
Pensions	Use benefits savings to design system with basic state pension at core; state pension age stays same; lump sums/higher payments for those working longer; special help for poorest	Restore link between state pension and earnings by replacing New Deal; fund free long-term residential care via three-year state sponsored insurance scheme	Boost basic state pension by £100+ a month and restore pensions-earnings link for over-75s; link pension to residency not National Insurance payments; free long-term personal care
Taxation and the economy (partially devolved in Scotland)	Takes credit for low mortgage rates, more jobs; would reform the 'unsustainable' council tax; say spending plans affordable without tax rises; tax reliefs for 'hard-working families'; abolished 10p tax rate but had to compensate with increased personal allowances	Would prevent 'Labour third term tax rises'; will use £4 billion to cut taxes including £1.3 billion cut in council tax for pensioners; also proposed cuts to inheritance tax, exempting all below £1million from payment, and also cut to stamp duty	Replace council tax with a local income tax; new 50 per cent tax rate on earnings over £100,000 a year (now dropped); raise stamp duty threshold to £150,000 to help first-time buyers
European Union	Wanted adoption of proposed EU constitution after referendum – negotiated replacement Lisbon Treaty ratified by Parliament only; support joining the single currency if five economic tests show it is in UK interests; UK should be at 'heart' of Europe	Opposed EU constitution and replacement Lisbon Treaty and wanted referendum; would let other nations integrate while UK gets powers back over fishing and quits Social Chapter; oppose adopting euro	Would work towards the right conditions for joining the euro and then call referendum; backed EU constitution and replacement Lisbon Treaty, saying it will make clear the limits on Brussels powers
Family life and welfare (partially devolved to Scotland, Wales and Northern Ireland)	'Universal, affordable and flexible' childcare for parents of all 3- to 14-year-olds; a Sure Start children's centre in every area; extend maternity pay from 6 to 9 months, allow fathers to share	Paid maternity leave extended to 9 months, or higher pay for 6 months; £50/wk childcare subsidies for all with children under 5; replace child tax credits with tax allowances	Maternity pay of £170 per week for first 6 months; create Early Years centres for pre-school education; no presumption in favour of mothers in child custody cases
Environment (devolved to Scotland, Wales and Northern Ireland)	Signed up to Kyoto and 60 per cent target for cutting CO_2 emissions by 2050; tax incentives for fuel-efficient cars; backing research into hydrogen-powered vehicles; committed to new nuclear power station programme and outlined plans to build 14,000 wind turbines as well as a tidal barrage in the Bristol Channel	'Better leadership' on Kyoto targets; make fly-tipping an offence which would mean arrest; push tidal, wave and offshore wind power; use taxes to make greenest fuels cheaper; protect green fields; change emphasis from personal taxation to carbon-using taxation	60 per cent CO_2 reduction target for 2050 and new global targets based on allocation by country; 20 per cent renewable electricity by 2020; 60 per cent household waste recycled in 7 years
Transport (devolved to Scotland, Wales and Northern Ireland)	Spending in 2015 to be 60 per cent up on 1997; rail reorganisation so ministers set strategy and Network Rail owns all track; road building but car-sharing lanes/road use charge plans too; Manchester chosen as one of the first experiments in road charging	Expand roads/speed up repairs; remove speed cameras which only make money; give best rail firms longer contracts; use retailers to fund improving train stations	Replace fuel tax/VED with national road user charging; congestion charging; shift spending from roads to public transport; free off-peak local bus travel for pensioners and disabled

Issue	Labour	Conservative	Liberal Democrat
Rural issues (partially devolved to Scotland, Wales and Northern Ireland)	Boost rural economy; save rural post offices (pushed through closure programme to 2000 local post office branches); build more new homes; more rural bus services; reform CAP; more aid for fishermen; enforce fox hunting ban	Greater say for local people in planning, stop illegal traveller sites; repeal hunting ban; ban GM crops; reform CAP to boost farm income	OFT check on farmers' prices; more reform of CFP and CAP; no GM crops without strict controls; more affordable shared-ownership homes
Constitution	Limited number of hereditary peers, further Lords reform promised; created Scottish parliament, Welsh and NI assemblies, want elected regional assemblies; new Supreme Court; parliament to have greater control over the use of the royal prerogative powers	Make House of Lords a mostly elected chamber; strengthen parliament; oppose postal voting; scrap supreme court plan; hold vote on future of Welsh Assembly; abolish the Human Rights Act and replace with a British Bill of Rights subservient to parliamentary sovereignty	Referendum on electoral reform; extend vote to 16-year-olds; make House of Lords elected chamber; PR for local elections; more powers for Welsh, NI assemblies; written Constitution
Equality and human rights	Equality commission set up 2007; passed Human Rights Act; introduced civil unions for gay couples; banned incitement to religious hatred; introduced stronger disability, sex, age and race laws	Reservations over equalities commission red tape; oppose 'politically correct' use of human rights laws; introduce disability discrimination act	A single, comprehensive equality act; action on age discrimination; played key role in 1998 Human Rights Act; wants UK Bill of Rights

DISCUSSION POINT ?

What do you see as the key areas for debate in a forthcoming election?

ExamCafé
Relax, refresh, result!

Relax and prepare

The following are example essay questions for unit F854. How would you go about answering th

- Compare and contrast classical and modern liberalism.

- Discuss whether there is more to liberalism than the safeguarding of individual rights and liberties.

- Discuss whether liberalism and democracy are fully compatible.

- Compare and contrast democratic and revolutionary forms of socialism.

- How important is social class to different forms of socialism?

- Compare and contrast liberal and socialist attitudes towards equality.

Refresh your memory

To help you with your revision, look at the following chart and consider the main liberal and socialist attitudes towards the various issues raised. Also try and link the views of relevant political theorists to each area.

Key issue	Classical liberal attitude	Modern liberal attitude	Democratic socialist attitude	Revolutionary socialist attitude
Human nature				
Freedom				
Political equality				
Economic equality				
State intervention				
Ownership of property				
Political reform				
Capitalism				
Democracy				

Get the result!

The following is an example of an exam essay question for unit F854.

Discuss the view that socialists differ more over the means than the ends of socialism.

Exam tips

To improve your chance of achieving a high mark you should plan your essay before you start writing it. To do this you might wish to think about the following issues. Remember your answer must include the ideas of relevant political thinkers in order to secure higher marks.

Introduction

Always start your answer by defining the key term related to the question; here it is socialism. Make sure you learn an appropriate definition.

Means to socialism

The reference here is to the various different ways of securing socialism; the clearest distinction is between revolutionary socialists and evolutionary or democratic socialists. Remember to include specific examples of relevant thinkers (these may include Marx, Lenin and Bernstein). You might also wish to consider utopian routes as well, as championed by Fourier and Owen. Don't forget to explain why different types of socialists advocate different methods.

The ends of socialism

Do all socialists advocate a similar outcome? That is, a classless society, collective ownership, equality primarily based upon outcome and an allocation of resources based upon needs, or are there actual differences in their belief as to what a socialist society should consist of. It would be a good idea to contrast the two extremes of socialist thought to examine this: Marxism and social democracy. Once again remember to use relevant theorists, for example Marx, Benn and Crosland.

Conclusion

Directly address the question. You don't have to agree with the assertion, but make sure your opinions are based upon what you have argued in your essay.

Unit F856

Relax and prepare

The following are example essay questions for unit F856. Discuss with your colleagues how you would go about answering them or try writing essay plans for as many as you can.

- Discuss the view that all mainstream British political parties are essentially liberal in ideology.
- How far have Liberal Democratic ideas and policies changed since 1997?
- Has liberal democracy triumphed?
- How socialist is the modern-day Labour Party?
- How coherent is the Third Way as a political ideology?
- Discuss the view that socialists in theory and in practice sacrifice individual liberty for equality of outcome.

Refresh your memory

Case studies on liberalism and socialism

To help you apply your theory knowledge of liberalism and socialism to modern politics for unit F856, think about how the following issues and events have significance for one or both of the ideologies.

- ✓ The extent of liberal elements within the UK political system (e.g. free elections, free media, independent judiciary, constitutional safeguards protecting individual liberty and limiting government actions).
- ✓ Liberal Democratic support for constitutional reform including electoral reform, a UK written constitution and a Bill of Rights.
- ✓ Liberal Democratic involvement in devolved administrations in Scotland and Wales.
- ✓ The rewriting of Clause 4 by the Labour Party in 1995.
- ✓ New Labour winning three general elections and thus becoming the longest-serving Labour administration in British history.
- ✓ New Labour's focus on health and education (expansion of education and health spending as a proportion of Britain's GDP, reforms seeking to give greater independence to individual schools and hospitals and the creation of targets to monitor performance).
- ✓ George Galloway's victory for the Respect Coalition in Bethnal and Bow in the 2005 general election.
- ✓ The coming down of the Berlin Wall and the demise of Soviet-style communism throughout Eastern Europe.

he following is an example of an exam essay question for unit F856.

ompare and contrast contemporary liberal and socialist attitudes towards welfare issues.

Exam tips

In any compare and contrast question you must make sure you identify similarities and differences between the two concepts. As this is an F856-style question this must be done for theory as well in practice. Remember the question says contemporary liberal and socialist attitudes – this means that your answer should not concentrate on earlier forms of liberalism and socialism (i.e. classical liberal and utopian-style socialism). A good guide for contemporary would be events post-1997, although your work would still be regarded for relevant examples drawn from before this date. To help you plan this essay you may wish to split up your points of comparison into the following areas.

Theory
Contemporary liberalism
Support both negative and positive aspects of liberty, thus showing willingness to countenance welfare spending and state intervention to tackle obstacles to the maximisation of personal development. Look at the views of T. H. Green and Lord Beveridge to illustrate this point. You may also want to consider more contemporary explanations of this, for example John Gray and John Rawls. Credit would be given for some comment on neo-liberal ideas championed by the New Right which seek to dismantle the welfare state as it inhibits individual freedom and distorts competition (e.g. Hayek and Nozick).

Modern socialism
Once again support for welfare issues, albeit from a different perspective, that is, less focus on self-development and more on egalitarianism. The socialist idea of the welfare state has tended to be to reduce wealth differentials instead of providing opportunities for advancement. Socialist ideas on the welfare state have tended to be more collectivist, state interventionist and redistributive in terms of wealth. Tony Benn and R. H. Tawney's ideas on democratic socialism would be relevant here. You would also be rewarded for examining social democratic attitudes to welfare issues, drawing parallels with contemporary liberal attitudes favouring a mixed-market approach and giving greater opportunities for personal development through assistance from the state – use the views of Crosland as well as the impact of the theorists such as Anthony Giddens upon the Third Way project (if this can be regarded as socialist!). Further credit could be given by extending socialism to consider international attitudes – for example, Cuba, China or Venezuela and their Marxist-inspired attitudes to state-monopolised welfare systems.

In practice
The creation of the welfare state by the 1945–51 Labour government based upon the Beveridge Report would be a good starting point. Your answer however should go on to consider specific welfare issues. These might include health, education, social security benefits, pensions and redistributive taxation. A good approach may be to compare Liberal Democrat Party policies with those of New Labour. The policies as laid out in their respective 2005 general election manifestoes would be useful. For more details on specific policies, see the comparison of party policies earlier in this chapter. By examining party policy you should find evidence that links party policy to the ideas outlined in the theory.

Specifically you might make the observation that New Labour policy tends to be more state focused than Liberal Democrat proposals (centrally imposed targets etc.), although issues of granting greater autonomy to schools and hospitals seems to move away from this. Redistribution also takes different forms, with New Labour offering directed tax credits to assist those poorest elements in society as well as reducing income tax but increasing National Insurance contributions, whereas Liberal Democrats have the aim of utilising income tax (and a local version to replace council tax) to differentiate over-contributions to the state. Indeed in some cases Liberal Democrat policy has appeared more radical than Labour over issues such as restoring the link between pensions and earnings as well as proposals to introduce a new top rate tax band of 50 per cent on all those earning over £100,000, however this latter policy has now been dropped by the party.

By examining the above this might lead you to conclude that whereas in theory contemporary liberalism and socialism in its mainstream forms found in the UK may have some ideological differences in their attitudes to welfare issues, in practice their policies ultimately add up to the same objectives, preserving the 1945 welfare state consensus.

A wave of reformist and radical feminist action against the inequalities women experienced in the legal, political, social, economic aspects of life in western societies began in the 1960s with the publication of Betty Friedan's book *The Feminine Mystique* in 1963. Feminist action was aiming not just at the gradual reform of the attitudes and the institutions of society but at the liberation of women in the sense of redefining their roles and relationships in society and achieving this through the radical transformation of that society. The first pursued the goals of equal pay for equal work, use of the law to prevent discrimination, use of positive discrimination, maternity leave and childcare facilities and legal protection against violence.

The radicals' pursuit of a social revolution was to alter the existing male dominance of the various facets of life and to establish that differences in sex and gender are not significant, so that the oppression of women can be resolved. Changing society was the only way to achieve these goals. The idea is that there should be equality in the relationships. Germaine Greer's view about the differences between men and women is that those differences should be celebrated. In doing this the inequalities in the relationship will cease to exist.

The environmental issues that confront humans and threaten the state of the planet and perhaps the existence of the human species have escalated into global significance. The focus is on the damage being done to the natural environment by the activities of humans, such as the stripping of forests and the generation of power using fossils fuels. The global nature of the problems requires them to be handled through international gatherings and protocols such as the UN Conference for the Human Environment, the Earth Summit in Rio de Janeiro and the Kyoto Protocol.

The ecologists take the view that the natural world is a self-regulating system of plants and animals that operate together in harmony to create a balanced state in which species do not threaten one another's existence. Humans, on the other hand, threaten the balance of this system through their pursuit of selfish materialistic ends.

Governments taking the threats to the planet seriously have proposed working out a system of human activity and controls that creates a state of sustainability. But the more radical environmentalists, the Greens for example, are unconvinced given the dedication to materialism, science and technology and utilitarian values rather than to the planet. For ecologists true sustainability demands setting limits on human activity in order to redress the balance. The Green realists accept that humans should pursue sustainability but they need to balance this against environmental costs. Green fundamentalists take the line that zero growth is necessary given that the problems occur because of economic growth, consumerism and materialism.

Another proposal is that humans should pursue a quality of life that relies less on economic needs. They should see themselves as part of nature and not as superior to it and use it for whatever material needs they seek to satisfy.

Religious fundamentalists view modern society as degenerate and their purpose is to regenerate that society through returning to core values of the faith. They are prepared to achieve this through political action, and militancy if necessary. Some fundamentalists believe that engaging in public life is essential for restoring the core values and preventing future descent into degeneracy. Fundamentalism is not restricted to any one religious faith: there are fundamentalist Christians, Muslims, Hindus, Sikhs and Buddhists.

A modern society like Britain has in recent times undergone major political, social and economic changes that have swept away much of the previous certainties of life. It is no longer an industrialised nation and is not so preoccupied with class. We are now consumers and individuals.

Our politics have changed from being ideological to being managerial in style, personality-driven and consensus-orientated. Public enterprises have been privatised and private expertise has been incorporated into the public services. Political party membership has declined and citizens are finding their political outlets through other forms of action, such as pressure groups.

These are some of the issues covered in this chapter, in which the following are key themes.

- The ideas and aims of feminism

- The alternative ideologies of environmentalism

- The nature and aims of religious fundamentalism

- The changes that have taken place in the post-modern world

- The place of political ideology in the modern world

- Radical environmentalism and anti-globalisation

- The challenges to religious fundamentalism in the modern world

- The problems of sexual equality in modern society and politics

In covering these themes the chapter is broken down into the following topics.

The chapter finishes with an exam café feature on page 274

Equality is at the heart of
feminism.

Origins and development

The term feminism is a relatively new one. However feminist ideas have been expressed for centuries. Although the first recognised feminist text was written in 1792 by Mary Wollstonecraft (*Vindication of the Rights of Women),* it was the *Book of the City of Ladies* written in 1405 that is credited with views that can be equated to modern feminism. Christine de Pisan's book advocated women's right to education and the right to exert political influence.

The first wave of feminism, in the mid-19th century, focused on attaining the right to vote. It also called for equal legal and political rights. The view was that once the vote had been won, women's influence would sweep away other forms of discrimination. The key events during this period include the following.

- The creation of the US Women's Rights Movement in 1848 at the Seneca Falls convention. It demanded female suffrage in its Declaration of Sentiments.

- The creation of the US National Women's Suffrage Association in 1869 by Stanton and Susan B. Anthony (later merged with the American Women's Suffrage Association in 1890).

- The foundation of the British organisation, the Women's Social and Policy Union, in 1903 by Emmeline and Christabel Pankhurst. They were to coordinate a series of attacks on property and organise public demonstrations.

- The extension of the right to vote for women over 30 in Britain in 1918 equalised at the age of 21 in 1928 (the US granted this in 1920).

Despite the belief that the vote would be the driving force for the women's movement, it did not work out this way. The battle to win the vote had united women's groups, now they fragmented into smaller competing organisations. Also, many women dropped out of the movement believing that the goal of equality had been achieved with the vote.

The movement gained new impetus in the 1960s. Betty Friedan wrote *The Feminine Mystique* (1963), in which she highlighted women's discontent with the dual roles of wife and mother. She called this 'the problem with no name'. This began what has been coined the Second Wave of feminism; it became increasingly more radical throughout the 1960s and the 1970s. Germaine Greer's *The Female Eunuch* (1970) and Kate Millett's *Sexual Politics* (1970) looked at all aspects of female oppression. No longer was emancipation the goal; it was liberation (as promised by the Women's Liberation Movement). The view was that liberation could not be achieved by staged reforms, but by revolutionary social change.

It was at this stage that feminism could reasonably be described as an ideology. Gender issues were now on the agenda and everywhere steps were being made to improve the consciousness of gender issues. Since the 1970s there have been two key developments in the feminist ideology.

- The movement and the general views are less radical, as most feminist goals have been achieved (this is known as post-feminism).

- The movement has fragmented and diversified and the feminist groups now lack common ideologies (fragmented groups include liberal, socialist, Marxist, radicals, psychoanalytical, black and lesbian).

Core themes

The emergence of radical feminism in the 1960s swept away the acceptance of conventional ideologies as the basis for furthering the advancement of women. Out of this emerged three key approaches: liberal feminism, Marxist (or socialist) feminism and radical feminism (see pages 250–51 for details). Common themes, however, do exist, as can be seen in the following table.

Theme	Explanation
Public/ private divide	This is the belief that politics exists wherever social conflicts exist. Millett defined politics as 'power-structured relationships, arrangements whereby one group of persons is controlled by another'. Prior to this the notion was that women should be political in public life, but non-political in their private lives. The argument also covers the nature of sexual inequality. In other words, feminists reject the notion that the sexual division of labour is natural; they claim it to be political. Feminists therefore challenge the notion of a public and private divide, radical feminists in particular. They aim to address all areas of the 'politics of everyday life', from domestic responsibility to child rearing, effectively calling for the state to take over responsibility for private life.
Patriarchy	This is a term used to describe the power relationships between men and women. Some will use the phrases 'male supremacy' or 'male dominance'. The implication is that male dominance encompasses not only family relationships and life, but also all areas of education, work and politics. Millett said 'male shall dominate female, elder male shall dominate younger'. Feminists do not have an all-embracing view of patriarchy, but recognise that there have been changes in politics, education, marriage law, divorce law and the legislation of abortion. Liberal feminists use the term to highlight the unequal distribution of rights. Socialist feminists focus on the economic aspects (although others reject the notion altogether as they see it as part of a larger problem). Radical feminists see patriarchy as a systematic, institutionalised way to ensure the continuance of male domination.
Sex and gender	Feminists challenge the notion that biology is destiny. They define sex as the biological differences between men and women, the important aspect being reproduction. Gender is defined as a cultural term, gender differences being typified by stereotypes of masculinity and femininity. Feminists deny that there is a direct link between sex and gender and argue that gender is socially and politically constructed. Feminists argue that the sex differences between men and women are not significant. Humans have both male and female characteristics (called androgyny). There is an acceptance that sex differences are biologically significant, but not politically, socially or economically significant. Feminists aim to promote genderless 'personhood'. Other feminists dispute this approach (called difference feminists). They suggest that social and cultural characteristics reflect deep biological differences. Post-modern feminists actually dispute that 'biological womanhood' cannot be applied to all women, as some cannot bear children and others are not attracted to men.
Equality and difference	Feminists have differing perspectives on equality and difference. Liberal feminists believe in equality with men, with an equal rights agenda. Socialist feminists believe that equal rights are useless without social equality; this extends to equality in economic power. Radical feminists focus on equality in both family and personal life; whilst some feminists champion equality and others focus on difference. They believe that equality with men implies that women have to be like men. They have no desire to model themselves on men (i.e. competitiveness and aggressiveness). They support being 'woman identified'. This highlights that sex differences are politically and socially important; it suggests that there are essential differences on a psycho-biological level (encompassing hormonal and genetic differences). They suggest that some experiences are unique to women and that a notion of sisterhood should be promoted.

DISCUSSION POINT (?)

To what extent could feminism be described as having an ideological basis?

Liberal feminism

Liberal feminists favour reform rather than revolution to achieve their key objectives. They reject the calls for a more radical (and socialist) revolution to secure equality. Liberal feminists believe that equality can be secured within the existing structures of society without sweeping away capitalism, pluralist democracies or multiculturalism. They also make a clear distinction between public and private life, choosing not to concern themselves with individuals' preferred lifestyles. However, if attitudes and behaviour impact more broadly on society and the state then this is a concern. Further, they accept that women have the right to decide how they live their own lives. They have taken the approach that gradual reform in both law and in changes of attitudes will bring about the intended impacts on society.

- The legal achievement of equal pay for equal work and additionally promoting the belief that women have the same capabilities as men.
- Legally ensuring that discrimination against women is unacceptable and promoting the importance of raising educational expectations for women.
- Encouraging the adoption of positive discrimination (or affirmative action) in favour of women (most voluntary schemes) and supporting a working environment in which women are held in the same regard at work.
- Securing guaranteed maternity leave, childcare facilities and assistance for lone parents by law and promoting the notion that putting career on an equal footing with childcare responsibilities is acceptable.
- The legal rights to abortion and promoting the concept that woman have a right to have control over their own bodies.
- Legal protection for women against violence in relationships and ensuring that the police and the courts take the matter seriously and are prepared to prosecute.

Liberal feminists have struggled with the issues of:

- securing rights and changes of attitudes on women's pensions, benefits and divorce
- coping with the backlash against political correctness
- eliminating stereotypes that still suggest female inferiority
- society accepts the existence of other cultural views, such as those in Muslim countries where women are considered (arguably) as inferior, subject to forced marriages and in some instances subjected to female circumcision.

Radical feminism

Emerging in the 1960s, radical feminism argued for social revolution rather than evolution. Central to their demands were that:

- patriarchy is dominant in all areas of life, public and private
- society accepts the biological differences between men and women and that any gender differences are not significant
- there is oppression in all relationships between men and women
- society as a whole has to be transformed in order to achieve their objectives.

Liberal feminists

Betty Friedan (1921–2006) is best known for starting what is known as the 'Second Wave' of feminism in her book *The Feminine Mystique* (1963).

Gloria Marie Steinem (1934–) is the founder and publisher of *Ms* magazine and was an influential member of the American National Women's Political Caucus.

Rebecca Walker (1969–) is a writer and has been named as one of the 50 future leaders of the United States.

Naomi Wolf (1962–) is a writer and political consultant, and public intellectual. She is a leading figure in the 'Third Wave' of the feminist movement.

Both Greer and Firestone believe that sexual relations are at the heart of oppression. Relationships are inherently exploitative and women are subservient. As far as Firestone is concerned, she adopts a basic Marxist approach, replacing class structures and conflict with sex. She believes that unless sexual equality is gained then there will be continued social conflict and that women would continue to be oppressed and alienated classes in society.

Greer takes another approach, believing that sexual differences should be highlighted and celebrated. If women's identity can be liberated from male dominance then the relationships between men and women will be vastly improved. In *The Whole Woman*, 1999, Doubleday, Greer wrote: 'Liberation struggles are not about assimilation, but about asserting difference, endorsing that difference with dignity and insisting on it as a condition of self-definition and self-determination.'

Distinctions between liberal and radical feminism

There is a clear distinction between liberal and radical feminism. However, there is some common ground in that:

- inequalities faced by women are not based on real inferiority
- there are biological differences between men and women, but in this respect there is no superior or inferior biological identity
- social conditioning underpins and reinforces male dominance
- social consciousness needs to be addressed to ensure that women's equality is accepted
- women need to take control of their lives and not allow men to do this for them
- any aspect of a relationship with men that leads to exploitation or control needs to be eradicated
- women need to be emancipated so that they are not controlled by male-dominated structures and society
- women should not be viewed as victims as this is an inherent acceptance of inferiority.

These issues were common ground until at least the end of the 1970s; by then there were clear distinctions. As far as the liberal feminists were concerned, many of the key objectives had been achieved, but as far as the radicals viewed it, there were still underlying oppressive factors in society. The two views are listed in the table.

Liberal view	Radical view
The liberals focused on the public sphere of inequality, making gains in this area.	They view patriarchy as pervading private and public lives. To ignore private life (family and sexual relations) is a mistake. The private sphere has to be addressed first.
They believe that society has already been transformed by key legal changes and attitudinal changes.	Their view is that without fundamental changes in consciousness (related to sex and gender) women can never have true freedom. The view that society is already transformed is false.
For the liberal feminist, economic equality and freedom are at the centre of women's liberation.	Their belief is that all forms of exploitation are linked; it is not just economic freedom that holds the key. Women are trapped in violent and alienating relationships; economic freedom will do nothing to solve this problem.

Shulamith Firestone on men's reproduction role

One of the most radical of feminists, Firestone believed that with artificial insemination men's reproductive role is outdated. Women are no longer reliant on men to bear children. Women-only communities are therefore possible and women can have full lives without men.

Germaine Greer on sexual liberation

Greer argues that women are oppressed and powerless as a result of exploitation by men. Women are under the control of men in every sphere of life. She proposed equality in relationships, arguing that the family should be replaced with communal living or women-only households.

DISCUSSION POINT

To what extent do liberal and radical feminists agree?

Landfill is a major environmental issue

Pastoralism

This is a belief in the simplicity of rural life and the closeness to nature, which is in sharp contrast to the corrupting influence of industrialised rural life. This was a theme taken up by fascists and nationalists in the 20th century.

Distinctions between environmentalism, ecologism and green politics

It is easy to confuse and to interchange these terms and it is difficult to be absolutely sure which strand is being referred to in certain cases. The following are the key distinctions.

- Environmentalism is not usually taken as being strictly ideological, but focuses on a concern for the environment without demanding any radical changes to society. However, environmentalists can be radical, but they are more often moderate.

- Ecologism is based on science and therefore ideological. Ecologists believe that there needs to be a fundamental change in human behaviour towards the environment.

- Green politics is not necessarily ideological, as it may not have a single, coherent approach suggesting a reform to society. Green politics includes green parties and a host of pressure groups (e.g. Greenpeace and Friends of the Earth). Both types of groups aim to influence opinion and decision-makers. The green parties, like other political parties, aim to gain representation through elections and may be prepared to cooperate by allying themselves with other broader-based parties.

Origins

Although modern-day environmentalism can only trace its roots back to the 1960s, ecological concepts can be tracked far further back. The pagans believed in the Earth Mother (essentially nature and the environment), whilst religions such as Taoism, Buddhism and Hinduism all have features stressing the importance of the earth and nature.

The term ecology is said to have been coined by Ernst Haeckel in 1866. He used the term to describe 'the investigations of the total relations of the animal both to its organic and its inorganic environment'. In the 19th century the term was used as part of the reaction against industrialisation and the growth of cities. In the eyes of libertarian socialists, such as William Morris and indeed the Russian anarchist Peter Kropotkin, ecology highlighted the concerns of this movement and the view that rural life was under threat, and that this traditional existence was somehow more desirable. This approach is often referred to as **pastoralism**.

From the 1960s, there was an increasing interest and concern regarding environmental issues. The first investigation into the damage being done by man to wildlife and the earth was written in 1962 by Rachel Carson. Other important books were written during the 1960s and the 1970s, and the environmental pressure groups Friends of the Earth and Greenpeace were founded. They were soon joined by a variety of campaigners focusing on deforestation, the use of fossil fuels and animal experimentation (e.g. animal liberation and eco-warriors).

By the 1980s, environmental issues had been pushed onto the political agenda and the understanding that the issues were not just related to single states, but were a transnational concern. This means that environmental crises are a global political issue, driven by new processes and developments that freely cross over national boundaries. In effect, this transnational process fuelled globalisation. In recognition of this, attempts have been made to tackle the environmental problems through the:

- UN Conference on the Human Environment (1972)

- Brundtland Report (UN World Commission on Environment and Development) – sustainable development (1987)

- Earth Summit in Rio de Janeiro (1992)

- Kyoto Protocol (1997).

Core themes

The first issue to note is that ecologism suggests that all other ideologies begin and focus on the wrong perspective, in believing that the only consideration is the actions of mankind. In 1978 David Ehrenfeld described this as the arrogance of **humanism**. This is a reflection of the comment by John Locke when he wrote that humans had become 'the masters and possessors of nature'. Rather than focus on strictly human-based ideology, ecologism stresses the importance of considering the relationships between all living creatures and the environment. There are, therefore, several strands of environmentalism that seek to address this approach.

The first core theme is ecology itself, but within it there are several key issues. Ecology grew out of biology and the recognition that plants and animals are all part of ecosystems, or natural, self-regulating systems. Through self-regulation they are in a state of harmony, called homeostasis. In the system everything is recycled and the number of animals and plants are governed by the available food supply. The world itself consists of a huge number of ecosystems which is known as the ecosphere or biosphere.

Humans have systematically destroyed or overwhelmed ecosystems because they believe that they are the masters of nature. By pursuing selfish goals, humans have compromised the balance of nature. Consequently, they have also compromised their own existence. The huge growth in human populations has seen the widespread use of chemicals, pollution, deforestation and the extinction of countless species of animals and plants.

In 1912 the Norwegian Arne Naess defined two differing approaches to ecology, both of which could be broadly described as being **ecocentric**. These are listed in the table.

Humanism

The view that human needs and achievements should be given absolute priority over all things.

Ecocentric

The belief that priority needs to be given to maintaining the ecological balance rather than focusing on human needs.

Arne Naess on the biosphere

His views are based on three elements: romanticism, science and philosophy. Romanticism means that humans have a deep, spiritual relationship with nature which has been lost in modern society. Science treats the earth as a biosphere in which all living things are interrelated. Philosophy, which has also been called ecosoply, is the desire for world harmony and the desire for all humans to achieve self-realisation.

Deep ecology	Shallow ecology
This rejects any notion of anthropocentricism and the fact that humans are in any way superior or more important than other species. It suggests that the role of humans is to support other species, not the other way round. At its most extreme, deep ecology is considered to be irrational and unrealistic.	This suggests that ecology should focus on conserving the natural world so that it can continue to support human life. This can be achieved by reducing the use of non-renewable resources and the reduction of pollution. In many respects shallow ecology is more associated with environmentalism, rather than ecologism.
This is based on ecocentrism, so the priority should be to maintain the ecological balance and not focus on human needs.	This is based on anthropocentricism, which is the opposite of ecocentricism in that the needs of humans are of overriding importance.
This is based on mysticism, with seemingly unsubstantiated beliefs that do not have broad appeal.	This is based on science, with empirical and provable tests, experience and experimentation.
This is based on nature and the needs of other species and ecosystems.	This is based on the needs of humans as a priority.
This is based on radical holism, that there is a more important 'bigger picture' and the issue can only be solved by addressing all relationships.	This is based on weaker holism, the acceptance that there are consequences of linked behaviour and impacts on parts of the earth and ecosystems.

Deep ecology	Shallow ecology
This is based on the assumption that nature in itself is important to preserve.	This is the view that nature needs to be sustained for the benefit of humans.
This holds that all species are equal (biocentric equality).	This holds that all species may not be equal, but they need to be protected and conserved.
This supports animal rights – i.e. species have inherent rights.	This supports animal welfare – i.e. species should be protected
This is implacably anti-growth as far as human society is concerned.	This supports sustainable human growth.
This focuses on the need to improve human consciousness of ecological issues as a major priority.	This accepts the importance of ecological awareness, but only in the context of more general personal development.

Holism is the second core theme, a concept that suggests that the whole is more important than the constituent parts. Holism also implies that understanding of the situation can be achieved by careful analysis of the relationships of the parts. Central to this is the conflict with scientism, this being an objective way of looking at a situation to understand its true nature. The key issues are outlined in the table.

Scientism (or Empiricism)	Holism
This is based on theories suggested by René Descartes and Isaac Newton.	This was originally coined as a concept by Jan Smuts in 1926.
The world is like a machine; parts can be analysed and understood through scientific methods.	The belief that science uses reductionism by looking at the constituent parts, whereas the world can only be understood as a whole.
The world can be amended, improved or repaired.	The holistic view to a problem would consider all the reasons that contribute to that problem.
The new physics and particularly quantum theory (Albert Einstein, Niels Bohr and Verner Heisenberg) view the physical world as a system or a network of systems.	This believes in a link between modern physics and eastern mysticism, which suggests a unity of all things. It is also linked to Christianity and Islam, where nature and humans are created by a divine force. Humans are seen as the protectors of the earth and charged with the responsibility of preserving the planet.

James Lovelock on Gaia

Lovelock sees the earth as a single organic entity, and humans are part of this entity. Humans, however, see themselves as superior beings and believe they can manipulate the earth. Earth is a self-regulating organism, capable of readjusting itself to survive. But humans have interfered too much and the basis of life is threatened by their actions.

Industrialism

The transition of production methods in order to create wealth.

James Lovelock developed the idea that the planet itself is a living entity (Gaia). Gaia acts to maintain its own existence, to maintain homeostasis despite changes. The overall health of the planet is far more important than the fortunes of any one species. A species that threatens Gaia is likely to face extinction and the species' that prosper are those that have helped the planet regulate its existence.

Sustainability is a concept that has been incorporated into the overall philosophies of a broad range of political parties and political ideologies. For the Greens, however, traditional socialist and capitalist supporters of **industrialism** are dedicated not to the earth but to materialism, science and technology, and utilitarian values. The key aspects of true sustainability as visualised by ecologists include the following.

- Kenneth Boulding (1966) suggested that the earth was like a spaceship, a closed system that will eventually be exhausted (entropy) and humans are accelerating this process.

- E. F. Schumacher (1973) suggested that humans consider energy sources to be income that can simply be added to when needed. It is not; most energy sources are non-renewable.

This approach has meant that finite fuel resources are being used up too fast and as yet there are no viable alternatives.

- Garrett Hardin (1968) suggested that humans are over-using the resources of the planet. His model 'tragedy of the commons' suggests that environmental resources are vulnerable because as people have common access to them they have used them in self-interested ways, and collectively the impact has been devastating.

- Humans therefore have to accept that they are only one part of a complex biosphere, and that sustainability means placing limits on human activity in order to reduce the damage being done to the delicate ecosystems.

- Green realists (known as light greens) accept that humans should adopt sustainable growth, balancing prosperity against environmental costs.

- Green fundamentalists (known as dark greens) believe in zero growth and argue that ecological problems are derived from economic growth, consumerism and materialism.

Ecologists take a different view from conventional ethics, as they maintain that they are essentially anthropocentric. Environmental ethics take the following views.

- Each generation of humans has an obligation to future generations.

- The interests of humans should take into account the entire human species (known as futurity).

- Humans should apply the same moral standards and values to all other species and organisms.

- Humans should not exhibit speciesism (a denial of the moral significance of other species and the belief that humans are superior).

- Humans should give due consideration to developed and self-aware animals and ensure that suffering is avoided.

- Robert E Goodin (1992) suggested that environmental ethics cannot be simply viewed by the value of the natural world to humans. It should be valued for itself so that humans see 'some sense and pattern in their lives' and are part of something greater.

- Aldo Leopold (1949) took the view that 'a thing is right when it tends to preserve the integrity, stability and beauty of the biotic community. It is wrong when it tends to be otherwise.' (*A Sand County Almanac*, Oxford University Press) Nature is an ethical community; humans have no more or no fewer rights than any other members of that community.

- Naess (1989) suggested a biocentric equality, meaning that all organisms in the ecosphere have equal moral value and they are all part of a related whole.

The final key theme of ecology is the concept of self-actualisation. This concerns personal fulfilment, basing the need for esteem above material or economic needs.

- The concept is based on the work of Abraham Maslow's humanity of needs.

- It was developed out of the work by Ronald Inglehart (1977) and post-materialism which suggests that as material affluence is achieved there is a focus on quality of life rather than economic needs.

- The post-material issues include morality, justice, equality and personal fulfilment.

- These concerns encompass ecology, racial tolerance and animal rights.

- Ecology is concerned with the apparent imbalance between humans' ability to create and innovate, but not whether these inventions and ideas are good ones or what their longer-term impacts may be. Schumacher (1973) summed it up by saying 'man is now too clever to survive without wisdom'.

- Shallow ecologists view this approach with scepticism, particularly if the wisdom is based on New Age beliefs or religious mysticism.

- Deep ecologists claim that this is part of a necessary paradigm shift, moving away from approaches used by traditional politics, to ensure that the same mistakes of the environment are not made.

- Deep ecologists believe that there should be a spiritual dimension to politics, that there should be an environmental consciousness in politics and the development of the ecological self.

- Warwick Fox (1990) suggested the concept of 'transpersonal ecology'. This means accepting that humans are part of a single reality.

- Naess suggested that self-actualisation means having a deep 'identification with others'.

- Eric Fromm (1979) suggested that consumerism and materialism is based on 'having', whilst sharing, personal growth and spiritual awareness is based on 'being'.

Origins

Although there have been periods of religious fundamentalism throughout history many modern commentators consider it to be a new phenomenon. In the past there were Puritans, Anabaptists and of course the religious fundamentalists who inspired the Crusades in the medieval period.

It is said by some that fundamentalism tends to emerge in countries with very deep problems, in societies that have crises of identity. Others believe it emerges from the clash of civilisations.

The three most likely factors are a combination of secularisation, host colonialism and globalisation. Fundamentalism often represents moral conservatism. This can be seen in countries as diverse as the United States and Iran.

In the past colonial rule, for example, may have devalued and suppressed a particular culture and religious fundamentalism is viewed as a resurgence of that culture. Globalisation, as a threat undermining nationalism and religion, has developed to possibly replace the nation as the source of collective identity. Secularism has been blamed for the decline of traditional religions and weakening the morals that underpin society. Fundamentalism seeks to retrieve this.

Core values

Religious fundamentalism represents a social movement created in reaction to crises created by secularisation, post-colonialism and globalisation. Religious fundamentalism becomes an ideology when it becomes inseparable from law and politics and attempts to regenerate and reconstruct society.

Fundamentalism represents protest against decadence and hypocrisy. Religious fundamentalism represents an anti-western political, post-colonial identity that claims to offer social emancipation after the failures of state socialism and nationalism. Religion provides a form of collective identity to substitute for the nation.

Fundamentalism consists of a set of simple principles providing exact and unambiguous definitions of identity extracted from a body of religious writings. Fundamentalist movements originate with a charismatic personality who claims the moral purity, spiritual insight and the experience of struggle to reduce the complexity of scriptures to a political project.

The following can be viewed as the core values.

- Mixing religion with politics – in the Iranian cleric Ayatollah Khomeini's words 'politics is religion'. Fundamentalists reject the divide between the public and the private life. To treat religion as only a private matter leaves the public domain open to immorality, corruption and crime. Fundamentalism seeks to replace the public sphere with underpinning religious principles.

- Fundamentalism – the commitment to particular ideas and values are seen as foundational or fundamental. They are immobile, original and classic. Most are taken from sacred texts and these form the basis of a political ideology. Interpretation is acceptable but the basic truths of the sacred texts are held close and at the heart of all activity.

- Anti-modernism – most religious fundamentalists turn their back on the modern world and seek a return to a past time that was the golden age. Fundamentalists reject liberal individualism. They see it as degenerate or amoral. They do not, however, shy away from using ultramodern technology in order to spread their views, such as televangelists in the United States and the use of Arab satellite television stations by Islamic fundamentalists.

Control and contention

Fundamentalists seek to take control of government to use it as an instrument of moral regeneration based on the original or classical form of the theoretical system as its core. Fundamentalism rejects both relativism and revisionism. It represents more than simple conservatism or scriptural literalism.

Fundamentalism generates intense passions by stimulating contention over core values and beliefs and uses identity politics to create an 'in-group' and a threatening 'other'. Fundamentalists seek to convince believers that they are fighting for the will of God against people who are actively opposing God's purposes.

A devout Sikh immersing himself in water at Amritsar

Religious fundamentalist groups

The ambitions for global activity conveyed by Islam and Christianity as transnational religions are based on a single sacred text. They promise believers direct access to spiritual wisdom in order to generate the potential for a global political movement. Other forms of fundamentalism represent ethnic mobilisations. The key types of religious fundamentalism include the following.

- Islamic fundamentalism derives from a religion based upon scriptural literalism; it is strong in predominantly conservative and sometimes xenophobic societies that are reacting to a recent history of western dominance and ongoing globalisation. Islamic fundamentalism can lead to a new political ideology called Islamism. Islamism represents a novel political ideology reacting to failed modernisation, autocratic states, globalisation and western ideological doctrines promoting the efficacy of political violence.

- Although most Christian fundamentalists seek only personal spiritual salvation and to avoid corrupt society rather than the political regeneration of society, some seek social reform. Fundamentalists are working within the pluralistic and constitutional framework of the American political system providing campaign finance and organising voter registration drives. Also there are legal campaigns seeking to overturn Roe vs Wade legal decision on abortion and outlaw stem cell research and same-sex marriages.

- Militant Hinduism has emerged to challenge the multi-ethnic and multicultural mosaic of India. They demand the cultural conversion of other communities.

- Sikh fundamentalism has created a chain reaction of threats and resentments, and inspired demands for recognition of other identity groups by closely linking ethnic identity to religious fervour.

- Buddhism purports to promote religious toleration and non-violence, however in Sri Lanka tensions between Sinhalese and Tamils has stimulated the spread of Buddhist nationalism in that country.

It is important to appreciate that few of these fundamentalist groups either have a great deal in common or are prepared to coexist alongside one another. All major religions have created some kind of fundamentalist movement. Some are more prone to this, such as Protestant Christianity and Islam. It is also important to note that fundamentalists arise from different societies, where the impact of social, economic and political factors is different. A prime example would be a comparison between Turkey and many of its near neighbours in the Middle East.

Fundamentalism also arises as a result of allied political causes. Sometimes religious fundamentalism is used as the means by which political renewal can be achieved by an oppressed ethnic or cultural group. It can also be used as a means of stabilising a situation for an unpopular leader or government. In effect fundamentalism is used in this case to create a unified political culture.

Finally, it can be used to strengthen a perceived weakness in a national or ethnic identity, essentially a defence mechanism that aims to differentiate and to unite.

Post-modernism

Post-modernism first came into existence as a term in architecture and culture. Essentially it is a social and political analytical tool. It looks at issues on the basis that society has moved away from dominant factors such as industrialisation and class and that we are now operating in a world where individuals are no longer producers but consumers. Class has been replaced with individualism and religion and ethnic loyalties are gone.

A post-modernist would suggest that there is no certainty and we can no longer rely on absolute truths. Instead there is debate and there is democracy.

Post-modernism can be used in a variety of contexts, as in:

- after modernism (subsumes, assumes, extends the modern or tendencies already present in modernism, not necessarily in strict chronological succession)

- contra-modernism (subverting, resisting, opposing, or countering features of modernism)

- equivalent to 'late capitalism' (post-industrial, consumerist, and multinational and transnational capitalism)

- the historical era following the modern (an historical time-period marker)

- artistic and stylistic eclecticism (hybridisation of forms and genres, mixing styles of different cultures or time periods, de- and re-contextualising styles in architecture, visual arts, literature)

- 'global village' phenomena: globalisation of cultures, races, images, capital, products ('information age' redefinition of nation-state identities, which were the foundation of the modern era; dissemination of images and information across national boundaries, a sense of erosion or breakdown of national, linguistic, ethnic, and cultural identities; a sense of a global mixing of cultures on a scale unknown to pre-information era societies).

Jean-Francois Lyotard on the role of the human narrative

In his best-known and most influential work, *The Postmodern Condition* (1979), Lyotard (1924–98) saw the post-modern era as one that has lost faith in all grand 'metanarratives' – the abstract ideas in terms of which thinkers since the time of the Enlightenment have attempted to construct comprehensive explanations of historical experience. Disillusioned with the grandiose claims such as 'reason', 'truth', and 'progress', the post-modern age has turned to smaller, narrower *petits récits* ('little narratives'), such as the history of everyday life and of marginalised groups.

Michel Foucault on critical theory

Michel Foucault (1926–84) is best known for his critical studies of social institutions (including psychiatry, medicine, the human sciences, the prison system and human sexuality). In the 1960s he was associated with the structuralist movement. Foucault sometimes described himself as post-modernist. He sought not to answer traditional and straightforward questions but to critically examine them and the responses they had inspired. He directed his scepticism toward those responses – among them race, the unity of reason or the psyche, progress and liberation.

The modern and the post-modern: Contrasting tendencies

Modernism/Modernity	Post-modern/Post-modernity
Master narratives and meta-narratives of history, culture and national identity	Suspicion and rejection of master narratives for history and culture; local narratives, ironic deconstruction of master narratives: counter-myths of origin

Modernism/Modernity	Post-modern/Post-modernity
Faith in 'grand theory' to represent all knowledge and explain everything	Rejection of totalising theories; pursuit of localising and contingent theories
Faith in, and myths of, social and cultural unity, hierarchies of social class and ethnic/national values, seemingly clear bases for unity	Social and cultural pluralism, disunity, unclear bases for social/national/ethnic unity
Master narrative of progress through science and technology	Scepticism of idea of progress, anti-technology reactions, New Age religions
Sense of unified, centred self; 'individualism', unified identity	Sense of fragmentation and decentred self; multiple, conflicting identities
Idea of 'the family' as central unit of social order; model of the middle-class, nuclear family; heterosexual norms	Alternative family units, alternatives to middle-class marriage model, multiple identities for couples and child raising
Hierarchy, order, centralised control	Subverted order, loss of centralised control, fragmentation
Faith and personal investment in big politics (nation state, party).	Trust and investment in micro-politics, identity politics, local politics, institutional power struggles
Root/depth tropes Faith in 'depth' (meaning, value, content, the signified) over 'surface'	Rhizome/surface tropes Attention to play of surfaces, images, signifiers without concern for 'depth'
Crisis in representation and status of the image after photography and mass media	Culture adapting to simulation, visual media becoming undifferentiated equivalent forms, simulation and real-time media substituting for the real
Faith in the 'real' beyond media, language, symbols, and representations; authenticity of 'originals'	Hyper-reality, image saturation, simulacra seem more powerful than the 'real'; images and texts with no prior 'original'
Dichotomy of high and low culture (official vs popular culture) Imposed consensus that high or official culture is normative and authoritative, the ground of value and discrimination	Disruption of the dominance of high culture by popular culture Mixing of popular and high cultures, new valuation of pop culture, hybrid cultural forms cancel 'high'/'low' categories
Mass culture, mass consumption, mass marketing	Niche products and marketing, smaller group identities
Art as unique object and finished work authenticated by artist and validated by agreed upon standards	Art as process, performance and production
Knowledge mastery, attempts to embrace a totality Quest for interdisciplinary harmony	Navigation through information overload, information management; fragmented, partial knowledge; just-in-time knowledge
Broadcast media, centralised one-to-many communications	Digital, interactive, client-server, distributed, user-motivated, individualised, many-to-many media
Centring/centeredness, centralised knowledge	Dispersal, dissemination, networked, distributed knowledge
Determinacy, dependence, hierarchy	Indeterminacy, contingency, polycentric power sources
Seriousness of intention and purpose, middle-class earnestness	Play, irony, challenge to official seriousness, subversion of earnestness
Sense of clear generic boundaries and wholeness (art, music, and literature)	Hybridity, promiscuous genres, recombinant culture
The book as sufficient bearer of the word; the library as complete and total system for printed knowledge	Hypermedia as transcendence of the physical limits of print media; the Web as infinitely expandable information system

Anti-ideology

Post-modernists reject the need for an acceptance of an overarching ideology, but many would say that this can only take place in a moral vacuum. To a large extent this is reflected in that the differences between conservative, liberal and socialist ideologies are becoming increasing blurred and post-modernists would claim less relevant. Equally, particularly in Britain and America, politics is becoming increasingly personality driven. Policies and ideologies take a backseat.

Relativism

Relativism is not a single doctrine but a group of views whose common theme is that some central aspect of experience, thought, evaluation, or even reality is somehow relative to something else. For example, standards of justification, moral principles or truth are sometimes said to be relative to language, culture, or biological makeup.

Discussions of relativism are also frequently marred by all-or-none thinking. Phrases like 'everything is relative' and 'anything goes' suggest versions of relativism that, as we will see, often are inconsistent. But to conclude that there are no interesting versions of relativism is to err in the opposite direction. Often the important question is whether there is a space for an interesting and plausible version of relativism between strong but implausible versions (e.g. all truth is relative) on the one hand, and plausible but trivial versions (e.g. some standards of etiquette are relative) on the other.

Managerialism

One of the features of contemporary society is the tendency under liberal democracies to define social, economic and political issues as problems to be resolved through management. There is also a generalised governmental concern to promote efficiency in what were previously non-governmental areas. During recent decades, these developments have been associated with the introduction of managerialism as a new method of governance under the restructured public sectors of many western societies. The restructuring has involved the reform of education in which there has been a significant shift away from an emphasis on administration and policy to an emphasis on management. This form of managerialism is known as new public management (NPM) and has been very influential in the UK, Australia, Canada and New Zealand. It has been used both as the legitimating basis and instrumental means for redesigning state educational bureaucracies, educational institutions and even the public policy process.

Managerialism has been characterised in a variety of ways. Willard Enteman (1993) describes managerialism as an international ideology on which rests the economic, social and political order of advanced industrialised societies and from which arises the impoverished notion that societies are equivalent to the sum of the transactions made by the managements of organisations. In this view, social institutions are primarily a function of the practices of management. For Peter Drucker (*Management*, 1974, Butterworth Heinemann) 'management has as its first dimension an economic dimension'. G. Davis ('Implications, consequences and future', in Davis, G., Sullivan, B. and Yeatman, A. *The New Contractualism*, 1997, Macmillan) claims that managerialism has swept aside 'an idyllic older bureaucratic world . . . reducing every relation to a mere money exchange'.

Managerialism has also been characterised as a 'set of beliefs and practices, (that) will prove an effective solvent for . . . economic and social ills' (C. Pollitt, *Managerialism and the Public Services: The Anglo-American Experience,* 1990, Basil Blackwell). 'In addition to its technical function, management is . . . an elite social grouping which acts as an economic resource and maintains the associated system of authority' (J. Child, *British Management Thought*, 1969, Allen and Unwin).

James Burnham on managerialist theories

The American philosopher and critic James Burnham (1905–87) also analysed shifts of power. In *The Managerial Revolution* (1941) he suggested a theory of bureaucratic revolution: the rulers of the new society, the class with power and privilege, will be the bureaucratic managers of 'super states'.

DISCUSSION POINT

Discuss the view that modern political executives are just like the boards of directors of a massive corporation.

Learning objectives

- Decline of ideology
- Personality-driven politics
- Decline of ideological differences
- Changes in the balance between parties and pressure groups

Decline of ideology

Ideology has dominated politics worldwide for a century or more, from communism on the extreme left to fascism on the extreme right.

However in modern-day politics arguments between left and right are no longer the defining features. After the Cold War and the increase of globalisation, many left-wing parties have struggled to obtain support for a socialist agenda amongst the western electorate.

Free markets are believed to deliver efficiency and value and this was previously the preserve of the centre-right. Since 1997 in Britain the Labour Party has pursued privatisation in air traffic control and for the London Underground, whereas it had bitterly opposed privatisation of industries like railways, telecoms, airways and coal. Private involvement has also been encouraged in public services like health and education, as market values of choice and efficiency are claimed to be the key to improved services.

It is not only those on the left who have adopted the rhetoric and beliefs of the right. In the areas of social services and welfare, many European centre-right parties now accept that whilst private enterprise and markets play a key role, government intervention is also essential for providing the development and services that the public wishes to see.

In many systems the role of government and the key areas for delivery consensus has emerged. There is increasing agreement about what is important and what is expected. The deep divisions in the fundamental role of the government have almost been breached.

Without these divisions politics becomes more pragmatic and policy decisions are taken on the basis of objective evidence. Bob Tyrell, a British specialist in forecasting political trends, suggested that politics now resembled a competition between two management teams; both were in effect offering the same product and had adopted similar managerial approaches. On the one hand, Labour focused on centralisation and target setting and on the other the Conservatives focused on greater autonomy. In reality, neither was suggesting major changes to what was being done or how it could be done.

In terms of the wider effects, an end to dramatic swings will allow for greater consistency and development. When reforms are introduced by one government and soon afterwards are swept away by another, few can have benefited because of the cost and time elements.

We already know that debate and discussion is essential in a healthy democracy. Building a consensus does not necessarily mean the opposition has to be suppressed. It means more respect and cooperation between the parties. Opposition parties sometimes oppose simply because they believe that is their role. They do have an essential role to scrutinise and hold the government to account. They can do this more effectively if their actions are not perceived to be driven solely by party political motivations.

The policy-making process can be improved and accusations that political parties oppose only for reasons of selfish political opportunism can result in cynicism about the entire political system.

The consensus can be driven from the bottom up or from the top down. Political leaders have to build the consensus, and the citizens also have a part to play by working as a nation to achieve the objectives.

Pessimists have lamented the end of vitriolic ideological disputes, claiming that a greater consensus in politics means that more will be content with the actions of the government, even if they did not vote for them.

Whilst this bodes well for the health of a democracy, it poses challenges for political parties retaining public support, involvement and interest. With this level of agreement on what must be achieved, political parties are free to debate on how best to achieve them. There is less room for ideological division and greater opportunity for considered analysis and evidence-driven policy-making. The result should be better policy, better outcomes, and less division.

Personality-driven politics

When David Cameron took over as Conservative Party leader in 2005, he was seen as the personification of centre-right politics. Many contend that Cameron is much, much more likely to succeed than his three immediate predecessors, and not only because the political climate has changed.

Cameron has been attacked for lacking policies, his sympathy with Blair's objectives but his growing doubt about his methods. History suggests this ability to personify the national mood is the most important component of political success.

Tony Benn was one who hated the collision between policies and personality. He saw press attacks on him as a person as a way of attacking his ideas. No one was interested in his ideas, the press simply attacked to prevent him from discussing the policies he proposed.

Personality politics is not new, after all how does a politician interest and excite the electorate. Years ago, Gladstone's Midlothian campaign transformed public attitudes to British support for the Ottoman Empire. The cause was not interesting in itself, however he transformed it with his energy, his charismatic oratory and his capacity for infusing the causes he adopted with a powerful sense of their morality.

Churchill is another prime example. He lost the Dundee seat he held as a Liberal in 1922, then was restored to frontline politics (and soon afterwards the Conservative Party) through a by-election in Westminster in which he drove around the constituency in a coach decrying socialism. He lost, but only after establishing himself in the public imagination as guarantor of the British constitution and irreconcilable enemy of socialism, a political identity that endured.

Clement Attlee may not have had a great deal of personality to drive his brand of politics forward, but Lloyd George was certainly charismatic, Baldwin was 'safe hands' and then Churchill returned again. After Churchill, the next dominant set of personalities was Harold Macmillan and Harold Wilson.

Edward Heath and James Callaghan may not have displayed true personality-driven politics, but certainly Margaret Thatcher did in overwhelming style. John Major was a return to normality, but then came Tony Blair, a dramatic personality.

Voters became less and less content with aspects of Blair's politics, but there was an enduring admiration for his style: they did not like Iraq, but they liked the fact Britain was led into it by a prime minister who thought he was right. They believed Blair should have compromised on the anti-terror legislation, but nearly half still thought he was right to stand up for what he believed in. There was a definite sense that Blair wanted what most voters wanted. He was in touch with the electorate. No so Gordon Brown, so long the bridesmaid and never the bride. Now prime minister, he has singly failed to project his image and personality, despite being clearly earnest and focused.

Brown has perceived personality failings and the Liberal Democrats moved relatively fast to remove Menzies Campbell. Meanwhile, the Conservative Party has been hard at work moulding the Cameron brand identity and, indeed, rebranding the Tory logo.

For the electorate it is Cameron who represents an engaging individual who personifies the fresh start, leading a party not overburdened with doctrine. It remains to be seen if there is any personality behind the image and whether the electorate is correct in assuming that he has the empathetic persona of a politician who understands and just happens to be a Tory.

Decline of ideological differences

Many now think that Britain's first-past-the-post electoral system for Westminster is unfair, however it is up to the political parties to educate voters, represent their interests and devise clear and systematic policy ideas that offer the electorate a definite choice between themselves and other parties.

Ideally, the voters should be capable of examining each policy so they can evaluate which political party they agree with most and will support. In reality, the system is less clear-cut. The political parties set out and announce their policies to the public with promises to implement the policies if they are voted into government. However, it is only at the end of their tenure in office that they can be fully judged on their success or failure in implementing the policies and how effective they were in dealing with specific issues that arose during that time. For individual MPs their futures in parliament are linked to the overall performance of the party to which they belong.

The present problem with British parliamentary politics is that it is very difficult for the electorate to clearly distinguish the differences between the policies of the parties. There were clear distinctions between the parties during Thatcher's prime ministership. The only time there are clear major differences is when the parties devise radical or extreme policy programmes. If both of the major parties appear to be broadly in accord on most policies then the voter's choice may be based on the relative merits of a party's national leader or the qualities of constituency candidates.

Following the demise of Thatcher, there developed a social market consensus across the three main parties. At times there was very little to distinguish the policies in key areas such as education, health, taxation and the environment. Indeed, this is a trend that has continued to some extent to date.

Another major consideration in terms of providing choice is that parties in seeking government are asking the electorate to vote for a national party rather than an individual member of parliament to represent their particular area of the country.

Changes in the balance between parties and pressure groups

In the mid to late 1990s Labour Party membership was around 400,000, but has since dropped to half that number. The Conservatives in 1997 had around 350,000 members; this too has fallen, to around 250,000. Liberal Democrat membership stands at around 70,000, down from 100,000 before the merger with the SDP. The Scottish Nationalists have some 17,000 members, Plaid Cymru 9000 and the Green Party 6000.

Several theories have been put forward to suggest why party membership has fallen, a trend that has been clearly identified since the 1950s. These are:

- people are participating in politics in different ways, such as joining pressure groups

- the specific objectives of pressure groups have greater appeal, rather than the broader political ideas and policies associated with parties (this is known as the particularisation of politics)

- the relatively poor image of politicians, particularly people not wishing to be associated with sleaze (recent examples include the loans for peerages scandals, the David Abrahams affair and Derek Conway)

- the perception that all parties have failed and make unpopular decisions, for example the Tory and Labour Party consensus over going to war with Iraq in 2003

- the increasing power of the European Union makes many political parties that focus on local or national policies appear irrelevant

- it is no longer necessary to join a party to stay up to date in terms of policies and ideas, as there are many other sources of information available especially via Internet political blogs and political chat rooms

- the membership of a party does not mean that an individual's views are heard or acted upon – in other words a lack of internal party democracy

- the politics of contentment – Galbraith argues that all mature democracies see a decline in political participation as citizens are in broad agreement with successive government policies.

An increasingly small percentage of parties' income is derived from membership fees. This is even more the case as national membership figures for all parties are in decline.

The parties have begun to rely on rich, personal donors or the support of businesses to boost their funds. This has not prevented the major parties from experiencing acute financial difficulties. For the Labour Party funding from trade unions dropped under Tony Blair (more recently, with Brown's unpopularity, political donations have significantly declined and levels of TU funding are above 61 per cent – the same as it was prior to Blair coming to power), partly due to a reduced trade union membership but also as a protest from the unions against what they see to be anti-union policies. Both businesses and unions feel in many cases that they do not get a sufficient return for their investment. Clearly any individual or organisation is bound to require something in return for a donation.

According to the Electoral Commission, covering the period March to June 2007, Labour attracted £5 million from individuals, businesses and unions. This was compared to £4.5 million donated to the Conservative Party (plus £1.78 million in government subsidies to opposition parties). Both parties, however, were heavily in debt, Labour owing £20.2 million and the Conservatives £16.3 million. The Liberal Democrats received nearly £600,000 in public funds, as well as donations of £1.3 million from individuals and businesses and owe just over £1 million.

An enquiry set up under Sir Hayden Philips reported in 2007 with proposals for party funding reform. He proposed that parties receive 50 pence each year for every vote cast for them in the most recent general election and an additional 25 pence for each vote received in the Scottish Parliament, the Welsh Assembly and the European Parliament. State funding would increase by £25 million per year. Individual donations would be capped. Due to a failure by both Labour and the Tories to reach a consensus on Philips' proposals the likelihood is that the proposals will be shelved.

At a time when the membership of political parties is in decline, membership of pressure groups is continually increasing. The RSPB has a membership of over 1 million and the National Trust 3.5 million. The two main political parties would struggle to show half a million members

The Snowdrop Campaign

On March 13 1996 Thomas Hamilton walked into Dunblane Primary School in Scotland and massacred sixteen children and an adult before he committed suicide. In response Ann Pearson founded the Snowdrop Petition or Campaign, which aimed to convince the Conservative government to introduce a ban on most handguns. The petition gained over 700,000 signatures. A separate petition raised another 430,000 signatures. Pearson made an impassioned speech at the 1996 Labour Party Conference and following New Labour's victory in the 1997 general election the government introduced the Firearms (Amendment) (Number 2) Act 1997. Generally, only antique or historic weapons were exempt. As a result, it is no longer lawful to buy, sell or own a handgun in Britain. Opposing pressure groups included shooting clubs, rifle clubs and gun enthusiasts. In all nearly 43,000 firearms and over a million rounds of ammunition were surrendered to the police across the whole of Britain. The campaign was particularly successful as it was one of the first to use email to distribute copies of the petition and information. Up to a third of all petition forms had been sent by email at some point.

between them. Cause groups like the RSPB have tended to be the principal beneficiaries of this trend. There are now over 17,000 recognised pressure groups operating in the UK today, a marked increase in numbers over the last decade.

Political parties must seek to appeal to the broadest possible range of interest groups. Their policies must therefore appear be attractive both to managers and employees, to the young and to the old, to the rich and to the poor and to as many other sections of society as possible, including ethnic and religious groups. The price to pay for not addressing the interests of the widest possible range of groups is that any party who does not do so is unlikely to be voted into power.

Pressure groups do not have to operate under these constraints. They are more focused, either on the sectional interests of their members or on a specific cause. Pressure groups exist or at least come into existence without necessarily having achieved positive public support. Their role is to build support in order to legitimise the influence that they seek to bring to bear on decision-makers. Obviously this means that pressure groups are reliant on publicity and attracting as many sympathetic supporters as possible, who may not only become activists but may also provide the necessary funds to continue and broaden campaigns.

DISCUSSION POINT ?

Examine the benefits and pitfalls of personality-driven politics.

Charter 88

Charter 88 was established in 1988 and has been influential in calling for constitutional and electoral reform. It has also been fundamental in the movement for other reforms, including devolution, the Human Rights Act and the Freedom of Information Act. It is currently supporting a campaign that calls for the election of individuals to the House of Lords. Jack Straw, the former prime minister Tony Blair and the former Liberal leader Lord Steel support this campaign. The group has been particularly successful blending campaigning, producing pamphlets, doing original research and organising seminars and public events to raise awareness.

To see more about Charter 88, go to www.heinemann.co.uk/hotlinks, insert the express code 6923P and click on the relevant link.

Ecologism strands

There are four significant sub-traditions of ecologism; each has its own political goals. In the case of the deep ecologists, they claim to have created an entirely new ideology (although some reject the concept of ideology, as it is associated with human-centred thinking).

Political ecology originated from an unexpected source, the far right, as exemplified by fascist ecologism in Germany during the Nazi period. The following are the key developments and roots.

- The main figure in political ecology's development was Walter Darré, who was Hitler's minister of agriculture between 1933 and 1942. His beliefs were based on Nordic racialism and an idealised view of rural life. His philosophy was known as Blood and Soil and had many features in common with National Socialism.

- In terms of policy, Darré introduced the hereditary farm law (giving farmers security of tenure) and setting up the National Food Estate (to keep food prices high to ensure rural property).

- Darré believed that life next to nature was desirable (not unlike the beliefs of modern-day ecologists, such as Edward Goldsmith).

- Darré supported organic farming and the organic cycle, which he borrowed from the anthroposophy movement (founded by Rudolf Steiner). This view of environmentally friendly farming is still a major part of modern-day ecological thinking.

- For Darré the approach was a failure, as Hitler's war machine relied on industrialisation to provide weapons and vehicles; the net result was rural poverty.

Eco-socialists draw their inspiration from pastoral socialists, such as William Morris, although modern-day eco-socialists have closer association with Marxism.

- Rudolf Bahro (1982) claimed that capitalism is at the root of environmental crises. Industrialisation destroys the natural environment as a result of capitalism's preoccupation with profits. The natural environment and human labour are considered just to be economic resources. A major social change is needed in order to protect the environment.

- Socialism is portrayed as the ally of the environment and capitalism its enemy. In order to save the environment, capitalism must be either radically changed or swept aside.

- Ecologists should not create new green parties; instead they should work within the socialist movement and focus on changing the economic system.

- Eco-socialists, however, can be of the opinion that the dangers to the environment are so great that it should take priority over the class struggle.

- They argue that if wealth is commonly owned then the environment will be used only in the long-term interests of all.

Eco-anarchists can trace their ideological roots back to the anarcho-communists of the 19th century, such as Peter Kropotkin (1914). These are the views they hold.

Learning objectives

- Ecologism strands
- Environmentalism and globalisation
- Environmental lobby and modern politics
- Ecologism – philosophy, politics or science?

Softer

A softer right-wing approach to ecologism was developed later.

- Eco-conservatives favour a return to pre-industrial society and a romanticised view of the rural life compared to urban existence. They seek to protect the natural environment, architecture and social heritage.

- They favour green capitalism or a market-based solution to environmental issues through advantageous tax regimes, incentives for eco-friendly behaviour, trading schemes and the manufacture of ecologically sound products (as they believe that long-term profitability can only be achieved if it is in the context of sustainable development).

- Murray Bookchin (1977) suggested the concept of social ecology where ecological balance is essential for social stability.

- Anarchists favour a stateless society with social solidarity, mutual respect and diversity. Eco-anarchists maintain that balance naturally exists in ecosystems.

- Bookchin saw parallels between anarchist communities and ecosystems.

- Anarchists see decentralised communities as being self-sufficient, depending on the natural environment and appreciating their relationships with nature and ecology. This can only be achieved when government and centralised authority are swept aside.

Eco-feminists based their view on the assumption that ecological problems are the result of a patriarchal society, that is, a society dominated by men. Patriarchy has effectively cut men off from any nurturing abilities, in the eyes of feminists who follow the androgynous view.

Mary Daly (1979) suggested women could liberate themselves from patriarchy by embracing female nature. This harks back to pre-Christian ideologies that focused on the earth mother goddess (later Gaia). The modern Gaia approach links women to their biological harmony with nature (bearing and nurturing children); women are bound by natural rhythms. The idea that a resource should be exploited is unacceptable, as they feel that nature operates through them. As women are creatures of nature, men are seen as creatures of the synthetic, a product of human ideas, and not natural ones. Gender inequality and ecological damage are part of the same man-made problem.

Environmentalism and globalisation

A radical anti-globalisation movement has developed in recent years, using mass demonstrations and attacks on property, particularly where international conferences involving world leaders are taking place, particularly the G8 summits. These are the consequences.

- Radical methods are used (anti-globalisation groups are quasi-anarchist) to demonstrate against globalisation. There has been considerable disruption of G8 summits and at the annual World Economic Forum meetings in Davos in Switzerland.

- Globalisation has united many environmental groups, promoting greater research.

- The groups, however, have found it difficult to combat the power of the massive corporations, which are backed by enormous funds of money.

- Anti-globalisation groups have tried to tackle the problem on an international basis, forming new tactics, for example the Global Justice Movement and the Anti-Corporate-Globalisation Movement.

- There is difficulty in balancing the rapid industrialisation of developing countries and their needs with the green calls for the development of a more natural and organic economic system in those countries.

Environmental lobby and modern politics

Rapid industrialisation and economic development in less developed countries is a major problem. Developing countries tend to take a shorter-term view in their efforts to raise their populations out of poverty, rather than taking a longer-term view on the environmental issues involved. They see the developed world as having prosperous and well-developed economies and understandably want to replicate this. This makes it difficult for the environmental lobby to persuade them to consider the effects economic development has on the environment. There has been a rise in green issues in British and German politics – the German Greens have participated in national coalitions with the SPD, and in Britain the Green Party has secured significant representation in local politics and seats in the European Parliament. They have also influenced the agenda for the mainstream political parties, with all of them stating their adherence to the Kyoto emissions targets and pledging greater focus carbon on emission taxes; for instance Labour announced in its 2008 budget large retrospective increases in rates of vehicle excise duties for the most polluting vehicles. Also note the drive towards expansion of renewable energy sources in order to meet EU targets of 20 per cent usage by 2020.

The key problems that environmentalists face are:

- competitive individualism and consumerism are deeply entrenched
- globalisation is a result of hyper-industrialisation
- environmental groups appear to be in favour of anti-growth, which is unattractive and electorally disastrous
- green politics is seen as an urban trend and somewhat romantic and unsupportable
- the scale of change is too drastic; ecologism is seen as too radical.

There are signs of greater environmental concerns in US politics. Former Vice-President Al Gore's film, *An Inconvenient Truth*, on the dangers of global warming did much to raise the political profile of the issue. Furthermore, Barack Obama has promised to sign up to an updated version of the Kyoto Protocol and place environmental concerns higher up the political agenda.

Ecologism – philosophy, politics or science?

There is considerable debate on this issue. These are the key arguments.

- Ecologism is a philosophy – it does not have specific ends and may have unforeseen consequences. It is seen by some as utopian and unrealistic.
- It is a philosophy as it is closely associated with mysticism and religion; ecologists would argue that to ignore environmental concerns is utopian and that it is they that are realistic.
- Deep and shallow ecology is both scientific and philosophical – key thinkers see no real difference between science and philosophy.
- Deep ecologists offer an alternative philosophy of science in the sense that they view issues as a whole, not as separate, isolated parts. Deep ecology is not just philosophy or science; the philosophy can be seen to be political.
- Deep ecologists seek to re-educate and have tried to transform their philosophy into concrete political action.
- Shallow and liberal environmentalists (such as Greenpeace) are political organisations with manifestos and a desire to influence decision-makers.
- Ecologism is not politics in the conventional sense, as it seeks to change the basis of ethics and human relationships with nature.

Global environmental groups

Major environmental groups have also become global organisations (such as Greenpeace and Friends of the Earth) and have to operate at an international level rather than trying to influence each state in isolation. Environmental issues are a global concern; solutions cannot be worked out by a single country alone; this makes the lobbying far more complex. The green movement in the United States has been particularly ineffective, although it received considerable publicity by Ralph Nader's participation in the 1996, 2000 and 2004 presidential elections as a Green Party candidate; successive US administrations have been resistant to environmental influence.

DISCUSSION POINT ?

How influential are environmental parties and pressure groups in modern politics?

Challenges to religious fundamentalism

Learning objectives

- Christian fundamentalism and right-wing politics
- Islamic fundamentalism and the west

Fundamentalism – seeking a return to traditional ways and beliefs

LCF

Andrea Williams' organisation, the LCF, has also developed a fruitful relationship with at least one well-resourced group in the US. Her partners are called the Alliance Defence Fund (ADF). The ADF fights its spiritual war in the US courts. It seizes on cases that can be used to challenge laws it sees as anti-Christian.

Christian fundamentalism and right-wing politics

While mainstream Christian worship has been in steady decline, evangelical Christianity has been increasing. Not all evangelical worshippers hold such hard-line beliefs, but the fundamentalists will almost certainly describe themselves as evangelical. Accurate figures quantifying the size of this movement are hard to come by the Carmel Church in Bristol says they are a Pentecostal Church, one of the most prominent and fundamentalist strands of evangelical Christianity. According to the Evangelical Alliance, more than two million people in Britain now claim to be Pentecostal worshippers. The ambitions of Britain's hard-line Christians go far beyond the borders of their local communities. Like most fundamentalist movements, the ultimate aim is a society built on their rigid belief system.

Christian Action Research and Education (Care) has borrowed the tactics of America's religious right in its attempts to affect public policy. Care describes itself as a 'mainstream Christian charity bringing Christian insight and experience to matters of public policy'. The organisation's published doctrinal basis is distinctly fundamentalist and among other things talks of 'the divine inspiration of Holy Scripture and its consequent entire trustworthiness and supreme authority in all matters of faith and conduct'. In other words, the Bible is the literal truth.

Lyndon Bowring, the charity's executive chairman, is on the board of Kensington Temple, one of London's largest Pentecostal organisations. He is also on the board of Care for the Family, the European arm of Focus on the Family. Focus on the Family is one of the largest and best-resourced pressure groups of America's religious right, and it is not coy about its fundamentalist agenda. Its mission statement talks of 'defending the God-ordained institution of the family and promoting biblical truths worldwide'. Like similar groups in the US, Care runs a parliamentary 'intern programme'. Interns are provided free to sympathetic MPs. They will work closely with the MP, doing research and helping to run the office. This additional staff member is worth thousands of pounds. There are currently 12 MPs, mostly Tories, who employ Care interns. The most powerful is Caroline Spellman, vice-chairman of the Conservative Party.

The intern programme is not only about rewarding friendly Christian parliamentarians, it is part of a plan to build a new generation of committed Christian politicians. The idea is that the interns will go on to become MPs furthering the Christian agenda. They have already had a degree of success. Stephen Crabb is the Conservative MP for Preseli in Pembrokeshire. He started his career as a Care intern.

Traditionally, British politics has been regarded as secular – Alistair Campbell, Tony Blair's Director of Communications and Strategy, famously said 'We don't do God'. This was in response to journalists wishing to investigate the extent to which Blair's policies, especially in relation to Iraq, were affected by his own deep Christian values. However, other politicians have been criticised for a potential conflicts of interest. Ruth Kelly, Minister for Women (2006–07) and also a member of the devout Catholic Opus Dei movement, was under pressure as to a potential conflict of interest when the government in 2007 pushed through anti-discrimination legislation preventing religious adoption agencies from discriminating against homosexual couples. She chose to remain a minister although in other free votes on moral issues she has revealed her religious views (e.g. she voted in favour of an attempt to reduce the age of legal abortions in 2008).

The Moral Majority was a political organisation in the United States with the agenda of evangelical-Christian-oriented political lobbying. It as dissolved in 1989, but re-launched in

2004. In the 1980 presidential election, it was credited with providing Ronald Reagan with two-thirds of the white evangelical vote over his opponent Jimmy Carter. Some issues for which the Moral Majority campaigned to outlaw abortion, oppose state recognition and acceptance of homosexuality and the Equal Rights Amendment, as well as to enforce a traditional vision of family life and the censorship of media that promotes an 'anti-family' agenda.

The evangelical right-wing influence continues with the Christian Coalition of America. In both the 2000 and 2004 presidential elections, voter mobilisation by conservative Christians tended to be focused within the Republican Party. In the 2000 presidential election, the organisation claimed that it distributed over 70 million voter guides in churches all across America, including over 5 million in Spanish. In 2004, the group claims to have distributed approximately 30 million voter guides, but this time in targeted states and congressional districts, choosing instead to focus its efforts on areas that were more politically competitive.

Islamic fundamentalism and the west

Islamic fundamentalism is a very diverse political and social movement in North Africa, the Middle East and South Asia. The primary goal is the creation of more Islamic-oriented states and societies based on the principles and values of Islam. For the west, the term 'Islamic fundamentalism' generates images of hostage crises, embassies under siege, hijackings and suicide bombers. Some Islamic militants try to reach their goals through violence, however the majority of Islamic activists work within mainstream society, participating in the electoral process. At the fringes are extremist groups, like the al-Qaeda network of Saudi-born millionaire Osama bin Laden, that engage in a global war of terrorism.

During the late 1980s and the 1990s, Islamic political groups began participating in elections. Candidates with an Islamic orientation were elected to high office in several countries. In Turkey, the leader of the Islamist Welfare Party held the office of prime minister from 1996 to 1997. In Malaysia, Anwar Ibrahim, a founder of the Malaysian Islamic Youth Movement (ABIM), served as deputy prime minister from 1993 until 1998. In the first democratic elections in Indonesia, Abdurrahman Wahid, leader of perhaps the largest Islamic movement, the Nahdlatul Ulama, was elected president in 1999.

Although the primary catalysts and concerns of most Islamic movements have been domestic or national, international issues also have shaped Islamic politics. Bin Laden and other extremists justify their use of violence with the claim that most Muslim and western governments are corrupt oppressors that resort to violence and terrorism. These extremists use Islam to motivate their followers and rationalise their actions. However, they misinterpret and misapply Islamic beliefs when, for example, they call for a jihad. In reality the term jihad refers to the right and duty of Muslims to defend themselves, their community and their religion from unjust attack; extremists use the term to legitimate acts of violence and terrorism.

Distinguishing between moderate Islamic groups that participate within society and violent revolutionaries is critical to understanding the resurgence of Islam. Many opponents of political Islam have charged that all Islamic movements are extremist groups that seek to 'hijack democracy' and manipulate the political system in order to gain power and impose their will. Some experts argue that this type of reaction contributes to the radicalisation of moderate Islamists.

There is conflicting evidence regarding the radicalisation of the British Muslim community in the aftermath of the September 2001 attacks in the United States, the war on Iraq and the London bombings in July 2005.

Post Pat

Since the departure of Pat Robertson as leader of the coalition, the religious right in the US has had less influence. In the 2008 presidential nomination for the Republican Party, the Christian right failed to rally around a single candidate and chose John McCain from the moderate wing of the party.

Sharia law in Britain?

In July 2008, Lord Phillips, the most senior judge in England and Wales, said there was no reason why sharia law principles could not be used in mediation in legal cases. However, he also argued that, where people failed to comply with the terms of mediation, any sanctions would be drawn from the laws of England and Wales.

DISCUSSION POINT

To what extent does the Christian right continue to dominate US politics?

Women's representation

Before the 1997 general election, women made up just 9 per cent of MPs. After the 1997 election, this figure rose to just over 18 per cent. This was largely due to the policy of all-women shortlists adopted by the Labour Party between 1993 and 1996. This policy was judged unlawful, in a case brought in 1996 under the Sex Discrimination Act 1975. Following this in the 2001 general election, the number of women elected to the UK parliament fell for the first time in 20 years. However, in the 2005 general election the figure rose to 20 per cent.

To facilitate progress towards increasing women's representation in government, the Sex Discrimination (Election Candidates) Act 2002 was introduced. It removed domestic legal barriers, that were in the 1975 Act and the equivalent Northern Ireland Order, to political parties wishing to adopt positive measures to reduce inequality between the numbers of men and women elected. The legislation covers elections to the House of Commons, the Scottish Parliament, the National Assembly for Wales, the Northern Ireland Assembly, the European Parliament and local government elections (excluding directly elected mayors and community councils in Scotland).

Sexual equality

Women around the world at every socio-political level are mostly under-represented in parliaments and find themselves far removed from decision-making levels. While the political playing-field in each country has its own particular characteristics, one feature remains common to nearly all: it is uneven and not conducive to women's participation.

Research indicates that political structures rather than social factors play a more significant role in women's parliamentary recruitment. The system of elections based on proportional representation, for example, has resulted in three to four times more women being elected in countries with similar political cultures, for example Germany and Australia.

Among the political obstacles that women face, the following feature prominently. The prevalence of the 'masculine model' of political life and of elected governmental bodies. The lack of party support, such as limited financial support for women candidates. The limited access to political networks. The lack of contact and cooperation with other public organisations such as trade (labour) unions and women's groups. The absence of well-developed education and training systems for women's leadership in general, and for orienting young women towards political life in particular. The nature of the electoral system, which may or may not be favourable to women candidates.

Political under-representation in Britain and the EU

The government does not believe that it would be right to make positive action compulsory in order to increase the number of women elected. It is for political parties to decide for themselves whether they wish to increase the number of women candidates standing for election for their party and, if so, how to achieve this increase. The government has legislated so that parties can legally use positive measures for this purpose.

The following table sets out the latest figures available for women's representation in Britain's governing institutions.

	Total number	Number of men	Number of women	(%)
Europe – European Parliament UK members (2004 election; January 2005 data)	78	58	20	25.6
Westminster – House of Commons	644	518	126	19.6
Westminster – House of Lords	753	605	143	19.1
Westminster Cabinet (June 2007 reshuffle)	22	17	5	22.7
Scotland – Scottish Parliament (2007 election)	129	86	43	33.3
Wales – National Assembly for Wales (2007 election)	60	32	28	46.7
Northern Ireland – Northern Ireland Assembly (May 2007 election)	108	90	18	16.7
Greater London Authority (GLA) – London Assembly	25	16	9	36
Local Authorities: – England (2004 data)	19,689	13,645	5,774	29.3
– Northern Ireland (2001 election)	582	456	126	21.6
– Scotland (2001 election)	N/A	N/A	N/A	21.6
– Wales (2004 data)	1,257	983	274	21.8

With women making up 19.6 per cent of our MPs, the UK is ranked 14th within the EU.

With the use of proportional representation in devolved assembly and European elections, it has been easier for the parties to promote an increase in female representation. An increase in the number of women elected to the Commons would, many argue, lead to a higher quality of decision-making, reflecting the greater diversity of experience of those making the decisions.

There is evidence in the newly devolved institutions in Scotland and Wales that the relatively high number of women have had a discernable impact on shaping their policy agendas. In both bodies, women parliamentarians have championed issues such as childcare, the social economy and equal pay.

In addition, Britain faces a serious problem of lack of interest among the electorate in the political system. If politics looks old, white and male, it can seem irrelevant and dull to many people, and lead to lower participation rates and a reduction in democracy. Research published by the Electoral Commission suggests that having more women elected encourages greater participation rates amongst women more generally.

Representation also plays a symbolic role. It is important for decision-makers to be effective role models and to be truly representative of their electors.

Positive discrimination

The term 'positive action' refers to a number of methods designed to counteract the effects of past discrimination and to help abolish stereotyping. Action can be taken to encourage people from particular groups to take advantage of opportunities; this can be done when under-representation of particular groups has been identified. The most visible case of such action was the Labour Party's decision to adopt all-female shortlists of parliamentary candidates. The other mainstream political parties have fallen short of adopting such compulsory tactics, instead encouraging the promotion of female candidates through national endorsement. This is apparent in David Cameron's promotion of the 'A-List' candidates, in which parity between male and female numbers is assured as well as significant representation of ethnic minorities. Cameron has however had trouble in getting local constituency associations to choose these candidates, so it is possible that at the next general election if Labour lose significant numbers of seats and even if there is an increase in the proportion of female Tory MPs, the overall percentage of female MPs might well decline.

Section 47 of the Sex Discrimination Act 1975 (the SDA) allows for the use of 'positive action' in a number of specific circumstances. Positive action is often confused with positive discrimination. Positive discrimination, which generally means choosing someone because they come from a deprived group in spite of whether they have the relevant skills and qualifications, is unlawful. Harriet Harman announced in June 2008 the government's intention to allow positive discrimination in certain circumstances in employment where there was a discernable under-representation based on race or gender. Her focus was primarily to encourage more women and ethnic minorities into the higher echelons of the business community and professions.

Member state (March 2007)	Percentage of women MPs (equivalents)
Sweden	47.3
Finland	42.0
Denmark	36.9
Netherlands	36.7
Spain	36.0
Belgium	34.7
Austria	32.2
Germany	31.6
Luxembourg	23.3
Lithuania	24.8
Portugal	21.3
Latvia	19.0
Poland	20.4
UK	19.6
Estonia	23.8
Italy	17.3
Slovakia	20.0
Czech Republic	15.5
Cyprus	14.3
Ireland	13.3
Greece	13.0
France	12.2
Slovenia	12.2
Hungary	10.4
Malta	9.2
Bulgaria	22.1
Romania	11.2

DISCUSSION POINT ?

What is the case for positive discrimination in politics and the use of 'women only' lists?

ExamCafé
Relax, refresh, result!

Relax and prepare

Here are several essay questions of the type that would occur in your exam for unit F854. How would you go about answering them?

- Discuss the coherence of feminism as a political ideology.

- Compare and contrast deep and shallow ecologism.

- Assess the extent to which ecologism can be seen as scientific.

- Discuss the main implications of post-modernist theory for traditional ideologies.

- How far can religious fundamentalism be seen as merely a reaction to the expansion of modern liberal values?

- To what extent are Christian and Islamic fundamentalism similar in their ideological outlook?

Refresh your memory

Unit F854 requires you to display knowledge and understanding of four alternative political ideologies. As there are four ideologies to learn, the depth of knowledge required for each is not going to be as detailed as for the other ideological sections in this unit. As a guide to revision, focus upon the following themes.

Feminism	Environmentalism	Post-modernism	Religious fundamentalism
Core ideas	Core ideas	Core ideas	Core ideas
Differences between liberal and radical feminism	Distinction between deep and shallow ecologism	End of ideology debate	Critique of liberal values
Distinction between sex and gender	Scientism versus holism	Managerialism	Comparison of Christian and Islamic fundamentalism
Key theorists	Key theorists	Key theorists	Key theorists

Get the result !

The following is the type of essay question for unit F854 that you may need to answer in your exam.

Compare and contrast liberal and radical feminism.

Exam tips

For the essay you will need to consider the relevant issues, including these in the table.

Area of comparison	Liberal	Radical
Reasons for inequality	Institutional patriarchal bias	Psychological and physical dominance by men
Attitude to female inequality	Focus on the public sphere and addressing female involvement in society	Focus on the domestic sphere and women's relationship with men
Changes needed in society	Legislation to ensure gender equality primarily focused on political change	Individual consciousness needs changing to end exploitation and female alienation – social change
Methods to achieve change	Focus on gradualism through positive discrimination in order to emancipate women	Need for radical/revolutionary restructuring of gender relations

Note that the above tends to focus on points of distinction. Your essay will also have to consider points of comparison. This should include the beliefs that society is fundamentally patriarchal and this needs tackling, that women are essentially exploited sexually, and that biological distinctions between the sexes are no longer relevant in modern society.

Don't forget to illustrate your comparison with the views of specific theorists.

Unit F856

Relax and prepare

Here are several essay questions of the type that could occur in your exam for unit F856. Discuss with y[our] colleagues how you would go about answering them or try writing essay plans for as many you can.

- Discuss the extent to which modern politics can be seen as patriarchal.
- Assess the justifications for and effectiveness of positive discrimination and action programmes in advancing the role of women in politics.
- Discuss the implications of environmentalism for modern politics.

- How compatible is environmentalism to the ideals of the mainstream political parties in the UK?
- To what extent can modern politics be regarded as managerial?
- Assess the extent to which liberal democracy is compatible with religious fundamentalist political ideas.

Refresh your memory

Case studies on alternative ideologies

Consider how events and issues such as those listed below are relevant to the theory you have studied on the alternate ideologies for unit F854. Remember, for unit F856 you must combine the theory you have studied for F854 with application to modern politics.

✓ The statistics on the extent of female participation in modern politics (as a guide compare representation in the UK parliament with the devolved regional assemblies, the European Parliament and international assemblies) – consider what factors are important in explaining differences.

✓ The comparison of UK party attitudes towards positive discrimination schemes to help advance female representation in politics.

✓ The international treaty obligations to tackle environmental issues (e.g. Kyoto Protocol 1997 and EU and G8 targets on reducing carbon emissions).

✓ The political party adoption of environmental policies (e.g. carbon taxes, increase in vehicle excise duty for large CO_2-emitting vehicles and support for increased use of sustainable energy sources).

✓ The evidence for ideological convergence in UK politics (consider if a social market consensus exists in areas such as education, health, taxation and regulation of industry).

✓ The evidence for the rise of personality-style politic[s] in the UK (consider media focus on party leaders, Foley thesis on rise of a British-style presidency and declining influence of ideology distinctions between the parties).

✓ The expansion of radical Islamist groups (e.g. Muslim Brotherhood and Hizb ut-Tahrir) assisting in the radicalisation of sections of Muslim youth i[n] the UK post-9/11 and Iraq war.

✓ The influence of Christian fundamentalists in US right-wing politics (consider campaigns to overturn legal abortions, outlaw same-sex marriages and ban stem-cell research).

Get the result !

This is the type of essay question that you may have to answer for unit F856 in your exam. To improve your chance of achieving a high mark you should plan your essay before you start writing it.

Analyse the validity of the post-modernist critique of modern politics both in theory and in practice.

Exam tips

For this essay you will need to examine how post-modernism interprets modern politics and analyses its validity through applying the ideas to modern society. Think about the following key areas and what evidence to use.

Decline in the role of traditional ideologies

Relate this to convergence in policies between the three major UK parties. Use examples from New Labour's acceptance of the free market and Conservative commitment to publicly-funded services. How similar are the views of Blair/Brown and Cameron? Do significant differences still exist (Europe, role of the state etc.)?

Moral relativism

Say whether traditional values disappeared from politics. Note the inclusiveness agenda from all major parties, accepting alternate lifestyles and beliefs. Do the mainstream parties still offer moral leadership especially on issues such as law and order, reasons for poverty and health concerns (obesity, smoking and alcoholism)?

Personality-driven politics

Compare the media focus on party leaders and importance of charisma for success (compare appeal of Blair and Cameron with 'less charismatic' Brown and Menzies Campbell). Has personality always been important in politics (Lloyd George and Churchill) and are charismatic politicians always popular (Blair and spin)?

Rise of managerialism

Discuss whether politics become purely about efficient management. Note that Labour's popularity 1997–2007 was partly based upon sound economic management and sustained economic growth. Has Brown's decline in popularity during late 2007 and 2008 been as a result of his government's loss of creditability as sound mangers (Northern Rock, loss of social security and other government records etc.)? Do modern politicians still offer leadership and innovative reform (note radical ideological agenda offered by Thatcher in 1979 and radical aspects of the Third Way agenda such as constitutional reform)?

Remember as you consider each theory question its validity by providing evidence for and against each aspect of the post-modernist critique. Don't forget also that for each area you will need to use the views of individual theorists where appropriate (e.g. Bell, Foucalt, Lyotard, Klein and Burnham).

The purpose of this qualification is to encourage you to develop a critical awareness of the nature of politics. Alongside this it aims to promote knowledge of rights and responsibilities. You will have realized that the demands of a GCE course are far greater than any other examined programme that you have ever encountered. The GCE Government and Politics specification requires you to:

- understand, synthesise and then interpret information related to politics
- to analyse and evaluate political arguments and explanations, the relationship between ideologies, concepts, behaviours and values, and political institutions and their processes and behaviours
- to identify connections, similarities and differences between different political ideologies and political systems
- to be able to find and organise relevant information that will assist you in building an argument or explanation and ultimately a reasoned conclusion
- to be able to communicate these arguments and explanations with relevant examples and be clear, coherent and, where possible, to always use the correct political vocabulary.

The two optional units related to political ideas and concepts are, in effect, an extension of the work that you will have examined in the AS units. At that point you will probably have tended to concentrate on British government and politics, along with the European Union. The political ideologies units extend your understanding of the British political system, but they also draw together other concepts, political systems and ideologies that have been or are features of other countries at various times.

Where possible this book has sought to identify the key theories, ideas and concepts for unit F854 and then to extend the coverage to illustrate unit F856, which looks at political ideas and concepts in practice and in contemporary situations.

Unit F854 aims to broaden your knowledge and understanding of political ideas and concepts, particularly those that relate to democratic systems and to the role of the state. The unit looks at how governments are able to rule and the relationships that exist between the individual and the state. Each of the political ideas has core themes, which should allow you to make valuable comparisons between them. The unit introduces you to a broad range of new political thinkers that you may not yet have encountered.

Unit F856 focuses on the operation of modern forms of politics and to this end it is valuable from the outset to monitor the media in whatever form, from newspapers and magazines through to television and the Internet. Modern political examples, key figures, trends and the relative successes and failures of different political ideologies in modern-day society can all prove to be valuable examples that you can use in a direct way in the examination.

Our final exam café should certainly be read far earlier than on the eve of your examinations. It contains a series of suggestions that will give you the best possible chance of being able to impress the examiner and to illustrate to them that not only you understand what you have been taught, but that you also know how to apply it, evaluate it and express it. Planning for your examinations is not something that should be left either to chance or to the last minute. It requires long-term preparation. Remember the fable of the hare and the tortoise – the race was won by the tortoise that systematically applied itself over a period of time to reach its goal and not by the hare that sprinted for the line at the last minute.

Suggestions for further reading

The following books are relevant to units F854 and F856. Refer to as many as possible because the more you read the greater will be your understanding.

Barry, N. (1989) *An Introduction to Modern Political Theory*, Macmillan, London.
Cole, A. (2006) *Democracy in Britain*, Edinburgh University Press, Edinburgh.
Goodwin, B. (1987) *Using Political Ideas*, John Wiley and Sons, Chichester.
Harrison, K. (2003) *Political Ideas and Movements*, Manchester University Press, Manchester.
Haywood, A. (2000) *Key Concepts in Politics*, Palgrave, Basingstoke.
Heywood, A. (2002) *Politics*, Palgrave, Basingstoke.
Heywood, A. (2003) *A Political Theory: An Introduction*, Palgrave, Basingstoke.
Heywood, A. (2003) *Political Ideologies: An Introduction*, Palgrave, Basingstoke.
Hoffman, J. (2006) *Liberalism,* Philip Allan Updates, London.
Hoffman, J. (2006) *Socialism*, Philip Allan Updates, London.
McNaughton, N. (2005) *Political Ideologies*, Philip Allan Updates, London.
Woodley, D. (2006) *Conservatism*, Philip Allan Updates, London.

For a greater insight into the ideas of key past political thinkers, you might consider reading some of the following works (all available with good explanatory introductions in the Penguin Classics series).

Plato, *The Republic*
N. Machiavelli, *The Prince*
T. Hobbes, *Leviathan*
J. J. Rousseau, *The Social Contract*
T. Paine, *Rights of Man*
E. Burke, *Reflections on the French Revolution*
J. S. Mill, *On Liberty*
K. Marx, *The Communist Manifesto*

Exam Café
Relax, refresh, result!

Relax and prepare

Now that you have read through the preceding chapters and practised some of the suggestions on how and what to write for the two units, the external exams are probably not too far away. What follows are a series of suggestions on what you can do to revise effectively and impress the examiner.

Preparing for your exams

Remember the motto: 'Fail to prepare, prepare to fail'. Revision requires careful planning, so think about the following suggestions.

- **Long-term preparation** – Create the right environment for revision. Remove the temptation of the television or sound system from your room if you need to. Make sure you have all the stationery required – revision cards, writing paper, highlighting pens etc.
- **Organise your notes** – Split your notes up into colour-coded sections or use chapter dividers. Do not forget to keep notes for the two modules separate. You should also make sure that you have no missing handouts – to do this, compare your files with fellow students.
- **Plan a revision schedule** – You will probably receive your exam timetable months in advance of the exams you will sit. When you know the exam dates, divide your revision for each module into blocks. Factor into your schedule some flexibility to take account of unforeseen circumstances such as illness. Do not attempt to do

all your revision for one module at any one time. You will probably accumulate a considerable amount of information to be revised, so leave yourself enough time to do this. Do not leave it to the last minute and do not stay up all night on the eve of the exam.

The big day arrives

Before entering the exam room

Make sure you allow plenty of time to get to the exam room. Remember to take all the materials you will need including more than one pen. Follow the exam board stipulations about taking electronic devices into exam rooms (mobile phones, electronic organisers etc.) – fail to abide by the regulations can disqualify you from all exams in that session. Do not get dragged into last-min cribbing discussions with others before entering the exam room.

In the exam room

Read the instructions on the exam paper carefully – this will help to calm your nerves. Once you turn over the exam paper, do not start writing an answer to the first question y think you know something about. Read all the questions f and answer the ones you feel most confident about. Keep to the timings for each question. As exams can be menta draining, you should keep your energy levels suitably high is a good idea to have water (in a clear bottle) and swee with you to help keep you going.

Refresh your memory

Rights and wrongs of revision

In the past you may have been told there is a perfect way to revise. This is wrong. We all learn differently, so it makes s for us to revise differently. However, psychologists argue that there are three main approaches to learning. These are:

- **auditory** – learning though listening to information
- **visual** – learning through reading and making sense of visual stimuli
- **kinaesthetic** – learning through active participation.

Most of us pick up information through all three methods but will tend to have a preference. Which is yours? Do you best understand something through hearing it (by listening to the radio or your teacher)? Do you retain more information from reading books or viewing things? Or do you need to participate in a learning exercise of some sort (perhaps a group discussion or role play)? Whatever kind of learner you are, these are the Do's and Don'ts you need to follow.

Do's

- If you are an auditory learner, make recordings of your notes so that you can play them to yourself on your MP3 player.
- If you are a visual learner, make prompt cards that are clear and visual – use a colour indexing system to differentiate between different topics and highlighting pens to differentiate between sections within a topic.
- If you are a kinaesthetic learner, transform your notes into activities (design posters, memory games etc.) and think up learning exercises, possibly with other students.
- Practise writing out answers – use past paper questions and answer them under exam conditions. Ask a teacher to look at your answers and make suggestions on how to improve.
- Use past mark schemes – these are available on the exam board website (www.ocr.org.uk and follow the links).
- Learn definitions and, if not actual quotes, then summaries of the key ideas of a range of theorists.
- Remember contemporary practical examples for use in module F856 – make sure you have at least one for each argument you intend to revise in each area.
- Focus upon improving your answering technique as well as your knowledge of the topics.

- ✓ If you have friends who also are revising for the same modules then form study groups.
- ✓ Make your revision schedule realistic – factor in personal treats and relaxation time (make them rewards for achieving targets in your revision).

Don'ts

- ✗ Don't think that you will be able to revise everything in a single session – split up your material into the different topic areas and revise each separately.
- ✗ Don't revise by reading your textbooks from start to finish – summarise the relevant section into personal notes that you can understand and directly relate to the question areas.
- ✗ Don't ignore issues you do not understand – this may lead to confusion that affects your understanding in other areas. Ask for help if necessary.
- ✗ Don't revise too late into the night as this will only lead to exhaustion and poor performance during the exams.
- ✗ Don't leave all your revision to the last minute – build it up gradually.
- ✗ Don't rely on one revision technique but try a variety – this will help to break up the tedium of revision and may improve your overall understanding of your learning style.

Get the result !

How to impress the examiner

Having undertaken extensive revision, you will probably have a thorough knowledge and understanding of the topic areas. It is now time to fine-tune your technique. Think about using the following points.

Learn definitions

Sharp and focused definitions, perhaps from an academic or theorist, are a good way to show the examiner you are aware of the key concepts covered in each essay.

Extend the range of theory you use

Do not rely on a standard list of a few theorists. Extend the range of theorists you use, especially some modern theorists. You may find articles in broadsheet newspapers by thinkers like George Monbiot and Francis Fukuyama; consider introducing their ideas into your essays.

Keep up to date with contemporary examples

To make your essays stand out, use up-to-date examples to illustrate your application to modern politics for module F856, instead of the tried and tested examples used in the textbooks. Using original and modern examples will show the examiner you have understood the consequences of an argument for modern politics.

Remember the importance of introductions and conclusions

An examiner will read numerous copies of the same essay. If yours stands out in the introduction and addresses the key issues in the conclusion, he or she will be more willing to tolerate the odd error or omission in the main bulk of the essay.

Above all, plan!

Stick to the time available for each essay in the exam and plan how you will answer each one. By doing this, you are more likely to produce an essay that is coherently and persuasively argued, and therefore gain more marks.

Absolutism This is a government that is not limited in any way by an agency internal to itself, in other words there are no constitutional checks and balances.

Anarchy A society that lacks institutions of state, rejects authority and favours spontaneous action.

Asymmetrical devolution This is a constitutional arrangement under which some of the constituent units within the system have more extensive powers than others relative to the central government.

Authoritarian A government that is determined that citizens should obey the authority of the state.

Autocracy This literally means self-rule, where an individual holds all the power and can exercise that power in an arbitrary way. Laws might appear to limit the power, but they can be revoked and disobeyed by the individual.

Bourgeoisie The ruling class in a capitalist society that owns the means of production and therefore wealth.

Capitalism An economic system in which wealth is privately owned and the market dictates prices for commodities.

Civil rights The fundamental freedoms that are guaranteed by law.

Confucianism This ideology focuses on individual morality and ethics, along with the correct exercise of political power by government. In many respects social ethics and morals based on Confucianism are blended with Taoist and Buddhist concepts.

Constitutional Reform Act This received Royal Assent in March 2005 and covered four areas: judicial independence, reform of the Lord Chancellor, the establishment of a Supreme Court and the creation of the Judicial Appointments Commission.

Ecocentric The belief that priority needs to be given to maintaining the ecological balance rather than focusing on human needs.

Egalitarian The belief that the promotion of equality is the main driving force in politics and public life.

Egalitarianism This is a vague term, but it is the belief that all individuals are or ought to be equal in almost every respect.

Ethnic cleansing The use of threat, terror or force to expel or kill those belonging to ethnic minority groups, for example the expulsion of the Greek population of Northern Cyprus in 1974.

Feudalism A system of organising and governing society based on the possession of land and service to the monarch.

Freedoms The freedoms guaranteed to individuals, such as the freedom of speech.

Functionalist The functionalism perspective is built upon twin emphases: application of the scientific method to the objective social world and use of an analogy between the individual organism and society.

Humanism The view that human needs and achievements should be given absolute priority over all things.

Human rights The rights that are guaranteed in the European Convention on Human Rights and the Human Rights Act.

Industrialism The transition of production methods in order to create wealth.

Laissez-faire In effect this means that government should not involve itself in trying to control the flow of money in an economy. This should be left to market forces and governments should not be trusted to have this amount of control over the economy. In effect it means a free market.

Night watchman state This is a state whose only role is to protect its citizens' rights. In other words government is limited to courts.

Obligation The things that a citizen ought to do, such as pay taxes.

Oligarchy A Greek term that means ruled by a few.

Pastoralism This is a belief in the simplicity of rural life and the closeness to nature, which is in sharp contrast to the corrupting influence of industrialised rural life. This was a theme taken up by fascists and nationalists in the 20th century.

Pluralist (or **Pluralism**) This is the notion that the distribution of political power limits the ability of any one group to dominate the political system.

Polity A Greek term that Aristotle intended to mean only a minority of adult males could have voting rights as citizens.

Pressure group A group of individuals who share a common interest or cause and try to influence government to further that cause or interest.

Proletariat This refers to not just the working class in a capitalist society, but to any individual who has to sell their labour to survive.

Right to silence The right to remain silent and not incriminate oneself by answering questions if arrested.

Satyagraha Gandhi used this term to describe non-violent resistance. To Gandhi, this meant truth-force, love-force or soul-force. He believed that violence was not an acceptable response to dealing with an opponent; rather, he believed that they should be slowly made to see the error of their ways through sympathy and patience. Gandhi recognised that truth as seen by one side would be seen as an error by their opponents. Hence, he maintained that to move them from the state of being in error, it was necessary to be patient and be prepared to suffer. Truth was borne out of self-suffering, rather than inflicting suffering on the opponent.

Totalitarian It means a dictatorship that pretends to be a democracy. In effect it is a state in which a single party rule and in which opposition is not tolerated.

West Lothian question This was a phrase used by Labour MP Tam Dalyell in 1977 when he said 'for how long will English constituencies and English honourable members tolerate at least 119 honourable members from Scotland, Wales and Northern Ireland exercising an important, and probably often decisive, effect on British politics while they themselves have no say in the same matters in Scotland, Wales and Northern Ireland?'

Actually, the West Lothian question as a term was coined by Enoch Powell MP in his response to the speech.

Page numbers in *italics* refer to illustrations.